BENCH AND BAR OF MONTGOMERY COUNTY MARYLAND

Early Lawyers of Montgomery County before 1900

Jane C. Sween
Montgomery County Historical Society

HERITAGE BOOKS
2017

HERITAGE BOOKS
AN IMPRINT OF HERITAGE BOOKS, INC.

Books, CDs, and more—Worldwide

For our listing of thousands of titles see our website
at
www.HeritageBooks.com

Published 2017 by
HERITAGE BOOKS, INC.
Publishing Division
5810 Ruatan Street
Berwyn Heights, Md. 20740

Heritage Books by the author:

Abstracts of Wills Montgomery County, Maryland, 1826–1875
Mary Gordon Malloy, Jane C. Sween and Janet D. Manuel

Abstracts of Wills, Montgomery County, Maryland, 1776–1825
Mary Gordon Malloy, Jane Sween and Janet D. Manuel

Bench and Bar of Montgomery County Maryland: Early Lawyers of Montgomery County before 1900

International Standard Book Number
Paperbound: 978-16-8034-479-0

THE BENCH AND BAR: EARLY LAWYERS

In Montgomery County Maryland before 1900

Abstract

Practioners before the bar, and members of the Bench

Montgomery County History library

library@montgomeryhistory.org

PART I: Practitioners before the Bench 1775-1825 1
HENRY ASHTON (1780-1834) 3
LEWIS PENN WITHERSPOON BALCH (1787 – 1868) 5
JAMES BOYLE (1784-1854) 6
WILLIAM LEIGH BRENT (1784-1848) 7
THOMAS BUCHANAN (1768-1847) 8
EDWARD BURGESS (1733 – 1809) 9
AENEAS CAMPBELL (1730-1812) 11
JAMES CAMPBELL (1754-1827) 12
WILLIAM CLAGETT (1768-1810) 12
JOHN COOK (1783-1847) 13
JEREMIAH CRABB (1760 -1800) 15
THOMAS CRAMPHIN, JR. (1740 – 1830) 16
THOMAS DAVIS (1768-1833) 17
CHARLES SAMUEL WORTHINGTON DORSEY (1797-1845) 18
WILLIAM HAMMOND DORSEY (1764-1818) 19
ALLEN BOWIE DUCKETT (1775–1809) 20
URIAH FORREST (1756-1805) 21
JOHN MACKALL GANTT (1762-1811) 22
WILLIAM GOLDSBOROUGH (1762-1826) 23
HENRY GRIFFITH (1720-1794) 24
HENRY HARDING (1782-1863) 26
WILLIAM PITT HUNT (1766 –1798) 27
BAKER JOHNSON (1747–1811) 29
JAMES JOHNSON (1736–1809) 31
CHARLES JONES (1712-1798) 32
FRANCIS SCOTT KEY (1779-1843) 33
PHILIP BARTON KEY (1757-1815) 35
CHARLES JORDAN KILGOUR (1790-1837) 37
DAVID LYNN (1698-1779) 38
ZADOK (or ZADOCK) MAGRUDER (1795-1831) 39

LUTHER MARTIN (1748-1826) 40
JOHN T. MASON (1765–1824) 41
EDWARD NICHOLLS (1743-1812) 42
ROGER PERRY (abt 1767-1835) 44
BENE SMALLWOOD PIGMAN (1776-1845) 45
RICHARD POTTS (1753-1808) 47
RICHARD RIDGELY (1755-1824) 49
DAVID ROSS (1755-1800) 50
FREDERICK AUGUSTUS SCHLEY (1789-1858) 51
ROBERT SMITH (ca. 1760 to ca. 1835) 53
ROGER BROOKE TANEY (1777 – 1864) 56
AUGUSTUS TANEY (1787-1823) 57
ARCHIBALD VAN HORNE (abt 1758-1817) 59
HENRY RIDGELY WARFIELD (1774-1839) 60
RICHARD KEY WATTS (ca. 1767--1826) 60
RICHARD WOOTTON (1741-1817) 62
THOMAS SPRIGG WOOTTON (1740-1789) 63
WILLIAM M. WORTHINGTON (1796-1842) 65
PART II: LAWYERS ADMITTED TO THE BAR, 1825-1875 66
CHARLES ABERT (1822-1897) 67
JAMES WALLACE ANDERSON (1797-1882) 68
JAMES WALLACE ANDERSON (1847-1881) 70
CHARLES W. BEACH (1819-1881) 70
SAMUEL WOOTTON BEALL (1807-1868) 71
MONTGOMERY BLAIR, SENIOR (1813-1883) 73
WILLIAM VEIRS BOUIC, JR. (1846-1906) 75
WILLIAM VEIRS BOUIC, SR. (1816-1896) 76
RICHARD JOHNS BOWIE (1807-1881) 77
JOSEPH BRADDOCK (1810-1843) 78
WILLIAM PERRY BRADDOCK (1817-1859) 79
JOSEPH HABERSHAM BRADLEY (1803-1887) 80

WILLIAM COTTRINGER BRENT (1824-1860) 81
JAMES CHISWELL BREWER (1815-1883) 81
JOHN BUCHANAN BREWER (1850 1908) 82
JOHN CHISWELL BREWER 1804-1866 84
NICHOLAS BREWER III (1828-1896) 84
WILLIAM BREWER (1847-1885) 85
JOSEPH ALOYSIUS CAHILL (1838-1902) 86
WASHINGTON CUSTIS CALVERT (1804--1868) 87
HUGH ELMWOOD CAPERTON (1821-1877) 88
JOHN A. CARTER (1798 – 1860) 88
ROBERT W. CARTER (1812-1890) 89
HAZEL BUTT CASHELL (1808-1886) 91
WASHINGTON BOWIE CHICHESTER (1828-1902) 92
RICHARD SMITH COXE (1792-1865) 94
LAWRENCE ALLNUTT DAWSON (1807 1875) 95
HENRY BRADLEY DAVIDSON (1860-1930) 96
ENOCH G. DAY (1808-1870) 97
SAMUEL WORTHINGTON DORSEY (1811-1875) 98
WILLIAM HENRY GOODWIN DORSEY (1819-1862) 99
JOHN GLISAN ENGLAND (1806-1883) 100
W. T. EWAN 101
BENJAMIN STODDERT FORREST (1792-1840) 102
URIAH FORREST (1803-1867) 102
WILLIAM COLLINSON GOTT (1816-1850) 103
EDWARD HAMMOND (1812-1882) 103
WILLIAM R. HARDING (1818-1843) 105
JAMES BARNES HENDERSON (1845-1917) 105
REVERDY JOHNSON (1796-1876) 107
SPENCER CONE JONES (1836-1915) 109
ALEXANDER KILGOUR (1799-1867) 110
JOHN A. T. KILGOUR (1795-1826) 112

JOHN MORTIMER KILGOUR (1822-1905) 113
BENJAMIN LINCOLN LEAR (1792-1832) 114
ZACCHEUS COLLINS LEE (1805 - 1859) 115
JOHN ALEXANDER LYNCH (1825--1904) 116
JOHN H. G. McCUTCHEN (1827- abt. 1885) 117
JOHN HAMMOND McELFRESH (1796-1841) 118
WILLIAM MATTHEWS MERRICK (1818 - 1889) 119
FRANKLIN MINOR (1823-1901) 119
JOSHUA MORSELL (1816-1883) 120
JOHN C. MOTTER (1844-1915) 121
CARRINGTON SCOTT NELSON (1853-1887) 122
ROBERT OULD, (1820-1882) 123
EDWARD W. OWEN (1808-1895) 124
MOSES GRAY PALMER (1825-1885) 125
GEORGE C. PATTERSON (1816-1889) 125
GEORGE ALEXANDER PEARRE (1819-1883) 127
THOMAS J. PEDDICORD (1839-1910) 128
RICHARD ROSS PERRY (1846-1915) 129
GEORGE PETER (1829-1893) 130
JOHN FREELAND PETER (1853-1878) 131
SOMERVILLE PINKNEY (1800-1843) 132
WILLIAM P. PRESTON (1811-1880) 132
ELIJAH BARRETT PRETTYMAN (1830-1907) 133
WILLIAM MONTGOMERY STEWART (1799-1872) 134
HATTERSLY WORTHINGTON TALBOTT (1842-1912) 134
WILLIAM THOMPSON (1812-1872) 136
ROBERT G. THRIFT (1836 -1877) 136
JOHN S. TYSON (1797-1864) 137
LYCURGUS C. (L.C.)VALDENAR (1822-1864) 138
JOHN WESLEY VEITCH (1833-1892) 138
JOHN T. VINSON (1825-1903) 139

RUDOLPH WATKINS (1844-1909) 140
RICHARD MORTIMER WILLIAMS (1841-1882) 142
FLAVEL SCOTT WOOTTON (1828-1853) 143
HENRY EDGAR WOOTTON (1837-1894) 143
LEWIS BEALL WOOTTON (1815-1839) 144
BRICE THOMAS BEALE WORTHINGTON (1820-1856) 144
PERRY WORTHINGTON (1811-1836) 145
JOHN EDWIN YOUNG (1833-1861) 146
PART III: 1875-1900 FORMATION OF BAR ASSOCIATION 148
FRANK ALMONEY (1854-1926) 149
GEORGE MINOR ANDERSON (1856-1927) 149
THOMAS ANDERSON (1835-1900) 150
WILLIAM WALLACE ANDERSON (1851-1922) 151
RICHARD ROBINSON BEALL (1859-1903) 152
GEORGE BIBB BROWN (1869-1959) 153
JAMES F. BYRNE (1858-1923) 154
WASHINGTON CATLETT (1852-1934) 154
WARREN RAGAN CHOATE (1865-1924) 155
REMUS RIGGS DARBY (1847-1916) 156
HENRY BRADLEY DAVIDSON (1860-1930) 157
JAMES D. DAWSON (1846-1909) 159
THOMAS DAWSON (1857-1924) 159
JAMES ALBY HENDERSON (1871-1926) 160
FRANK HIGGINS (1861-1922) 161
WILLARD HINKLEY (1862-1891) 162
HOBART HUTTON (1848-1896) 162
CHARLES M. JONES 1873-1957 163
ALEXANDER KILGOUR, JR. (1855-1917) 164
WILLIAM KILGOUR (1834-1907) 165
PHILIP DANDRIDGE LAIRD (1846-1920) 166
GEORGE HOLT LAMAR (1867-1945) 167

WILLIAM HARMONG LAMAR (1859-1928) ... 168
FRANCIS PRESTON BLAIR LEE (1857-1944) ... 169
STEPHEN MELTIAS LYDDANE (1817-1889) ... 170
ARTHUR PETER (1873-1943) ... 171
EDWARD C. PETER (1862-1923) ... 171
ROBERT BREWER PETER (1868-1936) ... 173
CHARLES WESLEY PRETTYMAN (1857-1921) ... 173
SAMUEL RIGGS (1869-1943) ... 174
HENRY MAURICE TALBOTT (1851-1934) ... 175
WILLIAM HYDE TALBOTT (1861-1941) ... 177
MILTON GEORGE URNER (1839-1926) ... 177
JAMES P. B. VEIRS (1866-1956) ... 179
BOWIE FRANKLIN WATERS (1870-1949) ... 179
RICHARD WHITE (1856-1927) ... 180
GLENN HOWARD WORTHINGTON (1858-1934) ... 181
BIBLIOGRAPHY: ... 183
MCHS REFERENCES ... 183
BOOKS/MANUSCRIPTS ... 183
INDEX ... 193

BENCH AND BAR OF MONTGOMERY COUNTY

PART I: PRACTITIONERS BEFORE THE BENCH 1775-1825

Scharf in his *History of Western Maryland* published the names in a register of those who were admitted to practice law in Montgomery County. This became the starting point in identifying the early lawyers in Montgomery County. This project has consumed many hours from many volunteers over the past fifteen or twenty years. A common problem is that many of those signing the register did not live in Montgomery County, but may have lived in Annapolis, Baltimore, Bladensburg, Frederick, Upper Marlboro or Geogetown (later Washington, D.C.) or elsewhere, often representing banks or other institutions.

Among the volunteers who initiated this project were Dorothy Pugh and Jane Sween. Their project concept was based on a manuscript done by Marion and Charles Jacobs on the *Early Doctors of Montgomery County,* which identified doctors in the county from 1776 to 1900, and was completed in 1989.

This volume of lawyer biographies has turned out to be a time monopolizer. Probably every library volunteer over the past ten to fifteen years has worked on it, although it has been put aside for years at a time. Lists and more lists of potential lawyers were identified. Finally two years ago it was decided that we needed to complete this project, Looking over the volunteer lists, we identify the following who contributed time to this project, researching, writing, editing, and or filing, including Dorothy Pugh, Jane Sween, Bill Hurley, Annette Fletchall, B.J. Digges, Ellie Hagner, Patty Elton, Dianne Jensen, Linda Kennedy, Jack Barnes, Shannon Bort, Anne Perrera, Bonnie Britton, Craig Diamond, Carolyn Sowinski, Tom Woodall, Rhoda Alderman and Kim Nguyen and others through the years, now forgotten.

We tried to follow a format, identifying our source for claiming this person's profession and then providing a brief biography, including birth information, education when available, career information (often political), marriage, children, death information, and other notes, including military service when appropriate. The family information is particularly interesting, as most lawyers were trained by reading law with another lawyer, often within their own family. They intermarried with other families of lawyers, or other learned professionals, and they often changed professional careers, from law, to medicine, to the ministry.

We also included many of the Clerks of the Court, and Justices, who often served as attorneys. A popular book in the colonial period was *Every Man Their Own Lawyer,* and most justices owned at least a book on writing deeds, and were proficient in basic law. Until

1811, Circuit Court Judges were not required to have studied law and Orphans Court Justices were often chosen for their sense and character.

We also had some difficulty in identifying the less famous lawyers who came in on the court's circuit, and perhaps were here for only one session, but signed the clerk's book. Among these were:

In 1780, we found two men named Robert Smith: one a prominent attorney/business man from Baltimore, who served in the James Madison administration, and Robert Smith who owned an estate here, which he later sold to the Bowies, his family had intermarried with them. They were written up in *Across the Years*[1]. He left the area in 1820. His biography would have nearly been impossible without additional information from *Ancestry.com*. He was also noted as a friend of James Madison and named two of his children Dolly and James. We opted to profile the Montgomery County resident.

Also in 1780, Thomas Wilson Ridgley, Jr.[2], signed the clerk's book. In spite of all the work done on the Ridgely families of Maryland, he remains unidentified.

In 1799, John Cottman is listed by Scharf, as in the clerk's book, but nothing else was found for him; in 1805 W. Chapman is listed; we've found one clue for, a William Chapman, who was presented for admission to the bar in Prince George's County at the September term 1806, by Philip Thomas Baker, who was appointed prosecuting attorney for Prince George's County. There is no biography for either of these men.

On one of our lists of attorneys created for this project is Jeremiah Crabb. He did not sign the clerk's book, but followed a legislative career, after serving as Justice of the Peace, and community militia leader. His biography is included.[3]

Other families with prominent members include the Key and Taney families, Catholics from Saint Mary's County, who have several representatives in the early period, including Francis Scott Key and Roger Brooke Taney. The Bowie Family of Prince George's County is also well represented here with Allen Bowie Duckett, and Robert Smith, by marriage, and by attorneys represented in the later time periods.

This compilation was completed in 2017 before my retirement.

Patricia Abelard Andersen, Librarian of Montgomery History.

---

[1] Bowie, *Across the Years in Prince George's County,* 470-471.
[2] Scharf, 667.
[3] Van Horn, *Out of the Past,* 244.

HENRY ASHTON (1780-1834)

Admitted to Prince George's County Bar 1812[1]
Admitted to Montgomery County Bar 1816[2]

BIRTH/PARENTS Henry Ashton was born ca. 1780 to Henry Alexander Ashton and Mary Dent of Charles County, MD, who were married on 25 May 1778[3]

EDUCATION He earned a Doctor of Medicine from University of Pennsylvania on 11 Jun 1803.[4]

LEGAL CAREER He was appointed Prosecuting Attorney for Prince George's County in 1815.[5] Several notices appear in the *National Intelligencer* naming him as trustee in real estate sales. Also he appeared on a list with Henry Clay, Francis Key, John Mason and other prominent men of DC as members of the American Society for Colonizing the Free People of Color.[6] In 1822, he was a candidate for county council in the second ward (DC).[7] In 1831 he was nominated as Marshall of DC.[8] At the time of his death he was Marshall of the District of Columbia and the Supreme Court.[9]

MARRIAGE 12 May 1804, in St. Mary's County to Cecelia Brown Key, daughter of Philip Key and Rebecca Jowles Sothoron. She was born ca. 1784 and died 2 Jul 1835 in Washington City, D.C.[10] Her will was presented for probate on 7 Jul 1835, and sets up a trust for her daughter Elinor Miles, to have ½ of furniture and wearing apparel; daughter Cecelia to have other ½ of wearing apparel and bed furniture; daughter Jane Walker, personalty, granddaughter Cecelia Stewart, her watch; to Rev. Mr. Mulledy of Georgetown College in trust for son Henry Ashton, books, bookcase, plate and two servants; money to be in hands of brother H.G.S. Key and son-in-law, Mr. Walker.

CHILDREN:

1. Eleanor Hawkins Ashton, b. 1807, d. after 1874, m. 15 Feb 1827 to James Miles, b. abt 1804, d. after 1870[11]
2. Mary Rebecca Latham Ashton, b. 26 Aug. 1809, Washington, D.C., d. 16 Sep. 1875 at Gaithersburg, MD,[12] m. 1. 20 Oct 1826 to Alexander Dyer, who d. about

---

[1] VanHorn, *Out of the Past,* 254
[2] Scharf, 667
[3] Newman, *The Maryland Dents,* 45.
[4] *National Intelligencer*, 20 Jun 1803
[5] Van Horn, *Op.cit.,* 265.
[6] *National Intelligencer*, 16 May 1820
[7] *National Intelligencer,* 29 Apr 1822
[8] *National Intelligencer,* 1 Feb 1831
[9] *National Intelligencer*, 1 Mar 1834
[10] *National Intelligencer*, 3 Jul 1835
[11] Pipenger, *District of Columbia Marriage License, 1811-1858.*
[12] Malloy, et. al., *Montgomery County Wills,* "Rebecca Bibb of Georgetown, D.C." names son George Lawrence Alexander Dyer, daughter Caroline Matilda Brown, and Ella Hunter, sister Eleanor Elizabeth Miles. A long obituary with birth & death dates was published in Pippenger, *Georgetown Courrier, 1865-1876,* 153.

1830 of consumption, m. 2. 22 May 1832, George R. Bibb,[1] b. 30 Oct. 1776, d. 14 April 1859, Georgetown. Judge Bibb served in the U.S. Senate from Kentucky, where he had a long judicial career[2].

3. Jane C. Ashton, b. 1808, d. 1854, m. 17 Jan 1832 to Dudley Walker, b. 1795, d. 1877, Providence, R.I.[3]
4. Mary Dent Ashton, b. ca. 1810, d. 10 Feb. 1880, m. 1. 31 Mar 1829,[4] Joseph Noble Stuart; m. 2. Johannis Greenfield Dent Storke, m. 3. after 1860, her brother-in-law, then widower, George Dent (1808-1885) of Charles County. She died testate in Gaithersburg, Montgomery County, making bequests to her daughter, Mary Jane Miles, and in trust for her son, Joseph Storke. [5]
5. Caroline Henry Ashton b. abt 1813, d. 1 Mar. 1852, m. 1. 30 May 1833 to Charles Rufus Ramsey, m. 2. 1 June 1841, George S. Watkins[6].
6. Cecilia Ashton, b. 1815-
7. Sarah B. Ashton, b. 1817, d. 1885, m. Oct 1831 to John Moore Todd, b. 1815, d. 1903[7].
8. Anna Sophia Ashton, b. 1817[8], d. 25 Sep. 1860[9], m. 21 Oct 1833 to George Dent. B. 29 Feb 1808, d. 30 June 1885, Montgomery County, MD. He married 2nd., his sister-in-law, Mary Dent Ashton, then a widow.[10]
9. Henry Ashton, b. abt 1823, d. 31 Jan 1846, on U.S. Frigate Cumberland, in Boston Harbor. Unmarried.[11]

DEATH 27 Feb 1834 in Washington, DC[12]

NOTES Henry Ashton served during the War of 1812 as a Major in 4th Regimental Cavalry Dist and as a Lieutenant-Colonel 45 Regiment.[13] His primary residence was Washington, D.C. He was listed as head of household in the 1820 Federal Census, Washington, D.C., Ward 2.

---

[1] Pippenger, District of Columbia *Marriage Licenses 1811-1858.*

[2] *Biographical Direcory of the American Congress,* 550.

[3] Pippenger, *Georgetown: Marriage and Death Notices, 1801-1838,* 215; *Find-A-Grave,* searched 12-2-2016.

[4] Pippenger, District of Columbia *Marriage Licenses, 1811-1858.*

[5] Malloy, *Genealogical Abstracts*, 10 lists her as Ashton, Mary Dent. More information in Newman, *Maryland Dents,* 82-83.

[6] Pippenger, District of Columbia *Marriage Licenses, 1811-1858* for 2 marriages, and Pippenger, *Daily National Intelligencer, Marriage and Death Notices, January 1, 1851-Dec. 30, 1854,* "in her 39th year, wife of Geo. L. Watkins, daughter of the late Col. Henry Ashton.

[7] Rosemaie Hill Stewart, *Charles County Maryland, 1850,* 258. She is 33 years old, he is 34, remarks include death dates, both buried Christ Church, Wayside.

[8] Rosemaie Hill Stewart, *Charles County Maryland, 1850,* she is 33 years old.

[9] Roberta J. Wearmouth, *Abstracts from the Port Tobacco Times and Charles County Advertiser, Vol. two: 1855-1869,* 118. [Bowie, Md., Heritage Books, 1991]

[10] Newman, Maryland Dents, 82-83..

[11] *National Intelligencer,* 16 Feb. 1846.

[12] *National Intelligencer,* 1 Mar 1834.

[13] Marine, *The British Invasion of Maryland,* 206.

LEWIS PENN WITHERSPOON BALCH (1787 – 1868)

Admitted to Montgomery County Bar 1809[1]

BIRTH/PARENTS: Lewis P. W. Balch was born at Georgetown on 31 Dec. 1787 to Stephen Bloomer Balch, D.D. (5 April 1747 to 22 Sep 1833) and Elizabeth Beall Balch (b. 18 Jan. 1765, d. 27 Jul 1827) who were married on 10 Jul 1781.[2]

EDUCATION He graduated from Princeton College in 1805. He studied law with Roger Brooke Taney and became a judge of the highest tribunal in West Virginia.[3]

LEGAL CAREER He began his law practice in Frederickstown, Virginia.[4] It was most likely his strong sentiments, in favor of the Union during the Civil War, that helped him secure the position of state circuit judge, within the northeast counties of West Virginia, in March of 1865. He would serve as a state circuit judge until March 1866.[5]

MARRIAGE 14 March 1811, to Elizabeth Willis Wever, b. 10 May 1790, d. 7 July 1874, daughter of Adam Wever of Jefferson County.[6]

CHILDREN Lewis and Elizabeth had 12 children and 6 survived to adulthood.[7]

1. Adam Weber Balch, b. 31 March 1812, d. 30 July 1813
2. Lewis P.W. Balch, b. 23 Feb 1814, Leesburg, Loudoun County, Virginia, d. 4 June 1875, Detroit, Wayne County, Michigan, m. 19 April 1839 in Bedford, Westchester County, New York, to Anna Jay, (b. 17 Aug. 1813, d. 5 Jan 1849, New York City). Had issue.
3. Catherine Elizabeth Spencer Balch, b. 28 Nov. 1815, Leesburg, Loudoun County, VA., d. 1 July 1850 in Leetown, Jefferson County, W.Va., m. 25 July 1844, Washington County, Maryland, to Freeman Clarkson.
4. Virginia Melancthon Balch, b. 18 Mar 1818, Leesburg, Loudoun County, Va., d. 22 Oct. 1898 in Washington, D.C., m. 21 Dec. 1841, Baltimore, MD, Charles H. Stephen (1816-1883).
5. Harriet Cornelia Balch, b. 26 Dec. 1819, d. 5 August 1820, Leesburg, Loudoun County, VA.
6. Thomas Balch, b. 23 July 1821, Leesburg, Loudoun County, Va., d. 29 Mar.1877, Philadelphia, Pa., m. Emily Swift, b. 26 Sept 1832, d. 6 Jan 1917, Philadelphia, PA. Had issue.[8]
7. Anna Beall Balch, b.25 May 1823, d. 12 Sep. 1824, Leesburg, Loudoun County, VA.

---

[1] Scharf, 667.
[2] MCHS Family File: Balch family.
[3] *Records of the Columbia Historical Society*, v. 15, Clark, "Rev. Stephen Bloomer Balch", 89.
[4] *Ancestry.com*, "Brief Biography of Judge Balch", 210 of *Colonial and Revolutionary Families of Pennsylvania: General and Personal Memoirs.*
[5] balchipedia.wikidot.com/lewispwbalch, accessed November3, 2015.
[6] MCHS Family File: Balch family
[7] Information on children from the MCHS Balch Family File..
[8] Historical Society of Pennsylvania, Balch Family Papers, finding aid on- line.

8. Sylvester Whitefield Balch, b. 9 March 1825, d. 22 Jun 1825, Leesburg, Loudoun County, VA.
9. John Wilson Balch, b. 22 July 1826, d. 15 August 1826, Leesburg, Loudoun County, VA.
10. Frances Carter Balch, b. 10 July 1827, d. 28 July 1827, Frederick, MD.
11. Alexandrine Macomb Balch, b. Sep 1828, Frederick, MD, d. 9 April 1900, Lutherville, Baltimore County, MD, m. 24 June 1847, Leetown, Jefferson County, W.Va., George David Cummins, (b. 11 Dec 1822, DE, d. 26 Jun 1876, Lutherville, MD).
12. Stephen Fitzhugh Balch, b. 14 March 1831, Frederick, MD, d. 20 May 1893, Philadelphia, PA, m. Aletha Matilda Boteler (b. 22 July 1836, Carroll County, MD, d. 8 Jan. 1913).

DEATH Lewis P. W. Balch death is reported as 29 Aug.1868 in Leetown, Jefferson Co., W.VA.[1]

NOTES In 1834 he was financially able to free his 27 slaves in Baltimore, and paid $1500 to send them to the American Colony in Liberia.[2]

JAMES BOYLE (1784-1854)

Admitted to Prince George's County Bar 1815[3]
Admitted to Montgomery County Bar 1816[4]

BIRTH/PARENTS: James Boyle was born 30 March 1784, to James Boyle (1744-1784) and Mary (Brewer) Boyle, (b. 1748).[5]

EDUCATION: Attended St. John's College, Annapolis, (B.A., M. A., 1800).[6]

LEGAL CAREER: Member, Executive Council; member of the House of Delegates, Annapolis, 1808-10; 1819-20; Mayor of Annapolis, 1823-25; State's Attorney for Anne Arundel County, 1848-51; member of the board of visitors and governors, St. John's College, Annapolis.[7]

---

[1] Ancestry.com "West Virginia Deaths Index", 1853-1973.
[2] *http://balchipedia.wikidot.com/lewispwbalch*, accessed November 3, 2015.
[3] Van Horn, *Out of the Past*, 265.
[4] Scharf, 667.
[5] McIntire, *Annapolis Maryland Families,* 75
[6] St. John's College, *Alumni Register, 1793-1967*
[7] Archives of Maryland: Biographical Series: James Boyle on-line, special collections.

MARRIAGE: on 12 May 1812,[1] Susan Maccubbin, b. 3 Sep. 1795, d. 27 Jan. 1864)[2] daughter of Samuel Maccubbin, b. 6 Mar. 1763, d. 27 Nov. 1838, and Mary Ann Rawlings Maccubbin, b 14 Dec. 1769, d. 5. Dec. 1835.

CHILDREN[3]

1. James Boyle, Jr., b. 13 June 1813, d. 17 Feb. 1889. (unmarried)
2. John Henry Boyle, b. 21 July 1815, d. 20 Feb 1866, m. 6 Mar 1838, Ellen Slemaker
3. Edwin Boyle, b. 26 Feb 1818, d. 29 Dec. 1900.
4. Mary Ann Boyle, b.30 Mar 1820, d. 8 Archives of Maryland: Biographical Series: James Boyle Oct 1836.
5. Llewellyn Boyle, b.30 Mar 1823.
6. Violetta Boyle, b. 29 May 1825, d. 5 Dec. 1831.
7. Susan Maccubbin Boyle, b. 8 Feb. 1828, d.10 Dec. 1831.

DEATH 28 Sept. 1854 in AnneArundel County, MD.[4]

NOTES Volunteered as a Private in Capt. Samuel Maynard's Company in Annapolis during War of 1812.[5] Gave address when Marquis de Lafayette visited Annapolis 17 Dec. 1824 as "Col. James Boyle, Mayor of the city."[6]

WILLIAM LEIGH BRENT (1784-1848)

Admitted to Montgomery County Bar 1803[7]

Admitted to Washington County Bar Prior To 1815[8]

BIRTH/PARENTS: William L. Brent was born 20 Feb. 1784 in Port Tobacco, Charles County, MD[9] to Robert Brent IV (1750-1810) and Dorothy Leigh Brent (1758-1790).[10]

LEGAL CAREER: He lived in Hagerstown, 1805-1815.[11] In *The History of Washington County, Maryland*, William L. Brent was listed as one of the principal Washington County lawyers of 1805. In 1809 William L. Brent was elected a member of the Maryland House of Delegates for Washington County. He spoke at a meeting in Hagerstown, MD celebrating the election of James Madison and he was appointed secretary of a committee to present "...a suitable address" to retiring president, Thomas Jefferson.[12] He was appointed by

---

[1] Barnes, *Marriages and Deaths from the Maryland Gazette, 1727-1839,* 15

[2] USDAR, *Tombstone Inscriptions of Southern Anne Arundel County,* 145

[3] McIntire, *op.cit.*

[4] McIntire, *op.cit.*

[5] Wright. *Maryland Militia War of 1812, Vol.4, Anne Arundel & Calvert,* 67

[6] Riley, *A History of Annapolis, 1649-1887,* 158.

[7] Scharf, 667.

[8] Williams, *History of Washington County,* 555. Scharf, 1131

[9] *Biographical Directory of the American Congress, (BDAC)* p. 595

[10] Ancestry.com, family trees "A Wise Man Said"

[11] Scharf, 1070

[12] Scharf, 1063,1070, 144

President Madison as deputy attorney general for the western district of the Territory of Orleans; elected to Congress from 1823 to 1829; practiced law in Louisiana and Washington, D.C.[1]

MARRIAGE: 4 April 1809, by Rev. John L. Fenwick[2] to Maria Fenwick of Welonton, Charles County, MD. (d. 31 Dec 1835). She was the daughter of Col. James Fenwick and Henrietta Lancaster[3].

CHILDREN: Joseph Lancaster Brent, b. 30 November 1826[4]

DEATH: 7 July 1848 in St. Martinville, LA.[5]

NOTES: In March 1807, William L. Brent and Otho H. W. Stull, both of Washington County, MD, fought a duel in Shepherdstown, VA. Both survived but Brent was wounded in his leg.[6]

THOMAS BUCHANAN (1768-1847)

Admitted to Montgomery County Bar, 1803[7]

BIRTH/PARENTS: Thomas Buchanan was born 25 Sept. 1768, near Port Tobacco, Charles County, the eldest son of Thomas Buchanan (1740-1787) and Anne Maria Cooke Buchanan. (1749-1836)

LEGAL CAREER First practiced law in Charles and St. Mary's counties until 1798 marriage. He then moved to Baltimore and then to Hagerstown. He was admitted to the bar of Montgomery County in 1803 and Washington County in 1815. He succeeded the Hon. Roger Nelson as judge of circuit court of Washington County in 1815, and was named chief justice of that court in 1825. [8]

MARRIAGE 11 April 1798, Rebecca Maria Harriett Anderson, b. Spring 1775, England, d. 27 Sep 1847, Washington County, MD, daughter of James Anderson, and Meliora (Ogle) Anderson. Rebecca was the granddaughter of Gov. Samuel Ogle.[9]

---

[1] *BDAC,* 595,

[2] Wright, *Western Maryland Newspaper Abstracts,* Volume 3, p. 77, item 418, *Maryland Herald and Hagerstown Advertiser,* 14 April 1809.

[3] SAR Application, tracing descent from Major Ignatius Fenwick Jr., of St. Mary's County from Ancestry.com.

[4] SAR Application, op.cit.

[5] *BDAC,* op.cit.

[6] Wright, op.cit., p. 55, item 314, *Maryland Herald and Hagerstown Advertiser,* 20 March 1807.

[7] Scharf, 667

[8] Scharf, op.cit., 1116, sketch of Judge Thomas Buchanan includes 1847 obituary notice.

[9] Baltz, *Chronicle of Belair*, p. 5 of part two Genealogies.

CHILDREN [1]

1. Anne Ogle Buchanan, b. abt 1799, d. 20 April 1839, m. 30 Sept. 1819, Hagerstown, Md., John Nevett Steele (1796-1853).
2. Meliora Ogle Buchanan, b. 24 Dec. 1800, d. 2 April 1879, m. 23 Feb. 1819, John Robert Dall (1798-1851)
3. Thomas Cribb Buchanan (unknown dates) disappeared from home as a minor but was, nevertheless, included in his father's will.
4. Harriett Rebecca Anderson Buchanan, b. 1803, d. 11 Feb. 1872. Buried St. John's Episcopal Church, Hagerstown. Never married.
5. James Anderson Buchanan, b. 21 Dec. 1804, d. 1844, m. 1. Anna Maria Nelson of Baltimore, she d. September 1836; m. 2 Ellenora Elder Miller (1821-1861).

NOTES Thomas was the elder brother of John Buchanan, who was named chief justice of the Fifth District court after his brother died.[2] Thomas Buchanan was active in civic and community affairs. He was a board member of the Hagerstown Academy, which was founded in 1810 and began operating in 1813. He was a co-founder and director of Conococheague Bank of Williamsport. He was also a member of the committee to aid Cumberland after most of the town was destroyed by fire in 1833.[3]

EDWARD BURGESS (1733 – 1809)

Justice of Montgomery County Orphan's Court, 1777-1790[4]

BIRTH/PARENTS: Edward Burgess was born ca. 1733, Anne Arundel County, MD, to John (b. 17 Nov. 1696, d. bef. 10 Jan.-1774) and Jane (McElfresh) Burgess[5] (b. 15 Mar. 1700, d. 16 Mar.-1833)

LEGAL CAREER He served as Justice of Frederick County, Maryland, 1773-1775; Justice of Montgomery County, Maryland, 1777-1792; and member of the House of Delegates, 1777-1795.[6]

MARRIAGE He was married by 1767 to Mary Davis, b. 21 Dec 1733, d. 1784, daughter of Thomas (1704-1749) and Elizabeth (Gaither) (1711-1773) Davis.[1]

---

[1] Baltz, op.cit., p. 5, 16-17 lists children and descendants.

[2] Scharf, op.cit., 1116

[3] Williams, *History of Washington County, MD*

[4] Papenfuse, *Biographical Dictionary, Vol. 1:181, sketch of Edward Burgess*

[5] Papenfuse, op.cit.

[6] Papenfuse, op.cit.

CHILDREN[2]

1. Edward Burgess Jr. d. bef. 4 May 1824[3], testate, in Montgomery County, naming sisters as heirs.
2. Elizabeth Burgess d. bef. 12 Nov. 1824[4], testate in Montgomery County, unmarried.
3. John Burgess, d. 1813, m. by license dated 19 Mar 1800[5], Eleanor (Helen) Maccubbin (b. ca. 1783) daughter of Zachariah Maccubbin (b. abt. 1751, d. bef. 1832) and Martha Needham Maccubbin (d. bef 1842)[6].
4. Ephraim Burgess, b. 1768, d. Allegany County, m. abt 1790, Elizabeth Magruder, daughter of Joseph Magruder and Mary (Jackson) Magruder.
5. Thomas Burgess "left Maryland".
6. Ann/Nancy Burgess, d. 1826, unmarried.
7. Jane Burgess, d. bef. Aug. 1824[7], unmarried.
8. Mary Burgess m. 9 Sep. 1785,[8] John Sheckles/Shekell and left Maryland
9. Sally/Sarah Burgess b. abt 1770, d. abt 1800, m. 19 Feb. 1787,[9] Daniel Hook b. abt 1760, d. 1809, in Virginia.
10. Margaret Burgess, b. 1772, d. 1844, m. 5 Sep. 1804[10], Ninian Magruder Clagett, b. 1774, d. 1841.

DEATH 5 December 1809 intestate, in Montgomery County, MD.[11]

NOTES Edward Burgess had property near present day Summit Hall in Gaithersburg; a store on the Frederick Road at Log Town (near Gaithersburg High School); and a residence west of Frederick Road near Ascension Church. He raised and became Captain of the first company of "minute men" in Montgomery County (Flying Camp).[12] He was Captain of the 7th Company, 29th Battalion, 1776-1781 and administered the Oath of Allegiance in 1778.[13]

---

1 Newman, *Anne Arundel Gentry*, Vol. 1, Burgess Family, 26-28

2 Newman, op.cit., and Papenfuse, op.cit. both list children with some data, including those who"left Maryland.".

3 Malloy, et.al., *Montgomery County Will Abstracts.*

4 Malloy, et.al., *Montgomery County Will Abstracts*

5 Manuel, *Marriage Licenses: Montgomery County,* 46

6 William M. LeoGrande and Jerome F. Collins, "The Maccubbin Family of Montgomery County," *Maryland Genealogical Society Bulletin,* Vol. 37, No. 1, Winter 1996.

7 In her will dated in August 1824, cited above, Elizabeth mentions her sister Jane's estate.

8 Myers, *Frederick County Licenses, 17.*

9 Myers, *Frederick County Licenses, 17.*

10 Manuel, op.cit., 47

11 Papenfuse, *op.cit.*

12 *Gaithersburg: The Heart of Montgomery County*, .

13 Peden, *Revolutionary Patriots, Montgomery County,* 45-46.

AENEAS CAMPBELL (1730-1812)

Judge of the Orphans Court, 1779-1792[1]

BIRTH/PAREMTS: Aeneas Campbell was born abt 1730[2], probably in St. Mary's County. He moved to Virginia by 1754. His parents have not been identified.

LEGAL CAREER Aeneas Campbell was active as Justice of the Peace in Frederick County by 1768, through 1774, and from 1777 in Montgomery County. He served as a Justice of the Peace, and Judge of the Orphans Court from 1779-1792. As Justice of the peace, he administered the oath of Allegiance, 1776–1777 and served as a Major in 16th Bn Militia, Sept 12, 1777, and as their Colonel from Oct 7, 1777.[3]

MARRIAGE(S):[4]

1. Abt 1753, Lydia Cartwright, (d. abt 1770) by whom he had at least five children.
2. 27 Nov. 1775[5], Margaret Hickman (b. abt 1731[6], d. bef. 1793) widow of Joshua Hickman (b.1730, d.bef. Dec. 1769) by whom she had four children.
3. 24 December 1793,[7] Henrietta Chaney (b. ca. 1747, d. 1828)

CHILDREN

By first wife[8]:

1. James Campbell b. in 1754, d. 14 September 1827, see following sketch.
2. Aeneas Campbell, b. 3 Oct 1757 in Loudoun County, d. 15 Oct 1828, Iredel County, N.C., m. 1. Abt 1778, Montgomery County, Sarah Hickman, daughter of Solomon Hickman (d. 1778)[9]; m. 2. Elizabeth Ann Belt (b. 20 Feb 1767, d. 3 Jan. 1853, Wilkes County, Georgia). Had issue by both wives[10].

---

[1] Scharf, 665

[2] Brumbaugh, *Maryland Records,* Vol. I, 206-207, from 1776 Census Frederick County, Eneas Campbell Senr age46, Eneas Jr., 18, Margrate 45, Hester 17, Lidia 15, Ann 8, and Kitty White 4 months

[3] Peden, *Revolutionary Patriots, Montgomery County,* 54.

[4] Campbell Family File, MCHS Library, information on Aeneas Campbell's marriages and children from Mrs. Glenn E. Freeman, Rte 1, Box 153, Windfall, Indiana, forwarded to us by Linda Layman

[5] *Montgomery County Orphans Court Liber A, transcript,* mss in Jane C. Sween Library, date of marriage noted in inventory of Joshua Hickman, delivered by Eneas Campbell.

[6] Brumbaugh, op.cit., age 45 in 1776.

[7] Myers, *Frederick County Marriage Licenses.*

[8] Andersen, *Frederick County Deed Abstracts, 1773-1778,* 53. Liber W:338-339, to James Campbell, Aeneas Campbell Junr., Esther Campbell, Lydia Campbell, and Ann Campbell, recorded 24 Nov. 1774, for natural love and affection, he confirmed to them various slaves, furniture; and part of a lease he had of Mary Elmendorf, called *Frozen Level* to his son James Campbell.

[9] *Montgomery County Orphans Court Liber A, transcript,* mss in Jane C. Sween Library, inventory presented by Aeneas Campbell, 17 Mar. 1778.

[10] Campbell Family File, MCHS library.

3. Hester Campbell, b. 1759, d. 1828, m. 14 July 1779[1], Leven Covington Beall (b. 1760, d. 1822)
4. Ann Campbell, b. abt. 1760, d. 23 Apr. 1808, m. 1. Abt 1780, Carlton Belt, (1744-1802), m. 2. 30 Mar. 1807, William Trail (b. 1770, d. 1833).
5. Lydia Campbell, b. 1761, apparently unmarried in 1812

By second wife:

6. Kitty White Campbell, b. 1776.[2] No other information.

DEATH Between 14 February 1812 when he signed codicil to will and 21 April 1812 in Montgomery County when will was probated[3]. In his will he named his sons James and Aeneas, daughter Hester Beall, wife of Leven Beall, and two great grand children Thomas Noland Davis and Catherine Noland, daughter of Thomas Noland, deceased.

JAMES CAMPBELL (1754-1827)

Judge of The Orphans Court, 1777-1779[4]

BIRTH/PARENTS: James Campbell was born between 1747 to 1754, probably in Loudoun County, Virginia to Aeneas Campbell (1730-1812) and his first wife Lydia [Cartwright] Campbell (d. ca 1770)

CAREER James Campbell served as a private, 8th co., Upper BN Militia on Aug 30, 1777. He took oath of allegiance before Aeneas Campbell on March 2, 1778 and recruited to serve as a private in Continential Army in 1780. Private in Virginia Line, who pensioned in 1818, "aged 71," while living in Montgomery County. [5]

MARRIAGE No record of marriage or children found.

DEATH 14 September 1827.[6]

WILLIAM CLAGETT (1768-1810)

Admitted to Montgomery County Bar 1797[7]

BIRTH/PARENTS William Clagett was born about 1768 to Alexander Clagett (b. 2 Sept.1742, d. 11 June 1821, Baltimore City) and his first wife, married 24 Dec. 1767 in Frederick County, Elizabeth Perry (b. about 1745, d. 1777), daughter of Benjamin Perry and Elizabeth Magruder Perry. Alexander Clagett married 2. abt. 1777, Eleanor Beall

---

[1] Mss. Copy of Montgomery County Marriages, of Minister's Returns from MSA. Rev.Clement Brooke.

[2] Brumbaugh, op.cit.,

[3] Montgomery County Wills, Liber H, folio 13. Copy in Family File, MCHS Library.

[4] Scharf, 665.

[5] Peden, *Revolutionary Patriots, Montgomery County,* p. 54-55

[6] *Ibid.,* Peden's reference is the *Maryland Pension Rolls of 1835...*

[7] Scharf, 667

(1755-1830), daughter of Samuel Beall and Eleanor Brooke. Alexander Clagett was elected Washington County Sheriff 13 October 1779.[1]

LEGAL CAREER In 1791 William Clagett was a member of the House of Delegates. He was appointed a chief justice on 28 Jan 1802 in the 5th Judicial District (MD) comprehending the counties of Frederick, Washington, Montgomery and Allegany. He qualified as an attorney in Washington County (MD) prior to 1805. He was admitted to practice law in Allegany County (MD) in 1791 after paying the State license fee of 3 pounds. [2]

MARRIAGE No record of marriage or children found for William Clagett.

DEATH He died 25 Mar 1810 in Hagerstown, Maryland "...after a lingering illness."[3] No will or estate distribution recorded. Index to wills indicates that there was an estate filed in 1810 in Washington County[4]

JOHN COOK (1783-1847)

Early Member of Montgomery County Bar[5]

BIRTH/PARENTS John Cook, b. ca.1782 in Frederick County, Maryland to Captain George[6] and Elizabeth (Johnson) Cook of Frederick County. Elizabeth was the daughter of Thomas Johnson (1702-1777) and Dorcas Sedgwick Johnson (1705-1770). She died 23 June 1806, and was buried in the Episcopal Church Yard in Frederick.[7] John's brother, Thomas Cook (who died 8 August 1826 in Georgetown, D.C.)[8] mentions his brother, John, in his will along with heirs of his sister Ann Cook Brashears. (1767-1839)[9] A third brother, James, was also probably a lawyer, who died in Georgetown before April 1798, when Thomas Cook presented his inventory which included law books purchased of J. Johnson. The final account of James Cook's estate was recorded in Montgomery County in December 1812.[10]

---

1 Peden, *Revolutionary Patriots of Washington County,* 62.

2 Scharf, *History of Western Maryland,* 988, 478, 1131, 1345-6.

3 *Ibid*, 1047

4 Morrow and Jensen, *Wills of Washington County, Index:1776-1890.* 7.

5 He is not listed in Scharf, but the register that is printed there is missing all entries from 1822-1829, theperiod in which he moved from Frederick County to Montgomery County. It is likely that he was practicing in Frederick before 1825.

6 MCLR, Liber Q:370-372. Anne Brashears, wife to Belt Brashears, recorded deed 23 June 1813 from Thomas Cook and John Cook, both of Frederick County, heirs of George Cook, for $454. Sells tract called *Rich Barrons.*

7 Wright, *Western Maryland Newspaper Abstracts, 1806-1810,* item 26, p. 6.

8 *Pippinger, District of Columbia Probate Records,* p.135, names wife Catherine Cook, brother Col. John Cook, and Dr. Belt Brashears executors, nephew Thomas Cook Brashear, also named in John Cook's will. Also Pippenger, *Georgetown District ofColumbia, Marriage and Death Notices 1801-1838.*

9 Brashear, *A Brashear(s) Family History,* Vol. 1, p. 223.

10 Montgomery County Orphans Court Records, Libers D: 105, inventory; D:386 list of debts; D:385, 1st account; G:522 final account.

LEGAL CAREER John Cook is identified as a practicing attorney in Rockville, from Information gleaned from articles in early Rockville newspapers. In 1819 his office was located in Judge Kilgour's former office; in 1822 he moved his office one door west of the Post office. There were advertisements for his services in 1826 and 1831.[1]

MARRIAGE On 24 April 1823 by Montgomery County license to Mary M. Campbell[2]. She appears to be the sister of Iver Campbell, and probably came with him into the county around 1810 from Winchester, Frederick County, VA. Her parents were probably John Campbell (1746-1807) and Elizabeth Sowers She was living in November 1848 when she sold her property in Montgomery County. She has not been found on the 1850 census, but since she owned property in Allegany County, and in Virginia, she may have moved there.

CHILDREN No children have been identified. His will named as heirs, his wife, Mary C. Cook, and nieces and nephews, children of his brothers and his sister Ann, and Iver Campbell and Alvin Cook Campbell, no relationship given. No later records were found on the Campbells.

DEATH "Died on October 8 [1847] in Rockville, Montgomery County, after a severe and protracted illness in his 64th year, Col. John Cook, one of the oldest members of the Montgomery Bar, for many years a highly respected citizen of the village."[3]

NOTES In John Cook's will, written on 21 Apr 1846 and probated on 16 Nov 1847, Mary M. Cook is listed as his wife and executor.[4] She filed an inventory of the estate and record of sales in 1847. In February 1848 she filed an account, which left her a balance of about $1200. He was a vestryman at Christ Church, Rockville, Prince George Parish[5]; president of the Second School District of Montgomery County in 1840, and in 1846, he became the first treasurer of the Brookeville Lodge, No. 50, I.O.O. F.[6]

The following summary of his military service during the War of 1812 was found for John Cook: Appointed "13 Feb. 1812 as capt. of a troop of horse; promoted 18 Sep. 1812, Major of 2nd Regt., 1st Cav. Dist.; promoted to lieut. col. in place of Henry Kemp 21 Dec. 1814."[7]

---

1 Jacobs and Malloy, *People, Places, and Potpourri*, 5.

2 MCLR Liber W:536-537. Johnson Hilton recorded deed of trust 24 April 1823 from Mary M. Campbell. Whereas a marriage is about to be solemnized between Mary M. Campbell of Montgomery County and John Cook; and the said parties agree for all property of which the said Mary M. Campbell now holds consisting of enumerated furniture, to be held in trust by Johnson Hilton. Manuel, *Marriage Licenses:*73

3 Dixon, *National Intelligenc*er, 15 Oct.1847

4 Malloy, et.al., *Abstracts of Wills: Montgomery County, Maryland, 1826-1875*, 33

5 In copies of the Vestry Minutes of Christ Church, Prince George's Parish, he is often listed as Col. John Cook, either going on or off Vestry, serving as Warden, and one year as delegate to the Episcopal Convention in the 1830s through early 1840s.

6 Scharf, *History of Western Maryland,* 748, 757, 782

7Mallick & Wright, *Frederick County Militia in the War of 1812*, 82.

JEREMIAH CRABB (1760 -1800)

State Representative 1788-1792, Associate Justice 1791-92[1].

BIRTH/PARENTS: Jeremiah Crabb was born about 1760 in Frederick County, MD to Henry Wright Crabb (b. 16 Jan. 1722/23, d. 12 June 1764) and Ann (Snowden) Crabb (1725-1775)[2].

LEGAL CAREER: He served as a Justice in the Montgomery County Court, 10 Jan. 1791, until 28 Dec. 1792.[3] He represented Montgomery County in the Lower House of the Maryland Assembly, 1788-1792, serving as speaker of the House in 1791.[4] He was the first Democrat to serve as U.S. Congressman from Montgomery County, in 1795-6.

MARRIAGE: 10 August 1785 to Elizabeth Ridgely Griffith (b. 10 Aug. 1764, Anne Arundel County, d. 31 Jan. 1824, "age 60"[5] daughter of Charles Greenberry Griffith (b. 17 May 1744, d. 12 Aug. 1792) and Sarah (Ridgely) Griffith. (b. 14 Nov. 1743)[6]

CHILDREN:[7]

1. Nancy (Anne) Snowden Crabb, (b. abt 1783) m. 10 Nov. 1800, Dr. Richard Johns Orme,(1771-1834) son of Col. Archibald Orme. (1730-1812) and Elizabeth (Johns).Orme.
2. Charles Henry Crabb, m. 28 Nov. 1811 to Mary L. Summers, daughter of Dr. Zadock Summers
3. Elizabeth Ridgely Crabb, b. 1789, d. 8 Nov 1821, m. 26 Mar 1807 to Thomas Worthington Howard (d. 1819). Buried in Crabb Family Cemetery.
4. Richard J. Crabb, b. 1792, m. 4 Nov 1813, Anne Arundel County, to Catherine Chase. Buried at St. Ann's Church Cemetery, Annapolis.
5. Sarah Griffith Crabb, b. 27 Jan. 1793, d. 27 Apr 1862, m. 27 Jan 1825 to Philemon Griffith as his second wife. Buried in Crabb Family Cemetery.
6. Matilda Crabb, b. `2 May 1795, d. 15 June 1860 in Missouri, m. 26 Dec. 1817 to James Cooper Lackland. (1791-1862, St Charles, Missouri).
7. Emeline Crabb, b. 12 July 1797, m. Nathan Nelson.
8. Lydia Ridgely Crabb, b. 24 June 1799, d. 20 March 1864 in Texas, m. 28 Aug 1823 to Michael Berry Griffith.

DEATH: 19 Feb. 1800. Both he and his wife are buried in the Crabb Cemetery, near Derwood, MD.[8]

---

[1]Papenfuse, et.al., *Biographical Dictionary,* 240-241.
[2]Papenfuse, et.al., *op.cit.* and Prall, *Crabb Family,* Vol. 1, 220.
[3]Prall, *Crabb Family, Vol 1, 226-227.*
[4]Hiebert and McMaster, *Grateful Remembrance,* 403.
[5]Brown, *Index to the Register of Prince George's Parish,* Section 2.
[6]Hurley, *Griffith Families, 15-18.*and Prall, *op.cit.*
[7] MCHS Crabb Family file; Prall, *Crabb Family,* 226.
[8] MCHS Cemetery File

NOTES: Served in the Revolutionary War; 1st Lt., and 2nd Lt., resigned after Valley Forge. Served as a Brig. General in the Maryland Militia, with active duty in the 1794 Whiskey Rebellion.[1]

THOMAS CRAMPHIN, JR. (1740 – 1830)

Orphans Court Judge 1792-1802[2]

BIRTH/PARENTS: Thomas Cramphin Jr. was born 26 Jan. 1740 in Rock Creek Parish, Prince George's Co., MD [3] to Thomas Cramphin, Sr, (1715-1783), "innholder", and his first wife Mary (Jackson) Cramphin[4]

LEGAL CAREER: He Represented Frederick County (before Montgomery County was formed) in Maryland Conventions of 1774 and 1775; served on the Committee of Observation for Frederick County, 1774 to 1775 and signed the "Hungerford Resolves" in Rockville. In 1777, he was chosen Justice for Montgomery County. He represented Montgomery County in the Lower House of the State Assembly 1778-1781; 1784-5; 1788. In 1788 chosen delegate to the Maryland Convention held in Annapolis to ratify the U.S. Constitution. From 1792-1802, he served as Judge of the Orphans' Court. [5]

MARRIAGE No known legal marriage, however in his will, which was not admitted to probate, he makes bequests to Caroline (mulatto) and her children, who were baptized as his mulatto children in Rock Creek Parish.[6] Litigation followed by his siblings, claiming the estate.[7]

CHILDREN :

1. Mary Etta, b. 15 Jan 1822, bp. 2 June 1822
2. Richard, b. 1 May 1824, bp.2 November 1824
3. Hannah, b. 23 November 1825, bp. 2 March 1826
4. Robert, b. 11 March 1827, bp. 2 May 1827

---

[1] Prall, *op.cit.,* and MCHS Library Crabb family file.

[2] Thomas Cramphin was a federalist. He inherited from his father 427 acres of the Hermitage, in vicinity of Glenmont, Montgomery County, today. Politically active and elected to public office from his 30s, he represented the voters in Annapolis in the house of delegates in 1778, 1780, 1784 and 1788. After serving as a delegate to Maryland's ratifying convention, he became Judge of the Orphans Court from 1792 to 1802. *Montgomery County Story,* Vol. 30, No. 2, May 1987, p. 8-9

[3] *Ibid.*

[4] *Ibid. Prince George's County, Indexes of Church Registers*, Vol. II, pg. 179; Jordan, *Early Families of Southern Maryland,* Vol. VI, p.193

[5] Papenfuse, et.al., *Biographical Dictionary,* Vol. I, 242; Peden, *Revolutionary Patriots of Montgomery County,* .79; Hiebert,*Grateful Remembrance,* 31,43, 44,71,76,121, 402, 403; Farquhar, *Old Homes,*. 14, 18, 20, 30, 82, 84, 179, 188

[6] Prince George's County, Indexes of Church Registers, Vol. II, pg. 230.

[7] Estate of Thomas Cramphin. Accession No.: 17,898-12355-1/2 MSA S512-15-12160 Location: 1/39/4/

DEATH Thomas Cramphin died Dec. 1830 "aged 90 years and 10 months" in Montgomery County, buried in Rock Creek Cemetery (Washington, D.C[1]

THOMAS DAVIS (1768-1833)

Judge of The Orphans Court

BIRTH/PARENTS: Thomas Davis was born 10 Dec. 1768 to Ephraim Davis (b. 3 Jan 1736/37, d. 13 Aug. 1769) and Elizabeth (Howard) Davis, (b. 1745, d. 4 Jan. 1793). She married 2nd. William Gaither (b. 15 Feb.1745/46, d. bef.1812).['

LEGAL CAREER: In 1794, and again from 1801-1803, he served as a member of the Maryland House of Delegates from Montgomery County. In 1801 he was on the Levy Court and County Commission; from 1812-1816 he served as a Judge on the Orphans Court.[2]

MARRIAGE:

1. On 21 April 1796, to Catherine Worthington[3] (b. ca. 1776, d. bef. 1802 without issue) daughter of Thomas Worthington (b. 7 Jun 1754, d. 1823[4]) and Margaret Mulliken Worthington.
2. On 21 Jan. 1802, to Elizabeth Bowie, b.11 Sep.1772, d. 23 Nov. 1840, the eldest daughter of Allen Bowie, Jr.,(1737-1803) and Ruth Cramphin (1742-1812) Bowie.[5]

CHILDREN:[6]

1. Catherine Worthington Davis, b. 26 Jun 1803, d. 1 June 1889; m. 14 Jan. 1830,Thomas Johns Bowie,her first cousin, son of Col. Washington Bowie and Mary Crabb Johns.[7].
2. Thomas John Davis, M.D., b. 1805, d. 11 Jul 1828, unmarried.
3. Allen Bowie Davis, b. 16 Feb 1809, d. 17 April 1889, m. 1. 1830, Rebecca Comfort Dorsey, (d. 8 July 1836, no issue) daughter of Judge Thomas Beale Dorsey (b. 17 Oct. 1780, d. 26 Dec. 1855) and Milcah (Goodwin) Dorsey (b. 1782, d. 28 Sept. 1850) of Elkridge. He m. 2. 8 Oct 1839, Anne Wilkins, daughter of William Wilkins of Baltimore.

DEATH: 8 Feb. 1835. He is buried on his farm, the historic Greenwood in Montgomery County[8].

---

[1] Wright, *Marriages and Deaths in the Newspapers of Frederick and Montgomery Counties 1820-1831,* p. 81
[2] Scharf, 664-666 and Farquhar, *Historic Homes, "Greenwood", 177-181.*
[3] Barnes, *Maryland Marriages, 1778-1820,* 54 from Montgomery County Prince George's Parish Records.
[4] Peden, *Revolutionary Patriots of Anne Arundel,* 231.
[5] Bowie, *Across the Years,* 667
[6] Bowie, *op.cit.*
[7] Hurley, *Davis Families,* 75-76.
[8] Farquhar, *Op.cit.*

CHARLES SAMUEL WORTHINGTON DORSEY (1797-1845)

Admitted to the Montgomery County Bar, 1821[1]

BIRTH/PARENTS: Charles S. W. Dorsey was born 6 Mar 1797, to John Worthington Dorsey (1751-1823) who served in the revolutionary army, and Comfort Worthington (1766-1837) Dorsey. They were a family of lawyers and judges[2], including Thomas Beale Dorsey (1780-1855) Charles' older brother, who was Attorney General of Maryland, 1822-1824 and from 1824, Chief Judge, first Judicial District, and from 1824, became an Associate Judge on the Maryland Court of Appeals until 1848 when he became Chief Judge until 1851.

EDUCATION: Princeton University, Class of 1808.

LEGAL CAREER In May 1828, Mr. Dorsey is listed as one of the directors of the Baltimore and Ohio Railroad Company. In February 1829, the General Assembly of Maryland incorporated the Cerralvo Mining Company of Baltimore; Mr. Dorsey was among the company's stockholders. In April 1836, the National Farmers and Planters' Bank of Baltimore was incorporated; Mr. Dorsey was appointed one of the commissioners to receive subscriptions to the bank.

MARRIAGE: On 4 December 1827, he married Mary Pue Ridgley, b. 13 Feb 1802 Hampton, Baltimore County, d. 18 Sep 1872, Howard County, daughter of Governor Charles Carnan Ridgley[3] (1760-1829) and Priscilla Dorsey (1762-1814) Ridgley. He was Governor from 1816-1819, and owner of Hampton, a 25,000 acre estate north of Towson. The house when completed in 1790 had 33 rooms.

CHILDREN:

1. Priscilla Ridgley Dorsey, b. 7 Jan. 1829, d. 12 Mar. 1847, buried St. John's Cemetery, Ellicott City, Howard Co.[4]
2. Comfort Worthington Dorsey, b. 29 Aug 1830, d. 16 Dec 1893[5], near Ellicott City, Howard County, MD. She married abt 1854, as his second wife, W. H. Goodwin Dorsey, b. 15 May 1819, d. 24 Oct. 1862, Ellicott City, Md.

---

[1] Scharf, p. 667, recorded as Charles L.W. Dorsey – since L & S are often confused in script, this is the likely person.

[2] Warfield, *Founders of Anne Arundel and Howard Counties, 495-496.*

[3] Warfield, *Op.Cit.*

[4] *Find-A-Grave* record of tombstone.

[5] An obiturary or death notice for her was published on 23 Dec 1893 and posted on *Find-A-Grave,com.* No newspaper sourced. "Mrs. Comfort Worthington Dorsey, aged 63 years, died at her residence, near Ellicott City, in Howard county. The deceased was the widow of the late W H Goodwin Dorsey. Her father was the late Colonel Charles S Worthington Dorsey. Her surviving children are Miss Comfort Worthington and Miss Mary Ridgley Dorsey. It was to the last named that Jefferson Davis left by will a valuable piece of real estate in Louisiana. The property had previously been devised to Mr. Davis by Mrs. Dorsey, widow of a brother-in-law of the deceased. He was the late Samuel W. Dorsey, who was a noted lawyer, and son of the late Judge Thomas B. Dorsey. The estate in question is situated in Tensas parish, and is a portion of the famous Limerick plantation. Mrs. Colonel George R Gaither is a sister, and Mr. John W Dorsey of Baltimore, and Mr. Samuel W Dorsey, of Howard County, are brothers. She leaves considerable property, much of which consists of real estate. She was buried in St John's Cemetery, Howard Co., MD next to her husband."

3. Rebecca Hanson Dorsey, b. Aug 1833, d. 1916, Baltimore, married 7 Aug. 1851, George Riggs Gaither.[1] (b. 21 Jan. 1831, d.11 May 1899). Both buried in Greenmount Cemetery, Baltimore.[2]
4. Charles Ridgely Dorsey, b. 20 Jan 1835, d. 10 Jun 187, Bowling Green, Caroline County, Virginia. On the 1860 census, he gave his occupation as a lawyer.
5. John Worthington Dorsey, b. 4 Sep 1836, d. 1901, Baltimore, m. 1882, Howard County, Eleanor Harrison, (b. abt 1855. In Catonsville, MD) daughter of Charles (b. 1810) and Mary Harrison of Catonsville. He was a law student in 1860, age 23; a farmer in 1870 & 1880, single with servants and assets; on 1900 census he was living in Baltimore.
6. Samuel Worthington Dorsey, b. 8 July 1838, d. 17 Mar. 1909[3] On the 1860 census, living with brothers Charles R., and John W., and his mother Mary P. Dorsey., he was a law student. He was single on the 1880 census, and a widower on 1900. No information on his wife has been found.

DEATH Died 9 July 1845, near Ellicott City, Howard County, Maryland.

WILLIAM HAMMOND DORSEY (1764-1818)

Admitted to Montgomery County Bar 1780[4]

BIRTH/PARENTS: William Hammond Dorsey was born 21 Feb 1764 at his parental estate "Oaklands" in Howard County[5] to John Dorsey (1736-1788) and Mary Hammond Dorsey (1738-1783).[6]

LEGAL CAREER: He was among the first trustees and president (1816-1818) of Brookeville Academy, chartered by the Maryland State Legislature in 1815.[7] In 1800 he was appointed Judge of the Orphan's Court in Georgetown by President Thomas Jefferson. In the early 1800's, he was on a committee to improve streets and roads in Georgetown.[8]

MARRIAGE: He married in March 1790, Anne Brooke (d.Nov. 1802) at Fair Hill, the Brooke homestead. She was the daughter of Colonel Richard Brooke (1736-1788) and Jane Lynn Brooke (d. 1776). W.H.Dorsey and his first wife, Anne Brooke, lived at the Oaks in Georgetown (now known as Dumbarton Oaks) and had 6 children. She died in November

---

[1]Warfield, *Founders of Anne Arundel and Howard County*, 421.
[2]*Find-A-Grave.com.*
[3]*Find-A-Grave.com.* Obituary in Baltimore Sun, Tuesday, March 16, 1909: Ellicott City Md., March 15 - Mr. Samuel Worthington Dorsey 70 years old a prominent resident of Howard county and a Confederate veteran {2nd Co.K,1st Va.Cav.Regt]. died today at his home near Ellicott City. He had been ill for a long time. Mr. Dorsey was a son of the late Charles S. W. Dorsey of Howard County, and a brother of Mrs. George R. Gaither, Sr. Mrs. Dorsey died several years ago. He is survived by a son, Mr. John W. Dorsey.
[4] Scharf, 667; question whether this is correct person, as he would only have been 16 years old!
[5] Newman, *Ann Arundel Gentry,* v. II, 152
[6] Newman, *op.cit.,* v. II, 130
[7] Scharf, 782
[8] Ecker, *A Portrait of Old Georgetown*, 50

1802. He married his second wife, Rosetta Lynn, in 1807., daughter of David Lynn (1698-1799) and Elizabeth Lamar Lynn (d. 1803). [1] She was the aunt of Dorsey's first wife, Anne. [2]

CHILDREN[3]

1. Richard Brooke Dorsey, b. 1791, d. 7 Jan. 1869, Washington, D.C., m. his first cousin, Ann Dorsey, (1800-1884) daughter of Clement Dorsey (1778-1848) and Priscilla Hebb Dorsey (1780-1812).
2. Ann Dorsey, b. 1792, died young.
3. Maria Ann Dorsey, b. 1794, d 6 Aug. 1832, m. 17 Sep 1822 William Johnson. (b. 26 Nov 1795, d. Mar. 1862)[4]
4. Robert E. Dorsey, M.D. ,b. 17 Jun 1796, d. 6 Feb. 1876, m. Sarah Ann Duvall (b. 28 Jan 1805, d. 18 Feb. 1882) daughter of Grafton Duvall (b. 10 Jun 1780, d. 22 Aug. 1841) and Elizabeth Whitaker Hawkins Duvall (b. 2 Oct 1785, d. 13 Apr 1831).
5. James M. Dorsey, b. 1798, d.1808
6. William Hammond Dorsey, Jr., b. 1800, d.12 Jun. 1833 in Maysville, Ky., m. 31 Oct 1825, Susan Robertson.

DEATH: Died 1 Oct 1818 at Oakley, near Brookeville, in his 55th year.[5]

ALLEN BOWIE DUCKETT (1775–1809)

Admitted to Prince George's County Bar 1795[6]
Admitted to Montgomery County Bar 1798[7]

BIRTH/PARENTS Allen Bowie Duckett was born about 1775 to Thomas Duckett (b. 26 Mar 1743, d. 2 Dec-1806) and Priscilla Fraser Bowie (b. 30 July 1750, d. 3 Jun-1786)[8]

EDUCATION: Read law and attended College of New Jersey (now Princeton University), 1790, where he was a member of the Cliosophic Society or debate club.[9]

---

[1] MCHS Family Files, see Lynn, Family File.
[2] Farquhar, *Old Homes,* 146-7, 153
[3] Newman, v. II, 152
[4] Holdcraft, *Names in Stone,* 626
[5] *National Intelligencer*, 7 Oct 1818.
[6] Van Horn, *Out of the Past,* 221
[7] Scharf, 667
[8] Doliante, *Maryland and Virginia Colonials,* 143-144, and 216-224 copies of Ducker family Bible Records.
[9] Ancestry.com, U.S., College Student Lists, 1763-1924 : Allen Duckett : accessed 27 May 2015

LEGAL CAREER: Granted a license to practice law in Prince George's County at the April 1795 court session. He was in private practice in Prince George's County. He served as the assistant clerk, Maryland House of Delegates, 1793-1795; State delegate, Maryland, 1796-1800; and a member of the Executive Council, State of Maryland, 1801-1806. He was nominated Judge of the Circuit Court of the District of Columbia by Thomas Jefferson on 28 February 1806. The Senate confirmed his appointment on 3 March 1806.[1]

MARRIAGE: On 17 October 1799, to Margaret Howard (b. 1774, d. 13 Sep.-1813),[2] daughter of Joseph Howard (b. 13 May 1749, d. 23 Dec. 1790) and Martha (Hall) Howard, (b. 1755, d. 11 June 1815)[3] She married 2nd, 14 Jan. 1812, Daniel Clarke (b. 1773, d. 2 Aug. 1815).[4]

CHILDREN:[5]

1. Infant son, stillborn, 18 Oct. 1801
2. Richard Jacob Duckett, b. & d. 29 Oct. 1802
3. Marcella Elizabeth Duckett, b. 11 Dec. 1803, d. 24 Sept. 1804
4. Thomas Duckett, b. 26 Oct. 1806, d. 18 Sep. 1849, m. 1. 13 Nov. 1827, Catharine Elizabeth Worthington Goldsborough, b. 25 Mar. 1807, d. 31 Sep 1836[6]; m. 2. 12 Nov. 1840, Catharine C Clarke, (b. 11 Jan 1815, d.1845) widow of Daniel Clarke (b. 1813, d. 1838)[7], daughter of William Bowie (b. 29 Jan 1776) and Kitty Beanes Duckett Bowie, (b. 4 Dec. 1783, d. 11 Aug 1819).[8]

DEATH 19 July 1809 "at his seat in Prince George's County."[9] He is buried at the Duckett Family Cemetery, "*Melford Farm*, situated northeast of intersection of Routes 3 and 450."[10]

URIAH FORREST (1756-1805)

State Senator from Montgomery County 1796[11]

BIRTH/PARENTS Uriah Forrest was born about 1746 in Saint Mary's County, to Thomas Forrest (b. 1710, d. 1782) and Henrietta Raley Forrest (b. 1714, d. 1791).[12]

---

[1] Federal Judicial Center : History of the Federal Judiciary : Biographical Directory of Federal Judges : Duckett, Allen Bowie, at fjc.gov. Accessed 27 May 2015

[2] Doliante, 217

[3] Bowie, *Across the Years,* 647.

[4] Doliane, 144.

[5] Doliante, 144 & 217 which pictures family bible record listing children's births.

[6] Holdcraft, *Names In Stone,* 346.

[7] He was Thomas Duckett's half brother, son of Daniel Clarke and Margaret Howard Duckett Clarke, see Doliane, 912.

[8] Bowie, *Across The Years*, 707-709.

[9] Dixon, *National Intelligencer,* 26 July 1809.

[10] Sargent, *Stones and Bones*, 614

[11] Scharf, 666

[12] Mann-Kenny, Rosedale, 2.

LEGAL CAREER: He was a member of the Continental Congress 1786-87, and an assistant to George Washington in the location of the Federal City to Georgetown. During the Revolutionary War, he served as an aid to the General.[1]

MARRIAGE: 11 October 1789 at Sotherby, St. Mary's County, to Rebecca Plater, (b. 8 Mar. 1765, d. 5 Sep. 1843) daughter of Maryland Governor George Plater (b. 8 Nov 1735, d. 10 Feb.1792)[2] and Elizabeth Rousby Plater (b. abt 1748, d. 1789).

CHILDREN [3]

1. Elizabeth Forrest, b. 6 Aug. 1791 at Sotherby, St. Mary's County, d. 1817, m. 30 Jun. 1814, Washington, D.C., Upton Scott Reed (d. 26 Jan. 1822, Taneytown, Frederick County, MD)..
2. Benjamin Stoddert Forrest, b. 22 October 1792, d. 12 May 1840, Montgomery County, m. 18 Feb 1823, Montgomery County, Ann Maria Summers[4], (b. 1799, d. after 1860). She was living in Rockville on 1860 census, age 61.[5]
3. George Plater Forrest, b. 14 July 1794, Rosedale, District of Columbia, d. bet 3 Feb. 1842-28 Feb. 1843,[6] with no issue.
4. Ann Forrest, b. 12 Jan. 1797, d. 13 Sep. 1870; m. 13 Nov. 1817 John Green, USN, d. 1850. Had issue.
5. Maria Forrest, b. 3 Mar. 1799, d. Nov. 1870[7]; m. 1. 11 Nov. 1817, John Tayloe of Virginia; m. 2. 9 Jan 1834, Dr. Benjamin Bohrer, (b. abt 1788, d. 19 Aug. 1862).

DEATH 6 July, 1805. Near Georgetown. "He embarked early in life in the Revolutionary War, until the battle of Germantown, in which he sacrificed a limb to his country."[8]

JOHN MACKALL GANTT (1762-1811)

Admitted to Montgomery County Bar 1780[9]

BIRTH/PARENTS: John Mackall Gantt was born by 1762 at White's Landing, Prince George's County to Thomas Gantt (1736-1808) and Susannah (Mackall) Gantt (1737-1782). [10] Thomas was a signer of the 1775 Declaration of Rights.[11]

---

[1] *Ibid., preface,* p. viii-ix.

[2] Papenfuse, et.al., Biographical Directory, *sketch of George Plater,* p.650-652 and White, *Governors of Maryland 1777-1970,* 29-31.

[3] Mann-Kenny, *Rosedale,* provides information on the children of Uriah and Rebecca Plater Forrest.

[4] Manuel, *Marriage Licenses,* p 113l

[5] Hurley, *1860 Census,* p. 231.

[6] Date of codicil of mother's will, revoking previous bequests, and giving house for him to live, and after his death to her daughter, Ann Green. Pippenger, *District of Columbia Probate Records, 1801-1852.*

[7] Pippenger, *Oak Hill Cemetery,* V. I, 165-166, with Benjamin S. Bohrer, her grave unmarked.

[8] Barnes, *Marriages and Deaths from the Gazette,* p.62 death notice published July 18, 1805.

[9] Scharf, 667

[10] Mackenzie, *Colonial Families, vol.* II, 782

[11] Mackenzie, *Colonial Families, vol* I, 187

LEGAL CAREER: Practiced in Prince George's County as early as 1783.[1] Served one year (1802-03) as general judge of the Court of Bankruptcy in D.C. He served as chief judge of the first Federal Court of Maryland for three years beginning in 1803,[2] From 1806 to 1808, and again from 1809 to 1811, served as chief judge of the Prince George's County Circuit Court.

MARRIAGE: 28 Dec. 1798, Mary Sprigg (Wooten) Hermance (b. 1771, d. 7 Feb. 1828)[3] widow of John Hermance, daughter of William Turner Wooten (b. 1736, d. 1777) and Ann Wooten (b. 1750, d. 1774).

CHILDREN[4]

1. Lucy Sprigg Gantt, b. 1799, d. 1825.
2. Edwin Thomas Gantt, b. 1801, d. 1801.
3. Dr. William Turner Gantt, b. 1802, m. 2 Dec. 1828, Catherine Mary Worthington, b. 18 Jan. 1811, daughter of John Brice Worthington (1874-1837) and Annie Lee Fitzhugh (1790-1824).
4. Benjamin Edward Gantt, b. 4 Feb.1805, d. 12 May 1871.[5] Lived in Anne Arundel County, District 4, married and had issue.[6]

DEATH 8 Mar 1811 after a lingering illness, at White's Landing near Taylorton, Prince George's County[7].

WILLIAM GOLDSBOROUGH (1762-1826)

Admitted to Frederick County Bar In 1795
Admitted to The Montgomery County Bar In 1797[8]

BIRTH/PARENTS William Goldsborough was born 5 Aug. 1762 at Horns Point, near Cambridge, Dorchester County, Maryland to Robert (1733-1788) and Sarah (Yerbury) Goldsborough (1734-1787). Robert Goldsborough was trained in law at the Temple in London. His family produced several men with distinguished Maryland political careers.[9]

---

[1] Van Horn, *Out of the Past*, 192
[2] Van Horn, *Out of the Past*, 239
[3] Mackenzie, *Colonial Families, vol*, II, 782
[4] Mackenzie, *Colonial Families, vol*, II, 782
[5] Baltz, *Marriages and Deaths, Vol. 1,* 228
[6] Powell, *1850 Census Anne Arundel Co.*, 134, District 4, wife Jane, age 43, and several children listed.
[7] Baltz, *op.cit.,* 229, references *Maryland Republican (*newspaper), 9 March 1811
[8] Scharf, 667
[9] MacKenzie, *Colonial Families*, 200-201; also see Papenfuse, et.al., *Biographical Dictionary,* vol. 1, 362, sketch of Robert Goldsborough, and *Maryland Genealogies,* vol. II, "Robert Goldsborough of Ashby", 1-22 for family.

LEGAL CAREER: William Goldsborough was a Frederick city councilman 1820 and 1821; represented Frederick as a Canal Delegate when the Chesapeake & Ohio Canal was being organized, 1822 and 1823[1]

MARRIAGE: 8 Nov. 1792 to Sarah Worthington, b. 13 Aug. 1770, d. 27 Jul 1854[2], daughter of Col. Nicholas Worthington (b. 29 Mar 1733, d. 1 Nov 1793) of Summer Hill, Anne Arundel County, MD and Catherine Griffith Worthington (b. 31 May 1732, d. 18 Dec. 1793).[3]

CHILDREN[4]

1. William Goldsborough, 1792-1813
2. Nicholas Worthington Goldsborough, 1795, d. 21 Apr.-1840[5]
3. Edward Yerbury Goldsborough , M.D., b. 1797, d. 13 Nov-1850, m. 21 Nov 1826, Margaret Schley,b. 1802, d. 28 Dec 1878, daughter of John Schley (b. 2 Jan 1767, d. 31 Oct. 1835), and Mary Schley (b. 29 Nov. 1773, d. 1 Mar. 1855). John Schley was Clerk of the Court in Frederick County from 1815[6].
4. Charles Henry Goldsborough, M.D., b. 14 Feb. 1800, d. 17 Aug.-1862, m. 25 Nov. 1836, Amelia Poe, b. 11 Aug. 1809, d. 2 Nov. 1887. Buried at Mt. Olivet Cemetery.
5. Leander W. Goldsborough, b. 21 May 1804, d. 28 Jun 1891, Philadelphia, PA, m. 8 Apr. 1830, Frederick, MD, Sarah Duncan (b. abt 1813).
6. Catherine Goldsborough, b. 25 March 1807, d. 31 Sep 1836,[7] m. 15 Nov 1827, Thomas Duckett of Prince George's County, had issue: Richard, and Allen Bowie Duckett.[8]

DEATH 22 May 1826 on his plantation "Richfields" Frederick County, Maryland[9] He is buried at Mt. Olivet Cemetery (Frederick, MD).[10]

NOTES William Goldsborough arrived in Frederick County, Maryland in 1790 and purchased about 1,000 acres north of the city of Frederick called Richfields.[11]

HENRY GRIFFITH (1720-1794)

Justice of Montgomery County Court 1777[1]

---

[1] Quynn, *Diary of Jacob Engelbrecht*, 7, 31,141

[2] Holdcraft, *Names in Stone,* 474.

[3] MacKenzie, 201

[4] MacKenzie, 201

[5] Holdcraft, *Names in Stone:,* 474

[6] Holdcraft, *Names in Stone,* 988. Hanson, *Old Kent, the Eastern Shore of Maryland, 281-283.*

[7] Holdcraft, *Names in Stone,* 346.

[8] Hanson, *op.cit., 281-283.*

[9] MacKenzie, 201

[10] Holdcraft, v.1, 474.

[11] *Portrait and Biographical Record,* 591.

BIRTH/PARENTS: Henry Griffith was born 14 Feb. 1720 in Annapolis, Anne Arundel County to Orlando Griffith (1688-1757) and Katherine Howard (1702-1783).[2]

LEGAL CAREER: Henry Griffith was a land speculator in Montgomery County. He built his home on "Tusculum" on Rte 650 between Unity and Etchison, now known as "Sundown Farms." He was a member of the Committee of Observation, and a signer of the Hungerford Resolves. At the formation of Montgomery County, he was appointed one of the Justices of the Court, and was on the committee to select a site for the Courthouse.[3]

MARRIAGE: 9 April 1741, to Elizabeth Dorsey, (b. 1721, Anne Arundel County, d. 24 Dec. 1749) daughter of Edward Dorsey (1701-1767) and Sarah (Todd) Dorsey (1705-1767); m. 2. 4 June 1751, Ruth Hammond, (b. abt 1733 in Annapolis, d. 27 June 1782) daughter of John Hammond (1701-1755) and Ann (Dorsey) Hammond (b. 1700).

CHILDREN[4]

By first wife

1. Sarah Griffith, b. 25 January 1742, d. 1794, married to Rezin Todd
2. Henry Griffith, b. 16 March 1745, d. 14 April 1809 in Anne Arundel County, m. 1. 13 Nov. 1766, Sarah Warfield (b. 1 Nov. 1746, d. 21 Jan. 1776), m. 2. 28 Feb. 1776, Sarah Davis (b. 21 Sep 1739, d. 25 Jun 1805).
3. Ruth Griffith (b. 18 May 1747, d. 24 September 1830, Montgomery County) m. Amon Edward Riggs (b. 11 April 1748, d. 16 March 1822).
4. Rachel Griffith (b. 28 Nov 1749, d. 1783 in Montgomery County) m. Samuel Welsh (b. 28 Nov. 1749, d. 21 Mar. 1822)

By second wife:

5. Samuel Griffith, b. 7 May 1752, d. 12 May 1833, m. Rachel Warfield, b. 1 Oct. 1757, d. abt 1778, daughter of John Warfield (d. 1773) and Rachel Dorsey (1717-1775).
6. John Hammond Griffith, b. 20 April 1754, d. abt 1794, m. 1778, Elizabeth Ridgely
7. Philemon Griffith, b. 29 August 1756, d. 29 Apr 1838, m. 18 Nov. 1782, Frederick County, Eleanor Jacob, b. 2 Oct 1762, d. 15 Apr. 1838, New Market, Frederick County, daughter of Mordecai Jacob (b. 24 May 1714, d. bef May 1771, and Jemima Isaac Jacob, b. 21 May 1722, d. aft. 1771.
8. Charles Griffith, b. 16 Dec. 1758, d. 1830, unmarried.
9. Ann Griffith, b.24 Feb 1762, d. 27 April 1791, m. 1 June 1779, Nicholas Hall, b. 1757, d. 29 Dec. 1821,

---

[1] Scharf, 666

[2] Papenfuse, et.al., *Biographical Dictionary,* 377-378. Sketch of Henry Griffith (ca. 1720-1794).They do give Feb. 14th birth day, but seem uncertain about year.

[3] *Montgomery County Story,* "Maryland and Montgomery County in the Evolution of the United States Constitution," by Jane C. Sween, Volume 30, no. 2, p. 273.

[4] Hurley, *Griffith Families,* Chapter 4, 37-57.

10. Joshua Griffith, b. 24 March 1764, d. 29 Nov 1845 in Owensboro, Kentucky, m. 1 Nov 1783, in Frederick County, Elizabeth Ridgely (b. 1765, d. 1797.)
11. Eleanor Griffith, b. 9 March 1766, d. 1 October 1821 in Frederick County, m. 27 Jul 1785, Anne Arundel County,[1] John Burgess, b. 24 Jan 1766, d. 5 Oct 1821, son of John Burgess (1705-1793) and Sarah Worthington Dorsey Burgess (1735-1768)..
12. Elizabeth Griffith, b. 16 December 1768, d. 13 September 1770.
13. Ruth Griffith, b. 1770, d. 21 May 1814[2], m. bef. 1794, Joab Waters, (b. abt 1769, d. 15 Aug. 1831, Perry County, Missouri. , had issue[3].

DEATH 28 September 1794, Laytonsville, Maryland. His will was dated 14 January 1794 and probated 10 October 1794. He named sons Henry, Samuel, Joshua and Philamon; grandchildren of deceased son John, of Amon Riggs and his wife Ruth, of Samuel Welsh and his late wife Rachel, of Nicholas Hall and his wife Ann and grandson Lyde Griffith; daughter Sarah Todd deceased, and legacies to John Burgess for his wife's part and Joale Waters for his wife's part. [4]

HENRY HARDING (1782-1863)

Judge of the Orphans Court, from 1818

BIRTH/PARENTS: Henry Harding was born in Rockville around 1782 to Edward Harding (abt 1755-1828) and his first wife, Ann Butler,(1760-bef 1814)[5].

LEGAL CAREER: "Harding served as a judge for the Orphan's Court from 1818-1820, 1828-1830, 1831-1839, and 1845-1847. He was also a member of the Maryland House of Delegates in 1820, 1830-1834, and 1836. Harding also served as sheriff and tax collector from around 1824 until 1843. He held the position of Register of Wills for Montgomery County from 1847 until at least 1851"[6]

MARRIAGE: On 2 June 1812, he wed Catherine Ann Robb (b. circa 1792, d. Aug. 1862), the daughter of Adam Robb (d. 1847) and Elizabeth Ann (Lansdale) Robb (d. bef. 1816) of Rockville.

CHILDREN:

1. Elizabeth Ann Harding, b. 4 July 1813, d.14 Jan. 1862, unmarried.

---

[1] Powell, IAnne Arundel County Marriage Records, 16.
[2] Wright, F. Edward, *Newspapr Abstracts of Frederick County, 1811-1815,* 75.
[3] R. R. Griffith, *Genealogy of the Griffith Family.* 132; Hurley, *Waters Family,* Chapter of Joab W. Waters, 259-280 for descendants.
[4] Malloy et. Al., *Wills, 1776-1825,* 58.
[5] Hurley, *Harding Families,* 7, 12-15.
[6] From the State of Maryland Archives website, on "Henry Harding"; accessed 23 March 2016, http://msa.maryland.gov.

2. Mary Anna Harding, b. 29 Oct 1815, d. 6 Jan. 1907, m. 19 Nov. 1839 to Robert W. Carter, (b. 2 Sept 1812, d. 12 Aug. 1890) who served as Register of Wills in Montgomery County, from 1870, for many years.
3. William R. Harding, b. 1818, baptized 23 Aug. 1818, St. John's Catholic Church, Forrest Glen, d. 3 April 1843, Augusta, Georgia.
4. Charles Adam Harding, b. 28 Sep 1820, d. 1 June 1892, m. 11 Jul 1865, Prince George's County, Violetta E. Lee, b. 1834, d. 24 Apr. 1910, daughter of Benjamin Lee (1787-1863) and Eleanor Lansdale Belt Lee (1800-1879).
5. Catharine Jane Harding, b. 23 Oct. 1824, d. 26 June 1897, m. 2 Oct. 1866, as the second wife of Charles J. Maddox (b. 31 Dec 1819, d. 26 Jul 1899) son of William Theobold Maddox (b. 1790) and Martha Harris Maddox.[1].

DEATH: June 1863, buried in St. Mary's Cemetery, Rockville.[2]

NOTES[3]: "He owned thirteen slaves in 1840 and 1850. In 1860, the census recorded fifteen slaves living in two slave houses. The names of Harding's slaves appeared in slave assessment records for 1853, 1855, and 1863. Catherine Harding had acquired another sixteen slaves when her father, Adam Robb, died intestate in 1847." "In 1852, Henry Harding sold eight of the late Robb's slaves to slave dealers, receiving $3,300 for Arabella Weems and her children, Sylvester, William Augustus, Thomas Richard, Charles Adam, Joseph, John Lewis, Ann Maria, and Catharine Ann."

WILLIAM PITT HUNT (1766 –1798)

Practicing Law in Montgomery County in 1790

BIRTH/PARENTS: William Pitt Hunt was born in Cecil County, abt. 1766 to Rev. James Hunt (b. abt. 1731, d. 2 Jun 1795) and Ruth Hall Hunt (b. abt. 1726, d. 17 May 1793),[4] daughter of Jacob Hall, and widow of Elisha Hall (d. 1757, Cecil County, MD).[5] Rev. James Hunt was called from Cecil County in 1769, by the Presbyterians to serve the churches at Bladensburg and Cabin John.[6]

EDUCATION: Attended school under the tutelage of his father, the Rev. James Hunt, who was the founder of Tusculum Academy, probably the first advanced school in Montgomery County. William P. Hunt took his bachelor's degree from Princeton in 1786[7].

LEGAL CAREER: After Princeton, William Hunt, returned to Montgomery County to finish his law study and set up an office at the Montgomery Court House. There he was joined

---

[1] Hurley, *Maddox,* 61-67.
[2] Cemetery Card File, MCHS.
[3] From the State of Maryland Archives, website, "Henry Harding," *op.cit.*
[4] Cemetery Records file, MCHS.
[5] *Maryland Genealogies,* Vol. II, "Hall Family", 27-28.
[6] Hienton, *Prince George's Heritage,* 202.
[7] Clark, *Spirit of Captain John,* 53.

briefly in 1790 by William Wirt. Scharf states that William Wirt studied law with William P. Hunt, son of Rev. James Hunt,[1] but record of admission to bar for Hunt was not located.

Marriage: 13 April 1790, Charlotte, Va., to Susanna Watkins (1768-1820), daughter of Joel Joseph Watkins (1739-1820) and Agnes (Morton) Watkins (1747-1804)[2]. On 24 Oct. 1803, Susanna married the prominent Presbyterian minister, Dr. Moses Hoge. (1752-1820).

CHILDREN[3]

1. James Watkins Hunt –(ca. 1790, d. 23 Nov. 1864, Mississippi) became a physician. May have married Harriett C. Hunt, b. 20 Jan 1794, d. 23 Feb. 1879, and had issue.
2. Ruth Hall Hunt (ca. 1793-, d. 16 Nov. 1821, Goochland County, Virginia).
3. Thomas Poage Hunt (b. 3 Dec 1794, d. 5 Dec-1876) became a Presbyterian minister, and may have been a missionary to China at the time of his death. Married Ann Meade, b. 1805, d. 11 Sep 1875[4], had issue.
4. William Hunt (ca, 1796-1800)

DEATH: His son, Thomas, related that his father "had intended to exchange the practice of law for the preaching of the Gospel. But getting overheated in assisting to extinguish a fire in Fredericksburg, Virginia., he caught a cold which settled in his lungs and consumption soon laid him in the grave"[5]. This seems to occur before June 1798, when there is a deed by the "children and co-heirs of William Pitt Hunt, deceased.[6]"

NOTES: In his father, James Hunt's will,[7] he and his brother James inherited their father's land – part of 'Brother's Industry,' part of 'Hopson's Choice,' part of 'Magruder's Industry,' (now 'Tusculum') and land in Halifax Co., Va. His father had already deeded him 174 acres of 'Tusculum' on Oct. 2, 1792 (Deeds, Liber E, Folio 182).[8] In advertising this land for sale, William P. Hunt described it as being 9 miles from Georgetown, 6 miles from the Montgomery County Court House, and 6 from Great Falls. He sold it to William Lodge, to whom he also executed a power of attorney, dated 15 March 1797, to settle other matters, including a dispute with Richard Hall, as he was planning a move to Virginia[9].

---

[1] Clark, *op.cit.,* and Scharf, 766

[2] *Ancestry.com,* several family trees sourced marriage reference.

[3] Clark, *Spirit of Captian John,* 61-62; *Ancestry.com,* accessed Dec. 16, 2016, and found conflicting information on several of the children, the best sourced data follows, but further research and verification recommended.

[4] *www.Find-A-Grave,* accessed Dec. 16, 2016. Buried in Luzerne County, Pennsylvania.

[5] Clark, *Spirit of Captain John, 61*

[6] Andersen, *Montgomery Land Abstracts, 1797-1803,* H;182-183, Lists James, Ruth, Thomas P. and Wiliam Hunt, children of William Pitt Hunt,

[7] Will of James Hunt, Liber C, Folio 222.

[8] Clark, *The Spirit of Captain John,*58-62.

[9] Andersen, *Montgomery Land Records, Libers A-E, F-G,* recorded in Liber G:397-8, and G:453.

BAKER JOHNSON (1747–1811)

Admitted to Montgomery County Bar 1777
Admitted to Frederick County Bar 1776
Admitted to Charles and Prince George's County Courts 1771[1]

BIRTH/PARENTS: Baker Johnson was born 30 Sep. 1747 at St. Leonard's in Anne Arundel County, the 11th child [2] of Thomas Johnson, b. 19 Feb 1702, d. 12 Apr 1777, and Dorcas Sedgwick Johnson[3] (b. 2 Nov 1705, d. 11 Dec. 1770). They were also the parents of Thomas Johnson, b. 4 Nov. 1732, the first Governor of Maryland.[4]

EDUCATION: He studied law in the Annapolis offices of his older brother, Thomas. He came to Frederick sometime before 1775.[5]

LEGAL CAREER: Appointed Clerk of Indictments, Charles County Court in 1773, County lieutenant, in office 1781, Commissioner, Frederick Town, appointed various years 1789-1802; Maryland senate elector, Frederick County, 1791; Justice, Orphans Court, Frederick County, elected 1793[6]

MARRIAGE: 9 Dec 1784, to Catherine "Kitty" Worthington (b. abt 1759, d. 9 Jun 1814, age 55[7]) daughter of Col. Nicholas Worthington (b. 29 Mar. 1733, d. 1 Nov 1793) of Anne Arundel County and Catherine Griffith Worthington (b. 31 May 1732, d. 18 Dec. 1793).[8]

CHILDREN:[9]

1. Catherine W. Johnson, b. 21 Sep 1785, Annapolis, Md., d. 1 May 1864, Frederick,Md., m. 4 March 1806, Frederick County, Md., to William Ross Esq. (b. 1 Mar 1772, d. 19 Dec 1852)
2. Baker Johnson, b. 30 Aug. 1787, d. July 1838 in Tallahassee, Leon County, Florida, m. 1810 in Baltimore, Md., Hannah Sophia Grundy (b. 1793)
3. Nicholas Johnson, b. 9 Aug 1789, d. 5 Nov 1790
4. Nicholas Worthington Johnson, b. 7 May 1793, d. 12 Jan 1798

---

[1] Maryland State Archives: Thomas Johnson (1732-1819):Governor of Maryland, 1777-1779 : MSA SC 3520-743 Notes from Baker Johnson's File : Family and Early Life
[2]Scharf, *History of Western Maryland,* V.I, 454
[3]Scharf, History of Western Maryland 8, V. I 454
[4] Delaplaine, *The Life of Thomas Johnson, .15.*
[5] MCHS Family File: Johnson Family : Thomas Johnson
[6] Maryland State Archives :Thomas Johnson Notes from Baker Johnson's LHP File : Family and Early Life
[7] Holdcraft, *Names in Stone,* 622.
[8] Scharf, V. I, 454 & 471, also Papenfuse et al., *Biographical Dicitonary of Maryland Legislature,* sketch of Baker Johnson, p. 491.
[9]Maryland State Archives :Thomas Johnson Notes from Baker Johnson's LHP File : Family and Early Life. Dates for children who died young, come from Holdcraft, *Names In Stone,* 622, buried with parents.

5. William Johnson, b. 28 Dec. 1795, d. 15 Nov. 1862, Frederick, Maryland, m. 17 Sep 1822, Frederick, Md., Anna Maria Dorsey (b. 11 Nov. 1797, d. 1832)[1] daughter of Walter Dorsey (1771-1823) and Hopewell Hebb (1773-1829).
6. Thomas Johnson, b. 1796, d. 1802
7. Juliana E. W. Johnson, b. 8 Oct 1798, d. 30 Aug 1836, m. 21 Nov. 1820, to Rev. John Johns (b. 10 Jul 1796, d. 4 Apr 1876, Fairfax, Va.). Rev. Johns was the new Rector of All Saints Parish, in Frederick when he married Juliana. He advanced to the Bishopric in Virginia before his death.[2]
8. Matilda Johnson, b. 29 May 1800, d. 16 Jul 1868[3], Frederick, Maryland, m. 8 Dec. 1818, Frederick,, Md.,[4] Alexander McPherson (b. abt 1798, d. abt 1830).
9. Worthington Johnson, b. 21 Nov. 1801, d. 13 Jul 1864, in Frederick, m.13 May 1822, Frederick, Md.[5], Mary Jane Potts (b. 22 Oct. 1800, d. 24 Jan 1835).
10. Caroline Worthington Goldsborough Johnson b. 1 Oct. 1803, d. 18 Dec. 1831, Frederick, Md., m. 10 Sep 1822, Frederick, Md.[6], to Thomas J. Grahame (b. 21 Nov. 1794, d. 24 Feb 1827).[7]

DEATH He died on 16 June 1811 and is buried at Mount Olivet Cemetery, Frederick, Maryland.[8]

NOTES In 1774, with his brothers Thomas, James and Roger , built Johnson Iron Furnace. After 1793 he was principal owner of Catoctin Furnace and after 1800 its sole proprietor.[9]

In September 1775, he was listed as a member of the Committee of Observation. He served during the Revolutionary War as a Colonel, 4th Battalion, Frederick County Militia, commissioned 1776 and Colonel, 34th Battalion, Frederick County Militia, re-commissioned 1777[10]

In November 1796, he was among a group of men appointed as school visitors for the newly formed Frederick County School.

---

[1] Holdcraft, *Names in Stone,* 626
[2] Helfenstein, *History of All Saint's Parish,* 48-53.
[3] Holdcraft, *Names in Stone,* 754. No record here of Alexander's dates.
[4] Myers, Marriage Licenses, 126
[5] Myers, Marriage Licenses, 126
[6] Myers, Marriage Licenses, 125
[7] Holdcraft, *Names in Stone*, 481
[8] Abstracts of Graves of Revolutionary Patriots, V. 2
[9] Scharf, V. I, 598
[10] Maryland State Archives :Thomas Johnson Notes from Baker Johnson's File : Family and Early Life

JAMES JOHNSON (1736–1809)

Admitted to Montgomery County Bar 1795[1]

BIRTH/PARENTS James Johnson was born 30 Sep 1736 to Thomas Johnson, b. 1702, and Dorcas Sedgwick Johnson (b. 1706). They were also the parents of Thomas Johnson, b. 4 Nov. 1732, the first Governor of Maryland.[2]

LEGAL CAREER: He was for many years justice of the peace in Frederick County, a member of the court, and in 1779, with Alexander C. Hanson and Upton Sheridine, composed a special court for the trial of the Tories who were executed on the Court House Creek in Frederick Town.[3]

MARRIAGE: In Sept. 1770 he married Margaret L. Skinner of Calvert County. (b. 1749, d. 3 Sep.-1813)[4].

CHILDREN:

1. James Thomas Johnson, b. 28 May 1774, Fort Frederick, Frederick County, Maryland, d. 22 Jul 1850[5]; m. 28 May 1807, in Balimore, Ann (Nancy) M. Richards (b. 1785, d. 17 Nov 1840[6]) daughter of Rev. Lewis Richards[7] pastor of First Baptist Church, and Ann Richards (b. 1853, d. 23 May 1798)[8].
2. Thomas Johnson, b. 11 Apr 1777, Bush Creek Forge, Frederick County, MD, d. 8 Feb 1815, Loudoun County, VA[9], m. 11 Feb. 1802[10], Rebecca Johnson. (b. 1781).
3. Rebecca Johnson, b. 07 Jan 1779, Frederick County, MD, d. Sep 1797.

DEATH: 3 Dec. 1809, age 74, Col. James Johnson of "Springfields."[11]

NOTES: He commanded a battalion of infantry in the Flying Camp, under his brother, Brig. Gen Thomas Johnson.

He built for the firm Jacques and Johnson, Green Spring Furnace, about a mile from Fort Frederick, where his son James was born, he then built with his brothers, Catoctin furnace

---

[1] Scharf, 666.
[2] Delaplaine, *The Life of Thomas Johnson, 13-15.*
[3]Scharf, History of Western Maryland, V. I: 454
[4] Holdcraft, Names in Stone, buried Mt. Olivet Cemetery, age 64.
[5] Eader & Long, *Engelbrecht Death Ledger,* 106.
[6] Eader & Long, *Engelbrecht Death Ledger,* 105.
[7] Barnes, Marriages and Deaths from Baltimore Newspapers, 1796-1807, 174 and Wright, *Western Maryland Newspaper Abstracts, 1806-1810,* paragraph 74.
[8] Barnes,op.cit., 270.
[9] Wright, Newspaper Abstracts, 1811-1815, paragraph 214 from *Fredericktown Herald.*
[10] Myers, *Frederick County Marriages licenses,* 81.
[11] Holdcraft, *Names in Stone,* buried in Mt. Olivet Cemetery; Wright, *Western Maryland Newspaper Abstracts 1806-1810,* paragraph 205, from *Fredericktown Herald,* and Bishop, *Frederick's Other City,* 46.

and Bush Creek Forge. Johnson Furnace near the mouth of Monocacy, and Potomac Furnace in Loudoun County, Virginia.[1]

We were rather slow to identify this James Johnson as the lawyer who was admitted to practice in Montgomery County in 1795, but failure to find another good candidate, with the same name, we have adopted him, as the last lawyer identified in this project.

CHARLES JONES (1712-1798)

Judge of the Orphans Court, 1777[2]

BIRTH/PARENTS: Charles Jones Of Clean Drinking Manor was born about 1712 to Charles Jones and Jane (Yates) Tyler Jones[3].

LEGAL CAREER In 1765, in Frederick County, he was one of the Judges who repudiated the Stamp Act[4]. In 1778, he was one of the magistrates who heard oaths of fidelity to renounce allegiance to Great Britain.[5]

MARRIAGE In 1747, he married Elizabeth Courts, daughter of John Courts (1691/92-1747/48) and Charity Henley, who subsequently married John Contee.

CHILDREN[6]

1. Henry Jones, d. bef 21 April 1797[7], leaving his estate to his sister Ariana Jones.
2. Mary Ann Jones, b. 12 Aug. 1752, Prince George's Parish, aka Rock Creek Parish.[8]
3. John Courts Jones, b. 11 Sept 1754, Prince George's Parish.[9] Resided at Nanjemoy Point, Charles County, married Dorothy Hanson Harrison, daughter of Robert Hanson Harrison. Had legislative career in the Lower House from Charles County,1785, and Maryland State Senator 1786. He died 20 May 1802[10].
4. Ariana Jones, died between 9 Nov 1807 and 8 March 1808, testate, unmarried.[11] She devised land near Rock Creek, inherited from her brother Henry, to her

---

[1] Scharf, op.cit., 454.
[2] Scharf, 665.
[3] *Montgomery County Story,* Mrs.Neal Fitzsimons, "The AudubonNaturalist Society and its home, Woodend," Vol. 17, No. 3, August 1974 and Steve Dryden, "Keeping Up with the Joneses" Vol. 49, no 2, May 2006
[4] Mrs.Neal Fitzsimons, *op.cit.*
[5] Peden, *Revoluionary Patriots Montgomery County,* 181.
[6] Malloy, et.al., 75, will of father Charles Jones of Clean Drinking Manor,names children Sarah and Ariana Jones, Sucky Courts Jones, Henrietta Bruce and Charles Court Jones (executor); grand children Jean Love, Jane Bruce, and Louisa Jones,
[7] Malloy, et.al., 76, Will of Henry Jones, dated 2 Jan. 1789, probated 21 Apr. 1797.
[8] *Prince George's Parish, Vol. II,* 187.
[9] *Prince George's Parish, Vol. II,* 187.
[10] Peden, *Revolutionary Patriots of Charles County,*159. Sketch in Papenfuse, et.al., 497-498, "John Courts Jones"
[11] Malloy, et.al., 75, will of Ariana Jones.

sister Susanna C. Jones. Also bequests to sister Eleanor Courts Jones, brother Charles C. Jones, and nieces Ariana Bruce and Susanna C. Jones.

5. Eleanor Courts Jones (Nelly Coats), b. 4 Nov. 1760, Prince George's Parish[1].
6. Charles Courts Jones (1763-1837), unmarried.
7. Sarah Jones, b. 11 Sept 1765, Prince George's Parish.[2]
8. Henrietta Jones m. bef 1792, Bruce.[3]
9. Susanna (Sucky) Courts Jones, b. abt 1768,[4] d. bet. 23 Nov 1810 and 29 Apr 1812, unmarried. Her will names brother Charles Courts Jones, executor. Bequests to nieces Maria Jones, Jane Bruce and Elizabeth Bruce; also to Samuel Forrest, Barney Gray and her sisters (not named).[5]

DEATH He was buried 8 March 1798. His will was probated 8 July 1801 in Montgomery County.

FRANCIS SCOTT KEY (1779-1843)

Admitted to the Montgomery County Bar in 1801[6]

BIRTH/PARENTS Francis Scott Key was born either August 1, 1779[7] or August 9, 1780,[8] at Pipe Creek, Frederick County, Maryland to John Ross Key (b. 1754, d. 20 Oct 1821) and Ann Phoebe Charlton (d. 8 Jul 1830).

EDUCATION Francis Scott Key was graduated from St. John's College, Annapolis in 1796 and read law with his uncle, Philip Barton Key.

LEGAL CAREER Francis Scott Key was District of Columbia Recorder from 1813 to 1816. He was a private in the Light or "Flying" Artillery commanded by Brigadier General George Peter. During the War of 1812, in 1814, as a civilian, Key was asked to represent friends of William Beanes, a physician taken prisoner by the British, in the matter of Beanes release in a prisoner exchange. Beanes was also a personal friend of Key's and he readily assented to visit the British fleet. The British granted Key's request, but Key was delayed overnight on the night of September 13-14, 1814. Aboard a British naval vessel that night he was inspired by the British naval bombardment of Fort McHenry, Baltimore to write a poem, "The Star Spangled Banner" rewritten within days, and set to a British drinking song, "To Anacreon in Heaven". Published on September 20, 1814 by the *Baltimore Patriot* newspaper, "The Star Spangled Banner," was treated by the U.S. Army and Navy as the national anthem until 1931, when Congress officially recognized the song as the national anthem. Some of Key's poetry was published posthumously in 1857.

---

[1] *Prince George's Parish s, Vol. II,* 187.
[2] *Prince George's Parish s, Vol. II,* 187.
[3] Malloy, et.al., 75, will of father, gives married name.
[4] Carothers,*1776 Census*, 67, has 8 year-old Susanna Courts Jones, will names "Sucky Courts Jones."
[5] Manuel et.al., Will Abstracts, 77.
[6] Scharf, p.667
[7] Scharf, p. 399, biographical sketch of prominent members of Frederick County Bar.
[8] *Ibid.,* p. 525, in section on Mount Olivet Cemetery

In 1833 Francis Scott Key was sent by his personal friend President Andrew Jackson to settle a dispute between Alabama and the American Federal Government, a dispute involving Creek Indian lands.[1] He was also an early supporter of the African Colonization Society.[2]

MARRIAGE: 19 Jan. 1802 in Annapolis, Mary Tayloe Lloyd b. 26 May 1784, d. 18 May 1859[3] daughter of Edward Lloyd (1744-1796) and Elizabeth Tayloe (1750-1825)[4] of Talbott County.[5]

CHILDREN:

1. Elizabeth Phoebe Key, b. 10 Oct 1803, d. 9 Sep 1897 in Baltimore,[6] married Charles Howard (1802-1869) a son of Gen. John Eager Howard. They lived at Charles & Monument Streets, Baltimore. The eldest of 11 children, she had two daughters and one son surviving her.
2. Maria Lloyd Key, b. 1805, d. 23 Jan 1897, Annapolis, MD, married Henry Steele, she was survived by three daughters and two sons.[7]
3. Francis Scott Key, Jr., b. 7 Oct. 1806, d. 4 Apr. 1866,[8] m. 26 Apr 1826, in Baltimore, Elizabeth Lloyd Harwood [1808-1902]. His widow was 87 in 1895, they had issue, including daughter Elizabeth Key, who was employed in Pension Office and supported aged mother.[9]
4. John Ross Key (1809-1837) married Virginia Ringold (b.4 Jun 1817, d. after 1898)[10] their son John Ross Key of Chicago, was an artist.
5. Anna Arnold Key, (1811-1884) m. 18 Feb 1829, in Washington, D.C., Daniel Turner, d. California.
6. Edward Key (1813-1822)
7. Daniel Murray Key (1815-1836)
8. Philip Barton Key (1818-1859), died in duel with General Daniel E. Sickles.[11] In his father's will he received his father's law library. Other children were to receive six books each of his personal library.

---

[1] Biographical material from *The New Encyclopedia Britannica, 1987; Encyclopedia Americana,* 1989; *and* Dictionary of American Biography, *Vol. 5.*

[2] Scharf, 399.

[3] Scharf, 525.

[4] Papenfuse, et. Al., *Biographical Dictionary, Vol* II:537, sketch of Edward Lloyd.

[5] Scharf, 402.

[6] *The Washington Post,* 10 Sep 1897, ProQuest Historical Newspapers, "Francis Scott Key's Last Child; Mrs. Charles Howard passes away at her cottage in Oakland."

[7] *The Washington Post,* 24 Jan 1897, ProQuest Historical Newspapers, "Mrs. Maria Doyd Steele Dead"

[8] Scharf, 525

[9] *The Washington Post,* 9 Aug 1895, ProQuest Historical Newspapers, "Money for Miss Key."

[10] *The Washington Post,* 24 Apr 1898, ProQuest Historical Newspapers, "Has a Famous Name, Venerable Mrs Key loves to hear the Star Spangled Banner"

[11] *The Washington Post, 22 May 1886,* ProQuest Historical Newspapers, "Mrs. Pendleton's Death" mentions her brother Philip Barton Key killed by Gen. Daniel E. Sickles.

9. Ellen Lloyd Key (b. 1821, d. 30 Mar 1884 at Fenby, Wales)[1] married 27 Jan1846, Washington, D.C., Simon Fraser Blunt (d. 27 April 1854, Baltimore City)[2] Had issue.
10. Alice Key (b 1825, d. 20 May 1886)[3] married 1846 in Baltimore to George Pendleton , had issue.
11. Charles Henry Key (1827-1869).

DEATH: On 11 Jan. 1843 of pleurisy at the home of his daughter, Mrs. Charles Howard in Baltimore. His body was placed first in St Paul's Cemetery, (or Greenmount Cemetery) Baltimore, and reburied in 1866 in Mt. Olivet Cemetery, Frederick, MD. His will, dated 9 Dec 1837 was presented for probate on 27 Jan 1843.[4]

NOTES: "Francis Scott Key's contemporaries esteemed him as a family man, poet, orator, civil leader, lawyer and churchman." He spoke publicly of the tie btween religion and patriotism. In addition to serving as a warden in his parish, "Key also was chosen to be a delegate to every General Convention of the Protestant Episcopal Church (held triennially) from 1814 to 1826."[5]

PHILIP BARTON KEY (1757-1815)

Admitted to the Montgomery County Bar 1804[6]

BIRTH/PARENTS: Philip Barton Key was born 12 April 1757 in Charlestown, Cecil County, MD[7] to Francis Key (1731-1770) and Ann Arnold Ross (1727-1811).[8] Key

EDUCATION: He received a private education and began to study law in Annapolis in 1775. When he was in England, he was admitted to the Middle Temple in 1784 (One of the four Inns of the British Court, which have the exclusive right to call men and women to the bar.)

LEGAL CAREER: He served in the British Army during the Revolutionary War; taken prisoner in Florida but paroled in Havana, he went to England. He returned to Maryland in 1787 and moved to Annapolis in 1790; member of the State house of delegates 1794-1799. He did not win re-election to the House of Delegates in 1800 but was appointed Chief

---

[1] *The Washington Post,* 5 April 1884, ProQuest Historical Newspapers, "Personal Intelligence."
[2] Scharf, 525
[3] *The Washington Post, May 22, 1886,* ProQuest Historical Newspapers, "Mrs. Pendleton's Death"
[4] *Mount Olivet Cemetery, Frederick MD, interment record, G-L,* mss. Printout at the Montgomery Co. Historical Society library; Scharf, 402; Pippenger, *DC Probate Records*, 269
[5] *Maryland Historical Magazine,* Vol. 84, No. 3, Fall 1989, Sam Meyer, "Religion, Patriotism, and Poetry in the life of Francis Scott, Key," 267-274.
[6] Maryland Biographical Dictionary, 315
[7] Early Anglican Church Records of Cecil County, (Westminster, Md. : Family Line Publications, 1990), 69
[8] Papenfuse, et.al., *Biograpnical Dictionary,* sketch of John Ross Key, provides her estimated dates.

Justice of the 4th Judicial Court and lived in Georgetown, D.C. His judicial office was abolished in 1802 and he began to practice law again. In the fall of 1806 he purchased one thousand acres of land in Montgomery County located on what is now Brookeville, near what is now the village of Norbeck, and became interested in agricultural pursuits. He was elected as a Federalist to the 10th, 11th, and 12th Congresses (1807-1813).[1]

MARRIAGE: Philip Barton Key was married 4 July 1790 to Ann Plater b. 23 Set. 1772, d. 18 Dec.-1834, daughter of George Plater (1735-1792) , governor of Maryland (1791-1792) and his second wife, Elizabeth Rousby[2] Plater (d. 1789)..[3]

CHILDREN:[4]

1. George Barton Key, b. 1793, d. in infancy.
2. Elizabeth Rousby Key, b.Mar.1796, d. 21 Nov 1860, m. 1 Oct 1829, Hon. Henry Johnson, Governor of Louisiana.
3. Mary Lloyd Key, b. Aug 1801, d. 8 Nov 1834, m. 13 Nov 1822, William Nevins, b. 17 Oct 1797, d.14 Sep 1835, of Baltimore.
4. Philip Barton Key, b. 2 Sep 1804, d. 4 May 1854 near Thibodeaux, Louisiana, trained as a lawyer with his cousin, Francis Scott Key, moved to Louisiana as a planter, and state legislator. He married 1. 4 Dec 1828, Mary Brent Sewell, daughter of Robert Sewell of Prince Georges, County; m. 2. 25 Apr 1833, Maria Louisa Sewell, daughter of Nicholas Sewell of Saint Mary's County.
5. Rebecca Ann Key, b. 2 Jun 1809, m.1. 14 May 1828, Dr. William Howard of Baltimore; m.2. 28 Sep 1837, Alexander H. Tyson of Baltimore.
6. Louise Emily Key, b. 22 Dec 1811, twin, d. 7 Mar 1830, Louisiana.
7. Emily Louisa Key, b. 22 Dec 1811, twin, d. 10 Jan 1891, New York; m. 19 Jan 1835, Dr. Philip Rogers Hoffman of Baltimore.
8. Anne Arnold Key, b. 28 Dec 1814, d. 18 Aug 1895, m. 21 Oct 1835, William E. Thompson of Louisiana

DEATH: He died 28 Jul 1815 in Georgetown, District of Columbia. He and his wife are buried in Oak Hill Cemetery in Georgetown.

NOTES Director of Bank of Columbia.

---

[1] *Biographical Directory of the American Congress, 1774-1961* (Washington, D.C. : GPO, 1961) 1161-1162

[2] Papenfuse, *Biographical Dictionary,* sketch of George Plater, 650-651..

[3] Maryland Genealogies, Vol. II, "Key Family", 121-127.

[4] Maryland Genealogies, Vol. II, "Key Family", 124-125, lists children with dates of b. d. and Marriages..

CHARLES JORDAN KILGOUR (1790-1837)

Admitted to Montgomery County Bar in 1809[1]

BIRTH/PARENTS Charles Jordan Kilgour, was born before 1790 in St. Mary's County, Maryland to James and Margaret (Jordan)[2] Kilgore[3]

LEGAL CAREER Rockville Attorney and Federalist leader. Judge of the County Circuit Court and Associate Judge of D.C.

MARRIAGE 16 Jun 1818 in Washington, D.C.[4], to Louisa McIlheny (b. 1799, d. 1 Jan 1822)[5] daughter of James McIlhaney (1749-1804) and Margaret Tribbey McIlhaney (1760-1837).

CHILDREN

1. James McIlheny Kilgour (b. 1818, d. 1902 Hillsboro, Loudoun County, Va.). Married 23 Nov 1843, at bride's home in Loudoun County, Va., Louisa T. McIlhany. (1827-1908) daughter of James McIlhaney[6] (1796-1866) and Elizbeth Johnson McIlhaney (1814-1901). James M. Kilgour was a farmer. Had issue.
2. John Mortimer Kilgour (b. 19 May 1822, d. 4 Apr 1905, Loudoun County, VA) He married to Martha Wilson Wootton (1827-1917),[7] daughter of Doctor John Wootton and Elizabeth Lynn (Magruder) Wootton. He was also an attorney.

DEATH: 22 Aug 1837. His death was assumed to be an accident in an overturned carriage, as he was found on the road, and his horse a mile further along the road, with the fragments of his carriage. He was returning to Rockville after visiting a farm he owned in Loudoun County, Va. He had spent the night at Mr. Chilton's near Conrad's Ferry on the Maryland side.[8]

NOTES He was a member of the vestry of Christ Episcopal Church. as shown in the following deed, BS1: 389-390. Rector and vestry of Prince Georges Parish

---

1 Scharf, p. 667

2 *Marriages and deaths, St. Mary's County, 1634-1900,* p. 176. Charles Kilgour, m. by 1794, Elizabeth Jordan, Ref. Chancery Papers, 2141 (7).

3 *Portrait and Biographical Encyclopedia of the Sixth Congressional District* in sketch of Col. William Kilgour, p. 758-759, gives his grandfather as William, father of Charles J., John A.T., Alexander and James; and death record of Charlotte Kilgour, one of Charles' sisters, who raised his sons, names her parents James and Margaret (Jordan) Kilgour, age 80, informant her nephew James M. Kilgour in January 1874, from Frain, Elizabeth R., *Loudoun County Virginia Death Register, 1853-1896,* 160

4 Dixon, *National Intelligencer,* June 23, 1818, 55.

5 Dixon, *National Intelligencer,* May 24, 1822, 198.

6 Jewell, *Loudoun County Marriages,* 125.

7 *Portrait and Biographical Encyclopedia of the Sixth Congressional district. Op.cit.*

8 Dixon, *National Intelligencer* August 26, 1837.

recorded deed 29 January 1828, made 1 November 1827 between John Tayloe of the District of Columbia, and the Reverend Thomas G. Allen of Prince Georges Parish in Montgomery County, and Charles I. Kilgour, George C. Washington, Benjamin S. Forrest, James Anderson Jr., Arnold T. Winsor, John Cook, Richard Butt and John Adamson Jr., Vestry of said parish for $5. Assigns part of tract of land called *Middlebrook,* being a parcel on the east side of the main road leading from Rockville to Frederick Town, near the end of 30 perches of a line of a tract called *Mill Tract,* containing 1 1/4 acres, for the purpose of erecting an Episcopal Church of Public Worship. Signed John Tayloe, Anne Tayloe, before R. S. Briscoe, James Ord.[1]

DAVID LYNN (1698-1779)

Montgomery County Justice and Judge 1777[2]

BIRTH/PARENTS: David Lynn was born in 1698 in Antrim, Ireland. He immigrated to Frederick County before 1751[3].

LEGAL CAREER: Justice and Judge of Orphans Court, 1777-1779. He served as a Justice in Frederick County from 1756-1775. He was one of three commissioners chosen to lay out Georgetown in 1751.[4]

MARRIAGE: On 24 August 1746, St. John's Parish, Baltimore, to Elizabeth Lamar, b. abt 1725, d. 29 Sep. 1803, testate, in Montgomery County, daughter of John Lamar (1703-1758) and Susanna Tyler Lamar, (1700-1761).

CHILDREN:

1. Jane Lynn, b. 16 Jul. 1747, d. 15 Sep. 1774, m. Richard Brooke, b. 8 Jul. 1736, d. bef 11 Jun. 1788, son of James Brooke (1705-1784) and Deborah Snowden Brooke (d. 1758).
2. Elizabeth Lynn, b. 25 Feb. 1749, d. 1818, m. Levin Magruder, b. abt 1756, d. Dec. 1801, son of Samuel Wade Magruder (1728-1792) and Lucy Beall Magruder. (1738-1795).
3. Sarah Lynn, b. 13 Apr. 1751, d. abt 1810.
4. Rosalie Lynn, b. 30 May 1753, d. 19 Mar. 1831.
5. Catharine Lynn, b. 17 Jul. 1756, d. bef 1810, m. 1780, James Lackland, b. 1756 in Charlotte, VA, d. bef 14 Nov. 1814, Montgomery County, MD, son of John Lackland (d. 1780) and Margery Edmonston Lackland, (1737-1801).

---

[1] "Middlebrook" was surveyed in 1811 by James M. Lingan, it is north of Rte. 124, about halfway up to Rte 188, Germantown Road, along 355. There is no church presence here at this time. Ascension Chapel is 2 or 3 miles further south, on the west side of the Main road from Frederick to Rockville.

[2] Scharf, 666

[3] Papenfuse, *Biographical Directory,* sketch of John Lynn, 558-559.

[4] Papenfuse, *Biographical Directory,* sketch of John Lynn, 558-559.

6. David Lynn, b. 15 Jul. 1758, d. 11 Apr. 1835, a member of the Lower House from Allegany County in 1794 & 1795, m, 28 Apr. 1795 in Anne Arundel County, Mary Galloway, b. 10 July 1774, d. 22 Mar. 1853, daughter of Joseph Galloway, (1740-1803) and his second wife.
7. John Lynn, b. 29 Aug 1760, d. 1813, resided in Allegany County until 1811, died in Garrett County, MD., m. 26 Feb 1780, Eleanor Edelin, (1762-1821) daughter of Christopher Edelin[1] (1723-1786) and Rebecca Johnson (1739-1785).
8. George Lynn, (1764 -1852), a practicing physician in Newton, Frederick County, VA, m. 31 Aug. 1790, in Charlotte, VA, to Ann Woodson (Nancy) Venable[2] (1769-1860) daughter of James Venable (1734-1814) and Judith Morton (1739-1826).

DEATH Before 16 Dec. 1779, when an inventory of his estate was presented by his son, David Lynn, administrator. Signing as next of kin were Caty Lynn and Sarah Lynn.[3]

ZADOK (or ZADOCK) MAGRUDER (1795-1831)

Admitted to Montgomery County Bar 1816[4]

BIRTH/PARENTS: Zadok Magruder is descended from an Alexander Magruder, who emigrated from Scotland to Prince George's County in 1662. He was born in 1795 in Montgomery County to Dr. Zadock Magruder, MD (1765-1811) and Martha Wilson Magruder, (1772-1837) the second of 10 children.[5]

LEGAL CAREER: Attorney at law, "engaged in an extensive and lucrative practice."[6]

MARRIAGE: 28 Nov 1822[7] to Rachel Cooke (1795-1855) daughter of Nathan Cooke (1768-1805) and Rachel Magruder (1768-1844), in Montgomery County, his first cousin.

CHILDREN:

1. Dr. Julian Magruder (b. 10 Oct. 1824, d. 9 Jan. 1888 in Ohio) graduated in 1846 in Medicine from University of Pennsylvania. Moved to Ohio in 1881[8]. Married 19 Apr 1853, in Washington, D.C., Margaret Ann Johnson (1835-1896) daughter of William Johnson and Ann Washington Johnson.
2. Harriet Elizabeth Magruder, b. 14 Jan 1826, d. 7 Aug 1907,[9] m. 5 Apr. 1849, Otho Zachariah Muncaster, b. 13 Nov 1814, d. 23 March 1893, Georgetown, D.C.[10]
3. Zadok Magruder IV (1829-1832).

---

[1] Papenfuse, *Biographical Directory,* sketch of John Lynn, 558-559.
[2] Papenfuse, *Biographical Directory,* sketch of John Lynn, 558-559.
[3] MCHS Lynn Family File.
[4] Scharf, 667.
[5] Sween, *All you want to know about the Magruder's,* and Magruder Family File, MCHS.
[6] Dixon, *National Intelligencer,* Sat., 31 Dec. 1831
[7] Manuel, *Marriage Licenses*
[8] Malloy, *Sentinel,* 237 (13 Jan. 1888)
[9] Malloy, *Sentinel,* 577 (9 Aug. 1907)
[10] Malloy, *Sentinel, 267.* (24 Mar 1893)

DEATH: Zadok Magruder died 7 Dec 1831, at his residence in Rockville[1] in his 37th year.

LUTHER MARTIN (1748-1826)

Admitted to Montgomery County Bar in 1780[2]

BIRTH/PARENTS: Luther Martin was born 20 Feb. 1748 in New Brunswick, Middlesex County, New Jersey to Benjamin and Hannah Martin[3].

EDUCATION: He graduated from the College of New Jersey (Princeton), first in his class of 35 graduates, in 1766. He began his legal career in 1771 having studied law in Accomac County, Virginia.[4]

LEGAL CAREER: In the years between graduation from college and admission to legal practice, Martin was a schoolmaster. Luther Martin was a soldier in the War of Independence, but did not participate in combat. In 1804-05 he was a defense attorney for Justice Samuel Chase in Chase's impeachment trial, which was brought by John Randolph of Virginia. Martin was one of Aaron Burr's defense attorneys in 1807, along with other lawyers. He was Maryland's first Attorney General from 1778-1805, and again from 1818-1822. Outstanding was his participation in the federal Constitutional Convention in 1787 as a Maryland delegate. Martin hated Jefferson. He believed that the federal government was only valid in the preservation of state governments[5]. Luther Martin appealed to the Constitutional Convention to stop America's participation in the Slave trade. He argued also that counting a slave as 3/5 of a free man for purposes of representation of whites in Congress was "inconsistent with the principles of the Revolution and dishonorable to the American character."[6] Luther Martin objected to the power of Congress to levy tariffs on imports. He felt that Congress would have state economies at its mercy. Although he refused to vote for the Federal Constitution he converted to the Federalist cause[7].

MARRIAGE: On 25 Dec 1783, to Mary Cresap daughter of Michael Cresap (1742-1775) of Western Maryland, and Mary Whitehead Cresap (? – bef. 1821) of Philadelphia, PA., who married 2) in 1781, John Jeremiah Jacob (1757-1839). Mary Cresap Martin died 2 Nov. 1796.[8]

CHILDREN:

1. Juliet Martin, died young.

---

[1] Dixon, *National Intelligencer,* Sat., 31 Dec.1831.

[2] Scharf. 667

[3] Papenfuse, et.al., *Biographical Dictionary,* 577-578.

[4] Papenfuse, et.al.,*.op.cit.,* 577-578.

[5] Papenfuse, et.al., *op.cit.,* 577-578.

[6] Scharf, History of Maryland, vol. III, 295-296

[7] *Ibid.* vol. II, 540-547

[8] *Maryland Historical Magazine,* June 1955, *Notes and Queries: The Autobiography of Luther Martin,* 152. Notice from *Federal Gazette, Nov. 3; and* Papenfuse, *op.cit.,* 577.

2. Maria Martin, m 8 April 1808. Lawrence Keene[1]. They later separated, and she died in insane asylum.[2]
3. Eleanora (Ellen) Martin, b. 1785, d. 16 Nov. 1807, m. 27 Jan. 1802, Richard Raynal Keene[3]
4. Infant, b.& d., 1789.
5. Elizabeth Sophia Martin b.1791, d. 1792

DEATH: 10 Jul 1826, New York, NY at home of Aaron Burr, with whom he had lived since 1823.[4]

JOHN T. MASON (1765–1824)

Admitted to Montgomery County Bar 1780[5]

PARENTS John Thomson Mason was born 15 Mar 1765 at Chopawamsic, Stafford County, VA[6] to Thomson Mason (b. 14 Aug.1733, d. 26 Feb. 1785) and Mary King Barnes, (d. 21 Oct 1771). He was a nephew of George Mason of Gunston Hall.[7]

LEGAL CAREER: Early in life John T. Mason moved to Maryland. He was offered the office of United States Attorney-General by President Thomas Jefferson. In 1806, the state of Maryland offered Mason positions as Chief justice and attorney general. He either declined the offers or occupied select ones only for a brief period. In 1811, he refused the office of United States Attorney-General a second time being offered by President Madison. In 1816, he was Democratic candidate for United States Senator in opposition to Robert G. Harper, but lost the election by a single vote.[8]

MARRIAGE: In 1797, to Elizabeth Beltzhoover b. 23 Feb 1781, d. 30 Jun 1836.

CHILDREN[9]

1. Mary Barnes Mason, b. c.1800, d. 11 May 1844
2. Elizabeth Ann Armistead Mason, b. 4 Apr 1803, d. 20 Jan 1857
3. Abram Barnes Mason, b. 21 Oct 1807, d. 10 Apr 1863
4. Melchoir Beltzhoover Mason, b. 3 Oct 1812 – n.d.
5. John Thomson Mason, Jr., b. 9 May 1815, d. 28 Mar 1873
6. Thomson Mason, b. 15 July 1818, d. 1848
7. Virginia Wallace Mason, b. 16 Apr 1820, d. 6 Oct 1858

---

[1] *Federal Gazette,* 13 April 1808.
[2] Papenfuse, *op.cit.*
[3] *Maryland Historical Magazine,* June 1955., Federal Gazette, *21 Nov. 1807*
[4] New York, Death Newspaper Extracts, 1801-1890; Papenfuse, *op.cit.*
[5] Scharf, 667
[6] "Mason family of Virginia". The Political Graveyard on-line, at the Political Graveyard.com.
[7] Gunston Hall, "John Thomson Mason" on line at gunstonhall.org.
[8] *The Colonial Dames of America* (1910). *Ancestral Records and Portraits: A Compilation from the Archives of Chapter I, the Colonial Dames of America*: Boston, MA, Grafton Press. pp. 808.
[9] Gunston Hall Archives, Mason Family Papers, on-line.

DEATH 10 Dec 1824 at age 59. He is buried at Montpelier Estate in Clear Spring, MD[1]

EDWARD NICHOLLS (1743-1812)

Admitted to Montgomery County Bar In 1780[2]

BIRTH/PARENTS: Edward Nicholls was born about 1743 in Cornwall, England. [3] Apparently he emigrated as a single man to Maryland before 1778.

EDUCATION: Reportedly Edward was fluent in French, so may have been educated abroad. This was a reason given for his move to Louisiana, as being a possible advantage

LEGAL CAREER: He was admitted to the bar in Prince George's County, by 1785.[4] In land records in Prince George's County he gives his occupation as Attorney at law[5], and in at least one instance, served as a trustee in an insolvent case, appointed by the State Chancellor[6]. He apparently lived in Upper Marlboro until 1799[7], when he removed family to Washington, D.C. From there, he went to England for several years to "settle an inheritance, and sell property," where it is implied by his son's letter, that he lived a dissipated lifestyle. He was appointed Civil Commandment in the County of Attapakas in Louisiana around 1805, and served until around 1809, when the system changed to a Parish System and another judge was appointed. His son reports the family lived with his son-in-law, who helped support the family with his brother, who labored to grow cotton.[8]

MILITARY: Took oath of allegiance before Hon. David Craufurd in 1778.

MARRIAGE: 15 August 1780, Prince George's County to Wilhelmina Hamilton, born 1759, posthumous daughter of William Hamilton (d. July 1759) and Martha Crawford (b. 1736, d. Oct 1778). Martha subsequently married Charles Clark, who died in 1767, and as

[1] Federal Writers' Project. *Maryland: A Guide to the Old Line State*. US History Publishers.

[2] Scharf, 667.

[3] Dates from Ancestry, ords of his grandson, Francis Redding Tillou Nicholls. The family papers, including genealogy, are reportedly at Tulane University. The family produced several judges and a Governor. Correspondence of Thomas C. Nicholls, Edward's son are among the papers.

[4] Bowie, *Across the Years in Prince George's County,* p. 162 gives April 1758. This date appears to be mistyped, as the earliest records in Heinton, *Out of the Past,* 202, indicates he was practicing law in Prince George's County, from 1786.

[5] Prince George's County Deeds, Liber FF2:276-278, recorded in 1785, to Thomas Clark, merchant, to whom he is indebted, to indemnify him as being his security to O'Neill and Deakins of Montgomery County, for 200 pounds, he assigns certain slaves. In 1791, he and his wife Willamina, sold a 100 acre lot in Prince George's County, "Sway" which may have been part of her inheritance.

[6] Prince George's County Deeds, Liber JRM7:112 & 179, as trustee for insolvent debtor.

[7] In 1796, he and Willamina sold a lot in Upper Marlboro, which he had acquired in a sheriff's sale. JRM4:335. He had previously executed a deed of trust to David Crawford for the benefit of his wife Willamina, and son Thomas, for other property and slaves. Prince George's County Land Records: JRM3:40.

[8] Lyle Saxon, *Old Louisiana,* 105-120, recounts family history written by Thomas Clark Nicholls.

her third husband, Osborn Sprigg (1741-1815). Her maternal grandfather and uncle, both named David Crawford, were prominent merchants in Prince George's County.

CHILDREN:

1. Martha Crawford Nicholls, b. abt 1781, Prince George's County, d. after 1850, Louisiana, Married in August 1808, New Iberia, Louisiana to Nathan Morse, an attorney.[1]
2. Robert Hamilton Nicholls, b. abt. 1783, d. 16 Jul 1813, Washington, D.C., where he worked as a clerk in the War Dept.[2]
3. Thomas Clark Nicholls, b. abt 1785, d. 1847 in Louisiana, married 21 Jun 1814, Louisa Hannah Drake and had issue. He was sent to Charlotte Hall School, and then read law with his brother in law, Nathan Morse in New Orleans, LA.
4. Mary Nicholls, b. bet. 1790-1794,[3] d. before 1800.

DEATH: 1812 in Louisiana.[4]

NOTES: It is possible that Edward was previously married, but unable to link him definitively with other records. There was an Edward Nicholls in Sugarloaf Hundred, up to 1780, who apparently had a wife Ann, and also appears in Prince George's County deeds as early as 1749, and as late as 1783, who patented *Resurvey on Pascalham* in 1770, and in 1783 had 4 white inhabitants in his household.[5] If he were born as early as 1728, then this could represent a first family. No probate records were found. It seems more likely however, that these are two separate families, and a case of identity confusion over the same names.

For further information regarding research on land records on Edward Nicholls, see the Nicholls family file. From abstracts from Prince George's Couny Deeds, it appears that he had financial difficulties, and from his son's notes published and sourced previously, he tended to live beyond his means, and was not successful in bringing home any of the inherited estate from England.

---

[1]Ibid., and Bowie, op.cit., p. 178, states marriage was recorded in National Intelligencer, of Aug. 22, 1808.

[2] Jean Dixon, *National Intelligencer & Washington Advertiser, Newspaper Abstracts 1811-1813,* pg. 294.

[3] Will of Mary Crawford, dated 19 Mar 1794 named great-granddaughter Mary Nicholls, to have a Negro girl "Phebe" daughter of Jenny. Her will also mentioned her granddaughter Willamina Nicholls, and other great grandchildren, Robert Hamilton Nicholls, Martha Crawford Nicholls and Thomas Clark Nicholls. *Prince George's County, Maryland Wills, Liber T, No 1, 1790-1796,* abstracted by Leslie & Neil Keddie. No child of Mary's supposed age appears in 1790 or 1800 census. No mention of her in brother's writings cited above.

[4] Lyle Saxon, *Old Louisiana,* Op.cit., pg. 105-120.

[5] MCHS Family Files.

ROGER PERRY (abt 1767-1835)

Admitted to Montgomery County Bar 1797[1]

BIRTH/PARENTS: Roger Perry was born about 1767 in Frederick (now Montgomery) County, to Charles Perry (1738-1818) and Priscilla Johns (1742-1824) who both died testate in Montgomery County, MD. Charles Perry was a wealthy and influential planter, who was often a signer for bonds for Upton Beall as Clerk of the Court. It seems likely that his wife was related in some way to Upton's mother, Margaret Johns Beall.[2]

LEGAL CAREER: Roger Perry moved to Cumberland as a young man, and was admitted to the bar at their first court sessions in 1791.[3] In 1805 he was among the committee that surveyed the town of Cumberland, MD. Roger Perry was a noted State's Attorney, counsel for the State in several important trials, the murder trial of Anthony Perkins, March 1820.[4] Counsel for State, Roger Perry in State of Maryland against Samuel Barnes, editor of the Political Examiner, March 1821.[5] Counsel for State vs. Shriver, Roger Perry, March 1821.[6] "James Dixon Esquire of this town is appointed States Attorney for the 5th Judicial District of Maryland, comprising Frederick, Washington, and Allegheny Counties, in the room of Roger Perry Esquire the present incumbent." February 25 1822[7]

MARRIAGE: Lucy Calmes daughter of George and Mary (Price) Calmes.[8] (b. 1780, d. 1832) early pioneers of Garrett County. Monument in Rose Hill Cemetery, Cumberland, MD.

CHILDREN[9]

1. George C. Perry, M.D., b. abt 1803, physician in Cumberland in 1850.
2. Charles Perry, b. abt 1806, moved to Hampshire County by 1850.
3. Thomas Johns Perry, b. 17 Feb 1807, d. 27 Jun 1871, m. 1835, Mary Louisa Van Lear (b. 1817, d. 27 June 1871) Attorney, noted Judge. Buried Rose Hill Cemetery, Cumberland.
4. Roger Perry, Capt. USN, b. 15 Jan 1814, d. 5 Nov. 1880, m. Estelle Frances Tayloe (1833-1867). Buried Rose Hill Cemetery, Cumberland.
5. Priscilla J. Perry, b. 1820, m. James R. Annan, b. 1815. Merchant in Cumberland.

---

[1] History of Western Maryland, Scharff, 1373-74.
[2] Portrait and Biographical Record of the Sixth Congressional District, Maryland, 522.
[3] Thomas & Williams, History of Allegany County, 309.
[4] Quynn, *Diary of Jacob Engelbrecht*, 9.
[5] Quynn, *Diary of Jacob Engelbrecht*, 32.
[6] Quynn, *Diary of Jacob Engelbrecht*, 33.
[7] Quynn, *Diary of Jacob Engelbrecht*, 82
[8] Hoye's Pioneer Families of Garrett County, 128
[9] Thomas & Williams, *History of Allegany County,* 309 names 9 children. Several Perry's found at *findagrave.com,* in Rose Hill Cemetery, Cumberland, MD.

6. William Perry
7. Marcus Perry
8. Magruder Perry
9. Mary M. Perry, never married.

DEATH: About 1835. Buried at Rose Hill Cemetery, Cumberland.

BENE SMALLWOOD PIGMAN (1776-1845)

Admitted to Montgomery County Bar 1803[1]
Admitted to Allegany County Bar 1805
Admitted to Frederick County Bar 1806

BIRTH/PARENTS: Bene Smallwood Pigman was born 20 January 1776, in that part of Frederick County, which later that year became Montgomery County, to Nathaniel Pigman (b. abt 1733, d. 1801)-and Anna Waters Pigman (b. 1735, d. 1810). [2]

EDUCATION: He had little or no formal education but read law under Roger Brooke Taney (5th Chief Justice from 1836 to 1864).[3]

LEGAL CAREER: He was admitted to Montgomery County, Allegany County and Frederick County bars[4] and presented several important cases before the U. S. Supreme Court. In 1819, Roger Brooke Taney and Bene S. Pigman successfully defended Rev. Jacob Gruber against charges of inciting slaves to riot.[5] He also argued "Lessee of Brewer v. Blougher - 39 U.S. 178 (1840)."[6] Construction of the Act of the Legislature of Maryland passed December session, 1825, entitled, "An act relating to Illegitimate Children," which provides that "the illegitimate child or children of any female, and the issue of any such child or children," are declared capable in law "to take and inherit both real and personal estate from their mother and from each other, and from the descendants of each other, as the case may be, in like manner as if born in lawful wedlock."

MARRIAGE: 27 March 1810 to Harriet Briscoe, daughter of Hanson and Elizabeth Mary Napier (Jordan) Briscoe of Allegany County.[7]

CHILDREN[8]

1. Philip Augustus Smallwood Pigman, b. 31 Mar 1812 in Frederick, d. 17 June 1840, m. 7 Mar 1833 Fanny Ann Burbage (1811-1873).
2. William Pinkney Pigman, b. 2 Jan. 1814, d. 23 Aug. 1815, buried at All Saints, Frederick, MD.

---

[1] Scharf, 667.
[2] Kelleher, et.al, *John Pigman and His Descendants*, 31
[3] Kelleher, *op.cit.,* 31
[4] Scharf, 667, 1353, 416
[5] Kelleher, *op.cit.,* 31
[6] openjurist.org/39/us/178/the-lessee-of-henry-brewer-v-jacob-blougher, accessed 2 Oct 2013.
[7] Kelleher, *op.cit.,* 31,
[8] Kelleher, *op.cit.,* 31-38 for children's information.

3. Hanson Briscoe Pigman, b. 12 Apr. 1815, d. 8 Sep. 1847 at sea; m. 23 May 1838, Mary Elizabeth Shriver (b. 1817).
4. Charles Henry Jordan Pigman, b. 27 Jan.1818, d. 2 Oct. 1842, never married, buried at Rose Hill Cemetery, Cumberland, MD
5. Bene Smallwood Pigman, b. 4 Sep. 1819, d. 2 Oct. 1855, m. 1 Mar. 1849, to Anne E. Gordon (1821-1865).
6. Summerfield Pigman b. 19 Aug.1824, d. 16 Nov. 1843, buried at Rose Hill Cemetery, Cumberland, MD
7. Nathaniel Pigman, b. 13 Aug. 1825, d. 10 May 1865, m. 20 Oct. 1853, Margaret Cecelia Morris (1831-1866). They lived in Wheeling , WV but both are buried at Rose Hill Cemetery, Cumberland, MD
8. Harriet Ann Pigman, b. 25 Apr. 1828, d. 30 Nov. 1861, m. 12 Aug. 1846 to Edwin Thomas Shriver (1815-1896). He was a lawyer in Allegany County, MD.

DEATH: 20 Jul 1845 in Cumberland, Maryland and buried at Rose Hill Cemetery.[1]

NOTES: He moved to Cumberland, Allegany County, Maryland and served as Postmaster from 1802 to 7 Jan 1807.[2] Shortly after his marriage in 1810, they moved to Frederick, MD where he practiced law. In 1817 he was on the Frederick Town Council. He represented Frederick County in the Maryland House of Representatives from 1817 until 1821. He returned to Cumberland in 1826 where he continued to practice law and he represented Allegany County in the Maryland Senate from 1831 to 1836.[3] He served on several commissions related to the early development of Cumberland.[4]

---

[1] Kelleher, *op.cit.,* 32
[2] Scharf, 1339
[3] Kelleher, *op.cit.,* 32
[4] Scharf, 1328, 1340, 1360

RICHARD POTTS (1753-1808)

Admitted to Montgomery County Bar In 1777[1]

BIRTH/PARENTS: Richard Potts was born 19 July 1753[2], Upper Marlboro, Prince George's County, to William Potts (b. 1718, Barbados, d. 1761, West Indies) and Sarah Lee Potts, (b. 1720, d. 1790, Frederick, Md., at son Richard's home) daughter of Phillip Lee of Prince George's County[3]

EDUCATION: His early education is unknown, but it is known that he studied law, most likely with Judge Samuel Chase

LEGAL CAREER: He was the holder of numerous offices in Frederick County and was one of the first two lawyers admitted to the practice of law in Montgomery County. He was a friend of John Hanson, who was called "The First President of the United States" because he was elected by the Congress as President under The Articles of Confederation[4]. Both friends were land speculators[5]. In 1784, he was appointed by the Honorable Luther Martin, Attorney General of the State, to act as State's Attorney for Montgomery, Frederick and Washington counties.[6] Potts was a member of the Maryland State Convention, which ratified the U.S. Constitution, and was the second U.S. Senator from Maryland's Western Shore. In 1801 he was a Court of Appeals Judge, appointed to fill a vacancy caused by the death of Judge James Murray[7].

MARRIAGE:

1. 15 April 1779, to Elizabeth Hughes (b. 1762, d. 28 Oct. 1793) of Hagerstown, Maryland, sister of Captain James Hughes "who bandaged Andre's eyes"[8] She is the daughter of Barnabas Hughes (1720-1765) and Elizabeth Waters Hughes (1730-1789).
2. 19 Dec 1799, to Eleanor Murdoch of Frederick, MD (b. 2 Nov 1773 d. 1 Oct 1842 daughter of George Murdoch (1742-1805) and Eleanor Charlton Murdoch (1748-1818). .

CHILDREN[9]

---

[1] Scharf, 667

[2] Williams, *History of Frederick County,* 1342-3, sketch of Arthur Potts gives ancestry of Richard Potts.

[3] Scharf, Vol. 1, 392

[4] Rice, *New Facts and Old Families*, 67

[5] Rice, *op.cit.,* 71

[6] Scharf, .393

[7] Scharf, 383b.

[8] Scharf, 393. Reference is to Major John Andre , a British soldier hanged as a spy, 2 Oct.1780. It was said Capt. James Hughes used his own scarf to bandage Andre's eyes

[9] Scharf states Elzabeth had nine children, and Eleanor four. He only named Richard, who followed the legal profession. Williams *History of Frederick County,* 1342-1343, in sketch of Arthur Potts, identifies 12 children named here. Some family trees on Ancestry, also list a "Patty or Polly" who

by Elizabeth, his first wife

1. William Potts, b. 26 Mar 1780, d. 04 Jun 1848, Baltimore, MD, m. 17 Mar. 1807[1], Susanna Campbell (b. 1785).
2. Elizabeth Potts, b. 1781[2], d. 03 May 1842., m. 3 Sep 1822, Frederick County,[3] Daniel Hughes, b. 1774, d. 1 Feb. 1854, both buried Mt. Olivet Cemetery.
3. Samuel H. Potts, b. 1783, d. 14 Feb 1812.
4. Rebecca Potts, b. 1785, d. 21 Feb 1801.
5. Richard Potts, b. 10 Mar 1786, d. 7 Apr 1865,[4] m.8 Apr. 1811[5], Ann Letitia Murdoch, (b. 1785, d. 9 Mar 1865[6], daughter of George Murdoch (1742-1805) and Eleanor Charlton. (1748-1818) Murdoch..
6. John Lee Potts b. 28 Sep 1788 d.1839.
7. Sarah Ann Potts b. 26 Sep 1791
8. Philip Thomas Potts b. 1793, d. 15 Jan. 1818.

by Eleanor

9. Mary Jane Fitzhugh Potts, b. 22 Oct 1800, d. 24 Jan 1835 (34y, 3m, 2days), m. 13 May 1822[7], Worthington Johnson (b. 21 Nov 1801 in Maryland, d. 13 Jul 1864 in Frederick, MD).
10. Harriet Murdoch Potts, b.. 06 Apr 1803, d. 18 Dec 1867 in Frederick, m. 12 Jun 1823, Richard H. Marshall[8] (b. 8 Mar 1799, d. 3 Sep 1884) both buried in Mt. Olivet Cemetery.[9]
11. George Murdoch Potts, b. 14 Jun 1805 in Frederick, d. 19 Aug 1893 in Frederick, MD., m. 16 Nov. 1826 in Washington County, to Cornelia Ringgold[10], (b. 2 Sept 1805, d 1868), daughter of Samuel and Anna Maria Cadwallader Ringgold.[11] He was a stock farmer and planter.
12. Eleanor Murdoch Potts b. 6 Sep 1807, d. 26 May 1882, buried Mt.Olivet Cemetery, unmarried.[12]

DEATH He died 26 November 1808, in Frederick, MD. His first place of burial was All-Saints Parish Cemetery, later remains were moved to Mount Olivet Cemetery, in Frederick.

---

married John Pack of Montgomery County, MD in 1801 in North Carolina, but this seems to be a mis-identification. No independent sources for her were found.

[1] Myers, *Frederick County Marriages, 1778-1810,* 118.

[2] Estimated birth year. Her tombstone gives her age as 68, which would place her birth in 1778.

[3] Myers, *Frederick County Marriages, 1811-1840,* 192.

[4] Eader and Long, *Englebecht Death Register,* 167.

[5] Myers, *Frederick County Marriages, 1811-1840,* 192.

[6] Eader and Long, *Englebecht Death Register,* p. 167

[7] Myers, *Frederick County Marriages, 1811-1840,* 192.

[8] Myers, *Frederick County Marriages, 1811-1840,* 192.

[9] Holdcraft, *Names in Stone,* 768.

[10] Quynn, *Diary Jacob Engelbrecht,* 253.

[11] Williams, *History of Frederick County,* 1343, sketch of Arthur Potts. George M. & Cornelia were his parents.

[12] Holdcraft, *Names in Stone,* 900.

NOTES: He served as Clerk of the Committee of Observation for Frederick County, in 1776, and served during an expedition as Aide to Thomas Johnson, who commanded the Virginia detachment of the Flying Camp. On 27 May 1777 he was appointed Clerk of Frederick County, which position he resigned in 1778[1]. There is one volume of Frederick County Land Records, RP1, which carries his initials.

RICHARD RIDGELY (1755-1824)

Admitted to The Montgomery County Bar 1805[2]

BIRTH/PARENTS: Richard Ridgely was born 3 August 1755 in Queen Caroline Parish, Anne Arundel County, to Greenbury Ridgely (b. 5 Dec 1726, d. bef. 13 Mar 1783) and Lucy Stringer Ridgely (b. abt 1738, d. Jun 1815).[3]

LEGAL CAREER: Admitted to the bar by 1779, practicing primarily in Baltimore and Anne Arundel Counties. Served in the Maryland Senate, Western Shore, 1776-1781, and appointed Clerk of the Senate in 1777[4]. Other Legislative service. Including serving as a Circuit Court Judge from Anne Arundel County.[5]

MARRIAGE: 3 Oct 1778, Anne Arundel County to Elizabeth Dorsey (b. abt 1759, d. 1811), daughter of Ely Dorsey (d. 1794) and Deborah (Dorsey) Dorsey (b. 1722, d. 1807)).

CHILDREN:[6]

1. Elizabeth Ridgely, b. abt 1782, m. Nathaniel C. Dare, (b. 1780 Calvert Co., d. 26 Aug. 1838.)
2. Richard Ridgely, b. abt 1783, d. bef. 1824 in Kentucky, m. 21 Jan. 1811 in Jessamine, KY, Jane Price, daughter of John Lewis Price and Sarah Bourne Price.
3. Sophia Ridgely, b. abt 1786, m. 25 Jul 1821, Richard Harwood Battee, b. abt 1785.
4. Daniel B. Ridgely, b. 1788 in Baltimore, d. 1814, m. 28 Jan. 1811, Baltimore, MD, Mary Hammond (d. 2 Jun. 1840).
5. Deborah Ridgely, b. 1790, d. 11 Sep 1831, m. 12 Sep 1816, in Baltimore, Robert Neilson, (b. 1785 in Donegal, Ireland, d. May 1850 in Baltimore.
6. Ann Ridgely, b. 25 Sep 1793, d. 19 Aug. 1879, in New York, m. 12 Oct. 1815, Rev. Alfred Henry Dashiell, b. 2 Aug 1793, d. 18 Mar. 1881.

---

[1] Scharf, sketch of Richard Potts, 392-393.
[2] Scharf, 667
[3] Papenfuse, *Biographical Directory,* sketch of Richard Ridgely, 689-691.
[4] Van Horn, *Out of the Past,* 177.
[5] Papenfuse, *op.cit.,* 690.
[6] Papenfuse, *op.cit.,* 689-690 and Newman, *Anne Arundel Gentry,* Vol , III, 139-141; and Arps, *Heirs & Orphans,i92,* Robert Neilson, exec. Richard Ridgely, and admin. Edward D. Ridgely, accounts 20 Aril 1836. There are differences in the children listed between Newman (who includes a William) and Papenfuse. Research on Ancestry.com helped fill in some dates from *Find-A-Grave.*

7. Edward Dorsey Ridgely, b. 1798, d. 4 July 1830[1], in Annapolis, in 32nd year.
8. Matilda Chase Ridgely, b. 7 Dec. 1800, in Baltimore, d. 10 July 1874, m. 27 May 1824, in Baltimore, MD, Michael Shellman Baer (b. in 1796, d. 8 Jun 1854, Baltimore, MD) son of Henry Baer and Elizabeth Shellman Baer.

DEATH: 26 Feb. 1824 in Anne Arundel County, MD, testate.

NOTES: He speculated heavily in land, and mortgaged and lost most of it in 1791. May have moved out of state for a short term in Georgia, before returning to Baltimore where he again acquired more property there and in Anne Arundel County, including becoming co-owner of Guilford Mills.[2]

,

DAVID ROSS (1755-1800)

Admitted to Montgomery County Bar 1780[3]

BIRTH/PARENTS: David Ross Jr. was born 12 Feb. 1755 in Prince George's County, MD to David Ross (1716-1778)[4] and Ariana Frisby Brice Ross, (b. 19 Jun 1732, d. 14 Apr 1797) daughter of John Brice (b. 4 Nov 1705, d. 24 Sep 1766) and Sarah (Frisby) Brice (b. 7 Dec 1714, d. 8 Apr 1782).

LEGAL CAREER: Admitted to the Frederick County Bar, in 1783. He was a delegate to the Continental Congress, 1786-1787[5] and a U.S. Representative from Maryland. He appears in listings of practicing attorneys in Prince George's County in 1783-84, 1786, 1789, and 1792.[6]

MARRIAGE: 9 May 1781, in Talbot County, to Henrietta Marie Bordley (b. 29 June 1762, Wye Island, d. 14 Nov. 1825, Chambersburg, PA) daughter of John Beale Bordley (11 Feb. 1727-26 Jan. 1804) and Margaret (Chew) Bordley (d. 11 Nov.1773).[7]

CHILDREN[8]:

1. John Bordley Ross (1782-1783)
2. Edmond Ross, (1783-1783)
3. Margaret Ariana Ross (1785-1831)
4. Sarah Corbett Ross (1786-1828)
5. Charles Bordley Ross (1788-1856)
6. James Brice Ross (1791-1872)

---

[1] Barnes, *Marriages and Deaths from the Gazette, 1727-1839,* 154.
[2] Papenfuse, *op.cit., 691.*
[3] Scharf, 667.
[4] Keddie, *Prince George's Wills, Liber T No #1, 1778-1783 p. 9-10.*
[5] Scharf, 469.
[6] Van Horn, *Out of the Past*, 192, 202, 207, 217.
[7] McIntire, *Annapolis Maryland Families,* 68.
[8] *Ancestry.com.,* 2nd Dan Higgins Family Tree lists children & dates. Unsourced.

7. Elizabeth Bordley Ross (1793-1828)
8. Thomas Bordley Ross (1796-1876)
9. William Stuart Ross (1799-1861)

DEATH About 1800, probably in Bladensburg. In August 1799, he assigned all his personal property to William Stewart to pay remaining legacies from his father's estate, and the remaining estate debts[1]. He appears in the 1800 census as head of household on the same page as William Stewart, with 15 white inhabitants and 17 slave. He was probably living in his father's house in Bladensburg, which was held in trust for the family. He apparently died insolvent, not having received his residual legacy of his father's estate.[2]

NOTES His father, Dr. David Ross of Bladensburg, Prince George's county patented over 12,000 acres in the 1760s, mostly in Frederick County.[3] He seems to have practiced multiple professions, also being a merchant with his brother in law Richard Henderson in Bladensburg, and an investor in an iron forge and furnace in what is today Washington County – coincident with his land speculation. His estate was still being settled and contested in Chancery Cases as late as 1814.[4]

FREDERICK AUGUSTUS SCHLEY (1789-1858)

Admitted to Montgomery County Bar 1810[5]

BIRTH/PARENTS Frederick Augustus Schley was born 14 May 1789 in Frederick, Maryland to John Jacob and Anna Maria (Shelman) Schley[6] In the 1790s the family moved to Georgia.

EDUCATION: He attended University of Georgia, but left at age 17, due to health reasons, and returned to Frederick where he was educated at the Frederick Academy. There he came to the attention of Roger B. Taney, who invited him to study law in his office in Frederick, where he was admitted to the bar around 1809/1810.[7]

---

[1] Prince George's County Deeds, Liber JRM7, 260, 264.

[2] Unable to locate gravestone or obituary for him. There is a chancery case at the MSA, dated 1799/10/29. #4614. William Stewart s. John Mason and James M. Lingan. PG. Estateof David Ross. Accession No. 17,898-4614 MSA S512-6 4783 Location 1/37/1 and also one dated 10/14/1800 #4383, David Ross of PG, insolvent estate of Ross.followed by 4383A, Horatio Ross, PG, insolvent estate of Ross. Accession No 17,898-4383 MSA 8512-6 4522 Location 1/37/1.

[3] Coldham, *Settlers of Maryland, 1751-1765,* p. 237-238.

[4] Chancery Case 1800/11/25, #4545 William Steuart and Notley Maddox vs. Honore Martin.PG. Estate of Dr. David Ross. Recorded Chancery Record 70, p. 365. Accession No. 17,898-4545-1/4 MSA S512-6-4714. Location 1/37/1/ Also 1814/03/30 William Stewart. AL. PG. Estate of Dr. David Ross. Luck, Addition to Spring Bottom, Workmans Desire, Johnsons Fancy in AL. Also lots in DC. Recorded Chancery Record. 48 p. 388. AccessionNo. 17,898-4580-1/3 MSA S512-6 4749. Location 1/37/1.

[5] Scharf, v.1,667

[6] Fogle, Frederick County Church and Cemetery Records, Vol. 4, 41

[7] Scharf, v.2. 1112-1113.

LEGAL CAREER According to Scharf, he built up an extensive and lucrative practice. Examples of his arguments can be found in the Court of Appeals, as reported in the *Maryland Reports*. "…in the full vigor of his professional life, had no superior at the bar of Western Maryland."[1]

MARRIAGES:

1. 27 April 1812, Frederick County, MD[2] Eliza Ashbuy McCannon (b 10 Sep 1794, d. 1816) daughter of James McCannon of Baltimore[3].

2. 17 Jan 1821, Cumberland, MD, Francina Cheston Lynn (28 Jan. 1798, -d. 4 April 1828)[4] daughter of David Lynn[5] (1758-1835) and Mary Galloway Lynn (d 1803).

3. 15 June 1843, Barbara Hall (b. abt 1820, d. 14 March 1850)[6] daughter of Thomas B. Hall and Ann Buchanan Pottenger Hall[7].

CHILDREN

By First wife:

1. George Schley, (Col.) (b. abt 1813, d. 11 Apr. 1890)[8] m. 29 Jun 1839, Hagerstown, MD., Mary Hall (d. 18 Jan. 1880),[9] daughter of Thomas B. Hall (b. abt 1779, d. 16 Jun 1822) and Ann Buchanan Pottenger Hall (b. 1800, d. 8 Feb. 1825).[10]
2. James McCannon Schley (b. abt 1815, d. 15 July 1885, Hagerston, MD[11]) m. 7 Feb. 1838, Hagerstown, Md., to Ellen N. Stull (b. abt. 1815, d. bef. 16 Dec. 1885)[12] [13] daughter of Otho Holland Williams Stull (b. 7 Mar. 1784, d. 23 Ju 1867) and Letitia Hall Stull (b. abt 1787, d. 2 Oct. 1862).[14][15].

By Second wife:

3. Frederick Augusta Schley, Jr., b. abt 1821, died 6 Oct. 1854 [16]
4. Fanny Lynn Schley, b. 1828, d. 3 June 1828[17]
5. William Henry Schley, b. ca. 1828, no occupation on 1850 census. No later records found.

---

[1] Scharf, v.2, 1401

[2] Myers, *Frederick County Marriage Licenses.*

[3] Holdcraft, 989, Scharf, 1128, sketch of George Schley.

[4] Quynn, *Englebrecht Diary*, v. 1, 6, 303

[5] Long & Eader, the Jacob Englebrecht Marriage Ledger,1820 – 1890, 107,

[6] Eader & Long,*The Jacob Engelbrecht Death Ledger, 1820-1890,* p192

[7] Bowie, *Across the Years,* 661.

[8] Morrow, Ed., *Washington County Cemetery Records, V. VII* 106. St. John's Episcopal Church Yard, Hagerstown.

[9] Morrow, *op.cit.,* 106.

[10] Morrow, *op.cit.,*106, buried near Schleys and Pottingers; Long & Eader, op.cit., 111.

[11] Bailey, comp., *The Stulls of "Millsborough",* 94.

[1212] Bailey, *op.cit.,* 95.

[13] Engelbrecht, v.1, 567

[14] Bailey, comp., *op.cit.,* 64-68.

[15] Scharf, 1401, sketch James M. Schley.

[16] Eader & Long,*The Jacob Engelbrecht Death Ledger, 1820-1890,* p194

[17] Holdcraft, *Names* In Stone, 989

By Third wife: After her death, these children were raised by their elder brother, George, and his wife, their mother's sister in Hagerstown.

6. Roger Brooke Taney Schley, b. July 1845[1], d.27 April 1854 in Hagerstown, 8 years, 9 months.[2]
7. Thomas Hall Schley, b.ca. 1846, d. 27 April 1849, age 3.[3]
8. Buchanan Schley (Col.) b. 7 Aug. 1848, d. 1916, m. 1869, Sarah Rebecca Roman (b. 1852, d. 1926) [4] daughter of Benjamin Franklin Roman (b. 1819, d. 1863)and Sarah Jacques Roman (b. 1826, d. 1872)[5]
9. Mary Buchanan Schley b. 22 Feb. 1850, d. 14 April 1854, Hagerstown, age 4 years 1 month, 21 days[6].

DEATH 5 February 1858 buried at Mount Olivet Cemetery, Frederick, Maryland[7]

NOTES 1st Lt. with Stempel's 3rd Regiment (MD Militia) during War of 1812[8] Served on the board of directors for the Frederick County Bank beginning in 1821[9]

ROBERT SMITH (ca. 1760 to ca. 1835)

Admitted to Montgomery County Bar In 1780[10]

PARENTS Robert Smith was born about 1760 to John Smith (d. bef 1798) of Prince George's County.[11] According to Bowie's source, Dr. Walter Wells of Washington, D.C., he came to America when his son Robert was 7 years old. There is no record in Prince George's county of his acquisition of land, but he did own several slaves, which he made a deed of gift to his son for in 1773. It was not necessary that Robert Smith be of age at that time. John Smith identified himself as a school master.

LEGAL CAREER Robert Smith was admitted to the Frederick County Bar in 1783.[12] He was on the list of justices and judges of the Orphans Court in Montgomery County from 1804

---

1 U. S. Federal Census, Maryland, Frederick County, Fredericktown, 1850
2 Eader & Long, *The Jacob Engelbrecht Death Ledger, 1820-1890,* 194
3 Eader & Long, *The Jacob Engelbrecht Death Ledger, 1820-1890,* 192
4 History of Washington County, sketch of Buchanan Schley, 787-789.
5 Morrow, ed., *Washington County Cemetery Records,* Vol. VI, 42, 82.
6 Eader & Long, *The Jacob Engelbrecht Death Ledger, 1820-1890,* 194
7 Holdcroft, 989
8 Mallick and Wright, Frederick County Militia in the War of 1812, 331
9 Engelbrecht, v.1, 41
10 Scharf, 667
11 MCLR, Liber H:254, Robert Smith manumits slave, given to him by his father, "John Smith, formerly of Prince George's County, now deceased." Prince George's County Deeds, BB3:319, 25 Nov. 1773, John Smith, schoolmaster to Robert Smith, in consideration of natural love and affection for his son, several slaves: Luce, Nell, Henry, Joan, Cloe, Rebecca, Rachel, Benjamin, and their increase.
12 Scharf, p. 416

-1810.[1] He owned over 300 acres, and more than 20 slaves. In April 1820 he sold his property to Washington Bowie of Washington, D.C., and it is written up as "Flint Hill II in Farquhar's Historic Homes."[2] He appears to have moved west with his second wife, and ended up in Missouri, where he shows up on the 1830 census in Scott County. In 1840, his wife Hannah Smith, with 3 daughters under 20, is in Cape Giradeau, Missouri, where one of his daughters, from his first marriage was married.

MARRIAGES:

1. 5 September 1785, Elizabeth Lanham of Piscataway Parish, who bore him 8 children. She died before 1812. She was the daughter of Edward Lanham (1731-1791) who died testate in Prince George's County, and Susannah (Page) Lanham (1732-1797) who died testate in Montgomery County.[3]
2. 13 December 1812, Hannah Walker (b, abt 1790) of Washington, D.C. in Fredericksburg, Virginia.[4] She is head of household in 1840 in Cape Giradeau, Missouri. No later records found.

CHILDREN[5]

By First Wife:

1. Robert Smith," who went west, and became the founder of Fort Smith, Arkansas." Unable to verify this.[6]
2. Jane Smith, b. 1786, d. Brighton, Montgomery County, Maryland, 19 Apr 1875[7]; m. 7 Jan1813,[8] Lloyd Adamson of Frederick County, MD, who died before 1840. She left a will, naming her son Robert and leaving him the house and furniture she inherited under the will of her brother John Smith of Washington, D.C.[9]

---

[1] Scharf, p. 665

[2] Farquhar, *p. 158.*

[3] Malloy, et.al, *Montgomery County Will Abstracts,* 81. Will dated 19 Jun 1797, probated 28 July 1797, among others names her daughter Elizabeth Smith, and names Robert Smith of Montgomery County one of her executors.

[4] *Marriages and Deaths, 1800-1820,* p. 39

[5] Bowie, *Across the Years in Prince George's County, 470-471,* lists the 9 children with some brief information.

[6] Bowie, *op.cit.,* Wikipedia gives the following history of the founding of Fort Smith: Fort Smith's name comes from General Thomas Adams Smith (1781–1844), who commanded the United States Army Rifle Regiment in 1817, headquartered near St. Louis. General Smith had ordered Army topographical engineer Stephen H. Long (1784–1864) to find a suitable site on the Arkansas River for a fort. General Smith never visited the town or forts that bore his name.

[7] Bowman, *Sentinel, April 23, 1875,* died on 19th instant at residence of son, Robt L. Adamson.

[8] Manuel, *Marriage Licenses, Montgomery County*

[9] Malloy, et.al, *Montgomery County Wills, 1826-1875.* 1; from book RWC 1, folio 110-111, on microfilm.

3. John Smith, b. abt 1789, d. 27 Jun 1857, testate, buried Rock Creek Cemetery[1]. Lived in Washington, D.C. where trustees William T. Duvall, and Robert L. Adamson claimed compensation for emancipated slaves in 1862[2].
4. Susan Smith, b. abt 1790, d. 27 Jul 1874,[3] m. 6 May 1813,[4] Walter Henry Hilleary (b. abt 1790, d. bef 7 Sep 1869[5]). Lived at Bladensburg, Prince George's County.[6]
5. Sarah Elizabeth Smith – no other information found.
6. Sophia Smith, b. 7 April 1805, d. 18 April 1893, Adams County, Ohio; married in 1827, in Cape Giradeau,Missouri, Greer Brown Grimes (b. 23 October 1803- d. 18 Feb. 1888) Adams County, Ohio. [7] Had issue.
7. Dolly Madison Smith, married Charles Davis of St. Louis – no other information found.
8. James Madison Smith, no other information.

By Second Wife: Possibly three daughters.

9. Andromeda Smith, married Governor Beardsley of New Jersey. Except for list in Bowie's, *Across the Year's inPrince George's county,* no records have been found.

DEATH: In April 1820 he sold his property in Montgomery County, and no later records have been found in Montgomery County. He may be head of household on 1830 census in Missouri, and was dead before 1840, when wife was head of household.

NOTES: Robert Smith is a very common name, and there was at least one other Robert Smith of approximately the same age, who was a good friend of James Madison, and held an appointment in his cabinet in the Dept. of State. He lived in Baltimore. He died 26 November 1842, at age 85. "The Hon. Robt Smith..[8] A Baltimore County will for this Robert Smith, and a biography in the Maryland Historical Society in 1919, make it unlikely that he extended his practice to Montgomery County. He only had one son, Samuel, and was quite active in the shipping business in Baltimore, as well as having a political career. He also had a prominent brother, Gen. Samuel Smith of Baltimore. From Baltimore County Wills, 1842-1844, Vol. 19, Will of Robert Smith, dated 18 June 1825, showed that he owned much property in Baltimore, from which he receives rents. The only child mentioned in this will is a Samuel W. Smith, who was also named executor. The will was presented for probate 16 January 1843. A codicil made 10 June 1826, names wife Margaret Smith, to whom he bequeathe domestic slaves. HE is buried in the Westminster church yard in Baltimore: Smith, Robert, b. Nov 3, 1757 d Nov 26, 1842;[9]

---

[1] Interment Record gave occupation as clerk, age at 68 years, b. Maryland. Pippenger*, District of Columbia Interments, 1855-1874,* 333.
[2] Provine, *Compensated Emancipation,* Petition No. 264.
[3] Balch, *Prince George's County Marriages and Deaths,* 287.
[4] Manuel, *Marriage Licenses Montgomery County.*
[5] PGCGS, *Index to Probate,* Will probate date, WAJ 1:426.
[6] Ancestry, 1830 & 1840 census records.
[7] Find-A-Grave has brief biographical material, found on Ancestry.
[8] Dixon, *National Intelligencer, 1842,* Tuesday, November 29, 1842, p 431
[9] *Find-A-Grave.com.*

ROGER BROOKE TANEY (1777 – 1864)

Admitted to Montgomery County Bar, 1801[1]

BIRTH/PARENTS Roger Brooke Taney was born 17 March 1777, in Calvert County, to Michael Taney V (1750-1820) and Monica (Brooke) (1752-1814) Taney[2]

EDUCATION: He was tutored by David English;. And graduated from Dickinson College, PA, with high honors in 1795.[3] Between 1796 and 1799 he studied law with Judge Jeremiah Townley Chase of Maryland General Court in Annapolis.[4]

LEGAL CAREER: He began his career practicing law in the Mayors Court of Annapolis, and served one term in the Maryland State Legislature 1799-1800. He joined both the Frederick and Montgomery County bars in 1801. After repeated attempts to win another elected office, he was elected to the Maryland State Senate in 1816 and led the Federalist Party in its final years.

President Andrew Jackson named him interim Attorney General in July 1833 and then Secretary of the Treasury in September 1833. In 1836, Jackson appointed him Chief Justice of the U.S., a position he held until 1864. His most famous decision on the court was in the Dred Scott case (Scott v. Sandford), in which he denied Scott's bid for freedom. Taney held that our founding fathers did not mean black people when they signed the Declaration of Independence with the words "all men are created equal," and that black people formed "no part of the people who framed and adopted this declaration."

Taney was planter aristocracy. As an attorney his language was simple and direct, contradicting a tendency to florid speech among the lawyers of his era. He freed his own slaves but retained a belief that blacks and whites could not be equals. As the Civil War approached, he believed that courts should defend state sovereignty against domination by the Federal Government. He had no sympathy for Lincoln's measures in the Civil War.

MARRIAGE

1. On 7 January 1806, at Tera Rubra north of Toms Creek, Frederick County, Maryland, Anne Phoebe Charlton Key, b. 17 Jun 1783, d. 29 Sep 1855, Baltimore, of yellow fever[5].daughter of John Ross Key (1754-1821) and Ann Phoebe Penn Charlton Key (1756-1830). She was the sister of Francis Scott Key (1779-1843).)

CHILDREN[6]

1. Ann Arnold Taney, b. 24 Aug. 1808, d, 18 Feb 1872,[7] m 27 May 1834, Washington, D.C.,[8] James Mason Campbell

---

[1] Scharf, 667

[2] Scharf, sketch of Roger Brooke Taney, 394-399

[3] Tyler, *Memoir of Roger Brooke Taney, LL.D.*.

[4]*American Biographical Dictionary*. Volume IX

[5] Scharf, op.cit., 398, *and Taney Family file, MCHS library.*

[6] MCHS, Taney Family file.

[7] Eader and Long, *Engelbrecht Death Ledger,*

[8] Quynn, *Englebrecht Diary,* 466.

2. Elizabeth Maynadier Taney b. 8 Apr 1810; m. 18 Nov. 1841, in Baltimore[1], William Stevenson.
3. Ellen Mary Taney, b. 29 Aug. 1813, d. 26 Sep 1871.[2]
4. Augustus Brooke Taney, b. 15 Sep 1815, d. 16 Aug. 1818, before his 3rd birthday
5. Sophia Brooke Taney, b. 13 Dec. 1817, d. after 1880, m. 15 June 1852, Lt. Col. Francis Taylor, U.S.A., (1805-1858).[3]
6. Maria Key Taney, b. 19 Feb. 1819, d. 15 Apr 1887,[4] m. 9 Feb 1852,[5] Richard Taylor Allison, b. 6 June 1823, Kentucky, d. 10 Apr 1909, Baltimore, MD.[6]. He served as a major in the Confederate States Marine Corps[7].
7. Alice Carroll Taney, b. 27 Jun 1827, d. 25 Sep 1855, in Baltimore of yellow fever.

DEATH 12 Oct. 1864, buried in the St. John the Evangelist Cemetery, Frederick, MD. Many notables, including President Lincoln, attended the funeral.[8]

AUGUSTUS TANEY (1787-1823)

Admitted to Practice in Montgomery County before 1816[9]

BIRTH/PARENTS: Thomas Augustine Taney, known as Augustus Taney, was born, about 1787 in Calvert County, to Michael Taney V (1750-1820) and Monica (Brooke) (1752-1814) Taney[10]

EDUCATION: Probably read law in his older brother's office, Roger Brooke Taney.

LEGAL CAREER: Practiced law in Montgomery County, Frederick County, and Washington, D.C.. He apparently was involved primarily in land transactions in Montgomery county and serving as a trustee in chancery case to sell real estate of William Holland of Capel, by 1816[11], as well as others.

---

[1] Long Eader, *Engelbrecht Marriage Ledger,* 111
[2] Eader & Long, *Engelbrecht Death Ledger,* 217
[3] Long Eader, *Engelbrecht Marriage Ledger,* 127
[4] Holdcraft, *Names in Stone,* 76.
[5] Long Eader, *Engelbrecht Marriage Ledger,* 3
[6] Arps, *Maryland Mortalities, 1876-1915.*
[7] Hartzler, *Marylanders in the Confederacy, 76.*
[8] Quynn, *Englebrecht Diary,*
[9] MCHS Taney Family file, letter from Dorothy Palmer Malloy addressed to Richard K. MacMaster, dated 12 April 1974, details career. Unsourced.
[10] Scharf, sketch of Roger Brooke Taney, 394-399
[11] Dixon, *National Intelligencer,* 5 April 1816.

MARRIAGES:

1. 10 Sep 1816, to Mary Young, daughter of Nicholas Young, of D.C.[1] (b. 1798, d. 16 Aug. 1817, Rockville, MD)[2]
2. 1 Feb. 1821, in Washington, D.C. by Rev. Mr. Hurley, Catherine (Kitty) Hurley, (b. 1796, d. 26 Feb. 1854)[3] daughter of the late Thomas Hurley, of Philadelphia[4]. She was apparently close to the Byrne family, and after becoming a widow, stayed with the Cloppers at the Woodlands, sending her children to school in Emmitsburg, before purchasing the Edgewood Plantation[5].

CHILDREN:

1. Roger Brooke Taney (named for Augustine's older brother) b June 1817, d. 16 Aug. 1817 by first wife.
2. Joseph Augustus Taney, b. 8 Nov. 1821 in Washington, D.C., d. 22 Nov. 1894, Montgomery County, Maryland, m.28 June 1855, Anne Louisa White, (b. 30 Mar. 1834, d. 23 Nov. 1913) daughter of Ambrose A. and Mary White of Baltimore County[6]. They are both buried at St. Rose Cemetery, Cloppers[7]. He became a farmer in Montgomery County.
3. Mary Henley Taney b. 1823, d. 21 Dec. 1886, at "Edgewood." Unmarried.[8]

DEATH: Died 21 Oct 1823 at 36 years of age. Buried in Georgetown. His death notice invited "the Judges of the Circuit Court of D.C.", to attend his funeral at his late residence.[9]

---

[1] Dixon, *National Intelligencer, 14 Sep 1816,* gave marriage date of 10 Sep. 1816, for Augustus Taney of Montgomery County.

[2] Dixon, *National Intelligencer,* 21 Aug. 1817, died same day as infant son.

[3] MCHS Cemetery Card file, Catherine Taney, buried in St. Rose Cemetery, Cloppers.

[4] Dixon, *National Intelligencer,* 6 Feb. 1821, marriage of Mr. Augustus Taney of Georgetown.

[5] MCHS Taney Family File, Letter to Richard K. MacMaster, from Dorothy Palmer Malloy. Montgomery County deeds to Catharine Taney recorded in BS11:299-301 in 1842 from William Musser and wife, for 177 ½ acres, parts of *Pleasant Fields and Resurvey on Pleasant Valley, Lost Jacket,* and STS1:175-176, in 1845 from John D. and Eleanor Freeman, for additional part of *Norway,* about 11 acres. There are two other Edgewoods in *Historic Homes* by Farquhar.

[6] Marriage record from Taney Famiy file, appears to be copy of Family Record from Bible.

[7] MCHS Cemetery Card file, buried with sons Roger B., d. 3 March 1865, 7 months and Roger Brooke, 1872-1896.

[8] MCHS Cemetery Card file, buried with Catherine Taney; Malloy, *Sentinel,* 24 Dec. 1886.

[9] Dixon, *National Intelligencer*, 23 Oct. 1823.

ARCHIBALD VAN HORNE (abt 1758-1817)

Admitted to Montgomery County Bar 1798[1]
Admitted To Prince George's County Bar 1796[2]

BIRTH/PARENTS Archibald Van Horne was born about 1758, probably in Baltimore County (or now Harford County) Maryland to Col. Gabriel Peterson Van Horne (d. 3 Mar 1814) and Mary (Van Sant) Van Horne. The family moved to Prince George's County around 1794, although Gabriel Van Horne knew the county well, as in 1785, the Maryland Assembly had granted him the exclusive right to set up schedules for the operation of stage carriages on the great public road from the Susquehanna River to the Potomac River, via Baltimore.[3]

LEGAL CAREER He was a member of the Maryland House of Delegates from Prince George's County, 1801-1803 and 1805 served as speaker, resigned 11 Nov 1805; elected to the 10th and 11th congresses, 1807-1811; chairman of the Committee on District of Columbia; returned to the State House of Delegates 1814-1816; elected to the State Senate in 1816 but died in Prince Georges County in 1817.[4]

MARRIAGE: On 26 Jul 1797, to Alethea Elizabeth Beall, b. abt 1775, d. bef. 17 May 1819, Prince George's County[5], daughter of Gen. Rezin Beall (1723-1809) and Amelia (Beall) (1749-bef 1809) Beall[6]

CHILDREN[7]

1. Mary Ann Van Horne, b. 1798 m 7 Aug. 1821, Washington, D.C. to John D. Emack.
2. Amelia Beall Van Horne, b.1799 m. 2 Jun 1818, Walter Truman Greenleaf Beall (b. 1795, son of George Beall (1770-1809) and Ann Trueman Greenfield Beall (d. 1832).
3. Alethea Van Horne, b.1801 m. 3 Mar 1825, Washington, D.C. to Robert Allen. Moved to Tennessee.
4. Eliza Van Horne, b. 1803 m. Alexander McCormick
5. Clarissa Van Horne, b. 1805, m. Rev. Carr
6. Rezin Van Horne, b.1807. d. 1838, never married
7. William Van Horne, b. 1809, d. 1820.

DEATH 13 Mar 1817 "...a member of the State Senate, and formerly a Representative in Congress from the second District, died at his seat in P. G. Co."[8]

---

[1] Scharf, 667
[2] Heinton, Out of the Past : 222
[3] Van Horn, *Out of the Past,* 207.
[4] *Biographical Directory of the American Congress : 1774-1961*, p.1749
[5] Keddie, *Prince George's Wills Liber TT, 1818-1822,* 18.
[6] Heterick, *Five Families "Beall" of Maryland,* 19
[7] Ibid, 19.
[8] Barnes, *Marriages and Deaths from the Maryland Gazette: 1777-1839,* 189

NOTES In 1799, on committee with his father to layout the village of Vansville Arranged construction of bridge over Cabin John branch. Appointed trustee of the Bladensburg Academy in 1816[1].

HENRY RIDGELY WARFIELD (1774-1839)

Admitted to Montgomery County Bar, 1797[2]

BIRTH/PARENTS: Henry Ridgely Warfield was born 14 Sep 1774 in Anne Arundel County to Charles Alexander Warfield and Elizabeth Ridgely Warfield.

LEGAL CAREER He was admitted to the bar in Montgomery County in 1797. At the time of his death he was the Auditor of Frederick County[3], and formerly a Representative in Congress from 3d Congressional District of Maryland, elected as a Federalist to the 16th, 17th & 18th Congresses (March 4, 1819-March 8, 1825)[4]. He, was in the memorable contest in Congress for the Presidency in 1825, he decided the vote of Maryland in favor of Mr. Adams and secured his election.[5]

MARRIAGE No record of marriage or children found.

DEATH on 18 March 1839 he was found dead in his bed in Frederick City. Reported to have died of apoplexy.[6]

RICHARD KEY WATTS (ca. 1767--1826)

Admitted to Montgomery County Bar, 1803[7]

BIRTH/PARENTS: Richard Key Watts is the son of Frances Rebecca Key (abt. 1751-1780)[8] of Saint Mary's County, and George Watts (abt 1735-1777) of Anne Arundel County. His grandfather was Richard Ward Key.[9]

LEGAL CAREER: He appears to have been part of the Key family group of attorneys, and he entered the bar in Montgomery County at the same time as his first cousin, Philip Barton

[1] Heinton, *Out of the Past* : 230, 251, 268.

[2] Scharf, 667

[3] Quynn, editor, Engelbrecht, Diary Vol. 1, 598.

[4] *Biographical Directory of the American Congess, 1774-1961,* 1776.

[5] Dixon, *National Intelligencer, 1838-1839,* 341.

[6] Dixon, *National Intelligencer, 1838-1839,* 341.

[7] Scharf, 667

[8] Anne Arundel County Deeds: **Error! Main Document Only.**NH1:27-28. Frances Rebecca Watts 2 July 1779, o beloved son, Richard Watts, for natural love and affection grants Negro Dick about 8 years old and Negro James 4 years old; one gold watch and silver ladle, and Negro girl Mill, 12 years old, from the day of my decease. At same time deeds of gift were made to George, Phillip, and Frances Watts, beloved sons and daughter.

[9] MCHS Key family file gives this lineage without dates. Approximate birth dates based on military service, which provided approx. dates for parents' births as well.

Key. On 1 April 1805, he, along with Francis Scott Key and others, were presented for admission to the bar in Prince George's County.[1] He apparently began his practice of law in Anne Arundel County, where he was living through 1803 when he sold his real estate, having sold in 1801 real estate owned jointly with his brothers, George Watts, and Philip Hammond Watts.[2]

MARRIAGE:

1. 15 Dec. 1789, Anne Arundel County, by Rev. Reed[3].to Mary Packer (b. abt 1770, d. after Feb. 1819)[4]

CHILDREN:

Richard K. Watts was listed as head of household in Annapolis in 1800, with 5 people under 15 –1 male 10-15; 2 males & 2 females under 10, and 1 male and 1 female 26-44. On the 1790 census, there is one male under 16, and one male & female over 16. Just 2 households away from Philip Key. The following have been identified:

1. Richard Key Watts Jr., b. ca. 1790, d. after 1849; m. 7 December 1820, Leesburg, Loudoun County, Virginia to Helen Rose, daughter of Capt. John Rose.[5] He was also an attorney, living in Washington, D.C. in the 1840's.
2. Mary Key Watts, b.ca. 1800, d. after 1860, m. 3 Oct. 1816, by license, Montgomery County, to Robert Wallace, (1775-1847)[6]. Living in Washington, D.C. with son in 1860.
3. Elizabeth Ann Key Watts.[7]

DEATH: Died in August 1826. His obituary in the *National Intelligncer* referred to him as Richard Key Watts, Jr., but in all the deeds he was party to, he never used "Jr." The obituary stated that he "was a practicing lawyer in Rockville for many years. He was

---

[1] Van Horn, *Out of the Past,* 240.

[2] Anne Arundel Deeds, Liber NH#11, 423-424. Deed dated 18 March 1803 from Richard Key Watts of the City of Annapolis, all his right to 158 acres, *Smith's Range Enlarged.* Mary, his wife released dower rights. Deed made 7 Sept 1701 fromfRichard Key Watts to Benjamin Ristou, for property mortgaged to him by George Watts, and jointly owned with Phillip Hammond Watts, conveyed for 5 shillings.

[3] Peden, *Anne Arundel Marriage Records, 1658-1800,* 250. Also NH11:245-246.

[4] MCLR in 1816, and Feb. 1819, Mary released dower right on deed from Richard K. Watts, mortgaging property in Montgomery County in. Liber S-19:471-475 and selling a parcel in Feb. 1819, in Liber U:431-432, as Richard Key Watts.

[5] Dixon, *National Intelligencer,* 20 December 1820; a prenuptial deed was recorded in Montgomery County Land Records, V:619: John Rose recorded deed from Richard Key Watts Jr. Between Richard Key Watts Jr., of the first part, Helen G. Rose of Leesburg, Va., of the second part and John Rose of Leesburg, Va of the third part. In consideration of a marriage about to take place between the said Watts and Helen Rose, in consideration of $5. it is agreed that all property in her name, shall be under her sole control and held in trust by John Rose.

[6] Pippenger, *District of Columbia Probate Records,* p.429, date of filing, Feb. 1847.

[7] MCLR Liber V:220-221. Elizabeth Ann Key Watts recorded bill of sale 25 August 1820. I gave to daughter some years past a Negro girl, Mary which was never recorded and in 1809 was sold with her consent, and then gave a Negro girl Mariah, but never executed bill of sale, so in consideration of the premises, I give her Mariah, aged about 20 years and her three children: James 4, William 2 and Kitty Ann 12 months. Signed Richard K Watts.

buried with full military honors in the Episcopal (i.e. Rockville) Cemetery, having served with the Lafayette Volunteers as an officer.[1]

NOTES: There has been some confusion between father and son. In 1818, it was reported that Richard K. Watts Jr., an insolvent debtor, was confined in the Washington prison for debt, by William Brent, clerk. A deed recorded between father and son in 1825, helps to clarify who is who: MCLR Liber X:531-532. At request of Richard K. Watts Sr., bill of sale recorded 25 January 1825: I, Richard K. Watts Junr of Montgomery County, for $147 paid by my father to sundry persons on judgments and notes and the futther sum of $70.11 for which my father now stands bound by judgments, I sell unto my father all my goods and chatells, one bedstead, bed mattress and furniture, thereto belonging, one easy chair, two bureaus, all my law and misc. books, one bathing tub, small table, one cupboard and one marsellais counterpane, all my kitchen furniture. Signed: R.K. Watts Jr. Before Samuel C. Veirs.

Earlier, it appears that Senior had his own difficulties: recorded in Liber S-19:471-475. Thomas S. Gantt's deed of trust dated 8 Feb. 1816, from Richard Key Watts. Whereas as Mallory and Watts of the town aforesaid, are indebted to the Bank of Georgetown in Washington, for $2000 and they have given joint bond to secure note, Richard Key Watts mortgages lot #22 of Bradford's Rest, and also tract called Saint Mary's sold him by Allison, for 113 acres. At the same time, Mary Watts, wife of Richard Key Watts, released dower. This was apparently redeemed, as it was sold later.

Military Service: Richard Key Watts, 32, Militia Coumpany of Richard Harwood of Thomas in Annapolis, in 1799 and Richard K. Watts, 32 atty at law, the Blew & Buff Co., being part of the 22nd Regiment, 20 March 1799.[2]

RICHARD WOOTTON (1741-1817)

Register of Wills, 1778

BIRTH/PARENTS Richard Wootton was born 22 June 1741, son of Turner Wootton (1695-1760) and his third wife, Elizabeth (Sprigg) Wilson Wootton (b. 1705) She had first married. Josiah Wilson who d. bet. 1726 and1731[3].

LEGAL CAREER From 1794 to 1797 he served as a justice and a Judge of the Orphans Court, and again from 1803-1804. In 1805 he was named as an Associate Judge.

MARRIAGE 27 April 1777 to Martha Perry (b.12 March 1755, d. 22 May 1845), daughter of James Wilson Perry (1700-1771) and Rebecca Harris (1712-1772) of Frederick County, MD..

---

[1] Dixon, *National Intelligencer,* Sept 1826.
[2] Wright, Maryland Militia War of d1812, Vol. 4, Anne Arundel & Calvert, p. 1 &2.
[3] Wootton Family File, MCHS.

CHILDREN

1. Margaret Wootton, b. 4 June 1779, d. 23 Aug. 1804, m. 22 May 1798, Montgomery County, Ignatius Davis (b. 23 Nov.1759, d. 4 May 1828) as his third wife; they had three children.
2. John B. Wootton, b. 2 Sept. 1782, d. 24 June 1840, m. 17 June 1806, Elizabeth Lynn Magruder, (1792-1861)
3. Elizabeth Wootton, b. 20 March 1785, d. abt 1840, m. 9 July 1801, Lewis Beall (b. abt 1780, d. bef. 11 Dec. 1811[1]), son of Brooke Beall (1742-1795) and Margaret Johns Beall (1740-1824), brother of Upton Beall, (1770-1827) Clerk of Montgomery County Court. She m. 2. 26 Mar. 1822, by Montgomery County license, to John Mines, installed as the Pastor of Bethesda Presbyterian Church in 1822 (b. abt 1774, d. bef. 1 July 1849[2], testate, in Montgomery County[3].)
4. Thomas Sprigg Wootton, b. 26 April 1788
5. Singleton Wootton, b. April 1790, d. 13 June1849, m.18 Nov 1817, by Frederick County License,[4] Elizabeth C. Brashears (b. 1 Sep 1798, d. 10 May 1853)
6. Richard Wootton, b. 22 June 1792, d. 1862, a lay brother in the Jesuit Order.
7. Mary Wootton, b. 4 May 1794, d. young.
8. Martha Wootton, b.21 Dec.1801, d.26 Dec. 1826, m. 29 Nov. 1821, by Montgomery County License[5], William Murdock Beall Willson.(b. 16 April 1800, d. 2 May 1858, buried Mt. Olivet Cemetery, Frederick County.

DEATH He died testate before 25 Nov. 1817, Montgomery County, MD.

NOTES In 1777 he served as a private in the Middle Battalion of Montgomery County Militia.[6]

THOMAS SPRIGG WOOTTON (1740-1789)

Justice and Judge of Orphans Court, 1777[7]

BIRTH/PARENTS: Thomas Sprigg Wootton was born about 1740 to Turner (or Turnor) Wootton(1696-1760) (1695-1760) and Elizabeth Sprigg (1703-1781) who was the widow of Josiah Wilson (1700-1726).[8]

---

[1] Cook, *The Brooke Beall Family and the Johns Family,* 88, 111, 121

[2] Church Card File, MCHS, funeral 1 July 1849, age 75(?), records of Bethesda Presbyterian Church.

[3] Malloy, *Will Abstracts, 1826-1875,* 106 will dated 13 Aug 1847, probated 3 July 1849, names wife Mary, who he married in 1842, and children. Including Samuel W. Beall and John L. Beall Mines.

[4] Myers, *Frederick County Licenses,* 273.

[5] Manuel, *Marriage Licenses, 351.*

[6] Peden, *Revolutionary Patriots of Montgomery County,* 637.

[7] Scharf, p. 665

[8] Most of the biographical material can be found in the Wootton family file in the MCHS library. Also see Biography in Papenfuse, *Directory of Maryland Legislature,* 910-911

EDUCATION: Possibly St. Omer's in France.

LEGAL CAREER: He was commissioned a Justice of the Peace for Frederick County in 1768 and served until the end of 1774. From December 1769 through 1773, he was a delegate from Frederick County to the lower house of the Maryland Assembly. He was a delegate to the State Constitutional Convention in 1776, which was called to establish a permanent government for the state of Maryland. At that convention, Wootton introduced the bill dividing Frederick County into three counties, one of which was Montgomery. He served as a judge of the Orphans' Court from 1777 to 1779.

MARRIAGE: About 1763 to Mary (Molly) Offutt (1740-bef. 1779) daughter of James Offutt[1] (1697-1750) and his second wife Sarah Beall[2]. (1717-1779). It was said that Molly was murdered[3].

CHILDREN: No children.

DEATH: He died between 11 Jan. and 30 Nov. 1789 in Montgomery County, where his will was probated. His estate was bequeathed to his nephew, Turner Wootton, of Queen Ann, Prince George's County[4].

NOTES: Wootton was a patriot who participated in the activities that led to the Revolutionary War. He was one of the participants in the committee that wrote the Hungerford Resolves in 1774, men who identified themselves with the causes of colonial America that led to the American Revolution. Also in 1774, he was a delegate to the American Continental Congress in Philadelphia, which resolved to break off commerce with Britain and its colonies in the Caribbean.[5]

---

[1] ***Maryland** Calendar of Wills,* Vol. 10, 70. James Offutt died testate, and in his will he devised to son William tract "William and James." He named daughters Elizabeth Lewis, Rachel, Rebecca, Hannah and Mary Offutt. To Mary he gave 200 acres of Dumfries, which formerly belonged to John Beall, (father of his 2nd wife Sarah) in addition to slaves.

[2] By the time she made her will, she apparently had no living children, as her bequests were to her nieces and nephews. Malloy, *Montgomery County Wills, 1776-1825,* 102.

[3] Papenfuse, *op.cit.,* 911

[4] Malloy, *Montgomery County Wills, 1776-1825,* 155.

[5] For more information on the Hungerford Resolves, consult the Montgomery County Story, a publication of the MCHS, in an issue published in May 1976 (v. 19, no. 2).

WILLIAM M. WORTHINGTON (1796-1842)

Admitted to Montgomery County Bar, 1816[1]
Admitted to Prince George's County Bar, 1824

BIRTH/PARENTS: William M. Worthington was born 31 Mar 1796 in Georgetown, District of Columbia to Dr. Charles Hathaway Worthington (b. 9 Oct 1759, d. 10 Sep 1836) and Elizabeth (Booth) Worthington (b. 26 Apr 1767, d. 19 Jan 1798). [2]

LEGAL CAREER He was admitted to the Prince George's County Bar in 1824 being presented for admission by Henry Ashton[3].

MARRIAGE: 26 June 1839, in Richmond, Va., Alice Brown[4] daughter of Henry Brown (1760-1841) and Frances Thompson (1775-1822) Brown. She married 2) 16 November 1848 in Richmond, VA., William Henry Haxall.[5]

CHILDREN: William Nicholas Worthington, b. 1841, d. 1871.[6]

DEATH: 22 February 1842, at Baltimore. Buried first at family estate in Brentwood, later removed to Oak Hill Cemetery, Georgetown[7].

---

[1] Scharf, p 667
[2] Pippenger, *Oak Hill Cemetery Records,* p. 104; and Dixon, *National Intelligener, 1842,* obituary, p. 64 "Lately a member of the New Orleans Bar, but formerly of Georgetown D.C. of which place he was a native."
[3] Van Horn, *Out of the Past,* 284.
[4] Wife and son named in Will as abstracted by Pippenger, *District of Columbia Probate,* p. 252
[5] Ancestry, *tree of William Nicholas Wothington.*
[6] Ancestry, *tree of William Nicholas Wothington.*
[7] Pippenger, *Oak Hill Cemetery,* Vol. 1, 104.

BENCH AND BAR OF MONTGOMERY COUNTY

PART II: LAWYERS ADMITTED TO THE BAR, 1825-1875

In Scharf's list for this period we had difficulty with several of the signatories as recorded from the Clerk's Record Book:

Beginning in 1828 – John J. Campbell and, in 1847, A. C. Campbell have not been positively identified although at least one record for each is identified. There is a marriage license issued for John I. Campbell to Martha J. Mines, 2 June 1836 in Montgomery County.[1] In his will, John Mines, notes that his daughter Martha Campbell, wife of John, is in Missouri. On 23 June 1845, the Maryland Journal announced that the reading room of the Lyceum is ready for circulation of books, A. C. Campbell, Librarian;[2]. and an Alvin Cook Campbell was mentioned in the will of John Cook (another of our attorneys) when he died in 1847. A.C. Campbell also witnessed a codicil to will. It would make sense that he was working with his relative John Cook, at the time of his death. He was not found on the 1850 census.

1830: W. M. Stuart. After much searching, he was identified as William Montgomery Stewart. His mother was Helen Beall Stewart, sister of Upton Beall, Clerk of Court. He appears in family deeds, as trustee of property inherited from Brooke Beall form 1830s, through 1848. He lived with his sisters in Georgetown after 1850 until his death.

1844: Hugh Carpenter – in a breakthrough moment, we found Hugh Caperton, who seems to fit the profile of an attorney living in D.C., but practicing in Montgomery County Court on occasion.

1845: John E. Addis – Not positive, but perhaps a misreading of John E. Adams, a farmer in Laytonsville, who also owned a town lot in Rockville.

1850: has Edward Ewen and W.T. Ewen admitted to the bar. They could not be located. We do have an Edward Owen, who was an Orphans Court Judge, that we included in his place, and we found a William Tecumseh Evans, included herein, who was a "Clerk" in government offices in Washington, D.C., married in Montgomery County in 1853.

Families of lawyers also show up – four of the five Brewers in this section were closely related. John Chiswell and James Chiswell Brewer, brothers, sons of an attorney William Chiswell, also had a brother Nicholas Chiswell Brewer – who became a doctor. The Lawyer Nicholas Brewer is a distant cousin from Annapolis, the 3rd Nicholas in his family line, b. 1828. He was 22 when he applied to the Montgomery County Bar – probably to serve in a specific case. He represented the county in the State Senate in 1864 and 1868.

---

[1] Manuel, *Marriage Licenses,* 53.

[2] Jacobs, *People, Places and Pot-pourri*, 3.

CHARLES ABERT (1822-1897)

Admitted to Montgomery County Bar, 1874[1]
Admitted to Washington, D.C. Bar, c. 1876[2]

BIRTH/PARENTS: Charles Abert was born 19 Sep 1822, in Mount Holly, Westmoreland County, NJ, to John James (Col., U.S. A., served in War of 1812) and Ellen Matlack (Stretch) Abert.[3]

EDUCATION: He graduated from Princeton University in 1840.[4] He continued the study of law in Washington, D. C.[5]

LEGAL CAREER: He was admitted to practice before the U. S. Supreme Court, the District Courts and the Court of Claims in Washington, D.C.[6] His partner with John W. Warner with an office in Washington, D.C.[7]

MARRIAGE: 16 April 1845 in Washington, D.C. to Henrietta Constantia Bache; daughter of Richard Bache (1737-1811) and Sophia Burrell (Dallas) Bache and great granddaughter of Benjamin Franklin (1706-1790)[8]. Her father was the son of Richard (1737-1811) and Sarah (Franklin) Bache (b. 1744), Benjamin Franklin's only daughter[9].

CHILDREN:[10]

1. Robert Walker Abert, b. 12 Feb 1846, d. 12 Feb 1928 (buried in Rockville Cemetery), m. 8 Nov. 1871 to Mary Warner of Baltimore, MD.[11] He graduated in law in Washington.
2. Ellen Abert, b. 6 Nov. 1847 m. 29 Jun 1893 to John S. Blair[12], an attorney in Washington.
3. Sophia Bache Abert, b. 4 Dec. 1849, m. 11 Nov. 1878[13] to James Mallory of North Carolina.
4. Charles Abert, Jr. (M.D.) b. 17 Nov. 1852, m. 12 Jan. 1880 to Martha "Mattie" Stonestreet, daughter of Dr. E.E. Stonestreet.[14]
5. Maria Bache Abert, b. 17 Mar. 1855, d. 10 Jan. 1940, m. 5 Aug. 1884[1] to William D. Baldwin, member of a prominent Washington, D.C. law firm.

---

[1] Scharf, 668.
[2] Bowman, *Sentinel,* 11 Feb 1876.
[3] MCHS, Family Files:Abert.
[4] Farquhar, *Old Homes,* 183-4, sketch of "Homewood".
[5] *Portrait and Biographical Record ...,* 750, sketch of his son Allan McLane Abert.
[6] Farquhar, op.cit.
[7] *Washington Post,* 11 Aug. 1897, obituary.
[8] MCHS, Family Files: Abert.
[9] Farquhar, 183, also *Portrait and Biographical Record ..., 750.*
[10] MCHS, Abert Family File, also *Portrait and Biographical Record ..., 750,* gives occupational information.
[11] *Sentinel*, 17 Nov. 1871
[12] *Sentinel*, 7 July 1893
[13] *Sentinel,* 239. 15 Nov. 1878.
[14] *Sentinel,* 1. 16 Jan. 1880.

6. Constantia Abert, b. 3 Oct 1858, d. 8 Jul 1934, unmarried
7. Allen McLane Abert, b. 27 Mar 1865, d. 7 Apr 1951, unmarried

DEATH: 9 Aug. 1897 at his home near Norbeck, Maryland.[2]

NOTES: He was a member of the Board of School Commissioners of Montgomery County; a member of the Board of Directors of the Chesapeake and Ohio Canal Company; assistant Marshall at the Smithsonian Institution's cornerstone ceremony;[3] director in the Montgomery County Mutual Fire Insurance Company and counsel of the corporation. He was active in the Episcopal Church.[4] The family lived at "Homewood" near Norbeck (purchased in 1849), now site of the Manor Club.[5]

JAMES WALLACE ANDERSON (1797-1882)

Justice/Judge of Orphans Court 1848-1851[6]

BIRTH/PARENTS: James Wallace Anderson was born 9 August 1797, to Dr. James Anderson (1760-1836) and Elizabeth Wallace Anderson (d. 1846). They were married 12 May 1796.[7]

EDUCATION: He attended Princeton University and afterward studied law under Augustus Taney, brother of Chief Justice Taney, and William Wirt, United States Attorney General.[8] He formed a partnership with Benjamin Forest in Rockville, MD.[9]

LEGAL CAREER In 1852 he served as a member of the Maryland State Constitutional Convention. James W. Anderson, served as Montgomery County Register of Wills, was Judge of the Orphan's Court, President of the Board of Trustees of Rockville Academy, Colonel of State Militia, and Vestryman in the Episcopal Church.[10] As part of a greeting committee, he met General La Fayette at a dinner in Montgomery County when the General was on his way to Washington, DC. James W. Anderson was a clerk in the War Department under President Buchanan.[11] Between 1854 and 1861 he worked in the Auditor's Office of the U.S. Post Office. His sympathies were with the Confederacy and he refused to sign the loyalty oath.[12] For the last several years of his life he lived in seclusion and was described in his Sentinel obituary as "...conservative in all his notions."[13]

---

[1] Malloy, *Sentinel,* 15. 8 Aug. 1884.
[2] Malloy, *Sentinel,* 1. 13 Aug. 1897.
[3] Dixon, *National Intelligencer,* 30 Apr 1847
[4] Washington Post, 11 Aug. 1897
[5] Farquhar, 183-184.
[6] Scharf, 665, although practicing attorney, not on Scharf's list of those admitted to bar in Montgomery County.
[7] MCHS Anderson Family File, includes bible records.
[8] Montgomery County Sentinel, 1883 Jan 5.
[9] Ibid.
[10] Portrait and Biographical Record of the Sixth Congressional District, Maryland, 1898, 691-2.
[11] MCHS Family File
[12] Maryland Historical Magazine, 88,2 : 182.
[13] Montgomery County Sentinel, 1883 Jan 5.

MARRIAGE: On 18 May 1830, he married Mary Minor, b. abt 1810, d. Sep 1865, daughter of George Minor (1774-1861) of Fairfax County, VA and Mary Thrift Mason (1771-1858). George Minor had commanded a regiment in the War of 1812.[1]

CHILDREN:[2]

1. Capt. James Anderson, b. 9 June 1831, d. 31 Dec. 1920, m. 12 Nov 1868, Montgomery County, Sarah (Sallie R.) M. Thrift (1843-1917). A civil engineer on the 1880 census.
2. Mary E. Anderson, b. abt 1834, d. 9 Jan 1910, m. 29 Dec 1882. Charles B. Rozer(1835-10 Dec. 1913). Both buried in Rockville Cemetery.
3. Thomas Anderson, b. 19 Sep 1835, d. 19 Jan 1900, m. 1. 7 Feb 1873,[3] Martha Wootton, b. 15 Apr 1833, d. 4 Jan 1882[4], daughter of Dr. Turner Wootton and Olivia C. Wootton; m.2. 18 April 1887, Ella Darne, (b. 19 Mar. 1850, d.10 May 1914)[5] daughter of the late Capt. Alexander H. C. Darne (1819-1907) and Mary A. Gassaway Darne (1824-1859);,[6] "niece of Sen. George Peter,"[7] - A lawyer on the `1880 census.
4. Richard Anderson, b. 1837, d. 1855.
5. Frances Virginia Anderson, b. 1839, d. 30 Jul 1913, m. 19 Sep 1860, Francis Whetenhall Rozer (b. 4 Oct 1838, d. Oct. 15, 1928). Buried in Rockville Cemetery.
6. Edward Anderson, b. 3 May 1841, d. 15 Aug 1917, m. 3 Dec 1883, Washington, D.C., to Alice M. Lawn (1851-21 Dec. 1928).
7. George Anderson, b. ca. 1845, d. in infancy.
8. Alice Anderson, b. 1849, d. bef 1860.
9. Lillie Minor Anderson, b. 21 Mar 1850, d. 6 Apr 1868.
10. George Minor Anderson, b. 9 Apr 1856[8], d. 7 Aug 1927, m. 14 Nov 1901, [9]Julia Prout Vinson, (b. 4 Apr 1865, d. 25 Jun 1950).[10] eldest daughter of Judge John Thomas Vinson (1825-1903) and Frances Rachel Prout Vinson (1835-1888).

DEATH He died 28 Dec 1882 in his 86th year at his residence near Rockville, MD.[11]

---

[1] MCHS Family File : Anderson Family compiled by Eleanor Cook
[2] MCHS Family File: Anderson Family.
[3] Malloy, *Sentinel Abstracts,* 8
[4] MCHS Cemetery Files, Rockville Cemetery..
[5] MCHS Cemetery Files, Rockville Cemetery.
[6] *Seninel Abstracts,* 15 May 1914.
[7] Malloy, *Sentinel Abstracts,* 8, 22 April 1887.
[8] Baptized Sept 8, 1865, age 9 years and 5 months, Records of Christ Episcopal Church, Rockville, MCHS Church files.
[9] *Sentinel Abstracts,* 15 Nov. 1901.
[10] MCHS Cemetery Files, Rockville Cemetery.
[11] Montgomery County Sentinel, 188333 Jan 5.

JAMES WALLACE ANDERSON (1847-1881)

Admitted to The Montgomery County Bar, 1874[1]

BIRTH/PARENTS: James Wallace Anderson was born 14 Mar 1847 to Dr. John Wallace Anderson (b. abt 1808, d. 8 July 1867) and Mira Magruder Anderson (b. abt 1813 d. 5 Apr 1872)[2].

LEGAL CAREER: The United States Federal Census for 1880 lists him as a lawyer, living with his wife and son in the household of his sister, Rose Williams (b. 13 Jul 1841, d. 2 Jan 1910), wife of a fellow attorney, Richard Mortimer Williams (b. 13 Mar 1841, d. 16 Jun 1882).[3]

MARRIAGE On 27 April 1876 in Washington, D.C.[4] to Mary Bowie Sprigg (b. 15 Apr 1842, d. 8 Nov 1920)[5], daughter of Osborn Sprigg and Carolina Lansdale Bowie Sprigg (b. 5 Feb 1820). Osborn Sprigg was the only son of Governor Samuel Sprigg (b. abt. 1782, d. 14 Apr.1855) and Violetta Lansdale Sprigg (b. 1788, d. 14 Apr 1865).[6]

CHILDREN:

1. William Bowie Anderson, b. 1877, d. 17 Aug. 1881
2. Osborn Sprigg Anderson, b. Nov. 1878, d. 15 Oct. 1880
3. Samuel Sprigg Anderson, b. Mar. 1880, d. Sep. 1881.

DEATH He died 22 Aug. 1881 at his home, a member of the Bar[7].

CHARLES W. BEACH (1819-1881)

Admitted to Montgomery County Bar 1874[8]

BIRTH/PARENTS: Charles W. Beach was born 15 Apr 1819 in Newark, NJ[9] His parents were not identified.

---

[1] Scharf, 668.
[2] MCHS Anderson Family File; approx.. birthdates from census records; obit. For Mira Anderson in *Sentinel.* She died testate in Montgomery County.
[3] Hurley, 1880 Census, 313.
[4] *Sentinel,* 5 May 1876.
[5] MCHS Cemetery Card File, buried in Rockville Cemetery.
[6] Bowie, *Across the Years,* 720.; also see White, *Governors of Maryland,* 78-79; Pippenger, *Oakhill Cemetery,* vol. 1, 105.
[7] Bowman, *Sentinel,* 26 Aug. 1881.
[8] Scharf, 668. For this year listed 18 admitted to the bar in Montgomery County – one of the largest "classes". No evidence of active practice of law.
[9] Ancestry.com: DAR member application for Robert Lee Swain, Jr.

LEGAL CAREER: "admitted to bar C. W. Beach of Darnestown."[1]

MARRIAGE: On 24 Nov 1847 in East Baton Rouge, LA, Frances Coleman Woodbridge.[2]She was born 3 Sept. 1824; she died 10 May 1895, buried in Springfield Presbyterian Church Cemetery, Sylesville, Carroll County, MD.[3]

CHILDREN[4]

1. Sylvester Beach, 1854, listed as a Presbyterian Minister in Baltimore, 1880-1888.[5]
2. Edwin Beach, 1855
3. Fannie Beach, 1857
4. Emma Virginia Beach, b. 24 Dec. 1858, d. 23 Feb 1934, buried Springfield Cemetery.[6]
5. John Newton Beach, b. 24 Dec. 1861, d. 17 Mar. 1895, buried Springfield Cemetery.[7]
6. Annie Lee Beach, b. 15 June 1865, d. 13 Aug.1934, m. Daniel Boteler Sprecher, b. 12 May 1855, d. 13 Aug. 1934. Both buried Springfield Cemetery.[8]

DEATH: 9 Mar 1881 buried in Springfield Cemetery, Sykesville, Carroll County, MD[9]

NOTES C. W. Beach is possibly Rev. Charles Beach, pastor of Darnestown Presbyterian Church, 1871-1877. As pastor of the Darnestown Presbyterian Church, Charles Beach was also head of the Andrew Small Academy associated with the church.[10] Children of Rev. Charles Beach attended the Small Academy.[11] The 1870 census finds the Charles Beach family in Snow Hill, Worcester, MD. In the 1880 census they are located in Carroll County, MD. No references to a legal career were located. He is listed as a minister at Snow Hill, 1869-70; Darnestown, 1870-77; and Springfield, 1877-1882.[12]

SAMUEL WOOTTON BEALL (1807-1868)

Admitted to the Montgomery County Bar in 1828[13]

---

[1] Sentinel, 27 Mar 1874

[2] Ancestry.com.

[3] *Carroll County Cemeteries, Vol. One,* 39, 103.

[4] US Federal Census, 1870: Snow Hill, Worcester, MD

[5] Kanely, *Directory of Maryland Ministers,* 38

[6] *Carroll County Cemeteries,* op.cit., 39.

[7] *Ibid.*

[8] *Ibid,* 43..

[9] Findagrave.com: Rev. Charles W. Beach

[10] Scharf, 762.

[11] Sentinel, 7 Jul 1876

[12] Kanely, *Directory of Maryland Ministers,* 38.

[13] Scharf, 667i

BIRTH/PARENTS Samuel Wootton Beall[1] was born 26 Sep.1807, Montgomery County, MD to Lewis Beall (1777-1822) and Elizabeth Wootton Beall (1782-1840) who married second John Mines.

EDUCATION He graduated from Union College in Schenectady, NY in 1827. He studied in the Law School at Litchfield, Conn., 1827-28.

LEGAL CAREER He was appointed Receiver for Public Lands and established a land office in Green Bay, Wisconsin from 1834-1836. He returned to live in the east from 1836-1840, but preferred life on the frontier. He returned to Wisconsin where he promoted statehood and in 1849 was nominated to served as Lt. Governor with Nelson Dewey as Governor.[2]

MARRIAGE: On 24 May 1829, Elizabeth Fenimore Cooper, (b. abt 1812, d. 14 Feb. 1879, Fond Du Lac, WI), daughter of Isaac Cooper (d. 1818) and Mary (Morris) Cooper (27 Aug 1784-16 Oct 1873)[3], buried Christ Church Yard, Cooperstown, NY; and niece of the author, James Fenimore Cooper.[4] He met her while a student in Schenectady.

CHILDREN [5]

1. Singleton Wooten Beall, b. July 1830, Green Bay, WI, d. 21 Mar. 1911, Washington State; m. in 1892, Luella Ophelia Doty (b. 1857).
2. Mary Morris Beall, b. 2 Mar 1832, d. 29 Mar.1866, m. Levi N. Hubbell, (15 Apr. 1807-8 Dec. 1876) a Wisconsin Judge.
3. John Beall age 16 on 1850 census, b. ca. 1834. No other info.
4. Emma Cooper Beall b. 22 Dec 1835, d. July 1926 in Juneau Alaska, m. 13 Sep 1855, George LeFevre (1828-1871)
5. Bessie W. Beall, b. abt 1838-42;age 8, 1850, age 22 1860. No other information.
6. Ellen Agnes Beall, b. 7 Nov. 1841, d. 21 July 1924, m. 1867, Elijah Cone, (1831-1900)
7. Louis Upton Beall b. abt 1844, d. 7 March 1868., of morphine, overdose, recovering from civil war injuries.
8. Roger Beall age 4, b. 1846 on 1850 census, no other records.
9. Fanny Beall age 3, b. 1847 on 1850 in Coopensus, no other records.

DEATH He died 25 Sep1868 in Helena, Montana from a fatal gun shot in the newspaper offices, where he went with a gun, and a disagreement regarding some

---

[1] Biographical data from MCHS Family Files, Lewis Beall file.

[2] *Daily Albany Argus*, 10 Sept. 1849, Courtesy of Special Collections, Schaffer Library, Union College.

[3] Find-A-Grave.com for death dates for Bealls in Taycheedah Cemetery, Fond Du Lac, and the Coopers buried in Cooperstown, NY.

[4] Ancestry.com: Marriage notices copied from the "Watch Tower" [Cooperstown, NY]; biographical material including "The Story of Cooperstown, pp 195-197, Courtesy of Special Collections, Schaffer Library, Union College

[5] Year: *1850*; Census Place: *Fond du Lac, Fond du Lac, Wisconsin*; Roll: *M432_997*; Page: *268A*; Image: *54*.

newspaper articles about him, which the Editor had refused to retract. The Coroner's Inquest ruled the shooting self-defense.

NOTES Partly because he loved adventure Samuel led an expedition to Pike's Peak in 1859 and assisted in the founding of Denver, CO. He enlisted in the Civil War as a Private, and rose to the rank of Lt. Col. of the 18th Wisconsin. He was wounded at the Battle of Shiloh, but recovered sufficiently to participate in the siege of Vicksburg. During the latter years of the war, Col. Beall was in command of the Confederate prisoners at Elimira, New York.[1] He had inherited land in Montgomery County from his mother but there is little evidence that he had a significant law practice here. In 1846, he and his brother, John Lewis Beall Mines, sold his mothers farm "Rosehill" to a trustee for his sister, Mary Mines.[2]

MONTGOMERY BLAIR, SENIOR (1813-1883)

Admitted to Montgomery County Bar in 1876

BIRTH/PARENTS: Montgomery Blair was born 10 May 1813, in Franklin, Kentucky, to Francis Preston Blair, born 12 April 1791, died Oct 1876 ln Silver Spring, and Eliza Violet Gist Blair, born 1794,[3] died July 1877, Silver Spring, Md.; both buried in Rock Creek Cemetery. [4] In 1830, Francis Preston Blair was invited by President Jackson to come to Washington to publish a newspaper to promote his policies. The Blair home, located at the edge of Montgomery County on Eastern Ave, was built in 1842. He bought the Blair House on Pennsylvania Avenue around 1843.[5]

EDUCATION Transylvania College, Lexington, Kentucky[6] and West Point 1831-1836[7] After his graduation from West Point, he served in the Seminole War in Florida. He resigned from the Army in 1836, and went to University of Pennsylvania to study law. He began his practice in Saint Louis.[8]

LEGAL CAREER Prior to 1844, he served an apprenticeship under Thomas Hart Benton in St. Louis. In 1844 he was Judge of the Court of Common Pleas in St. Louis; in 1852 he was appointed Solicitor to the Federal Court of Claims. Montgomery Blair came to Montgomery County from Missouri, in 1854 and established his home near that of his father, at "Falkland."[9] In 1856 he served as an attorney to Dred Scott, taking no payment.

---

[1] "Class of 1827, Samuel Wotton Beall [sic] , Courtesy of Special Collections, Schaffer Library, Union College

[2] Montgomery County Land Records, Liber STS2:57-59 and 231-233.

[3] Smith, *Francis Preston Blair,* 3, 7, 10.

[4] Malloy, *Sentinel, 32* death notices for Francis P. Blair and Mrs. Francis Preston Blair.

[5] Farquhar, *Old Homes,* "Silver Spring,′201-203.

[6] Smith, *op.cit.,* 92.

[7] Ibid., 93-94.

[8] Malloy, *Sentinel,* 33. A long obituary of Montgomery Blair was abstracted.

[9] Farquhar, *op.cit.*

He was discharged as Federal Solicitor in 1858; and in 1860 served as President of Republican State Convention in Baltimore. In 1861 he was elected Postmaster General; in 1864, he resigned from position at request of President Lincoln. He was Nominated by National Union Party of Maryland for Congress, in 1866 but he refused; in1867 he attempted to get elected as U.S. Senator (Democrat) by the Legislature of Maryland; in 1874 he attempted to get the Democratic nomination for Congress and in 1882 he was nominated as Democrat for MD Congress but lost[1]

MARRIAGE

1. In 1836, to Caroline Rebecca Buckner, She died in childbirth Jan. 4, 1844[2]
2. 6 July 1846, in Portsmouth, N.H., Mary Elizabeth Woodbury[3] (b. 1826, d. Jan. 1887, Washington, D.C.[4]) daughter of Hon. Levi Woodbury, a former Secretary of the Treasury and Supreme Court Justice.[5]

CHILDREN[6]:

1. Betty Blair, b. 1844. (mother was Caroline). Adopted by paternal grandparents.[7]
2. Minna Blair, b. 1849, m. 15 Nov 1884, Dr. Stephen Olin Ritchie of Washington.
3. Woodbury Blair, b. 1 Sep. 1852 in St. Louis; m. 6 July 1907, Emily N. Wallach, daughter of Richard Wallach, former Mayor of Washington, D.C. Woodbury studied law at Harvard, and was admitted to the D.C. bar and the Supreme Court.
4. Maria Blair, 1854-1862.[8]
5. Gist Blair, b. 10 Sep. 1860, m. 3 Mar 1813, Mrs. Laura Lawson Wills. He graduated from G. W. Law School in 1882, and was living in Saint Louis in 1887.
6. Montgomery Blair Jr., b. 14 Mar. 1865[9] in Washington, D.C., living in St. Louis in 1887, m. 26 Feb. 1895, Edith Draper, daughter of William Draper of Massachusetts. He was an 1886 graduate of Princeton and afterwards of G. W. Law School. Member of D.C. Bar.

DEATH Montgomery Blair died 27 July 1883 at his home in Silver Spring.[10]

---

[1] *Ibid.,* 178, 213, 240, 259, 271, 401, 405, 439, 454.
[2] Ibid., 155.
[3] Ibid., 178.
[4] Malloy, *Sentinel,* 32, obituary of Mary E. Blair, published 4 Feb. 1887.
[5] Malloy, *Sentinel,* 33, obituary of Montgomery Blair.
[6] The four children of his second wife were listed in her obituary in 1887. Malloy, *Sentinel,* 32-33. Their birthdates and marriages were found in Proctor, *Washington Past and Present,* Vol. IV, 630-631.
[7] Smith, *Francis Preston Blair,* 155.
[8] Smith, *Francis Preston Blair.*
[9] Hurley, 1870 Census, 428.
[10] Ibid., 439 and Malloy, *Sentinel,* 33.

WILLIAM VEIRS BOUIC, JR. (1846-1906)

Admitted to Montgomery County Bar 1870[1]

BIRTH/PARENTS: William Veirs Bouic, Jr. was born 20 July 1846 at *Meadow Hall* near Rockville, MD. He was the only son of Judge William Veirs Bouic, Sr. (1816-1896) and Mary Ann Matilda (Veirs) Bouic.[2]

EDUCATION His earliest education was in a private school taught by the wife of the clerk of the court. Later, he attended the Rockville Academy for 7 years. At age 17, he entered Columbian University on 14th St. in Washington, D.C. He studied there from 1863 – 1868. Three years later he completed a Master of Arts degree. He then studied law with his father and in June 1870 was admitted to the Bar of the Circuit Court of Montgomery County.[3]

LEGAL CAREER: He was admitted to the Montgomery County Bar in 1870. He entered the practice of law with Thomas Anderson, forming the firm of Anderson & Bouic. He was a founding member of the Maryland State Bar Association and served for a while as its vice-president. He was a member of the Supreme Court, District of Columbia, the U. S. Circuit Court for the district of Maryland, the Bar of Washington, Frederick, Howard, and Anne Arundel Counties, and of the court of appeals, of Maryland[4].

MARRIAGE: On 6 July 1870, he married Alice A. Almoney, b. 26 Dec. 1845, d. 22 Aug. 1922,[5] daughter of Jarrett (1816-1861)[6] and Mary Ann (Burke) Almoney (1822- 1884)[7] proprietors of the Montgomery House Hotel in Rockville.

CHILDREN[8]

1. Louis Aubrey Bouic, b. 12 May 1871, d. 14 Feb. 1872.
2. Henry Vauclin Bouic, b. 23 Nov. 1873, d. 9 Feb. 1929, m. 17 May 1905, in Washington, D.C. to Eva (Russell) Carter, daughter of Catherine Russell and widow of Harry Lee Carter of Virginia. Buried in Rockville Cemetery.
3. William Garner Bouic, b. 28 July 1875, d. 6 Nov. 1947, m. 22 Feb. 1904 in Pine Bluff, AR to Margaret Wilbourne. Practiced law in Arkansas.
4. Isabel Bouic, b.18 April 1878, d. 12 April 1918, m. 21 Jun 1905 to Harry Herbert Buck
5. Charles Norman Bouic, b. 26 May 1880, d. 4 January 1919

---

[1] Scharf, 668.
[2] MCHS Bouic Family File.
[3] *Portrait and Biographical Encyclopedia*, 158-159.
[4] *Portrait and Biographical Encyclopedia, 158-159.*
[5] MCHS Cemetery Files, card of William Veirs Bouic, Jr. Family plot at Rockville Cemetery.
[6] Malloy, *Sentinel,* 4, 13 Dec. 1861. Stated he was Rockville resident for 9 years.
[7] *Washington Post,* 3 July 1884.
[8] MCHS Family File: Bouic Family; and Cemetery File card of Family of William Veirs Bouic,Jr in Rockville Cemetery.

6. Albert Manoury Bouic, b. 20 Aug. 1882, d. 1 May 1969, m. Frances Vinson Peter (b. 29 Apr. 1889, d. 29 Jan. 1964) daughter of Edward and Mary V. Peter.

DEATH He died 12 Oct. 1906 at his residence, Meadow Hall in Rockville, and is buried in Rockville Cemetery.[1]

NOTES[2] He was active in the Democratic Party of Montgomery County. He served in the state senate from 1898-1902. In 1873 he was appointed one of the commissioners of Rockville and served for 17 years. In 1888, he was elected first mayor of Rockville. During his tenure many improvements were made to Rockville's infrastructure. He was for many years, secretary and treasurer of the Agricultural Society, a trustee of the Rockville Academy, and secretary of the Library Association. He served as local counsel for the B & O Railroad. He owned and managed many buildings in Rockville as well as the home farm *Meadow Hall* consisting of 400 acres.

WILLIAM VEIRS BOUIC, SR. (1816-1896)

Admitted to Montgomery County Bar 1840[3]

BIRTH/PARENTS: William Veirs Bouic, Sr. was born 12 May 1816 near Poolesville in Montgomery County, son of Peter Amiable Tranquille Bouic a native of France, (b. abt 1770, emigrated in 1785, d.24 Aug. 1823, Whites Ferry, Montgomery County, Maryland) and Dorcas Veirs Fletchall Bouic[4] b. abt 1775, d. bef. 1823. She had married first John Fletchall (b. abt 1770, d. Mar. 1808). After the death of his parents, Samuel C. Veirs, became his guardian.

LEGAL CAREER He was admitted to the Montgomery County Bar in 1840, but moved first to Jefferson County, Missouri, where he practiced law briefly. He returned to Rockville in 1843. From 1849 to 1867, he served as State's Attorney for Montgomery County. In 1867 he was elected Associate Judge of the Sixth Congressional District and served for 15 years.[5]

MARRIAGE On 2 Jan. 1844, in Montgomery County, to Mary Ann Matilda Veirs, b. 2 June 1821, d. 1 Oct. 1888, daughter of his guardian, Samuel C. Veirs and Juliana (Diffendorfer) Veirs.

CHILDREN[6]

1. Mary A. Rosetta Bouic, b. 24 Dec. 1844, d. 19 May 1849.
2. William Veirs Bouic, b. 20 Jul 1846, Rockville, Md., d. 12 Oct.1906,Rockville, Md., m. 6 Jul 1870, Alice Almony, (b. 26 Dec.1845, d. 22 Aug. 1922) daughter of

---

[1] *Sentinel*, 19 Oct 1906, 23 Nov 1906; Farquhar, *Historic Homes,* 212.

[2] McGuckian, *Rockville: Portrait of a City*, 85, 90

[3] Scharf, 668

[4] MCHS, Bouic Family and Veirs Family Files; Aud, *Our Ancestors,* 93.

[5] *Portrait and Biographical Encyclopedia,* 158-159.

[6] MCHS Family File: Bouic Family; and Cemetery File card of Family of William Veirs Bouic.

Jarrett (1816-1861)[1] and Mary Ann (Burke) Almoney (1822-1884)[2] proprietors of the Montgomery House Hotel in Rockville.

3. Ella Clark Bouic, b. 16 Oct. 1849, d. 20 Sep 1931, Adamstown, Frederick County,MD, m. 19 Oct. 1882, Dr. Nathan Smith White, b. 28 Mar. 1840, d. 21 July 1885, son of Nathan Smith White and Evalina Wailes; both buried in Monocacy Cemetery, Beallsville, Md.[3]
4. Mary Anna Bouic, b. 12 Apr. 1855, m. 3 Dec. 1879, George William Beale, minister of the Baptist Church. They lived in Bowling Green, VA.[4]
5. Rosetta Vauclin Bouic, b. 24 Jul 1857, d. 29 Mar. 1925, m. 7 Dec. 1881, Charles Wesley Prettyman,.b. abt 1857, d. 5 May 1921[5], also a lawyer, son of Elijah Barrett Prettyman, Clerk of Court in Montgomery County and Lydia Forrest Johnston Prettyman.[6]
6. Eulalie Louise Bouic, b. 24 Nov. 1861, d. 2 Feb. 1945, unmarried.

DEATH: He died 4 May 1896 and is buried in Rockville Baptist Cemetery at Jefferson and Falls Road, Rockville, MD.

RICHARD JOHNS BOWIE (1807-1881)

Admitted to Montgomery County Bar In 1828 [7]

BIRTH/PARENTS: Richard Johns Bowie was born in Georgetown, D.C. on 23 Jun 1807 to Col. Washington Bowie (1776-1826) and Margaret Crabb Johns (1775-1840) Bowie[8] and moved to Rockville, MD in 1820.[9]

EDUCATION: He was a pupil of Dr. Caranahan in Georgetown, at the Brookeville Academy, and studied law in Georgetown in the office of Clement Cox. He graduated from Georgetown University in 1826.[10] He was admitted to the Washington, D.C. bar around 1828.[11]

LEGAL CAREER: He was admitted to the Montgomery County bar in 1828 and began a law practice. His practice was small because the county's population was declining due to low agricultural productivity.[12] He became active in state politics and served 2 terms as delegate and then state senator from 1837-1841. In 1839 he was elected by Montgomery and Frederick County Whigs as representative to the National Convention in Harrisburg.

---

1 Malloy, *Sentinel,* 4, 13 Dec. 1861. Stated he was Rockville resident for 9 years.
2 *Washington Post,* 3 July 1884.
3 MCHS Cemetery Card file, Manuel, *Marriage Licenses.*
4 Aud, *op.cit.,* MCHS Bouic Family File.
5 Malloy et. Al., *Sentinel,* 13 May 1921.
6 Hurley, *1880 Montgomery County Census*, 258.
7 Scharf, 668
8 MCHS Family File, Bowie Family.
9 *Sentinel*, Malloy.
10 MCHS Family File, Bowie Family.
11 Scharf, 755-6.
12 MCHS Family File, Bowie Family.

He served 2 terms as the States' Attorney of Montgomery County. In 1849 the Whig Party nominated him as a candidate for the House of Representatives. He was re-elected in 1851. He served as Chief Judge of Maryland 1861-1867 and again 1871-1881.[1]

MARRIAGE: Married on 7 May 1833, to Catharine L. Williams (b. 16 Nov. 1808, d. 8 Dec. 1891.[2]) by Rev. Drane (license dated 5 May)[3] She was the daughter of Gen. Otho Holland Williams and his first wife, Elizabeth Bowie Hall Williams of Hagerstown, MD.

CHILDREN No children[4]

DEATH He died on 12 Mar 1881 in Rockville, MD and was buried in the Episcopal Cemetery.[5]

NOTES As a Congressman he lived at the Glenview Estate, which is now the Rockville Civic Center. The mansion was one of the local free houses on the Underground Railroad. An ardent abolitionist, his views were not popular in the Rockville of that day. Bowie was one of several prominent men of the town who were taken hostage by Jeb Stuart as the Confederates rounded up horses and supplies before joining Lee at Gettysburg.[6] He was active in the Montgomery County Agriculture Society, and nominated for Maryland Governor in 1852 but was not elected.[7]

JOSEPH BRADDOCK (1810-1843)

Admitted to Montgomery County Bar 1832[8]

BIRTH/PARENTS: Joseph Braddock was born ca. 1810 to John Braddock (1790-1846) and Mary Hilton Braddock, who were married 23 Feb. 1809 in Frederick County, Maryland[9] John Braddock, built a home in Rockville in 1817 on the northeast corner of Commerce (Montgomery Ave.) and Washington St. His house later was known as the England Store. Braddock was issued a license as a storekeeper in 1820.

LEGAL CAREER: He is listed in Scharf as admitted to the bar.

MARRIAGE: On 6 Feb. 1839 in Montgomery County,[10] to Laura Locke, (b. abt 1820, Prince George's County) She was the daughter of William Bruce Locke (1785-1834) and Sarah Mary Smith Locke (1795-1834) of Prince George's County.

CHILDREN

1. Mary Braddock, b. 1840.

---

[1] MCHS Family File, Bowie Family.
[2] Montgomery County Cemetery File, Bowie, Richard Johns.
[3] Manuel, Marriage Licenses, 32; Dixon, *National Intelligencer,*25 May 1833.
[4] *Sentinel.*
[5] *Sentinel.*
[6] MCHS Vertical File, Glenview File.
[7] Schaarf, 755-6
[8] Scharf, 668.
[9] MCHS Braddock Family File.
[10] Manuel, *Marriage Licenses,* 35

2. Joseph Braddock, b. 1843, d. 20 July 1844, age 9 months, Montgomery County, MD.[1]

DEATH 29 Sep.1843, in his 34th year in Rockville.

NOTES His obituary notes he was Principal of the Rockville Academy. "His knowledge of the Latin & Greek languages, of the higher mathematics, & of science generally, was profound & discriminating. The whole community feels that a grievous loss has fallen upon them..."[2]

WILLIAM PERRY BRADDOCK (1817-1859)

Admitted to Montgomery County Bar 1843[3]

BIRTH/PARENTS: William Perry Braddock was born ca. 1817 to John Braddock (1790-1846) and Mary Hilton Braddockwho were married 23 Feb. 1809 in Frederick County, Maryland.[4] By 1820 John Perry had moved to Rockville and had a store on the corner of W. Montgomery Ave. and Washington Ave. in Rockville.

LEGAL CAREER: He is listed in Scharf. On the 1850 census, he is listed as a farmer in St. Mary's County with wife and two children. His father and brother were shop keepers in Rockville, and from land records, it appears that he may have functioned briefly as a lawyer in Rockville. There was no mention of it in the Sentinel when he died, which did mention his membership in I.O.O.F..

MARRIAGE: On 15 June 1843 in Montgomery County,[5] to Elizabeth Sothoron Smith Locke, (b. 26 Feb. 1826, Prince George's County, d. 3 July 1898, buried at All Faith Episcopal Church, Mechanicsville, St.Mary's County, Maryland)[6]. She was the daughter of William Bruce Locke, (1785-1834) and Sarah Mary Smith Locke (1795-1834) of Prince George's County. She married secondly, in 1860, Hezekiah Leonard Burroughs (b. 1831, d. 1888) of St. Mary's County.

CHILDREN[7]

1. Charles Braddock, b. 1844 Montgomery County, Maryland. Not found after 1860.
2. Joseph Braddock, b. 1848 St. Mary's County, Maryland. Not found in 1860.
3. William Locke Braddock, b. October 1850, d. 25 March 1931, Washington, D.C.[8] He became an Episcopal Priest, and never married.

---

[1] MCHS Braddock Family File.

[2] Dixon, *National Intelligencer, 1843,* 467.

[3] Scharf, 668 as W.P. Braddock

[4] MCHS Braddock Family File.

[5] Manuel, *Marriage Licenses,* 35

[6] Find-A-Grave, com. From Ancestry.com.

[7] Ancestry.com, St. Mary's County, 1850 Census.

[8] Death Certificate, on Ancestry.com, buried All Faith Cemetery listed Wm Perry Braddock & Elizabeth Locke as his parents. On 1900 Census, his half siblings lived with him.

DEATH 31 Oct. 1859 in his 42nd year.[1] Buried at Rockville Baptist Cemetery and later moved to Rockville Cemetery.[2]

NOTES His brother Joseph Braddock married 6 Feb 1839, Laura Lock, and his brother John Braddock, Jr., married in July 1839, Sarah Ann Locke.

JOSEPH HABERSHAM BRADLEY (1803-1887)

Admitted to Montgomery County Bar 1868[3]

BIRTH/PARENTS: Joseph Habersham Bradley was born 22 March 1803 in Washington, D.C., to Abraham and Hannah (Smith) Bradley.

EDUCATION Graduated from Yale College at the age of 18 and then studied law for three years under Mr. Caldwell (Clerk of the Supreme Court) and Richard S. Cox, of Georgetown.[4]

LEGAL CAREER He was admitted to the Washington, D.C. Bar in 1824. He was among lawyers who defended John H. Surratt in the conspiracy charge arising from the assassination of President Abraham Lincoln[5]. Nominated in 1872 for Chief Judge for the 6th Congressional District but defeated by Judge Richard J. Bowie.

MARRIAGE:

1. On 5 Dec. 1825[6], to Lucy Sherman Tuttle (21 Jan. 1804-9 Apr. 1870) daughter of Asahel Tuttle of New Haven, CT.
2. On 31 Oct. 1883, Mary Harrissin Philadelphia,PA.

CHILDREN[7]:

1. Sarah D. Bradley, b. abt 1826, d. 22 Aug 1886, bur. Oak Hill Cemetery, m. 21 Nov. 1855, Charles A. Sherman.
2. Hannah T. Bradley, b. abt 1828, d. Sep 1870, bur. Oak Hill Cemetery, m. 24 Dec. 1851, William H. Saunders. (d. 11 Feb. 1857, age 37).[8]
3. Abraham Thomas Bradley, b. 9 Sep. 1829, d. 15 Jul 1895,.m. Mary d. 15 Oct. 1864[9].

---

[1] Malloy, *Sentinel,* 11 Nov 1859, Concord Lodge no 73, I.O.O.F.
[2] MCHS Cemetery Card File.
[3] Scharf, 668.
[4] Bradley Family file, MCHS, copy of obituary from *Sentinel*, April 8, 1887.
[5] Bradley Family File, MCHS, copy of obituary from *Sentinel*, April 8, 1887.
[6] Dixon. *National Intelligencer* 1824-1826, 14 Dec. 1825.
[7] Five children mentioned but not named in obituary, only three were then living. On1850 Census in Washington, D.C., the five children below appear in the household.
[8] Pippenger, *Daily National Intelligencer Index to Deaths, 1835-1870.*
[9] Pippenger, *Oak Hill Cemetery, vol. 1,* 157.

4. Joseph H. Bradley, Jr., b. 4 Sep. 1831, d. 21 Aug. 1874, m.1. 25 Nov. 1856, Eliza M. Thomas (b. 12 Dec. 1837, d. 12 Mar. 1859), m. 2. 4 Jun 1863, Mary Duncan (b. 6 Jun 1834, d. 30 May 1901).[1]
5. Alice Bradley, b. abt 1836, m. 24 Feb 1859, Rev. Walter W. Williams[2].

DEATH 3 April 1887. Buried in Oak Hill Cemetery, Georgetown, D.C.

WILLIAM COTTRINGER BRENT (1824-1860)

Admitted to Montgomery County Bar 1845[3]

BIRTH/PARENTS: William Cottringer Brent was born 12 Aug.. 1824[4] to Robert Young Brent (1788-7 Dec. 1855)[5] and his second wife, Harriet Cottringer Brent (1801-10 Oct. 1865), who were married 6 Jan. 1824 in Washington, D.C.[6]. Robert Y. Brent was the son of Robert Brent (1763-1819), the first mayor of Washington. He was appointed in 1802 by Thomas Jefferson, and reappointed each year until 1812[7]. Harriett Brent was the daughter of Garrett Cottringer, the bookkeeper and cashier for Robert Morris, the Philadelphia financier.[8]

LEGAL CAREER: Admitted to Montgomery County Bar in 1845.

MARRIAGE: No record of marriage or of children.

DEATH: 13 Sept. 1860. Buried in St. John the Evangelist Catholic Church Cemetery, Forest Glen[9], Montgomery County.

NOTES: Believed to have been born at the family's house, "The Highlands," the site of which is now occupied by the Mormon Temple overlooking the Capital Beltway.

JAMES CHISWELL BREWER (1815-1883)

Admitted to Montgomery County Bar 1836[10]

BIRTH/PARENTS: James Chiswell Brewer was born 16 April 1815, in Montgomery County, MD to William Brewer, M.D., (b. 24 Jul. 1777, d. 14 Oct. 1861) and Mary Robertson Chiswell (b. 13 Dec. 1782, d. 7 Feb. 1867).

---

[1] Pippenger, *Oak Hill Cemetery, vol. 1,* 157.
[2] Pippenger, *District of Columbia Marriage Licenses, 1858-1870, 318.*
[3] Scharf, 668.
[4] Find A Grave, on Ancestry.com.
[5] Cemetery Card File, MCHS, buried St. John's Forest Glen.
[6] Pippenger, *D.C.Marriage Licenses, 1811-1858,* 63.
[7] Proctor, *Washington Past and Present,* 78.
[8] Papers of Robert Morris, 1781, p. 297, footnote 3
[9] Cemetery Card File, MCHS.
[10] Scharf, 668.

They were married in Montgomery County on 5 Feb. 1800. They are buried at Monocacy Cemetery. He was a prosperous farmer.

LEGAL CAREER: After admission to the bar in Montgomery County, he removed to Jefferson, Louisiana, where he met his wife, married in 1841, raised a family, and became a prominent lawyer in New Orleans according to his obituary.[1]

MARRIAGE: On 4 March 1841, he married Sophia Bradford (b. 1 Nov 1820, d. 27 Jun 1887)[2] daughter of James Morgan Bradford and Sophia Elizabeth Bradford of Louisiana.[3]

CHILDREN[4]

1. William Peale Brewer, b. 1843, d. 5 May 1909, buried Matarie Cemetery, New Orleans, LA.[5]. No record of marriage.
2. James Brewer, b. 1845, d bef. 1883.
3. Nicholas Brewer, b. 1848., d. bef. 1883.
4. Joseph Brewer, b. Aug. 1850, d. after 1900, occupation attorney, married to Lucy Turner Harris, b. 1855.
5. Mary Octavia Brewer, b. 1853, d. after 1900, living with brother, William P. Brewer, listed as single.
6. Elizabeth Sophia Brewer, b. 6 Jan 1856, d. Mar 1860 (Scarlet Fever)[6]

DEATH: 20 Aug 1883,[7] buried at Metarie Cemetery, New Orleans, Louisiana.

JOHN BUCHANAN BREWER (1850 1908)

Admitted to Montgomery County Bar 1873[8]

BIRTH/PARENTS: John Buchanan Brewer was born on 4 Dec. 1850 in Montgomery County, MD to John Chiswell Brewer (b. 14 Sept. 1804, d. 10 July 1866)[9] and Elizabeth Stewart (Buchanan) Brewer (b. 16 Sep 1813, d. 18 Apr. 1882) who were married 30 Jan. 1838.

EDUCATION: Academy of Rockville, Washington and Lee University, graduated from Law Department at University of Maryland in 1873[10]

---

[1] "Age 69 yrs., prominent lawyer of New Orleans, died in that city Mon. of last week. His father was Dr. William Brewer, and his brother, John Brewer, was a lawyer of Rockville. He leaves a wife, a daughter and 2 sons, Dr. William P. Brewer and Joseph Brewer, a lawyer" published in Malloy, *Sentinel,* 47.

[2] Orleans Death Notices, 1877-1895, v.91, 488.

[3] Ancestry.com, Family Trees.

[4] 1860 Census: Louisiana (Ancestry.com).

[5] *Find-A Grave*, accessed 31 May 2016.

[6] U.S. Federal Census Mortality Schedules, 1850-1885.

[7] Malloy, *op.cit.,*, 47.

[8] Scharf, 668.

[9] MCHS Cemetery Card File, buried Rockville Cemetery.

[10] Portrait and Biographical Record of the 6th Congressional District, 740-1

LEGAL CAREER: In 1871, studied law at the firm of Brown and Brune in Baltimore, MD. Shortly after his marriage he went to St. Louis, MO to practice law, but returned to Montgomery County due to his wife's health[1].

MARRIAGE 9 Oct. 1874 to Virginia Fletcher Russell (b. 11 Feb. 1854, d. 16 Oct. 1943) daughter of Major William W. Russell and Virginia (Fletcher) Russell of Alexandria, VA. She was active in the Women's Christian Temperance Union and the Burden Bearer's Circle of the Kings Daughters of Rockville.[2]

CHILDREN:[3]

1. Virginia Fletcher Brewer, b. 25 Jul. 1875, d. 2 July 1933.[4] Buried in Rockville Cemetery.
2. Ellen Russell Brewer, b. 21 Sept. 1876, d. 1968, m. 12 Dec. 1906, William Brewer Waters (b. 19 Oct. 1875).
3. John Brewer, b. 31 Aug. 1878, d. 15 Mar.-1954. He was admitted to the Bar in 1903., m. 3 June 1916, to Rosalind Caldwell. Buried in Rockville Cemetery.
4. William Russell Brewer, b. 6 Apr. 1880, d. 12 Mar.1941, m. 17 Aug. 1910, Maude Stalnaker.
5. Mary McPherson Brewer, b. 3 Aug. 1881, d.19 Jul. 1936.
6. Lloyd Archibald. Brewer, b. 30 Nov. 1882, d. 6 Jan.1968, m. 12 July 1909, Eureka Springs, AR, to Amelia Alexander, (b. 30 Nov. 1882, d. 29 May 1957).
7. Nicholas Brewer, b. 21 Mar. 1884, d. 20 Oct.-1958, m. 18 Dec. 1908, Bessie Stonestreet Greene.
8. George Brewer, b. 31 May 1885, d. 1 Feb.1949
9. Elizabeth Stewart Brewer, b. 23 Apr. 1891, d. 18 Aug. 1971[5], unmarried. Buried in Rockville Cemetery.
10. Lucy Briscoe Brewer, b. 1892, d.-24 May 1982, m. 8 Nov. 1924 to Stanislaus Murray Hamilton. (b. 29 Sep 1892, d. 25 May 1949.)

DEATH: 22 Oct. 1908, buried in Rockville Cemetery.[6]

NOTES: Upon returning to Montgomery County, he took up farming and continued for twelve years. He was appointed assistant postmaster at Rockville, MD. He was a member of the Montgomery Lodge #195, AF&AM.[2] John Buchanan Brewer was the son of John Chiswell Brewer, the nephew of James Chiswell Brewer and the grandson of William Brewer, M.D. Both his father and uncle were practicing lawyers as well as his brother William, and are included in this manuscript.

---

[1] *Ibid.*

[2] Obituary of Mrs. Virginia R. Brewer, 89, dated 18 Oct 1943, in Brewer Family File, MCHS..

[3] Hurley, William N., "Brewer Families," in Brewer Family File, MCHS, published in Montgomery County Families.

[4] MCHS, Cemetery Card File, buried Rockville Cemetery, with her parents.

[5] Brewer Family File, MCHS.

[6] MCHS Cemetery File : Brewer, John B.

JOHN CHISWELL BREWER 1804-1866

Admitted to Montgomery County Bar 1828[1]

BIRTH/PARENTS John Chiswell Brewer was born 14 Sep 1804 near Poolesville, MD to William Brewer (b. 24 Jul. 1777, d. 14 Oct. 1861) and Mary Robertson Chiswell. (b. 13 Dec. 1782, d. 7 Feb. 1867) They were married in Montgomery County on 5 Feb. 1800. They are buried at Monocacy Cemetery. He was a prosperous farmer.

EDUCATION He read law in Frederick, MD with William Ross.

LEGAL CAREER Later he practiced law in Rockville and was associated with George Peter. He had an active legal career until his death in 1866. He was a member of the 1850 Maryland constitutional committee, being the first Democrat to carry Montgomery County. In 1856 he was counsel for the government of the Chesapeake & Ohio Canal until the Civil War. During the Civil War he was kept in prison at General Bank's camp, at Darnestown, MD because of his political opinions.[2]

MARRIAGE 30 Jan. 1838 to Elizabeth Stewart Buchanan (b. 16 Sep. 1813 in Baltimore, MD, d. 18 Apr. 1882).

CHILDREN[3]

1. Mary Brewer, b. 4 Oct. 1839, d. 19 Apr. 1845.
2. Catherine Brewer, b. 4 Nov. 1842, d. 25 Apr. 1845.
3. Eleanor Brewer, b. 22 Jul. 1845, d. 21 Jul. 1876, m. 21 Dec. 1871 to Spencer Cone Jones (b. 3 July 1836, d. 1915 in Frederick County), son of Rev.Joseph Hawkins Jones and Elizabeth Clagett Jones.[4]
4. William Brewer, b. 14 Feb. 1847, d. 16 Apr. 1885. Also an attorney. See sketch.
5. John Buchanan Brewer, b. 4 Dec. 1850, d. 22 Oct 1908. Also an attorney. See sketch.

DEATH 10 Jul 1866. Originally buried in Baptist Church Cemetery. Family monuments in Rockville Cemetery.[5]

NICHOLAS BREWER III (1828-1896)

Admitted to Montgomery County Bar 1850[6]

BiRTH/PARENTS: Nicholas Brewer III was born 12 Jul 1828 in Annapolis to Nicholas Brewer, Jr., b. 23 Nov. 1795, d. 16 Oct. 1864, and his second wife, Catharine Musser Medairy of Baltimore, MD, b. 20 Jun. 1807, d. 16 Nov. 1862. They were married on 11 Sept. 1827.[7]

---

[1] Scharf, 667.
[2] *Portrait and Biographical Record,* 739-740, in sketch of "John Burchanan Brewer."
[3] MCHS Cemetery Card File in Rockville Cemetery.
[4] MCHS Brewer Family File, manuscript by William N.Hurley.
[5] Scharf, 752. MCHS Cemetery Card File.
[6] Scharf, 668.
[7] McIntire, *Annapolis Maryland Families*, 84

EDUCATION: He was educated at St. John's.

LEGAL CAREER: He served as Mayor of Annapolis in 1855; federal auditor; state law reporter, Court of Appeals, 1862-1869; and member State Senate, 1884 and 1886

MARRIAGE: On 30 April 1861 to Harriet Carolina Batcheller, b. 2 Jan. 1840, d. 22 Mar. 1906.

CHILDREN

1. Nicholas Brewer, IV, b. 17 May. 1862, d. 17 Jan. 1901.
2. Hattie Batcheller Brewer, b. 29 Dec. 1863, d. 19 Jun. 1865.
3. Charles Brewer, b. 27 Dec. 1865, d. after 1935
4. Hattie Batcheller Brewer, b. 4 Aug. 1867, d. 9 July 1868.
5. Thomas Leverett Brewer, b. 24 Jan. 1871, d. after 1935.
6. Sarah Caroline Brewer, b. 7 Sept. 1872, d. 8 Oct. 1872.
7. Catharine Susanna Brewer, b. 6 Nov. 1873, d. 21 Aug. 1914, m. Morris Whitmore Torrey.
8. Elizabeth Morris Brewer, b. 7 July 1875, d. 9 Jan.1935, m. 9 Mar. 1907, Ashley Molgram Gould..

DEATH: 9 Dec. 1896.

WILLIAM BREWER (1847-1885)

Admitted to Montgomery County Bar 1870[1]

BIRTH/PARENTS: William Brewer was born 14 Feb. 1847 in Rockville, MD to John Chiswell Brewer (b. 14 Sept 1804, d. 10 Jul 1866) and Elizabeth Stewart Buchanan Brewer (b. 16 Sep 1813, d. 18 Mar 1882). [2]

EDUCATION: Rockville Academy, Rittenhouse Academy (Washington, D.C.), and Columbian College.[3]

LEGAL CAREER: Listed as a lawyer in the 1870 Federal Census[4]; advertised in the *Sentinel* as an attorney beginning in 1871 and in 1873 with offices "in the parlor of the old Washington Hotel" in Rockville;[5] William Brewer and P.D. Laird became law partners.[6]

---

[1] Scharf, 668.

[2] MCHS Cemetery File, dates from John & Elizabeth Stewart Brewer Family Card.

[3] *Sentinel,* 24 Apr. 1885.

[4] Federal Census : Maryland: Montgomery County : Rockville : 4th District : Brewer, Elizabeth

[5] Thompson, *Western Gateway*, 95.

[6] Sentinel, 6 Jan. 1882.

MARRIAGE: 13 Feb. 1878, Christ Episcopal Rectory, Rockville, MD, to Matilda Provost Russell[1] (b. 16 Jan. 1857, d. 17 Apr. 1940) She was the daughter of William W. Russell (USMC) and Virginia (Fletcher) Russell.[2]

CHILDREN:

1. John Brewer, b. 8 Dec. 1878, d. 19 Jul. 1962, unmarried. Buried in Rockville Cemetery. Trained as a lawyer, he graduated from Princeton University in 1901. Practiced as a patent attorney, then, left in 1905 to an appointment at the American consulate in Caracas, Venezuela. In 1910, he became vice deputy and then deputy Counsul General in Santo Domingo. From 1924 to 1947, he served as legal secretary of the West Indies Sugar Company. After returning to the United States, he resided at 2900 Connecticut Avenue, Washington, D. C.[3]
2. William Brewer, Jr.[4]

DEATH: 16 Apr. 1885 in Rockville, Maryland. Buried in Rockville Cemetery.

NOTES: He purchased *The Montgomery Advocate* in 1875 from the founder, William B. Green.[5]

JOSEPH ALOYSIUS CAHILL (1838-1902)

Admitted to Montgomery County Bar in 1876[6]

BIRTH/PARENTS: Joseph Aloysius Cahill was born 6 December 1838 to Philip J. Cahill, b. 10 Aug 1804, d. after 1860, and Sophia Ann Cecilia (Elder) Cahill, b. 27 Feb 1807, d. 17 Jan. 1872.[7]

LEGAL CAREER: He grew up in Cumberland in Allegany County, Maryland, and was admitted to the Allegany County Bar in 1860.[8]

MARRIAGE: No known marriage or children.

DEATH: 31 Oct. 1902, Baltimore, MD. Buried in Loudoun Park Cemetery.[9]

NOTES: During the Civil War he crossed the river to the south at Cumberland, and walked to Springfield, VA., from there to Romney and by regular mail stage to Winchester, where he enlisted about 20 August 1861 as a private in Company F, 7th

[1] MCHS Church Records Card File.
[2] MCHS Family file, Brewer Family : unpublished manuscript by William N. Hurley, Jr.
[3] MCHS Biography file : Brewer, John.
[4] MCHS Family File,"Brewer Family" *op.cit.,* reports he was married and had two children. On the 1900 Census, his mother reports only one child, then living.
[5] Thompson, *Op.Cit.,* 52.
[6] Scharf, 668.
[7] Donnelly, *Maryland Elder Family,* 48, 49, 82.
[8] Scharf, 1353.
[9] www.find-a-grave.com via *Ancestry.com*

Virginia Cavalry. He was at the named battles of Romney, Blue Gap, Winchester, Kernstown, Fishers Hall, and all skirmishes his command was engaged in until his transfer to the Quarter Master Dept., where he was at the time of surrender of General Lee. He was paroled at New Market, VA[1]. He later entered the Christian Brothers at Ammendale, Prince George's County, Maryland, and was known as Brother Gabriel. On the 1900 census, he can be found as an inmate in the Confederate Soldiers Home in Baltimore.

WASHINGTON CUSTIS CALVERT (1804--1868)

Admitted to Montgomery County Bar 1832[2]
Admitted to Prince George's County Bar 1829

BIRTH/PARENTS: Washington Custis Calvert was born 27 September 1804 to Edward Henry (1766-1846) and Elizabeth (Biscoe) (1780-1857) Calvert][3] Edward Henry Calvert was a member of the Maryland General Assembly for several years.[4]

LEGAL CAREER: Court records show that Richard Peach moved for Calvert's admission to the Prince George's bar during the October 1829 term.[5] He was admitted to the Montgomery County Bar in 1832.

MARRIAGE:

1. Sophia Oden Mullikin, 17 Jun 1851[6]
2. Elizabeth G. Randolph, n.d.[7]

CHILDREN:: No children survived from his marriage to Sophia Mullikin and there were no children from his marriage to Elizabeth G. Randolph.[8]

DEATH: 14 January 1868 at his home, Avalon, in Prince George's County.[9]

NOTES: On February 10, 1835 he was named among others to lay out and supervise the construction of a road from Calvert's Old Mill to Winckler's Gate.[10]

---

[1] Excerpted from Autobiography written in January 1900, quoted in Toomey, *Maryland Line Confederate Soldier's Home,* 42-43.
[2] Scharf, 668.
[3] Ancestry.com: Johnson, Robert Winder, *The* ***Ancestry*** *of Rosalie Morris Johnson: daughter of George Calvert Morris and Elizabeth Kuhn, his wife:* Philadelphia: Ferris & Leach, 1905-1908, 31 (accessed 19 Nov 2014)
[4] Callcott, *Letters of Rosalie Stier Calvert,* 70 & other references to her brother in law Edward & his wife.
[5] Van Horn, *Out of the Past,* 290
[6] Brown, *Marriage Licenses, Prince George's County* 40
[7] Ancestry.com: Johnson, Robert Winder, 32 (accessed 19 Nov 2014)
[8] Ancestry.com: Johnson, Robert Winder, 32 (accessed 19 Nov 2014)
[9] *Washington Star,* 17 Jan 1868 as reported in Baltz, *Prince George's Marriage & Deaths in 19th Century Newspapers,* 106.
[10] Van Horn, *Op.Cit.,* 306

HUGH ELMWOOD CAPERTON (1821-1877)

"HUGH CARPENTER" Admitted to Montgomery County Bar 1844[1]

BIRTH/PARENTS: Hugh Elmwood Caperton, Esq., was born 11 January 1821, Morgan County, Virginia (now West Virginia) to Representative Hugh Caperton (1781-1847) from Virginia and Mary Jane Erskine(1786-1836.). He was elected as a Federalist, in the thirteenth congress, 1813-1815.[2]

LEGAL CAREER: He was primarily a lawyer in Washington, D.C. He did purchase some real estate in Montgomery County[3]. He was appointed General in the Militia by President Buchanan.

MARRIAGE: 27 December 1842 to Eliza Jane Mosher,[4] b. 10 Sept 1821, Baltimore, Maryland, d. 1875, daughter of James Mosher and Elizabeth Magruder Mosher. Buried in Holy Rood Cemetery, Georgetown, Washington, D.C.[5]

CHILDREN:[6]

1. James Mosher Caperton, b. 1843, d. 1905.
2. Jane Caperton, b. 1851, d. 1872.
3. Hugh Caperton, b. 1854, d. 1915.
4. Imogene Caperton, b. 1855, d. 1879.

DEATH: 14 September 1877, buried in Holy Rood Cemetery, Washington, D.C.[7]

JOHN A. CARTER (1798 – 1860)

Admitted to Montgomery County Bar c.1826[8]

BIRTH/PARENTS: John Alexander Carter was born about 1798 in Washington, D.C. He was probably the son of John Carter (b. ca. 1772 d. 13 Oct. 1830[9]) and his first wife, who is unknown. In 1822, John Carter made a deed for his 328 acres in Prince George's County

---

[1] Scharf, p. 668 – name is listed as Hugh Carpenter, but no such lawyer was found.

[2] *Biographical Directory of the American Congress, 1774-1961.*

[3] There are several deeds in which he is the grantee between 1858 and 1874, some as trustee: JGH6:521; EPB6:256, EBP7:180, EPB9:270, EPB10:244; EBP11:373, EPB12,277. Later deeds to and from his son Hugh and others settling the real estate. There are also several deeds as grantor, one in 1860, identifying him as Attorney, others as trustee. The Hugh Caperton Estate deed is cited below.

[4] *Washington D.C. Marriage Licenses, 1811-1855.*

[5] *Find A Grave,* accessed September 6, 2015.

[6] 1870 Census, Georgetown, Washington, D.C., listed four children with parents, James M., agd 26, Jennie 18, Hugh 16 and Imogene, 14. All are listed on marker in Holy Rood Cemetery, as found on www.findagrave.com. Montgomery County deeds, Liber EBT21:291-293 is from the heirs of Hugh Caperton, James M. Caperton and Ella his wife of Baltimore, and Imogene Caperton and Hugh Caperton of Wahsington, D.C., dated 6 November 1879.

[7] *www.findagrave.com, op.cit.*

[8] Maryland Journal, advertisement, 13 Jun. 1826

[9] Dixon, *National Intelligencer, 1830-1831,* 13 Oct 1830, died at Billingsley, Prince George's County, MD aftera short but painful illness, Capt. John Carter in his 59th year.

, by the names of *Grey Eagle Enlarged* and *Maidens Dowery* to John Alexander Carter, and executed a bill of sale to him for his slaves, livestock, and furniture[1]. In Maryland Chancery Court, December term 1828, John A. Carter is involved in proceedings regarding the sale of these lands[2]. John Carter had acquired the property around 1809 by deed from Trueman Tyler, trustee appointed to sell the real estate of Samuel Hepburn[3].

LEGAL CAREER: John A. Carter, residing in Rockville, Montgomery County, was listed as a delegate to the May 7, 1832 to the Young Men's Republican Convention[4]. In 1844, "[Major John A. Carter] Appointed Clerk of the Court, began his duties on Tues. "[5] Listed as a "Lawyer" on the 1850 Federal Census for Arkansas.
MARRIAGE On 11 May 1830 to Mary Catherine Holmes Magruder. Her parents were Lloyd Magruder (d. 1837) and Ann Holmes (d. 1835). Mary was born 18 Jul 1808 and died 1 Dec. 1894 in Washington, DC. She is buried at Hermon Chapel, Potomac, Maryland.[6]

CHILDREN[7]

1. Rebecca J Carter, b. 1833, in Maryland[8]

DEATH John A. Carter, half- brother of Robert W., died January 23, 1860 in his 61st year. He read law in the office of the late John A. T. Kilgour. He went to Arkansas in 1849 and to Louisiana in 1855, where he died.[9]

ROBERT W. CARTER (1812-1890)

Admitted to Montgomery County Bar 1834[10]

BIRTH/PARENTS: Robert W. Carter was born 2 Sept. 1812 in Prince Georges County, Maryland.[11] Because the father of John A. Carter, his half brother, has been identified, it is believed that he is also the son of John Carter (1772-1830) by a second wife. See John A. Carter sketch.

---

[1] Prince George's County Land Records, AB2:190 & AB2:217-219, made 30 March 1822..

[2] Dixon, *National Intelligencer, 1827-1829,* 341. Bill to obtain decree for sale of land, notice 6 March 1829 for benefit of Margaret Johns Key, widow of Edmund Key, trustees appointed by will of Benjamin Mackall. Reference contract in March 1822..

[3] Prince George's County Land Records, JRM 15:357-359. Recorded in 1812. In 1810 John Carter posted a bond as constable, with Dennis Burgess as surety. See AB13:567.

[4] Dixon, *National Intelligencer, 1832-1833,* p. 71 & 90.

[5] Maryland Journal, 24 Apr. 1844

[6] MCHS Cemetery File : Mary C. H. Carter

[7] The 1840 Census, for Rockville, MD, shows that he may have taken on the guardianship of his wife's younger siblings, as there were 4 teenage boys in the household, and other young females.

[8] On the 1850 Federal Census for Ruddell, Arkansas the following were listed as residing with John A., Mary C. H., and Rebecca J. Carter: Lucy B. Magruder, 33, Ann H. Magruder, 30 years and Agdin C. Magruder, 20 years old.

[9] *Sentinel,* March 1860.

[10] Scharf, 668.

[11] *Sentinel, 1855-1899,* 68..

EDUCATION: Educated in Rockville, Maryland, while residing with his half-brother, John A. Carter.[1]

LEGAL CAREER: Went to Arkansas to work but returned to Rockville where he was elected Register of Wills in 1863.[2] He was serving his 5th term at the time of his death.

MARRIAGE: On 19 Nov. 1839, to Mary Ann Harding, b. 28 Oct. 1815, baptized at St. John's Catholic Church, Forest Glen, in Montgomery County, MD, d. 6 Jan. 1908.[3] She was the daughter of Henry Harding and Catherine Ann Robb Harding. She died at home of her daughter , Mrs. Dove, "of old age; in her 94th yr. bur. 8 Jan."[4]

CHILDREN :

1. Henry Harding Carter, b. 10 Sep. 1840[5], d. Dec. 1895[6], m. 15 Oct. 1873, Mary M. Gunton of Prince George's County[7].
2. William John Carter, b. 26 Jan. 1842.[8], died young.
3. Robert W. Carter, Jr., b. 8 July,1844, d. 30 Jan. 1865, POW Camp Chase, Ohio of pneumonia. He enlisted 25 Aug. 1862, at Charlottesville, Va. In 1st Bn., Md. Cav., Co. A.[9]
4. Charles Adam Carter, b. 10 Oct 1846, [10] d. 17 Mar. 1880 of typhoid fever. He was deputy Register of Wills in Rockville.[11]
5. John Alexander Carter, b. 26 Dec. 1848,[12] d. March 1890[13]
6. James Caldwell Carter, b. 26 Dec. 1848, d. 26 Mar.1877, typhoid fever.[14]
7. William Carter, b. 26 Nov. 1853,[15] d. 1 Sep 1874.
8. Elizabeth Ann Harding Carter, b. 18 July 1856,[16], m. 6 Sep. 1882, John Maury Dove.[17]
9. Catharine Carter, b. 1851, bp. 6 Oct. 1851, d. 1856.[18]

---

[1] Ibid.
[2] Sentinel, 1863 Jun 15
[3] Guide to selections from the Montgomery County Sentinel, Maryland,January 1, 1905-December 31, 1908, 139.
[4] MCHS Cemetery File, Carter, Robert W.
[5] MCHS Church Card file, records of St John's Catholic Church, Forest Glen, baptized 18 Sept. 1840.
[6] Malloy, *Sentinel,* 68, 3 Jan. 1896.
[7] Malloy, *Sentinel,* 68
[8] MCHS Church Card file, records of St. John's Catholic Church, Forest Glen, baptized 3 March 1842.
[9] Jacobs, *Confederate Soldiers and Allies, 28.*
[10] MCHS Church Card file, records of St. Mary's Catholic Church, baptized 15 Oct 1846.
[11] Malloy, *Sentinel,67,* 26 March 1880.
[12] MCHS Church Card file, records of St. John's Catholic Church, Forest Glen, baptized 5 Jan. 1849.
[13] Malloy, *Sentinel,* 68,
[14] MCHS Church Card file, records of St. Mary's Catholic Church, baptized 5 Jan. 1849, buried at St Mary's Cemetery, Rockville.
[15] MCHS Church Card file, records of St. Mary's Catholic Church, baptized31 Dec. 1853.
[16] MCHS Church Card file, records of St. Mary's Catholic Church, baptized 7 Sept 1866.
[17] MCHS Church Card file, records of St. Mary's Catholic Church., Rockville, MD.
[18] MCHS Cemetery File, Carter, Robert W

DEATH: He died 15 August 1890 in his 78th year. He is buried at St. Mary's, Rockville.[1]

NOTES: "Resolutions of Respect" by the Orphans Court and the Bar of Montgomery County on 12 Sep. 1890. [1]

HAZEL BUTT CASHELL (1808-1886)

Judge of Orphans Court

BIRTH/PARENTS: Hazel Butt Cashell was born about 1808 to George (b.1776, d. 20 Aug.1862) and Elizabeth B. Edmonston (b. 1789, d. 12 Aug. 1866) Cashell.[2]

LEGAL CAREER: From 1847-51 he was a County Commissioner (Democrat); in 1854, he was appointed Judge of the Orphans' Court to fill out term of Judge Magruder. Continued for four 4-year terms.[3]

MARRIAGES:

1. Jan. 28, 1834 (lisc. dtd.) to Catherine Groomes (b. 2 Dec. 1804, d. 15 Jan. 1859[4]) d/o James & Eleanor (Fish) Groomes[5]
2. About 1869, At Ruther Glen, VA, Harriet Amelia Jones (1832- 12 March 1915 at Ruther Glen, Va.)[6] daughter of Hill Jones, and Mary Courtney Jones. On the 1860 census, she was a teacher, and Hill Jones was living in same household. On the 1850 census in father's family with siblings, Hill Jones and others[7].

CHILDREN
by 1st wife

1. Amanda E. Cashell, b. 1837 (tombstone and censuses) d. 25 Oct. 1915,[8] m. 24 Oct. 1876 to William Metzger. Buried in Monocacy Cemetery, Beallsville.
2. James Groomes Cashell, b. 9 Mar. 1839, d. 22 Sept. 1903[9] m. 13 Nov. 1902 at the Church of the Holy Name of Jesus, Wash., DC to Mary Ellen Hodges, d/o Henry and Mary Catherine (Bailey) Hodges, [she m. 2nd Alfred Ray, Jr.].

---

[1] Genealogical Abstracts, 68

[2] *Portrait and Biographical Record of the Sixth Congressional District,* p. 629; Cashell family file, MCHS.

[3] *Portrait and Biographical Record of the Sixth Congressional District,* p. 629

[4] Malloy, *Sentinel,* 21 Jan 1859.

[5] Groomes Family file, MCHS; *Sentinel,* op.cit., Jan. 21, 1859.

[6] *Sentinel,* 1915.

[7] Ancestry.com, census records, 1850, 1860, death record for Hill Jones; other researchers family tree.

[8] Cemetery File, MCHS.

[9] *The Hodges of Green Hill, Montgomery County, MD* by Kenneth F. Hodges, unpublished Mss. MCHS.

3. Thomas Franklin Cashell, b. 17 June 1841, d. 29 Dec. 1901, buried in Rockville Cemetery[1] m. 13 Feb. 1874 (lisc. dtd) to Elizabeth Emily Groomes d/o Hanson and Elizabeth Henrietta (Cashell) Groomes, his 1st cousin.
4. William Lycurgus Cashell, b. 27 Nov. 1843, d. 17 May 1915, buried in St. John's Episcopal Cemetery, Olney,[2] m. 25 April 1874 to Ellen Rebecca Groomes, d/o Hanson and Elizabeth Henrietta (Cashell) Groomes, his 1st cousin.

By 2nd wife

5. Francis Hazel Cashell, b. 1871, d. 14 Feb. 1930, buried In Rockville Cemetery[3] m. 29 Nov. 1894 to Ella Virginia Ferry.
6. Edgar Hill Cashell, b. 18 Apr. 1872, d. 9 Oct. 1933,[4] m. 8 Apr. 1896 to Marie Catherine/Kathryn Weller at the parsonage of St. Mary's Catholic Church,[5] Rockville.

DEATH: 26 October 1886 at age 78[6]

NOTES: His primary occupation was Farmer.[7] He also dealt in real estate and owned land in both Montgomery County and ington, D.C. He was arrested for "treason", i.e. Southern sympathies during the Civil War. Tried and released on parole.[8] Methodist Episcopal.[9]

WASHINGTON BOWIE CHICHESTER (1828-1902)

Admitted to Montgomery County Bar 1849[10]

BIRTH/PARENTS: Washington Bowie Chichester, Sr. was born 11 Feb 1828, in Leesburg, Loudon County, VA to George Mason Chichester and Mary A. Bowie (b. 1802) (daughter of Washington Bowie). They were married 23 Dec. 1824, in Loudon County, VA. George Mason Chichester died in 1835. Although the obituary for Washington Bowie Chichester has his father's name as Nathan Chichester[11] other sources name George Mason Chichester as his father.[12] He came to live at Oatland, Montgomery County, Maryland as a boy with his Aunt Margaret and Uncle Washington Bowic II.[13]

---

1 Malloy, *Sentinel,* 19 Mar. 1915, MCHS Cemetery File, Groomes Family File, MCHS.
2 *Ibid.*
3 MCHS Cemetery File; Cashell family file.
4 *Sentinel Abstracts.*
5 MCHS Church Records File.
6 Sentinel, obituary Oct 29, 1886.
7 Montgomery County Census Records.
8 National Archives, Group 153, Stack 6W4, Row 6, Compartment 6, Shelf B., from Cashell Family file, MCHS.
9 MCHS Church Records File.
10 Scharf, 668
11 Malloy, *Sentinel,* 239.
12 Bowie, *The Bowies and and Their Kindred*, 98; Duncan, *Loudon County Will Abstracts,* 278
13 Farquhar, 239.

EDUCATION: He attended the Rockville Academy and studied law under his uncle Judge Richard Johns Bowie.[1]

LEGAL CAREER: He never practiced law.[2] He attended the [Maryland] State Constitutional Convention in 1851 and served as the Assistant Secretary.[3]

MARRIAGE He married 17 Jan. 1854, in Baltimore, to Lydia Brown b. 7 Jul 1831, d. 1 Jul 1888[4],daughter of Amos Brown (d. 1845) and Sarah Ridgely (Griffith) Brown (b.19 Sep. 1792, d. 31 Mar 1866)[5]; sister of Ridgely Brown. (1833-1864)[6] She is buried at St. John's Cemetery, Olney, MD.

CHILDREN[7]

1. Margaret Bowie Chichester, b. 1856, m. 29 Jan. 1890, at St. John's Church, Olney, Warrington Gillet Smith of Baltimore, MD.[8]
2. Lydia W. Chichester, b. 1859, m. Jun. 1894, St. John's Church, Olney, William Sawtell Muir of Philadelphia, PA[9]
3. Harriet Ridgely Chichester, b. 20 Nov 1859, d. 31 Dec. 1938.[10] Unmarried.
4. Washington Bowie Chichester, Jr., b. 7 July 1868, d. 21 Dec. 1918, m. by license in Montgomery County, 21 Dec. 1891, Eliza Miller Hallowell, b. 31 Oct. 1869, d. 19 Jan. 1943, both buried at St. John's Olney.[11]
5. Mary Richards Chichester, b. 1877, m. April 1902, in Philadelphia, Alexis Felix DuPont, son or the late Francis G. Dupont , of Wilmington, DE.[12]

DEATH Washington Bowie Chichester died on 2 Nov. 1902, in his 75th year at his home, near Olney, MD He is buried at St. John's Cemetery, Olney, MD.

NOTES He bought Oatland from his Aunt Margaret Bowie and built a new home there c. 1875.[13]

---

[1] Ibid, 239.

[2] Sentinel, 1902 Nov 7, 3.

[3] Scharf, 1549.

[4] MCHS Cemetery card file, Chichester, Washington B. & family.

[5] Hurley, *1850 Census,* 26; and Hurley, *Griffith Families,* 93-95.

[6] Bowie, *Op.cit. and* Sentinel, 1902 Nov 7, .3.

[7] Hurley, *The Griffith Families*, 95 lists children with some data, 1850 census gives approx. birth dates..

[8] Malloy, Sentinel,7 Feb 1890

[9] Malloy, Sentinel, 8 Jun 1894.

[10] MCHS Cemetery card file, Chichester, Harriet Ridgely at St. John's Olney.

[11] MCHS Cemetery card file, Chichester, Washington B. & family.

[12] Malloy, *Sentinel,* 18 April 1902.

[13] Farqhuar, 239.

RICHARD SMITH COXE (1792-1865)

Admitted to Montgomery County Bar 1831[1]

BIRTH/PARENTS: Richard Smith Coxe was born in January 1792 in Burlington, NJ, son of William Coxe, Jr. (b. 3 May 1762, d. 25 Feb. 1831)[2] and Rachel Smith Coxe (He was the great grandson of Col. Daniel Coxe)[3]

EDUCATION: He attended Burlington (NJ) Academy, and was prepared for college by a private tutor; he entered the College of New Jersey (Princeton) in 1805 and graduated in 1808. He read law in the office of Judge William Griffith for three years at Burlington. He went to Philadelphia to study with Horace Binney. In December 1812, he was admitted to the bar of the Supreme Court of Pennsylvania. He was admitted to the New Jersey bar in 1817 when he returned there after his marriage to Susan B. Griffith.[4]

LEGAL CAREER: He was appointed deputy attorney-general for Burlington County (NJ). In 1822, he moved to Washington, D. C. and was admitted to the bar of the circuit court of D.C. He specialized in real property law "...he was employed in more cases upon the docket of the Supreme Court than any other lawyer in the country." He was admitted to the Prince George's County bar in Sept 1823; In 1831 he served as a delegate to the Republican Convention held in Baltimore, MD. Between 1813 and 1840 he wrote various publications regarding scholarly, historical and legal issues.[5]

MARRIAGE:

1. He married on 23 Jan. 1816 to Susan Boudinot Griffith, daughter of Judge William Griffith She died 17 Sept. 1837.[6]
2. On 12 March 1840 in New York City, to Susan Warren Wheeler daughter of John Warren of New York[7].

CHILDREN all by first wife:

1. Susan Bradley Coxe, b. 27 Aug. 1818 Burlington, NJ, d. 20 Feb. 1864, m. 29 Mar. 1842 in Washington, D.C., to Col. Richard Hanson Weightman (1816-1861).
2. Mary Griffith Coxe, b. 6 Mar. 1823, d. 12 Mar. 1914, m. Alexander M. Mahan, (1821, d. 22 Feb. 1873).
3. Richard Daniel Coxe, b. 5 Nov. 1828, d. 13 Oct.1831.[8]

---

[1] Scharf, 667.
[2] *Biographical Directory of the American Congress, 1774-1961,* 746.
[3] *Dictionary of American Biography*, Vol. II, 487-488.
[4] *Dictionary of American Biography*, Vol. II, 487-488.
[5] Van Horn, *Out of the Past,* 280; *Dictionary of American Biography*, Vol. II, 487-488
[6]Dixon, *National Intelligencer,* 29 Sep 1837
[7] *Dictionary of American Biography*, Vol. II, 487-488
[8] Dixon, *National Intelligencer* "...died yesterday Richard D. Coxe, s/o R.S. Coxe, aged about 3."14 Oct. 1831

4. William Griffith Coxe,,b. 14 Sep. 1831, d. 20 Sep.1832.[1]

DEATH 28 April 1865, in Washington, DC[2]. Buried Congressional Cemetery.

LAWRENCE ALLNUTT DAWSON (1807 1875)

Admitted to Montgomery County Bar 1828[3]

BIRTH/PARENTS: Lawrence Allnutt Dawson was born 2 Oct. 1807 in Dawsonville, MD to James Mackall Dawson (b. 11 June 1775, d. 11 Jan. 1867) of Prince George's County, MD and Ann Allnutt Dawson (b. 1783, d. 5 Aug. 1854).[4]

EDUCATION: Educated in public schools. At the age of 16 he began teaching at Old Bethel School. After two years of teaching he went to Rockville and studied law with Benjamin Forrest. After completing his studies he was admitted to the bar and began to practice while also maintaining his farm.[5]

LEGAL CAREER: He was a member of the Maryland House of Delegates in 1837. He was first a Whig and the joined the Republicans. He gave up the practice of law when the war broke out as his role as auditor of the court and Commissioner of the Draft consumed his time. He and his wife supported the Union cause. During JEB Stuart's march through Rockville Dawson and several other Union supporters took refuge in Christ Episcopal Church. Stuart's troops discovered the group and took them hostage but released them during the first night[6].

MARRIAGE: On 16 June 1844, to Mary Elizabeth Kiger, b. Oct. 1814, d. 31 Dec. 1877, only daughter of George W. and Rebecca (Rice) Kiger, of Winchester, VA.[7].

CHILDREN[8]

1. James D. Dawson, b. 16 Feb. 1846, Rockville, MD, d. 30 Jan. 1909, m. 21 Oct. 1895, Henrietta Hoffman, (b. Nov. 1847, d. 17 May 1926) of Spokane, Washington. He was a member of the Rockville Bar, listed as a lawyer in 1880. He moved to Seattle in the fall of 1889.
2. George C. Dawson, b.18 Nov. 1847, d. 17 May 1926, m. 4 Jan. 1883, Louise Weaver in Washington, D.C. (b. 1863, d. 21 Feb. 1913.)
3. John Lawrence Dawson, b. 14 Nov. 1849, d. 5 Oct. 1926, m. 7 Sep. 1871, Amelia Hollyday Somerville, (b. 5 March 1849, d. 28 Sep 1898) daughter of James Somerville and Priscilla Beall. The marriage took place at the home of her

---

[1] Dixon, *National Intelligencer*, "...died yesterday ...., Wm. Griffith Coxe, s/o Richd S. Coxe, aged about 1 yr 21 Sept. 1832

[2] Dixon, *National Intelligencer Newspaper Abstracts, Civil War Years, Vol. 2,* 404. 29 April 1865.

[3] Scharf, 667.

[4] MCHS, Dawson Family File,

[5] *Portrait and Biographical Record of the Sixth Congressional District of Maryland,* 607.

[6] *Portrait, Op.Cit.,* 607.

[7] MCHS Cemetery Card File and Dawson Family File..

[8] MCHS Family File, "Descendants of James Mackall Dawson."

cousin, Margaret Beall, in Rockville, and the Dawson family lived with her, on 1900 census.

4. Mary (Mollie) Dawson, b. 6 Oct. 1852, d. 17 Aug. 1933, Rushville, Neb., m. 27 Oct. 1897, George C. Comer.
5. Henry A. Dawson, b. 2 Aug. 1854, d. 28 Oct. 1937, Rockville, Md.[1], He m. 1. 3 Dec. 1879, Josephine Baker (b. 1855, d. Dec. 1880); m. 2. Rose Newell Williams (b.1861, d. 29 April 1889); m. 3. Fannie Knight Williams (b. 1869, d. 1948).
6. Anne E. Dawson, b. 8 Sep.1856, d. 1926, m. 27 Nov. 1889, William M. Willson, Christ Church, Rockville, MD.
7. Thomas Dawson, b. 6 Oct.1857, d. 24 Sep.-1924.

DEATH: He died at his farm, Rocky Glen, on 6 Aug 1875. About 1840 he had bought Benjamin Forrest's house and a small parcel of land for farming on the outskirts of Rockville.

HENRY BRADLEY DAVIDSON (1860-1930)

Admitted to Montgomery County Bar in 1882

BIRTH/PARENTS: Henry Bradley Davidson was born 30 June 1860[2] to Dr. James Henry (2 Sep. 1828-8 Mar. 1886) and Sarah (Slater) Davidson[3] (13 Nov 1838, 7 July 1889).[4]

LEGAL CAREER: Admitted to practice law in Montgomery County in 1882.[5]

MARRIAGE:

1. June 1887 in Baltimore to Nannie Cunningham,[6]. b. 25 September 1862, d. 22 October 1888,[7] at her home at 3024 Q St., Washington, DC of "Typhoid fever"[8]
2. On 2 January 1890 (license date in Montgomery County) to Mary Stannard Porter. b. 1 April 1862, in Indiana, PA, d. 5 Sep. 1935 in New Bedford, PA. After the death of her husband she lived with her stepdaughter Louise in Edgemore area of Bethesda.[9]

CHILDREN:

by 1st wife:

1. Louise Armstrong Davidson, b. 17 May 1888 in Georgetown, Washington, DC, unmarried, d. 18 Dec. 1973. Buried in Oak Hill Cemetery. Lived in Bethesda, MD.

---

[1] *Sentinel Abstracts,* card file, 1835-1845.
[2] Pippenger, *Oak Hill Cemetery*, Vol. 1, 301.
[3] Martin, *James Davidson of the Maryland Line,* 14,she lists birthdate as August 30, 1860.
[4] Pippenger, *Oak Hill Cemetery*, Vol. 2, 166.
[5] *Sentinel,* 9 June 1882.
[6] Martin, *Op.Cit.*
[7] Pippenger, *Oak Hill Cemetery*, Vol. 2, 166.
[8] *Sentinel,* 26 October 1888
[9] Martin, *Op.Cit.*

by 2nd wife:

2. Henry Bradley Davidson, Jr., b. 10 Sep. 1892, in Bethesda, married 1. Jessica Alward (divorced), 2. Elizabeth Bishop Dunn of Philadelphia, and probably 3. Elva Statler.[1]
3. Richard Porter Davidson (Lt. Col.) b. 7 September 1900 in Washington, D.C., d. 2 Nov. 1957, Cooperstown, N.Y.;[2] m. 1, 5 April 1824, in Washington, D.C. to Elizabeth Gordon Hannah (b.1 Dec. 1901, d. 9 Apr. 1943 Fairfax County, VA) daughter of David Hannah, married 2. in Cooperstown, NY to Mabel Elmore Rucker. Lived near Fairfax, VA; assistant to Gen. Louis B. Hershey, director of the Selective Service.

DEATH 21 July 1930 in Atlantic City, N.J.. Buried in Oak Hill Cemetery, Georgetown,D.C. The Davidson family owned property in Montgomery County between Bethesda and the District Line. Henry Bradley Davidson [3] was an elder of the Bethesda Presbyterian Church.

ENOCH G. DAY (1808-1870)

Admitted to the Carroll County Bar 1848[4]
Admitted to the Montgomery County Bar 1850[5]

BIRTH/PARENTS: Enoch G. Day was born ca. 1808 in Maryland. Unable to identify parents.

LEGAL CAREER: The United States Federal Census for 1850-1870 lists him as attorney-at-law. In 1850 he resided in Carroll County, Maryland; 1860 Ritchie, Virginia, and; 1870 Wheeling, West Virginia.[6]

MARRIAGE: 9 May 1831 to Julia Ann (or Juliann) England.[7] She was born in Frederick, MD c.1808 and died in Mexico, MO, 6 Jun 1884.[8] Identified as the daughter of Andrew England (1778-1812) and Catherine (Buckey) England[9] (1772-1848). She was a widow and was living with her son Thomas Day in Missouri at the time of her death.[10]

CHILDREN[11]

1.Thomas E. Day, b. ca.1832

---

[1] *News,* March 4, 1935.
[2] *Find-A-Grave,* via Ancestry, accessed 24 June 2016.
[3] MCHS Church Records file.
[4] Scharf, 819.
[5] Scharf, 668.
[6] United States Federal Census, 1850: Maryland, Carroll County, District 9; 1860, Virginia, Ritchie, Ritchie Court House; 1870, West Virginia, Wheeling, Ohio County (www.ancestry.com)
[7] Quynn,*The Diary of Jacob Engelbrecht*, 378.
[8] Missouri Death and Burials Index, 1873-1976 (www.ancestry.com)
[9] www.ancestry.com, family tree on line, she was the fourth of five daughters. Andrew was married in Frederick County by license dated 5 Sep. 1801. Myers, *Marriage Licenses,Frederick, 1778-1810*, 44.
[10] Federal Census : 1880, Missouri, Mexico City, Audrain County (www.ancesty.com).
[11] U.S. Federal Census, 1860, Virginia, Ritchie, Ritchie Court House (www.ancestry.com), 53.

2.Charles A. H. Day, b. ca. 1838

3.Mary C. Day, b. 6 Nov. 1840, m. Johnson Baltzer Mallory[1].

4. John E. Day, b. ca. 1842

5. William H. Day, b. ca.1844

DEATH: He died 12 Sep 1870 at the age of 64 in Wheeling, West Virginia.[2]

SAMUEL WORTHINGTON DORSEY (1811-1875)

Admitted to the Montgomery County Bar, 1832[3]

BIRTH/PARENTS: Samuel Worthington Dorsey was born 23 April 1811 in Elkridge, Anne Arundel County, (now Howard County) Maryland[4] to Thomas Beale Dorsey (1780 - 1855), Attorney General 1822-24, Chief Judge of the Maryland Court 1848-1851, and Milcah Goodwin Dorsey (1782 - 1850). His younger brother, William H. G. Dorsey (b. 1819), was also a lawyer, who married as his second wife, Comfort Worthington Dorsey, daughter of Charles S.W. Dorsey.

EDUCATION: Studied in Ellicot City with Isaac Sams ; Yale School of Law, 1830; studied law in Baltimore with John Glenn, 1830-1832

LEGAL CAREER: In 1838, he moved to Vicksburg; practiced law there for a decade and then moved on to become a manager of plantations in Tensas Parish owned by his family and the Routh and Ellis families.) He inherited the cotton plantation from his father Thomas Dorsey.

MARRIAGE: In 1853, he married Sarah Anne Ellis (1829-1879), a popular American novelist (6 novels) and historian from the prominent southern Percy family. They settled first in Maryland but soon moved to a Routh family plantation near Newellton in Tensas Parish, Louisiana[5]. No children were identified.

DEATH: Died 18 October 1875,[6] near Natchez, Missisippi in Tensas Parish, Louisiana. Buried in Saint John's Cemetery, Ellicott City, Howard County, Maryland

NOTES: Around 1840, Sarah Ann Ellis Dorsey had attended Madame Deborah Grelaud's French School in Philadelphia, Pennsylvania, founded in the 1790s by a refugee from the French Revolution. There she became good friends with Varina Banks Howell, later the wife of Jefferson Davis.

---

[1] www.ancestry.com_– various family trees on line, not independently verified.

[2] West Virginia Death Index, 1853-1970 (www.ancestry.com).

[3] Scharf, 667

[4] Warfield, *The Founders of Anne Arundel and Howard Counties, Maryland;* p 495

[5] Wikipedia, "Sarah Dorsey"; citing Bertram Wyatt-Brown, The Literary Percys: Family History, Gender & The Southern Imagination, Mercer University Lamar Memorial Lecture, University of Georgia Press, 1994; The House of Percy: Interesting comment by Sarah's stepfather regarding his daughter on her marriage: "It was like wedding the living to the dead." (from "Sarah Anne Ellis Dorsey: A Woman of Uncommon Mind", Bertram Wyatt-Brown, Missisippi History Now, online magazine; mshistorynow.mdah.state.ms.us/.../sarah-anne-ellis-dorsey).

[6] *Find-a-Grave.*

Soon after her husband died in 1875, Dorsey learned that Jefferson Davis was ill and bankrupt. She invited him to visit at the plantation in December 1876. Davis had been married since 1845 to his second wife, Varina Howell. The Davises had been living with their eldest daughter and her family in Memphis. Davis moved into Beauvoir on a permanent basis, where Dorsey provided him with a cottage on the grounds for his use.

There he began to write his memoir, *The Rise and Fall of the Confederate Government.* Rumors quickly began to fly that the two were having an illicit affair, and it was nearly "an open scandal," but they refused to yield to it. Varina Davis became enraged and refused for a long time to set foot on Dorsey's property. Eventually she accepted Dorsey's invitation to live there and moved into one of the guest cottages at Beauvoir.

In the summer of 1878, Sarah Dorsey nursed Varina through a long debilitating illness. Soon afterward, Sarah Dorsey learned that she had inoperable tumors in her breast. As her health declined, Varina Davis became her primary nurse. Recognizing that she was dying, Dorsey rewrote her will in 1878. She bequeathed all her capital and, more importantly, the family plantation to Jefferson Davis.[1] After the Davis's death, the estate was bequeathe to Misses Comfort and Mary Dorsey of Ellicott City, daughters of WHG Dorsey, listed below.[2]

WILLIAM HENRY GOODWIN DORSEY (1819-1862)

Admitted to Montgomery County Bar 1842[3]

BIRTH/PARENTS: William Henry Goodwin Dorsey was born 15 May 1819 in Elkridge, Anne Arundel County, (now Howard County) MD[4] to Thomas Beale Dorsey, b. 17 Oct. 1780, d. 26 Dec. 1855, Attorney General 1822-24, Chief Judge of the Maryland Court 1848-1851, and Milcah Goodwin Dorsey, b. 1782, d. 25 Sep. 1850. His older brother, Samuel Worthington Dorsey, also an attorney is listed above.

MARRIAGE:

1. Elizabeth Worthington Dorsey, b. May 1823, d. Apr. 1847, daughter of Charles Worthington Dorsey (1785-1864) and Mary Tolly Worthington Dorsey (1791-1868).
2. Comfort Worthington Dorsey, b. 29 Aug. 1830, d. 16 Dec. 1893, daughter of Charles Samuel Worthington Dorsey, b. 6 Mar. 1797, d. 9 Jul. 1845, and Mary Pue Ridgely Dorsey, b. 13 Feb. 1802, d. 18 Sep. 1872.

CHILDREN:

1. Thomas B. Dorsey, b. Jan. 1855, d. 17 Dec. 1855.
2. Mary Ridgley Dorsey, b. 7 Oct. 1856, d. 25 Aug. 1907, unmarried.
3. Comfort W. Dorsey, b. 10 Oct. 1857, d. 19 Aug. 1910, unmarried.

---

[1] From the above Wikipedia article and Notable American Women - 1607-1950, A Biographical Dictionary, Edward T. James, Harvard University Press, 1971, Vol. I, p.505.

[2] Warfield, *Founders of Anne Arundel and Howard Counties,* 495.

[3] Scharf, 668.

[4] Warfield, *Founders of Anne Arundel and Howard Counties* 495

4. John T.W. Dorsey, b. Mar. 1860, d. 3 Feb. 1861

DEATH On 24 Oct. 1862, Ellicott City, Howard County, MD.

JOHN GLISAN ENGLAND (1806-1883)

Admitted to Montgomery County Bar 1830[1]
Member of House of Delegates from 1839

BIRTH/PARENTS: John Glisan England was born 20 Oct. 1806 in Frederick County to Amos England (d. bef. 1830) and Rebecca Glisan England,[2] b. 18 Aug. 1786, d. 17 Feb. 1828. They were married in Frederick County on 20 Jan. 1806.

LEGAL CAREER: He was elected to the Maryland House of Delegates in 1839 and served two terms. He was twice nominated to the Maryland Senate but declined to run for office. He served for many years on the Board of Trustees of the Rockville Academy.[3]

MARRIAGE On 4 May 1830, by license in Montgomery County, Emily Howard, b. 12 Feb. 1812, d. 18 June 1852, daughter of Thomas Worthington Howard (b. , d. 29 July 1818)[4] and Elizabeth Ridgely (Crabb) (b. 1789, d. aft 1850[5]) Howard, who were married by license in Montgomery County, 26 March 1807.[6]

CHILDREN:[7]

1. Susan R. England (1832-1898) unmarried. Died at her home in Rockville, June 1898[8].
2. Thomas H. England (1834-1919) unmarried. "age 88, died Apr. 9th at his home near Rockville."[9]
3. Harriet V. England (1838-1925) unmarried "age 86, died on Jan. 26th at the home of her nieces in Rockville."[10]
4. Henry Clay England (1840-1895) unmarried. Identified as a lawyer in Rockville, he was killed when struck by an electric car in Kensington[11].

---

[1] *Portrait & Biographical Record*, sketch of John Glisan England Jr., 685,
[2] England, *John England,* 19.
[3] *Portrait & Biographical Record,* p. 685-6.
[4] MCHS cemetery files, Family Cemetery on Derwood Road
[5] She lived with family on the 1850 census.
[6] Manuel, Marriage Licenses, p.160. *Sentinel,* Feb. 2, 1883. Obituary for John G. England, stated his wife was Emily Howard, daughter of Thomas Worthington Howard and granddaughter of General Jeremiah Crabb.
[7] MCHS Cemetery Card file – the five unmarried children, along with birth and death years, are listed on a stone with their mother, in the Derwood, Crabb Family Cemetery.
[8] Malloy, S*entinel,* 24 Jun 1898.
[9] Malloy, *Sentinel,* 11 April 1919.
[10] Malloy, *Sentinel,* 30 Jan. 1925.
[11] Malloy, *Sentinel,* 5 July 1895.

5. Mary Ridgely England (1843-1923) unmarried. "An aged resident of Rockville died Thursday of last week."[1]
6. John Glisan England, Jr., b.19 Feb. 1845, d. 28 Feb. 1913,[2] married 22 April 1867 by Montgomery County license,[3] Annie L. Griffith, (b. 29 Sept 1847, d. 3 June 1905), daughter of Uriah Griffith, (1825-1896) and Henrietta Elizabeth Wilcoxin Griffith (1821-1905). Fifteen children.

DEATH 30 January 1883 at age 76.[4]

W. T. EWAN

Possibly William Tecumseh Evans (1830-1915)
Admitted to Montgomery County Bar in 1850[5]

BIRTH/PARENTS: William Tecumseh Evans was born about 1830 [6], probably in Washington, D.C. His parents have not been identified.

LEGAL CAREER: On 1870 Census, listed occupation as Clerk. His obituary stated he had worked in the War Dept., later transferring to the Pension Office, where he served for a third of a century.

MARRIAGE: 27 October 1853 in Washington, D.C. [7] to Josephine L. Anderson, b. 1837 in Montgomery County, Maryland, daughter of Richard S. Anderson (1803-1847) and Martha C. (Love) Anderson[8] "sister of Charles Anderson of Berry's District, she died May 1886."[9]

CHILDREN[10]

1. Susan Evans b, ca. 1865
2. Madge Evans b. ca. 1874

DEATH 5 May 1915. Beginning in 1907, he had received an Army Pension. He was a member of the Lincoln Post GAR.

[1] Malloy, *Sentinel,* 21 Dec. 1923.
[2] MCHS Cemetery File, Rockville Cemetery.
[3] Manuel, *Marriage Licenses,* p.105.
[4] *Sentinel,* Feb. 2, 1883.
[5] Scharf, 668
[6] 1870 Census, Washington, D.C., from Ancestry.com – the only census year in which he was found.
[7] Pippenger, *National Intelligencer, Marriage and Death Notices, 1851-1854.* P. 191.
[8] Cook, *Anderson-Brown Family of Montgomery County, MD.,* April 1984.
[9] *Malloy, Genealogical Abstracts,* Sentinel, May 14, 1886. Died last Friday.
[10] 1870 Census, Washington, D.C. lists himself, wife and two probable children, Susan 15 and Madge age 6.

BENJAMIN STODDERT FORREST (1792-1840)

State Delegate and Senator from Montgomery County 1817-1834

BIRTH/PARENTS: Benjamin Stoddert Forrest was born 22 October 1792, at Rosedale, in Cleveland Park, Washington, D.C.[1] to Col. Uriah Forrest (1756-1805) and Rebecca Plater Forrest. (1765-1843).

POLITICAL CAREER: Benjamin S. Forrest served in the Maryland House of Delegates from 1817-1821 from Montgomery County and in the Senate from 1826-1836, serving as the Senate President from 1831-1834[2]. In 1828, Benjamin S. Forrest, Esq. was the Presidential Elector for the 2nd District.[3]

MARRIAGE: 18 Feb. 1823, in Montgomery County, to Anna Maria Summers,[4] b. 8 Feb. 1799, d. May 1874[5], Washington, D.C., daughter of John Letton Summers, 1764-1802 and Anna Maria Letton Summers, b. 14 Jan. 767, d. 18 Dec.1843 testate, who married 2. Thomas Linstead (1760-1814) and 3rd to William Willson (1760-1832). Anna was a sister of Rueben Summers.

CHILDREN None identified.

DEATH: 12 May 1840[6], testate, in Montgomery County, Maryland.[7]

URIAH FORREST (1803-1867)

Admitted to Montgomery County Bar 1826

BIRTH/PARENTS: Uriah Forrest was born about 1803 in Virginia to Henry Forrest (1772-1826) and Jane [Love] Forrest (1777-1861).[8]

LEGAL CAREER: 9 June 1826. "Uriah Forrest, Atty at Law, will practice in Montgomery County Court[9]. He was listed as a lawyer on the 1850 census. Served as Clerk to Commissioners of Montgomery County in 1860[10]

MARRIAGE: No record of marriage or family. Single in 1850 & 1860 censuses.

---

1 Mann-Kenny, *Rosedale*, 32.

2 Maryland State Archives, biographical series, MSA SC 3520-1589.

3 Maryland State Archives On-Line, Vol. 208, p. 50. "Proceedings of the Electors of President and Vice President of the United States in Maryland, 1789-1980."

4 Manuel, *Marriage Licenses,* p 113

5 Pippenger, *District of Columbia Interments, 122;* Pippenger, *Oak Hill Cemetery,* V. 2, p. 102, she was removed from Presbyterian Cemetery in 1883. She was on the 1860 census in Rockville, age 61 (Hurley) and she was active in Montgomery County Deed Records, the last one recorded in 1872, at which time she was living in Washington, D.C.

6 On memorial tablet in *Oakhill Cemetery*, Pippenger, V.2, p. 101.

7 Malloy, *Wills,* 1826-1875, p. 53

8 www. Find-A-Grave. Accessed 12 Aug. 2016.

9 Dixon, *National Intelligencer,* 9 June 1826

10 Scharf, p 667

DEATH: 15 July 1867, in Washington, D.C., at the residence of his brother on I St., Uriah Forrest of Rockville, Montgomery County[1]. Buried in Rock Creek Cemetery, Washington, D.C. On tombstone with parents and two brothers: Charles Wayman Forrest, 1802-1883 and Henry Forrest (1806-1860)[2].

WILLIAM COLLINSON GOTT (1816-1850)

Admitted to the Montgomery County Bar 1839[3].
Member House of Delegates from Montgomery County, 1840-1841[4]
Montgomery County Levy Court/County Commission in 1850-1851[5]

BIRTH/PARENTS: William Collinson Gott was born 10 Feb. 1816, in Anne Arundel County, to Richard Gott (1776 - 1858) and his second wife, Sarah Collinson (1784 – 1826). Richard Gott first married Lydia Nichols and then Sarah Collinson in 1802

LEGAL CAREER: Only one reference, noted as taking a seat as a member of the Slave-Holders Convention. See "Proceedings of the Slave-Holders Convention", Niles National Register, Vol. 61, February 5, 1842, p.356. "The Slave-holders' Convention assembled in Annapolis from January 12-14, 1842. The convention recommended numerous measures to the Maryland Legislature, many of which became law, tightening the bonds of slavery and increasing restrictions for free blacks.[6]

MARRIAGE: No record of marriage or children.

DEATH: Not mentioned in 1856 will of Richard Gott.[7] Family files on Ancestry give date as 1850-51. Not located on 1850 census.

EDWARD HAMMOND (1812-1882)

Admitted to Montgomery County Bar 1834[8]

BIRTH/PARENTS: Edward Hammond was born 7 Mar. 1812 in Ellicott City, MD, to Lloyd Thomas Hammond, b. 11 Aug. 1779, d. 12 May 1839, and Elizabeth Meriweather Hammond, b. 22 Oct. 1787, d. 17 Dec. 1820[9].

---

[1] Dixon, *National Intelligencer, 1967,* p. 303, 16 July 1867.
[2] Died in Feb. 1860 of paralysis, occupation clerk in bank. From *Ancestry.com,* Mortality census
[3] Scharf, 668.
[4] Scharf, 667.
[5] Scharf, 665.
[6] William H. Marriott , MSA SC 3520- 1588,msa.maryland.gov/megafile/ms and Scharf, History of Maryland, Vol. III, p.325-326.
[7] Manuel et.al., *Wills of Montgomery County, 1826-1875*
[8] Scharf, 668.
[9] MCHS Hammond Family File.

EDUCATION: Attended the common schools, Rockhill Academy, and Yale College, from which he graduated in 1830. Studied law for one year at Yale Law School, and two years in Baltimore with Reverdy Johnson[1].

LEGAL CAREER Served in the Maryland House of Delegates from Anne Arundel County in 1839, 1841 `and 1842, and also served as a member of the Maryland Senate in 1848. Late in 1848, he was elected as a Democrat to the 31st and 32nd Congresses. Elected to the House of Delegates from Howard County in 1861 and 1867. Later elected Associate Judge of the fifth judicial district of Maryland in 1867 and served until his death.[2]

MARRIAGE On 2 Jun. 1842, Married Mary Catherine Mackubin, b. 4 Jun. 1822, d. 23 May 1900, daughter of George Mackubin, b. 9 Mar. 1789, d. 11 Jan. 1853, and Eleanor Carroll Maccubbin Mackubin, b. 11 May 1795, d. 9 Dec 1858[3]. It is interesting to note that she is a descendant of Nicholas Maccubbin and Mary Clare Carroll Maccubbin, daughter of Charles Carroll, who had no male descendants, so some of Maccubbin's sons, took the name Carroll.

CHILDREN[4]

1. George Maccubbin Hammond, b. Nov. 1844, d. 29 Jan. 1852.
2. Alice Hammond, b. 4 Oct. 1847, d. 10 Aug. 1893, m. 2 Jan. 1872, William Allen Hammond (b. 10 Apr. 1847, d. 28 Sep. 1892).
3. Frank Lloyd Hammond, b. 2 Mar. 1850, d. 19 Aug. 1913, m. 6 Dec. 1870, Frances Maria Cook, b. Jul. 1845.
4. Dr. Richard Creagh Hammond, b. 25 Aug. 1852, d. 13 Jun. 1909.
5. Lola Augusta Hammond, b. 10 Jan.1856, d. 18 Jan. 1921, m. 20 Nov. 1879, Frederick Boller Graf Whelan (b. 21 Jun. 1849, d. 3 May 1914).
6. Elizabeth Merriweather Hammond, b. 1 Jul. 1861, d. after 1910, m. 5 Jun. 1888, George Thomas (b. 12 May 1858, d. 1 Jun. 1897).
7. Edward Hammond, b. 3 Apr 1865, d. 12 Apr 1947, m. 1. On 16 Jun. 1904, Emily Potter Cuyler, (b. 21 Apr 1870, d. 23 Jun 1906); m. 2. on 14 Jan 1909, Agnes Cuyler, (b. 23 Apr. 1869, d. 19 Jun. 1936)

DEATH: On 19 Oct. 1882 at "Font Hill," near Ellicott County, MD, in the house where he was born. Buried St. John's Cemetery near Ellicott City.[5]

---

[1] *Biographical Directory of the U.S. Congress, 999.*
[2] *Biographical Directory of the U.S. Congress, 999*
[3] MCHS Maccubbin Family File.
[4] MCHS Hammond Family File, "Descendants of Lloyd Thomas Hammond"
[5] www.Find-A-Grave.com

WILLIAM R. HARDING (1818-1843)

Admitted to the Montgomery County bar in 1839[1]

BIRTH/PARENTS: William R. Harding was born about 1818 in Rockville to Henry Harding (1782-1863) and Catherine Ann (Robb) Harding (1792-1863) They were married on 2 June 1812. Catherine's sister Jane Robb had married Upton Beall, the first resident Clerk of the Court of Montgomery County. Henry Harding was a Judge of the Orphans Court.

EDUCATION: No record was found, but it is likely that he learned his law practice with his father and uncle in the Montgomery County Court.

CAREER: W.R. Harding is listed as a clerk in 1841 at the Arsenal in Augusta, Georgia. He served in the Quartermaster's Department and as a Military Storekeeper under Captain H. A. Fay[2].

MARRIAGE/CHILDREN There is no record of a marriage or children.

DEATH: He was wounded in a gun fight in Augusta, Georgia on 30 March 1843, dying two days later, Saturday, 1 April 1843.[3] The fight and death were reported in various newspapers; there also appears to exist a book on the subsequent trial of the other man, W.H. Platt, which concluded that Platt was not guilty.

JAMES BARNES HENDERSON (1845-1917)

Admitted to Montgomery County Bar in 1868[4]

BIRTH/PARENTS: James Barnes Henderson was born 23 Mar. 1845 in Neelsville, MD, on his grandfather's farm to James S. H. Henderson (1815-1882) and Rosanna Neel Henderson, (daughter of Joseph Neel (1787-1855) and Isabella Barnes Neel (1787-1833)[5] of Neelsville).[6]

EDUCATION: He attended public schools and the Normal School in Pennsylvania. He taught school in Pennsylvania when only 17 years old. He returned to Maryland and continued to teach for 3 years while studying law.[7]

LEGAL CAREER: He began at the law office of Brewer and Peter of Rockville. After being admitted to the Montgomery County Bar in 1868, he started practice in Berkeley Springs, WV. In 1869 he returned to Rockville as a partner with George Peter. In 1880 he began the first of two terms as Maryland States' Attorney. On 1 Jan 1895 he was appointed Associate Judge of the 6th Judicial Circuit by Maryland Governor Frank Brown and he was elected and served a 15 year term. He was a director of the Montgomery

---

[1] Scharf, 668.

[2] *Official Register of the United States, 1841*, Page 119.

[3] *The Southern Banner,* 7 April 1843 (made available online by a very unexpected source: MacQaurie University of Sydney, Australia) "From the Augusta Constitutionalist of the 1st inst".

[4] Scharf, 668.

[5] MCHS Neel Family File.

[6] Portrait and Biographical Record, 749-750.

[7] MCHS Henderson Family File.

County National Bank since its founding in 1883. He served as a directory of the Rockville Cemetery Association and as trustee and treasurer of the Rockville Academy.[1]

MARRIAGE: On 11 Aug. 1870, Clara Smith Adamson, b. 13 July 1846, d. 8 Dec 1926, daughter of Walter Hilleary Adamson (1821-1858) and Margaret Ann Alby Adamson (1824-1853)[2].

CHILDREN[3]

1. James Alby Henderson, b. 7 Jun. 1871, d. 2 Nov. 1926; m. 3 Feb. 1915, Washington, D.C., to Mabel Anderson Spencer, (b. Dec. 1895, still living in 1940 in Washington, D.C.) daughter of Thomas H. Spencer (b. 10 Apr. 1867, d. 5 May 1913) and Cora Caroline Couch Spencer (b. 15 Nov. 1863, d. 4 Aug. 1937). He was also an attorney.
2. Rose Mary Henderson, b. 1873, d. 29 Nov. 1944, Rockville, MD, unmarried.
3. Margaret Adamson Henderson, b. 6 Jan. 1875, d. 15 Feb. 1958, Rockville, MD, unmarried.
4. George Peter Henderson, b. 2 Feb. 1877, d. 14 Oct. 1954, m. Nov. 1899 in Charlestown, WV, to Mary M. Welsh (b. 8 May 1879, d. 31 Mar. 1962) daughter of Warner W. Welsh and Anna Jane Clagett Smith Welsh..
5. Sarah Isabella Henderson, b. 9 Jul.1878, d. 21 May 1953, m. 26 Nov. 1904 in Berkeley Springs, WV, James Taliafero Bridges. (b. 8 Jul 1872, d. 10 Jan. 1954) of Hancock, MD.
6. Frederick Neel Henderson, b. 2 Sep. 1880, d. 7 Apr 1918, Camp Oglethorpe, GA; m. 30 Oct 1912, Memphis, TN, Gussie Glenn Lamar (b.24 Jun 1891, d. 15 Nov. 1973), dau. of Major William Harmong Lamar (also an attorney, see sketch) and his wife Virginia Longstreet Lamar. She m.2., before 1928. Robert Lytle of College Park, MD (b. b. 3 Aug. 1887 in Washington, D.C., d. 3 Oct. 1940). He was buried in Arlington Cemetery with his wife.
7. Walter H. Henderson, b. 2 Jun 1882, d. 18 Nov. 1911, unmarried.
8. Vernon Lee Henderson, b. 31 Dec. 1886, d. 27 Dec.1890, buried Rockville Cemetery.

DEATH: 27 May 1917 in Rockville, MD. Buried in Rockville Cemetery.

---

[1] *Portrait and Biographical Record*, 749-750.

[2] Her parents dates are from a stone erected in the James B. Henderson cemetery plot. MCHS Cemetery card file.

[3] MCHS Henderson Family File.

REVERDY JOHNSON (1796-1876)

Admitted to Montgomery County Bar 1835[1]

BIRTH/PARENTS: Reverdy Johnson was born 21 May 1796 in Annapolis, MD, to John Johnson, b. 12 Sep. 1770, d. 30 Jul. 1824, and Deborah Ghieselen Johnson, b. 1770, d. 19 Nov. 1847. John Johnson served Maryland in both houses of the Legislature,[2] and he was a Judge of the Court of Appeals and Attorney-General of Maryland. Deborah was the daughter of Reverdy Ghiselin, Commissioner of the Land Office at Annapolis.

EDUCATION: Graduated in 1811 from St. John's College in Annapolis; read law with his own father and later with Judge Stephen.[3]

LEGAL CAREER: Admitted to the Bar in 1815 in Upper Marlborough, Prince George's County, MD. During his career of almost sixty years he had a reputation for a fine memory, cross-examination, and oratory. In the time of his early legal career he kept records of the Maryland Court of Appeals, along with clerk Thomas Harris. In November 1817 he moved to Baltimore. In 1854, with Thaddeus Stevens, he successfully protected the reaper patent of Cyrus McCormick. His most famous case was in arguing in Dred Scott vs. Sanford against freedom for bondsman Scott. In 1821 he became a State Senator from Baltimore for two terms but resigned during his second term. In 1849 he became President Taylor's attorney-general but was affected by a scandal involving his decision on the "Galphin claim." He sympathized strongly with the Union during the Civil War, was again elected US. Senator in 1863. In 1868 he was appointed Minister to Great Britain. When President Grant was elected he returned to his law practice and defended the Ku Klux Klan in South Carolina.[4]

MARRIAGE: On 16 November 1819 to Mary Mackall Bowie, b. 12 Dec. 1801, d. 19 Mar. 1873, in Baltimore, MD. Her parents were cousins, John Contee Bowie (1771-1813), and her namesake, Mary Mackall Bowie (1775-1825), the daughter of Robert Bowie, the 1st Democratic Governor of Maryland, and Priscilla Mackall[5]

CHILDREN[6]

1. John Johnson (1820-1887).[1]

---

[1] Scharff, 666.
[2] *Dictionary of American Biography,* Vol. V., 112-114.
[3] *Biographical Cyclopedia of Representative Men,*. 677-678.
[4] Doliante, *Maryland and Virginia Coloni*als, 914-918.
[5] Bowie, Across the Years ..., p. 698-698 & 743-744.
[6] *Ibid,* and Doliante, op.cit., who confuses the Bowie generations and skips John Contee Bowie in lineage. The 1850 Census (Ancestry) lists Camilla, 22, Matilda 20, Emily 17, Reverdy 22, Louis E., 13, Ella 11, Bowie 9 and Edw C. 6.

2. Mary Bowie Johnson (1822-1915)[2] m. 1 Jan 1846, Thomas Hollingsworth Morris of Baltimore (1817-1872). Had issue.
3. Eliza Johnson, b. abt 1823, d. 28 Dec. 1897,[3] Alexandria, VA. m. as his second wife, Henry Daingerfield (1802-1866).[4] He was first married to Susan Sewell, (1803-1837), sister in law of Philip Barton Key, another prominent lawyer.
4. Reverdy Johnson, Jr.[5] (1825-1907)[6] m. Caroline Patterson, who d. bef 1870, no children. He also was an attorney.
5. (Frances) Camilla Johnson (1826-after 1870) m. 20 May 1857 to Andrew Sterrett Ridgely (1826-1877). His occupation in 1870 was Attorney at law; in 1860, Lawyer. Educated at Johns Hopkins Lived in Baltimore. His father, Charles Sterrett Ridgely, was Speaker of Maryland House of Delegates.
6. Maria Louisa Johnson (1827-1893), m. 1846 in Baltimore to William Riggins Travers (1819-1887).[7]
7. Matilda Elizabeth Johnson (1830-1915) m. 26 Jan 1858, Charles J. M. Gwinn (1822-1894).
8. Emily Contee Johnson (1832-1909, Berryville VA)[8] m. 25 March 1852, George Washington Lewis (1829-1885).[9]
9. Louis Eichelberger Johnson (1837-1905), m. 1. Mary Hamilton, and 2 Mary Bostwick in Washington, D.C. By 1900, he was divorced. [1] Had issue.

---

[1] Listed as a child with these dates, but no information to substantiate this found. He may be one of several children who died young.

[2] Dates from www.Findagrave.com, Greenmount Cemetery, Baltimore. Found on Ancestry, 1870 Census, in Baltimore.

[3] *The Washington Post,* December 30, 1897, *Proquest Historical Newspapers,* obituary for Mrs. Henry Daingerfield, identifies her as the second daughter of the Hon. Reverdy Johnson, 76 years old, interment in Greenmount Cemetery, Baltimore. She was not found on Find A Grave, as were many of the other Johnsons buried in Greenmount.. The name "Eliza" is from the 1860 Census, in Alexandria, found on Ancestry.com, where she is found living with Henry W. Daingerfield, and daughters from his first marriage and her children, including a Reverdy J. Daingerfield.

[4] Sargent, *Stones and Bones,* Buried at Poplar Hill, the Sewell Family Cemetery in Prince George's County.

[5] Reverdy Johnson, Jr., who lived in Baltimore, MD. He enlisted in the Union Army during the Civil War and was transferred to the Navy 1864 Apr 17 and served until he was dismissed in 1865 Jan 10.[5] The 1860 US Federal Census for Baltimore, MD lists him as a lawyer.[5] He appears in the 1900 US Federal Census for Baltimore, MD and is a widower.

[6] *The Washington Post,* July 16, 1907, *Proquest Historical Newspapers.* "Reverdy Johnson Dead. Baltimorean was son of Maryland's Famous Senator and Diplomat.." Details education, gives information on his wife;s family and her earlier death, and states that there were no children.

[7] *The Washington Post,* March 29, 1887, ProQuest Historical Newspapers, obituary: "The Late Wm R. Travers" lists his wife as "Miss Lulu Johnson, daughter of the late Reverdy Johnson" and lists their nine children, as well as eleven children for Reverdy Johnson, including his wife, "his fourth daughter." On census records, she is generally named Louisa Travers.

[8] *The Washington Post,* April 4, 1909, ProQuest Historical Newspapers, "Mrs. Contee Lewis Dead, Daughter of Late Senator Johnson and Related to Washington," died Berryville, Va. April 8, Mrs. E. Milley Contee Lewis, widow of George Washington Lewis and daughter of Reverday Johnson, ...aged 78. Four sons and five daughters (named) survive.

[9] Cemetery Records on Find A Grave, Census records on Ancestry.

10. Ella Johnson (1839-1898), m. Charles Goldsborough Kerr (1838-1898).[2]
11. (Thomas) Bowie Johnson, (1841, d. 29 Sep. 1893 Garrett County MD.) m. Virginia Mary Thayer, daughter of Ralph Thayer of Allegany County, merchant.[3]
12. Maj. Edward Contee Johnson, (1844-1905), m. abt 1869, Kate (Catherine) Moore (1845-after 1920) of Virginia.[4]

DEATH: On 10 May, 1876, from an accidental fall in Annapolis, MD. Buried at Green Mount Cemetery, Baltimore, Md.[5]

SPENCER CONE JONES (1836-1915)

Admitted to Frederick County Bar 1860
Admitted to Montgomery County Bar 1868

BIRTH/PARENTS: Spencer Cone Jones was born 3 July 1836 in Rockville Maryland to Rev. Joseph H. and Elizabeth (Clagett) Jones. His father was a Baptist minister.[6] The family moved to Frederick, MD when he was nine years old.[7]

EDUCATION: He attended Rockville Academy, Frederick College, and studied law under J. W. Ross.[8]

LEGAL CAREER: He was admitted to the Frederick County bar in 1860[9]; and admitted to the Montgomery County bar in 1868;[10] when he established a law office in Rockville[11]; elected States Attorney and served 2 terms, 1871-1879; served as Maryland State Treasurer;[12] president of the Maryland State Senate, 1871-1879; clerk of the Maryland Court of Appeals and served 12 years.[13]

MARRIAGE: On 21 Dec. 1871, to Ellen Brewer, (b.22 July 1845, d. 21 July 1876) daughter of to John Chiswell Brewer (b. 14 Sept. 1804, d. 10 July 1866)[14] and Elizabeth Stewart (Buchanan) Brewer (b. 16 Sep 1813, d. 18 Apr. 1882).[15] Her father and brother were also attorneys. See sketches.

---

[1] Ancestry.com 1900 census Washington, D.C., and family trees, Buried at Greenmount Cemetery.
[2] Ancestry.com, Framily Trees, census records.
[3] *Ibid.*
[4] *Ibid.* 1870 Census in Baltimore gives her name as Catherine. His occupation as a Lawyer. Living in Catonsville.
[5] Find A Grave records.
[6] *Portrait and Biographical Record,* 139, 140.
[7] *Portrait and Biographical Record,* 139.
[8] Steiner, *Men of Mark in Maryland, V.1,* 228.
[9] Scharf, 416.
[10] Scharf, 668.
[11] *Portrait and Biographical,* 139.
[12] *Portrait and Biographical,* 140.
[13] Steiner, 228.
[14] MCHS Cemetery Card File, buried Rockville Cemetery.
[15] *Sentinel,* 5 Jan. 1872.

CHILDREN: Elizabeth Jones, b. 1875, d. 1940, m. Thomas R. Falvey of New Orleans, La. Elizabeth and Thomas are buried at Mt. Olivet Cemetery, Frederick, MD.[1]

DEATH: 1 April 1915 "...at the home of his daughter in New Orleans."[2] He and Ellen are buried at Mt. Olivet Cemetery, Frederick, MD[3]

NOTES: He was unable to begin the practice of law because of the onset of the Civil War; he was arrested as a Southern sympathized and imprisoned for 8 months; after which he enlisted in Co. D. 1st Maryland Confederate Cavalry and served until the end of the war.[4] After the war, he taught school in Texas for 2 years before he returned to Rockville in 1867 or 1868.[5] He was elected Mayor of Rockville, In May 1898 and resigned Nov 1901;[6] Helped to establish and was president of Montgomery County National Bank in 1892;[7] he was a mason and a charter member of the Ridgeley Brown Camp of the Veterans of the Civil War; "He conceived the plan and was a most helpful assistant in the building of the monument to our departed comrades, which adorns the public square in this town."[8] (It is held that he was the model for the Confederate statue on the lawn of the Montgomery County Court House, 1891.); vice-president of the Visitors of the State School for the Deaf in Frederick, Md. [9]

ALEXANDER KILGOUR (1799-1867)

Admitted to the Montgomery County Bar in 1826
Member of House of Delegates 1843[10]

BIRTH/PARENTS: Alexander Kilgour was born about 1799, to William and Sarah (Edgerton) Kilgore[11] of Saint Mary's County, MD.

EDUCATION: He graduated from Charlotte Hall and from Union College in 1819.[12]

LEGAL CAREER: In politics, he was an old line Whig. He moved to Rockville in 1822, practiced law in Leonardtown and Rockville, and was elected to the State Legislature from Leonardtown and Rockville, 1847-1855.[13] He was Episcopalian.

---

1 Holdcraft, *Names In Stone,* 394
2 *Sentinel*, 9 Apr 1915
3 Holdcraft, 630
4 *Portrait and Biographical Record,* 139. Also see Jacobs, *Confederate Soldiers,* 90.
5 Steiner, 228
6 MCHS_Vertical File : Rockville History File : Mayors.
7 Portrait and Biographical..., 140
8 *Sentinel,* 17 Aug. 1917
9 Steiner, 229
10 Scharf, 667.
11 Kilgore Family File, MCHS.
12 Kilgore Family File, MCHS.
13 Hiebert & McMaster, *Grateful Remembrance,* p.146-148

MARRIAGE: On 1 November 1832 in Loudoun County, VA, to Margaret Ann Stribling, (b. 1815 Frederick County, VA; d. 6 May 1903, Rockville, MD[1]), daughter of Francis and Cecelia (McIlhaney) Stribling.

[1] Church Records File, MCHS Records of Christ Episcopal Church, age given as 86 years.

CHILDREN :

1. William Kilgour, b. 24 July 1834, d. 14 July 1907;[1] m. 27 October 1858, at Rockville[2], Rose Ellen Queen (ca. 1834, buried 12 Sept. 1886.).[3]
2. Cecelia Kilgour (1835-1902) m. 27 Oct. 1863, St. Mary's Catholic Church, Samuel Jones.[4]
3. Francis Stribling Kilgour, b 10 Oct 1836, d. 22 July 1917,[5] m. Margaret McIlhany Heaton (23 Aug 1848-26 Aug. 1909)[6] daughter of Dr. James Decatur Heaton and Cecelia, his wife.
4. Charles J. Kilgour, (1840-1863).
5. Martha Matilda Kilgour (1842-1900), m. 21 February 1865, Alexander Chilton of Virginia at her father's home.[7] He followed a legal career in Alexandria, VA.
6. Sarah Edgerton Kilgour b. 5 Feb. 1845, d. 24 Mar. 1934,[8] unmarried. In 1880 she was a teacher, her mother Margaret was head of household. In 1900, at age 55, she and her mother age 84, were both listed as Capitalists, living with her brother Francis and his family.[9]
7. Virginia Kilgour, b. 1847, d. 21 Oct. 1878, m. Charles Vandervender.[10]
8. Alexander Kilgour, Jr., b. 1855, d. 13 Apr. 1917, [11] m. 9 October 1924, in Rockville, Md., [12] Elizabeth Barrett Prettyman. (1866-1954).[13] He was also an attorney, see biography.

DEATH: 1 September 1867 "in his 68th year" buried at the Baptist Church Cemetery.[14] Tombstone in Rockville Cemetery with wife, son Francis and daughter Sarah.[15]

JOHN A. T. KILGOUR (1795-1826)

Member of House of Delegates from Montgomery County, 1822

BIRTH/PARENTS: John A. T. Kilgour was born about 1795 to William Kilgour of St. Mary's County. In one sketch, listed as the brother of Charles, Alexander and James

---

[1] Record of interments in St. Mary's Cemeteries. No marker. Cemetery card file, MCHS.
[2] Church Records File, MCHS, St. Mary's Catholic Church Records.
[3] *Ibid.*
[4] Church Records File, MCHS.
[5] *Sentinel,* 27 July 1917.
[6] *Sentinel* 3 Sept 1909.
[7] Church Records File, MCHS, records of Christ Episcopal Church.
[8] *Sentinel,* March 29, 1834.
[9] Hurley, I 1880 Census, *and 1900 Census, p.* 552.
[10] Kilgore Family File, MCHS.
[11] Cemetery Card File. Rockville Cemetery.
[12] *Sentinel, 9 Oct 1914.* In his sketch in the *Portrait and Biographical Encyclopedia,* op.cit., *p. 775-776,* published in 1898, he was not married, the author noted "he has had little time for participation in matters of a fraternal, social or public nature."
[13] *Ibid.*
[14] Records of Christ Episcopal Church in Church Records File, MCHS.
[15] Cemetery Card File, MCHS.

Kilgour. If he is a brother of Charles, then he would be a son of James, and sketch of either Alexander or Charles in this volume is incorrect.[1]

LEGAL CAREER: Admitted to Prince George's County Bar in April 1814[2]. A Rockville lawyer and federal leader, served as member of House of Delegates from Montgomery County, 1822.[3]

MARRIAGE: 4 Dec. 1817, in Baltimore to Ann Elliza Shelmerdine,[4] (b. abt 1798, d. after 1840) daughter of Stephen Shelmerdine (d. Apr.1809, Frederick County) and Eunice Phillips Shelmerdine (1778-1812). As a widow she removed to Baltimore, where she was living in 1839, when in the deed she mentions she was planning to go abroad, and she released her dower to her property[5]. At a sheriff's sale, Charles J. Kilgour purchased the property that John bought from Suter.

CHILDREN:

1. John Allen Thomas Kilgour, Jr., b. abt 1826, d. 11 Apr. 1863, Rockville; m. 6 Feb. 1849, Montgomery County, to Harriett Jones (b. abt 1830), daughter of Evan Jones of Nathan.[6]

DEATH: 14 April 1826, at his residence in Rockville, 31 years of age, "an able lawyer and advocate"[7]

NOTES: Ann E. Kilgour, consort of John A. T. Kilgour, recorded deed 19 March 1818, from Alexander Contee Hanson of Ann Arundel County for 5 shillings, assigned lot #4 of Rockvile. This lot was mentioned in deed above, along with other property deeded to John A. T. Kilgour.

JOHN MORTIMER KILGOUR (1822-1905)

Admitted to Montgomery County Bar 1849

BIRTH/PARENTS: John Mortimer Kilgour was born 19 May 1822 near Rockville, MD; baptized November 26, 1823,[8] son of Judge Charles Jordan Kilgour (1790-1837) born in St. Mary's County, Maryland, and his wife, Louisa McIlhany Kilgour (1799-1822) of Loudoun

---

[1] *Portrait and Biographical Record,* p. 758, sketch of Col. William Kilgour, son of Alexander. "John A.T. was a prominent forensic advocate."

[2] Van Horn, *Out of the Past,* 254.

[3] Scharf, 666.

[4] Barnes, *Maryland Marriages, 1801-1820.*

[5] Montgomery County Land Records, BS9:519-521. William Darne recorded deed of trust 23 Sept. 1839 from Ann E. Kilgour of Baltimore, who is about to go abroad. Widow of Judge Kilgour, her right of dower in lot in Rockville, and other real estate.

[6] Montgomery County Land Records, JGH6:333-334. Sarah Jones, widow of Evan Jones of Nathan recorded deed 28 Dec. 1857 from among others, the heirsof Evan Jones of Nathan, including Harriett N. Kilgour, wife of John A. T. Kilgour. Montgomery County Marriage Licenses.

[7] Wright, F. Edward, *Marriages and Deaths in the newspapers of Frederick and Montgomery Counties, Maryland, 1820-1830,* item 628.

[8] Prince George's Parish Records.

County, Virginia. They were married in Loudoun County on June 16, 1818, but came to Rockville to make their home. After the untimely death of their parents, the two brothers, John Mortimer and James McIlhaney were reared in Rockville by Judge Kilgour's two maiden sisters, Misses Isabella and Charlotte Kilgour.[1]

EDUCATION: Attended Rockville Academy and Harvard Law School

LEGAL CAREER. Practiced law in Montgomery County. Member of the Maryland Constitutional Convention of 1850-1851. Practiced law in Leesburg, Va., after the Civil War and Commonwealth Attorney for Loudoun Co., VA.

MARRIAGE: 5 May 1847 in Montgomery County to Martha Wilson Wootton (1827-1917),[2] daughter of Doctor John and Elizabeth Lynn (Magruder) Wootton.[3]

CHILDREN:[4]

1. Charles Jordan Kilgour (b. Feb 1849, d. after 1910) Episcopalian Minister, married Fannie Claiborne Beaufort, moved to Schuykill County, Pennsylvania.
2. Elizabeth Cornelia Wootton Kilgour (1852-1934) unmarried
3. James McIlhany Kilgour (1855-1937) unmarried
4. Mary Adelaide Wootton Kilgour (1858-1925) unmarried

DEATH: 4 April 1905, near Hillsboro, Virginia.[5]

NOTES Served in the Confederate Army, as Private, Captain and Quartermaster. Member 35th Bn., Va. Cavalry Co. D[6]

BENJAMIN LINCOLN LEAR (1792-1832)

Admitted to Montgomery County Bar 1829[7]

BIRTH/PARENTS: Benjamin Lincoln Lear was born 11 Mar. 1792 to Tobias Lear (1762-1816) and Mary Long Lear, of Portsmouth, NH. She died in 1793. He then married Frances (Bassett) Washington who was Martha Washington's niece and the widow of George Washington's nephew. She died in 1795. Tobias then married Frances Dandridge Henley, another of Martha's nieces[8]. She died on 2 Dec.1856 at the age of 77 years. Tobias Lear graduated from Harvard College in 1783. He was engaged as George Washington's secretary after the war when Washington retired to Mount Vernon, VA.

---

[1] See Jacobs, *Confederate Veterans of Montgomery County,* sketch of John Morimer Kilgour.
[2] *Portrait and Biographical Encyclopedia of the Sixth Congressional District.*
[3] Jacobs, *op.cit.*
[4] Jacobs, *op.cit*
[5] *Sentinel, 7 April 1905.*
[6] Myers, *The Comanches,* p. 84 & 156. This was Lige White's regiment.
[7] Scharf, 667.
[8] *Dictionary of American biography, Vol. VI,* 76< sketch of Tobias Lear.

LEGAL CAREER: In 1815, he placed an advertisement in *National Intelligencer*, "Benjamin L. Lear offers his services as atty at law, Penn av Wash City."[1] He also served as a director of the Bank of Columbia.

MARRIAGE:

1. Maria Morris in July 1826 [2] (died March 1828)[3]
2. On 9 Aug. 1831, Elizabeth (or Louisa) Bomford.[4]

CHILDREN: None mentioned in his will, which divided most of his property between his mother Frances and his wife Louisa, with other bequests to cousins.[5]

DEATH: 1 Oct. 1832 "member of the Washington Bar, after a short illness."[6] Buried at Congressional Cemetery.

ZACCHEUS COLLINS LEE (1805 - 1859)

Admitted to Montgomery County Bar 1832[7]

BIRTH/PARENTS: Zaccheus Collins Lee was born 5 Dec. 1805[8] in Fairfax County, VA, to Richard Bland Lee (1761-1827) and Elizabeth Collins Lee (1768-1858). His first cousin was Robert E. Lee, his uncle was Henry "Light Horse Harry" Lee.[9]

EDUCATION: University of Virginia (where he was a classmate of Edgar Allen Poe)[10] and at Henry St. George Tucker's Winchester Law School, 1827-1828

LEGAL CAREER: Established law practice in Baltimore. Also admitted to the Prince George's County Bar, in April term, 1834[11]. He was United States District Attorney for Maryland from 1841 to 1845, and from 1850 to 1853. Judge of the Superior Court of Baltimore from 1855 to his death

MARRIAGE: 14 June1837 in Baltimore, by Archbishop Eccleston, to Martha Ann deValcourt Jenkins (1819-1864) daughter of Thomas Courtney Jenkins (1802-1881) and Elizabeth (Gould) Jenkins[12].

[1] Dixon, *National Intelligencer,* 15 Jan. 1815.
[2] Dixon, *National Intelligencer,* 31 Jul.1826.
[3] Dixon, *National Intelligencer,*24 Mar. 1828.
[4] Dixon, *National Intelligencer,* 7 Aug. 1831.
[5] Pippenger, District of Columbia Probate Records, 178.
[6] Dixon, *National Intelligencer,*2 Oct. 1832.
[7] Scharf, 667.
[8] SAR membership application, 1889-1970, from Ancestry.com.
[9] Edward Felix Jenkins, *Thomas Jenkins of Maryland, 1670...,* p. 50, 51.
[10] Scharf, *The Chronicles of Baltimore,* p. 530.
[11] Van Horn, *Out of the Past, 305.*
[12] Jenkins, op.cit.

CHILDREN[1]

1. Richard Henry Lee, b. 28 April 1839 in Baltimore, d. 20 March 1883; married Isabella George Wilson.[2] Served as a Private in the Confederate Army. Father of 4.
2. Mary Elizabeth Lee (1840-1904) was born in Baltimore. She first married William Buchanan Perine (1823 - 1863), the son of David Maulden Perine and Mary (Glenn) Perine of "Homeland," Baltimore, MD. William was a lawyer, and his home was at Charles and Eager Streets in Baltimore City. Mary then married in1889, Bernard John Cooper. a Post-Captain in the British Navy. Mary, a mother of 4, died in Rome.
3. Mary Ida Lee (b. c. 1843); died at 6 months of age

DEATH: 28 November 1859 in Baltimore, MD. Buried at Congressional Cemetery, Washington, D.C.[3]

JOHN ALEXANDER LYNCH (1825--1904)

Admitted to Montgomery County Bar 1851

BIRTH/PARENTS: John Alexander Lynch was born 3 October 1825 near Jefferson in Frederick County, MD, to William Lynch (b. 15 Feb. 1788, d. 9 Aug. 1857) and Eliza Boteler Lynch, b. 1797, d. 14 Jan. 1832), all buried in Mt. Olivet Cemetery, Frederick, MD.[4]

EDUCATION: He attended college in Gettysburg, Pennsylvania, and then studied law in the City of Frederick with Montjoy B. Luckett.

LEGAL CAREER: Admitted to the Frederick and Montgomery County Bars in 1851. He served in the Maryland Legislature for three terms, as a Democrat, and served as States Attorney two terms. He was appointed a Judge in the 6th Judicial Circuit in 1867 and served for 30 years.[5]

MARRIAGE: On 17 Nov. 1856 to Isabella C. Beckenbaugh, b. 8 Mar. 1820, d. 18 Jan.1901,[6] daughter of George Beckenbaugh, b. 5 Dec. 1801, d. 14 Apr. 1878 in Baltimore, MD and Martha (Vanes). Beckenbaugh, b. 25 Aug.1798, d. 17 Jan. 1862. Both buried in Mt. Olivet Cemetery, Frederick.[7]

CHILDREN: None.

DEATH: Sunday, 31 Jan. 1904[8].

---

[1] "Zaccheus Collins Lee," Wikipedia.
[2] SAR, op.cit.
[3] *Find A Grave,* which cites *The Evening Star,* 29 November 1859.
[4] Holdcraft, *Names in Stone,* V II, p. 734.
[5] Portrait and Biographical Record, 245-246.
[6] *Sentinel,* 1901, and Holdcraft, *op.cit.*.
[7] Holdcraft, *Names in Stone, V. 1:129.*
[8] Bowman, *Sentinel,* 4 Feb. 1904; Holdcraft, *Names in Stone, V. 2,* 734.

NOTES: He was a Royal Arch Mason in the Masonic Fraternity, an Episcopal Church Vestryman, a director of the Fredericktown Savings Institution and Central National Bank, and President of the Frederick County Historical Society.

JOHN H. G. McCUTCHEN (1827- abt. 1885)

Admitted to Montgomery County Bar 1847[1]

BIRTH/PARENTS John H. G. McCutchen was born abt 1827 in Washington, D.C., to John McCutchen, b. abt. 1800, d. 1862, buried in Oak Hill Cemetery, Georgetown, D.C.[2] and his wife, Ann Bacon McCutchen, (b. 1807, d. after 1860) who he married in 1824 in Washington, D.C.

LEGAL CAREER In 1870 census, Washington, D.C and 1880 Census, Albuquerque, N.M. occupation Lawyer. Admitted to the Montgomery County Bar in 1847[3].

MARRIAGE 28 Dec. 1863 in Washington, D.C. to Annie E. Dawes, b. abt 1833, Maryland, d. after 1885,[4] daughter of Isaac Dawes and Juliana Darby Dawes. (b. 1805, d. bef 1850).[5]

CHILDREN[6]

1. John McCutchen, Jr., b. abt. 1865, d. after 1910 in Texas, m. abt 1894, in Albuquerque to Mary Martin, b. abt.1864, d. 1941 in Los Angeles, CA.
2. Julia McCutchen, b. abt 1868. No other information found.

DEATH After 1880 Census (living at that time in New Mexico) and before 1885, when his widow and two children are found on the state census[7].

---

[1] Scarf, p 668

[2] Pippenger, Oak Hill Cemetery, 87

[3] 1870 & 1880 Census from Ancestry

[4] Washington, D.C. Marriages Licenses, 1858-1870

[5] Darby, *All About Darbys,* Author, 209.

[6] 1870 & 1880 Census from Ancestry

[7] New Mexico Territorial Census, 1885," database with images, *FamilySearch* (https://familysearch.org/ark:/61903/1:1:QV98-NKWJ : 30 September 2014), John H Mccutchen in entry for N E Mccutchen, 1885; citing p. 29, line 25, household ID 455, NARA microfilm publication M846 (Washington D.C.: National Archives and Records Administration, n.d.); FHL microfilm 16,610.

JOHN HAMMOND McELFRESH (1796-1841)

Admitted to Montgomery County Bar 1834[1]

BIRTH/PARENTS: John Hammond McElfresh was born 27 May 1796, near New Market, Frederick County, son of Henry McElfresh(b. 21 July 1776, d. 22 June 1846) and Ariana Hammond McElfresh (b. 15 Sep 1768, d. 7 Jul 1827) .[2].

EDUCATION: Finished his education in Classical Dept. of Frederick College, and in 1813, began the study of Medicine under Dr. L. T. Hammond of Anne Arundel County. In 1816-1817 he attended a course of lectures at the University of Maryland, and was graduated with a Doctor of Medicine in February 1817. In 1822 he abandoned the profession of medicine for law, having previously been chosen register of Frederick Town and a trustee of Frederick Academy. He studied law in Frederick with John Nelson for 3 years..[3]

LEGAL CAREER: Admitted to the Frederick County Bar in 1825. Elected to the House of Delegates in 1830. He had an extensive law practice in Frederick, Washington and Montgomery Counties, as well as the Court of Appeals of the State.

MARRIAGE: On 27 March 1820, to Theresa Mantz[4], (b. 11 Dec. 1794, d. 29 May 1846) daughter of Francis Mantz (b. 26 Jan. 1749, d. 22 May 1823) and Anna Mary Burkhardt Mantz (b. 3 June 1754, d. 12 May 1818)[5].

CHILDREN:

1. Anna Mary McElfresh, b. 14 Mar. 1821, d. 12 Dec. 1878, m. 3 Jan 1848, Jacob M. Kunkel. (b. 24 Jul 1822, d. 7 Apr. 1870.)
2. Francis McElfresh, b. 9 Aug. 1824, d. Feb. 1825.
3. Henry McElfresh, b. 22 Feb. 1826, d. 25 Mar. 1852, at Annapolis, while representing Frederick County in the Assembly.
4. Ariana McElfresh, b. 7 Apr. 1828, d. 8 Jan. 1892, m. Feb. 1851, Charles Edward Trail. (b. 28 Jan. 1825, d. 8 May 1909)[6].
5. Casper Mantz McElfresh, b. abt 1830, d. 25 Dec.1851[7].

DEATH 4 August 1841.

---

[1] Scharf, 667
[2] Scharf, 415; Holdcraft, *Names in Stone,* 745.
[3] Scharf, 415.
[4] Scharf, 415.
[5] Holdcraft, *Names in Stone,* 745, 762.
[6] Williams, *History of Frederick County,* 720-722, sketch of Charles Edward Trail; *Holdcraft,* Names in Stone, *1156.*
[7] Engelbrecht Diary, Vol. II, 715-716.

WILLIAM MATTHEWS MERRICK (1818 - 1889)

Admitted to Montgomery County Bar 1855[1]

BIRTH/PARENTS: William Matthew Merrick was born 1 September 1818, near Faulkner, Charles County, MD[2] to William Duhurst Merrick (1793 – 1857), United States Senator from Maryland, serving from 1838 to 1845, and his second wife, Catherine Boarman Thomas (1800 - 1850).

EDUCATION: He graduated from Georgetown College (now Georgetown University), in 1831 and studied law at the University of Virginia, Charlottesville.

LEGAL CAREER: Private practice, Baltimore, Maryland, 1839-1844, where he was admitted to the bar in 1839; private practice, Frederick, MD, from 1844-1854; Deputy Attorney General, Frederick County, MD, 1845-1850, Judge from 1854, of the U.S. District Court of the District of Columbia, until the court was abolished in 1863.[3]. Senior professor of law, Columbian College, (now GW University), Washington, D.C., 1866-1867. Private practice, Howard County, 1863-1870, and 1873-1886., Maryland State representative, 1870; U.S. representative from Maryland, 1871-1873; Associate Justice, U.S. District Court for the District of Columbia [Supreme Court of the District of Columbia] 1885-1889

MARRIAGE: Married 15 October 1844, Mary B. Wickliffe (b. ca. 1820) of Kentucky.[4]

CHILDREN : No children.

DEATH 4 February 1889.[5] Buried in Oak Hill Cemetery, Washington, DC, in an unmarked grave.

FRANKLIN MINOR (1823-1901)

Admitted to the Montgomery County Bar 1843[1]

---

[1] Scharf,668.

[2] *BDAC,* 1322, sketch of both William Matthew Merrick and his father. Also see Betas of Achievement; being brief biographical records of members of the Beta theta pi who have achieved distinction in various fields of endeavor, Baird, William Raimond), 1914, The Beta publishing co., New York as reported in Wikipedia article on William Matthew Merrick, 2015. Archives of Maryland (Biographical Series); William Matthew S. Merrick (1818-1889) MSA SC 3520-2091.

[3] William Matthew Merrick's Biography from the Federal Judicial Center; Merrick became notorious in the early years of the Civil War by issuing writs of habeas corpus at the instigation of parents demanding that underage sons who had illegally enlisted be sent home; he was legally correct but politically exasperating and the Lincoln administration finally acted against him...see "Sweltering with Treason", The Civil War Trials of William Matthew Merrick, Jonathan W. White, 2007, Prologue Magazine, Summer 2007, Vol. 39, No. 2. It should be noted that his wife came from a rebel family in Kentucky.

[4] Trudie Davis Long & Edith Olivia Eader, *The Jacob Engelbrecht Marriage Ledger of Frederick County, Maryland, 1820 – 1890, p.82.*

[5] *The Washington Post,* 5 February 1889. "Judge Merrick is Dead." ProQuest Historical Newspaper. He was married to the daughter of Judge Wickliffe, Mary Wickliffe of Kentucky, but had no children. At the time his two nieces, Miss Wickliffe and Miss Beckham constituted part of his household.

BIRTH/PARENTS: Franklin Minor was born 4 December 1823 in Fairfax County, VA to George Minor (1771-1862) and Mary Thift Minor (b. abt 1771, 18 Jan 1858). He was baptized 11 Nov. 1827 in Rock Creek Parish, in Montgomery County.[2] His sister, Mary Minor, was married to attorney James W. Anderson, 18 May 1830.

LEGAL CAREER . Although signing the clerks book in Montgomery County in 1843, in 1850 he is found as a School Teacher in Putnam County, Virginia. On the 1880 census, he is a lawyer, in Providence, Fairfax County, Virginia.

MARRIAGE:

1. 29 June 1847, in St. James Church, Leesburg, VA [3],to Eleanor Anderson, (b. abt 1827, d. 1755 in Putnam County (WV)).
2. 25 Aug. 1859, in Washington, D.C. to Mary Driscoll, b. abt 1835 in Ireland, d. after 1920 in Washington, D.C.

CHILDREN:

1. Robert Minor (by first wife) b. 1849 in Virginia, on 1850 census no later records.
2. Mary Virginia Minor, b. 2 June 1869, Washington, D.C., d. 27 Aug. 1920, unmarried, Washington, D.C[4].

DEATH: 1901, Washington, D.C.

NOTES: The Washington Post reported on 2 Dec. 1899 that he was committed to the insane asylum by his daughter, Virginia Minor, formerly a prosperous lawyer, suffering from senile dementia.[5]

JOSHUA MORSELL (1816-1883)

Admitted to Montgomery County Bar 1837[6]

BIRTH/PARENTS: Joshua Morsell, b. ca. 1816, was identified as the son of James S. Morsell Esq. James S. Morsell, acted as a trustee in Montgomery County in 1831 in a deed transaction, at which time he was resident in Washington County, District of Columbia.[7]

EDUCATION: Probably Joshua learned the law profession in his father's office, but he did not remain in the practice of law. In 1839-40, he was a student at the Protestant

---

[1] Scharf, 668

[2] *Prince George's County, Maryland, Index to Register of Prince George's Parish (also known as Rock Crekk) 1791-1845, in two parts, Part II, Montgomery County,* 274.

[3]Vogt & Kethley, compilers, *Loudoun County Virginia Marriages, 1760-1850,* 115.

[4] *The Washington Post,* ProQuest Historical Newspapers, 28 Aug 1920, "she is survived by her mother."

[5] *The Washington Post,* ProQuest Historical Newspapers, 2 Dec. 1899.

[6] Scharf,668.

[7] MCLR, BS4:433 & 437.

Episcopal Theological Seminary in Virginia, and by 1840-1842 he was rector of All Saint's Parish, Frederick County. His second call was St. James Parish, Ann Arundel County, 1843-1855.[1]

MARRIAGE: 25 January 1844, at Upper Marlboro, by Rev. J. Trapnell, rector of Trinity Church, to Jane G. Chesley, daughter of the late Rev. William Fitzhugh Chesley (d. 1843), former rector of St. James[2].

CHILDREN:

1. William F. C. Morsell, b. ca. 1845, d. 1918.

DEATH: 16 Dec. 1883, New York.

JOHN C. MOTTER (1844-1915)

Admitted to Montgomery County Bar 1874[3]

BIRTH/PARENTS: John Columbus Motter was born 14 Dec. 1844[4] in Emmitsburg, Frederick County, MD, to Jacob Motter (b. 2 Mar. 1814, d. 7 Dec. 1872) and Jemima (Troxell) Motter[5] (b. 13 June 1810, d. 11 June 1881).[6]

EDUCATION : Dickinson Seminary, Williamsport, PA. Studied law in office of Grayson Eichelberger of Frederick.[7]

LEGAL CAREER: After his admittance to the Frederick County Bar in 1868, he built a prosperous law practice in Frederick.[8] He was also active in Republican politics. In 1871 he was appointed counsel to the Board of County Commissioners of Frederick County, and in 1875 he was elected state's attorney of Frederick County. In 1882 he ran unsuccessfully for associate judge of the Sixth Judicial Circuit. He ran again for the same position in 1897 and won by a large margin.[9]

MARRIAGE: Married 20 May 1875, to Effie Buhrman Marken, b. 19 Oct. 1853, d. 21 Jun 1911, daughter of Josiah Recher Marken (1825-1903) and Ann Buhrman Marken. (1830-1913)[10].

---

[1] Kanely, *Maryland Ministers,* Vol. II, 105.
[2] *Baltimore American & Commercial Daily Advertiser,* 8 Feb. 1844.
[3] Scharf, 668.
[4] Holdcraft, Names in Stone, v. 2, 820.
[5] *Portrait and Biographical Directory*, 765-766.
[6] Holdcraft, *Names in Stone, v. 2, 820.*
[7] *Portrait and Biographical Directory, 765-766.*
[8] Scharf, 816
[9] Scharf, 817
[10] *Find-A-Grave,* Memorial.

CHILDREN:[1]

1. Roger Motter, b. 14 Mar. 1876, d. 28 Jan. 1958, Frederick County, MD.
2. Bessie Estella Motter, b. 15 Oct. 1878, d. 22 Aug. 1958.
3. Alan Motter, b. 30 Aug. 1879, d. 17 May 1934.
4. Jessie Motter, b. 18 Oct. 1881, d. 15 May 1883.
5. George Motter. b 16 Feb 1883, d. 4 Jul. 1904.
6. Lola Motter, b. 11 May 1884, d. 2 Feb. 1970.
7. Aimee Rebecca Motter, b. 15 Jan. 1887, d. 10 Oct. 1973, Braddock Heights, MD, m. 22 May 1922, Major Francis Asbury Awl (1876-1936). According to her memorial from Find-A-Grave, they had no children, but she was survived by two nieces and great nieces and nephews.
8. Emily Motter, b. 8 May 1889, d. 24 May 1912.
9. Helen Motter, b. 6 Feb. 1892, d. 21 Dec. 1956.

DEATH: 12 June 1915.[2] Buried in Mt. Olivet Cemetery in Frederick.

NOTES: He served as attorney for Citizens National Bank, Frederick; and as a director of the Frederick & Middletown Railroad, Frederick County.

CARRINGTON SCOTT NELSON (1853-1887)

Admitted to Montgomery County Bar 1874[3]

BIRTH/PARENTS: Carrington Scott Nelson was born about 1853 in Pennsylvania,[4] to Rev. John Scott Nelson, b. abt 1823 in New York, d. 5 Feb. 1859, Union, Kentucky, a Presbyerian minister; and Martha Anna Carrington Belt Nelson, b. 26 Aug. 1828, d. 13 Feb. 1901, buried in Rockville Cemetery[5]. After her husband's death she returned to her family home in Rockville with her two sons.

EDUCATION: Rockville Academy and Georgetown College. Studied law in the office of Peter and Henderson of Rockville.[6]

LEGAL CAREER: Member of both the Montgomery and District of Columbia Bar Associations. "He practiced with marked success in the courts of the District of Columbia, having his office in Washington. However, owing to the fact that his mother was alone, he spent much of his time at the homestead."[7]

MARRIAGE No record of marriage or of children.

---

[1] *Find-A-Grave Memorial,* and copy of records of Mt. Olivet Cemetery, Frederick MD identifying children's dates. Only one of the nine children is known to have married and had children.

[2] Abstracts of Sentinel Newspapers, 1900-1935, p. 568

[3] Scharf, 668, listed as "G. Nelson". "Admitted to bar November 14, 1874," according to *Portrait and Biographical Record,* 745.

[4] Obituary, Sentinel newspaper, 14 Oct.1887, age 34 at death, also Hurley, 1860 Montgomery County Census, age 7, living in Rockville.

[5] MCHS Cemetery Card File.

[6] *Portrait and Biographical Record,* "sketch of Rev. John Scott Nelson", *743-745.* .

[7] *Portrait and Biographical Record,* "sketch of Rev. John Scott Nelson, *743-745.* .

DEATH: 10 Oct. 1887, at age 34. Believed to be buried in Rockville Cemetery with his mother.[1]

ROBERT OULD, (1820-1882)

Admitted to Montgomery County Bar 1843[2]

BIRTH/PARENTS: Robert Ould was born about 31 Jan. 1820 in Georgetown, District of Columbia[3], to Robert Ould, Sr., b. 1 Mar. 1788 in London, England, d. 22 July 1840, Georgetown, D.C. and Pauline Gaither Ould , b. 3 May 1794, Montgomery County, MD, d. 1 Mar. 1876 Robert Ould Sr. was the Preceptor of the Lancaster Free School in Georgetown[4].

LEGAL CAREER: Ould and Peachy Law Offices[5]; Judge Advocate, Georgetown, Oct. 1844[6] ; Common Council Member, Feb. 1845.[7]

MARRIAGE:

1. On 3 Dec. 1846 to Sarah Turpin, b. 1828, d. 15 Mar. 1870, daughter of Thomas J. Turpin of Richmond, VA.[8]

2) Madge Dorsey, b. 1835, d. 1888).[9]

CHILDREN:

By first wife:

1. Robert C. Ould, b. 1848.
2. Martha Gwynn Ould, b. 1850, d. Apr. 1877, m. Oliver J. Schoolcraft (d. Apr. 1877).
3. Samuel Riggs Gaither Ould, b. 1853, d. 1854, Georgetown, buried Oak Hill Cemetery.
4. Sarah Turpin Ould, b. 1855, d. June 1921, m. George M. Donaldson.
5. Jessie Bright Ould, b. 1859.

By second wife:

6. Madge Ould, *b. 1873, d. 1955,* m. William Francis Powers.
7. Kate Ould, d. in infancy.

DEATH: 13 December 1882,[10] buried in Hollywood Cemetery, Richmond, Va.[11]

---

[1]Bowman,.*Sentinel,* 14 Oct. 1887,
[2] Scharf, Pg. 668.
[3] Virginia Death and Burial Index 1853-1917 (Ancestry).
[4] Dixon, *National Intelligence,* 24 July 1840.
[5] National Intelligencer 1846, Aug 7
[6] National Intelligencer 1844, Oct. 16
[7] National Intelligencer 1845, Feb. 25
[8] National Intelligencer 1846, Dec. 7
[9] Findagrave.com
[10] Virginia Death and Burial Index 1853-1917
[11] Findagrave.com

NOTES: Moved to Richmond in 1860, ad to sell house in Georgetown Jan. 5, 1860[1] Civil War Confederate Government Official. He served as Assistant Secretary of War the first three months of 1862, but later that year became the chief of the Bureau of Exchange of Prisoners. Represented Richmond authorities in their dealings with Washington over the formal parole and exchange of prisoners of war until its collapse in early 1864. Captured in April 1865, he was held by Federal Authorities for eight weeks until cleared of charges that he misappropriated the funds of captured Federal prisoners.[2] Lived in Richmond, VA. in 1870.[3]

EDWARD W. OWEN (1808-1895)

(Possibly the Edward Ewen admitted to the Bar in 1850)[4]
Judge of the Orphans Court

BIRTH/PARENTS: Edward W. Owen was born 6 May 1806 to Col. Washington Owen (1777-1846)[5] and Ruth (Gassaway) (1773-1846) Berry Owen,[6] who had married first, Jeremiah Berry.

LEGAL CAREER: Judge of the Orphans Court for 16 years.

MARRIAGE: On 2 November 1830, to Elizabeth Ann Clagett[7] (c. 1808-19 Aug 1887) daughter of Nathaniel (1751-1809) and Margaret Ann (Wilcoxin) (1776-?) Clagett[8], who were married in 1807.

CHILDREN:

1. Margaret Owen, b. 1841, d. 30 Oct. 1909[9], m. 6 Nov. 1866 to Gustavus Warfield Dorsey, C.S.A, son of Samuel Owings Dorsey (1814-1902) and Mary Riggs Griffith Dorsey (1816-1880).

DEATH: 21 March 1895. He is buried in the Owen Family Cemetery on Cashell Rd.[10]

---

[1] National Intelligencer 1860, Jan 5
[2] Findagrace.com
[3] 1870 Census
[4] Scharf, 668.
[5] Montgomery County Land Records, STS2:117-119 and STS2:119-122,between children of Washington Owen..
[6] MCHS Family Files, Owen Family; *Sentinel,* 29 Mar 1895
[7] Dixon, *National Intelligencer,* 8 Nov. 1830
[8] Jacobs, *Confederate Soldiers & Allies,* typescript, 47.
[9] Malloy, *Sentinel Abstracts,* 3 Dec.1909.p.51.
[10] MCHS Cemetery Card Files.

MOSES GRAY PALMER (1825-1885)

Admitted to Montgomery County Bar 1846[1]

BIRTH/PARENTS: Moses Gray Palmer was born 26 Aug. 1825, at "Woodlawn"in Sandy Spring area, the home of his father, William P. Palmer (b. 19 Nov. 1792, d. 27 Dec. 1869) and his first wife Martha Gray Palmer, (b. abt 1793, d. 31 Aug.-1825)[2].

EDUCATION Attended Westtown Boarding School in Pennsylvania in November 1836.[3] His father was also a student there[4].

LEGAL CAREER Admitted to Montgomery County Bar in 1846. He moved to Quincy, IL between 1846 and 1854 where he continued to practice law. At the time of his death he was the clerk of the Court of Appeals in Missouri.[5]

MARRIAGE:

1. 8 Oct. 1854 to Henrietta M. (Reed) Richardson daughter of Elijah and Eleanor Reed, as her 2nd husband in Adams County, Illinois. She died 26 Mar.1857, in Quincy, IL[6].
2. 18 July 1865, Carrie Gear (dau. of Carter and Rebecca Gear). She died 24 Mar. 1902.[7]

CHILDREN:

1. Walter Gray Palmer, b. 29 Aug. 1866, d. 22 Jul.1901, buried Woodland Cemetery, Quincy, IL.
2. Jessie Palmer, b. 26 Dec, 1869, d. 21 Nov. 1936, buried Woodland Cemetery, Quincy, IL.[8]

DEATH: 6 Sep. 1885 in St. Louis, MO. Buried in Quincy, IL.[9]

GEORGE C. PATTERSON (1816-1889)

Admitted to the Montgomery County Bar 1838[1]

---

1 Scharf, 668.
2 Palmer, *Descendants of John and Mary Palmer,* Lewis Palmer, comp., Chester, PA: 1910, 25, 30 and Jacobs, *Medical Doctors of Montgomery County, 1776-1900*, 173
3 www.Ancestry.com : U.S. High School Student Lists, 1821-1923 (accessed 21 May 2014)
4 Jacobs, *op.cit.,* 173.
5 Jacobs, *op.cit.,* 173 and www.ancestry.com: Missouri Death Records (accessed 21 May 2014)
6 www.ancestry.com: Illinois Marriages, 1851-1900 (accessed 21 May2014), and Palmer, *op.cit., 30.*
7 Palmer, *op.cit.,* 30.
8 www.findagrave.com, accessed 22 Sept. 2016.
9 Palmer, *op.cit.,* 30. Also see *Find-A-Grave.*

BIRTH/PARENTS: George C. Patterson was born 3 August 1816, Hagerstown, Maryland to Dr. Thomas Patterson (ca. 1767 - 1848)[2] and Jane Clarke Patterson (ca. 1778 - 1858). He Came to Gaithersburg in 1833 with his parents.

LEGAL CAREER: He was a member of the 1841 meeting in Baltimore of the Colonization Convention, a group founded and funded by the Maryland State Legislature in 1832 to encourage free blacks to leave Maryland. [3] He served as the Librarian of the House from 1842-1843;[4] and then was elected to the Maryland Assembly in 1844-45 and 1880. [5] In 1852 he was nominated by the Maryland Senate to be a Justice of the Peace in Montgomery County, [6] and for a number of years was deputy clerk to the Circuit Court, under Mr. E. B. Prettyman,.[7] In 1879 he was again elected to the Legislature with Messrs. Thos. Owen and Wm. Grady. For a number of years he was a writer on agricultural topics and was employed by the Baltimore newspapers.

MARRIAGE(S)

1. 18 July 1848, marriage license in Montgomery County, to Prudence Bean (b. 1824, d. 30 July 1855).[8]
2. 13 December 1859, married Julia Belt (b, 1834), daughter of the Reverend Addison Belt (ca 1788-1857) and Elizabeth Ann (Carrington) Belt in Washington, D.C., Fourth Presbyterian Church.[9]

CHILDREN by First Wife[10]:

1. Virginia Patterson, b. 1850 in Virginia
2. Henry Patterson, b. 1855 in Montgomery County, Maryland.

---

[1] Scharf, 668.

[2] Rosenthal, Janice, "Read the paper www.amazonedit.com" re THOMAS PATTERSON SR.(c. 1724 - 1822) of Lancaster Co., PA & of Washington Twp., Fayette Co., PA. updated on 24 Sept 2014, and Gaithersburg: The Heart of Montgomery County, 1978, Jane Clarke was the sister of Matthew St. Clair Clarke (1790 - 1852), a clerk of the House of Representatives, sometimes understood to be the first Librarian of that institution.

[3] Maryland Colonization Journal, Baltimore, June 15, 1841, Vol. 1; reprinted APA Society, Maryland State Colonization. (2013). Maryland Colonization Journal, 1841. London: Forgotten Books. (Original published 1841)

[4] Rosenthal , op.cit.

[5] Scharf, History of Western Maryland, p. 667 and p. 2253

[6] Journal of the Proceedings of the Senate of the State of Maryland, p.48

[7] 1870 Census, Rockville, he was listed in Montgomery Hotel, occupation: Deputy Clerk. No family was with him.

[8] *Marriage Licenses, 1798-1898.*

[9] *Genealogical Abstracts, Montgomery County Sentinel, 1855-1899,* p.286.

[10] 1860 Montgomery County Census, shows him living in Rockville with his two children. Although recently married to Julia Addison, she appears to have been staying with her mother and siblings at the time nearby, in Rockville.

DEATH 6 March 1889, as a result of a train accident at age 76.[1] Buried in Rockville Baptist Cemetery.

GEORGE ALEXANDER PEARRE (1819-1883)

Admitted to Montgomery County Bar in 1844[2]

BIRTH/PARENTS: George Alexander Pearre was born in 1819 in Montgomery County, MD to William Pearre (1795-1864) and Catherine Marian (Springer) Pearre (1785-1864). George Alexander Pearre was partly raised by his mother's uncle, George Baer of Frederick, MD. Mr. Baer was a Representative to Congress in 1814 and 1815.[3]

EDUCATION: George attended the Barnesville Academy, then called Hayes School House. William Schley, a Frederick Town lawyer, tutored George.[4]

LEGAL CAREER: Practiced in Frederick, Maryland with Hon. William Motter, he was admitted to the Frederick County Bar in 1838[5]. He moved to Cumberland, Allegany County, Maryland in 1839 and was admitted to the bar there that year.[6] He was appointed Judge of the Circuit Court at the death of Judge James Smith by Gov. Bradford of Maryland. He was elected to the position in 1871[7].

MARRIAGE: On 31 Oct. 1843, to Mary Worthington (b. 4 Aug 1823, d. 30 Apr 1871) daughter of Reuben Worthington (b. 25 Mar. 1799, d. 31 Dec. 1871 in Cumberland, Maryland) and Ruth Perry Worthington (b. abt 1802, prob. d. bef. 1850).

CHILDREN: The Pearre Family File mentions nine children. Only seven have been identified in census and/or other records.

1. Elizabeth Smith Pearre, b. abt. 1845 in Maryland.
2. Mary Pearre, b. abt. 1847 In Maryland.
3. Georgia Pearre, b. abt.1853 in Maryland.
4. William Pearre, b. abt. 1855 in Maryland.
5. Florence Worthington Pearre, b. Sep. 1857, d. 10 Mar. 1915 in Philadelphia, PA.
6. George A. Pearre, Jr., b. 16 Jul. 1860, Comus, Montgomery County, MD, d. 1948 in Cumberland, Allegany, MD, m. 1898, Elizabeth G. Shoup, no children. He followed his father into the law and into politics, serving as a Republican State Senator.[8]

---

[1] Genealogical Abstracts, Montgomery County Sentinel, 1855-1899.
[2] Scharf, 668.
[3] ACHS Summary Form, "William Pearre Farm and Cemetery", *Statement of Significance, and attachment A, which records gravestones for William Pearre and Catherine M. Pearre, and others. See MCHS Library Historic House File, and copy of one page in MCHS Pearre Family File.*
[4] ACHS Summary Form, "William Pearre Farm and Cemetery."
[5] Scharf, 416.
[6] Scharf, 1353.
[7] Scharf, 1349, 1402.
[8] MCHS Family file, bio sketch.

7. James Graham Pearre, b. abt. 1863

DEATH: He died 22 May 1883 and his buried with his wife, Mary, at Rose Hill Cemetery, Cumberland, Maryland.

NOTES: Ran for Maryland State Legislature in 1842 but lost. Ran again in 1861 as a Republican and served until 1867 when he resumed his law practice;[1] Vestryman of Emanuel Episcopal Church, Cumberland, MD and Board of Trustees of Allegany County Academy (MD).[2]

THOMAS J. PEDDICORD (1839-1910)

Admitted to Montgomery County Bar 1871[3]

BIRTH/PARENTS: Thomas John Peddicord was born 9 Nov. 1839 in Lisbon, Anne Arundel County (now Howard County) MD to Washington Asbury Peddicord (b. 14 Nov. 1815, d. 2 Mar. 1882) and Rebecca Crawford Peddicord, (b. 1814, d. bef. 1880), daughter of John Crawford of Howard County[4].

EDUCATION: He attended school in Anne Arundel County until age 16, then William T. Crapster, a Harvard graduate, tutored him for 2 years. He studied medicine under Dr. John H. Owings but gave it up to manage a farm given to him by his father. After 5 years he sold the farm and moved to Montgomery County to accept a position as deputy sheriff under his father-in-law, Sheriff James H. Clagett. While serving as deputy sheriff from 1868-1869 he studied law and was admitted to the Montgomery County Bar in January 1871.[5]

LEGAL CAREER: He practiced law in Montgomery County until 1873. At that time he moved to Oakland in the newly created Garrett County, MD and opened a law practice there. In 1878 he formed a law partnership with H. Wheeler Combs.[6]

MARRIAGE:

1. 27 Oct. 1860, to Ara Rebecca Claggett (b. 5 Mar.1843, Gaithersburg, MD; d. 20 Nov.1900 in Oakland, MD)[7] daughter of James H. Clagett (b. 22 Feb. 1818, d. 5 Aug. 1896) and his first wife, Mary Thrift Clagett (b. 5 Dec. 1819, d. 31 Mar. 1877).[8]
2. In1901, to Harriet (Lindley) Whipps, b. 8 Oct 1854, d. 6 May 1937) daughter of John Clark Lindley and Elizabeth King Lindley, widow of Henry Whipps, who d. 1880.[9]

---

[1] Scharf, 1352.
[2] MCHS Family File.
[3] Scharf, 1539-40. Sketch of Thomas J. Peddicord.
[4] www.ancestry.com, "Skylar Brown Family Tree" accessed 10 July 2016.
[5] Scharf, 1539-40, *op.cit.*.
[6] Scharf, 1539-40, *op.cit.*.
[7] www.ancestry.com, "Find-A-Grave" reference, to her in Oakland Cemetery.
[8] MCHS Cemetery Card File, James H. Clagett and wife in Forest Oak Cemetery, Gaithersburg.
[9] www.ancestry.com, "Skylar Brown Family Tree" accessed 10 July 2016.

CHILDREN:

1. Ella May Peddicord, b. abt 1862, MD, d. 20 May 1913, Oakland, MD.
2. Maggie Washington Peddicord, b. 31 Mar. 1863, Oakland, MD, d. 25 May 1927, Oakland, MD.
3. Mary Rebecca Peddicord, b. abt 1865, d. 1937.
4. James Clagett Peddicord, b. abt 1867, d. 3 Feb. 1935, Oakland, MD, m. Mary Edward Lewis (1868-1917).

DEATH: 5 Nov. 1910, In Garrett County.[1]

NOTES: During his years in Rockville he was active in the Masonic Lodge and an elected officer in 1871. He was listed among the patrons of the Montgomery Female Institute in 1873. He was one of the officers of the Sons of Temperance in 1872.

RICHARD ROSS PERRY (1846-1915)

Admitted to Montgomery County Bar 1871[2]

BIRTH/PARENTS: Richard Ross Perry was born in 1846[3] in Washington, D.C., to dry goods merchant, Augustus Emory Perry (b. 27 Jan. 1820, d. 16 Jun.1876) and Mary Jane Ross Perry (b. 29 Jan.1825, d. 9 Aug. 1908), buried in Rock Creek Cemetery[4].

EDUCATION: BA, Georgetown University, 1864; and MA, Georgetown , 1865. In 1866[5], traveled in Europe and studied at the University of Paris. On return to U.S., he studied with Richard T. Merrick, the son of William D. Merrick, a member of the Maryland Legislature and the U.S. Senate.

LEGAL CAREER: Admitted to the bar of the Supreme Court, 1876. Appointed to Rock Creek Park Commission, in1890. In 1897 wrote and published "Common-Law Pleading: Its History and Principles," Boston: Little, Brown. He was a member of the board of directors of Riggs Bank, Columbia Institute for the Deaf, Corcoran Gallery of Art, Carnegie Public Library, and American Society of International Law.

MARRIAGE: Married in 1870 to Mary Callie Thaw (b. 1848, d. 30 July 1839) daughter of John Thaw (b. 1804, d. 1887) and Jean Hood Thaw (28 Jun 1815, d. 20 Aug. 1896) of Washington, D.C..

CHILDREN:

1. Richard Ross Perry (1871-1953).
2. Edith Perry (1873-1881).

---

[1] www.ancestry.com, buried in Oakland Cemetery.
[2] Scharf, 668.
[3] www.ancestry.com, age 4, 1850 Federal Census, Washington, D.C.
[4] Hurley, *The Perry Families,* 45 and www.find-a-grave.com.
[5] *General Register of Georgetown University*, Washington, DC 1916.

DEATH 17 July 1915. Buried in Rock Creek Cemetery, Washington, DC[1].

NOTES Lived at 1635 Massachusetts Ave., Washington.

GEORGE PETER (1829-1893)

Admitted to Montgomery County Bar 1850[2]

BIRTH/PARENTS: George Peter was born on 28 Nov 1829 in Montgomery County, at Montevideo, to Maj. George Peter, b. 28 Sep. 1779, d. 22 June 1861, and his third wife, Sarah Norfleet (Freeland) Peter, b. 5 Dec. 1805, d. 16 Dec. 1846.[3]

EDUCATION: Studied law with John Brewer and became his partner in law practice.

LEGAL CAREER: After Brewer's death, he partnered with James B Henderson. George Peter was a trial lawyer held in great regard by the legal circles of the county. In politics he was a Democrat and a member of the Maryland Constitutional Convention of 1864. In 1868, he was elected State's Attorney for Montgomery County and was re-elected in 1872. Twice he was elected to the Maryland State Senate. He was nominated by his party for the U.S. Senate but was defeated by the Republican candidate, Milton G. Urner.[4]

MARRIAGE: On 13 Oct. 1852, by Montgomery County license, to Eliza Lavinia Gassaway, b. 26 April 1831, d. 11 May 1909,[1] daughter of John Gassaway (1790-1845) and Eliza Dorsey Gassaway (1798-1857).

CHILDREN:

1. John Freeland Peter, b. 15 Nov 1853, d. 31 Mar 1878, buried Oak Hill Cemetery, noted to be a lawyer. Unmarried.
2. Sarah N. Peter, b. 30 May 1856, d. 16 May 1935, m. William Dunlop, (b. 15 May 1850, d. 23 Oct. 1916) an attorney.
3. Mary A. Peter, b.23 Feb 1859, d. 19 Oct 1928, m. Thomas Dawson, (b. 6 Oct.1857, d.24 Sep. 1924) an attorney.
4. Edward Compston Peter, b. 18 Jun 1862, d. 22 Aug 1923, m. 27 Jun. 1888 to Mary Gordon Vinson (b. 10 Sep 1867, d. 20 July 1947), daughter of Judge John Thomas Vinson (b. 6 Jan. 1825,[5] d. 7 Feb. 1903) and Fannie Rachel Prout Vinson (b. 1837, d. 27 Dec. 1888), both buried at Oak Hill Cemetery.[6]
5. George Gibson Peter, b. 21 Nov 1865, d. 2 Oct 1870, buried Oak Hill Cemetery.

---

[1] Proquest Historical Newspapers, *New York Times,* 18 July 1915, "R.R. Perry Kills Himself; Washington Lawyer Follows Example of his Two Brothers."

[2] Scharf, 667.

[3] *Biographical Cyclopedia of Representative Men*, 30-31; Pippenger, *Oak Hill Cemetery,* 2

[4] *Montgomery County Story,* Vol. 51, No. 4, November 2008, Jane C. Sween, "The Peter Family of Montgomery County, 45."; *Portrait and Biographical Record,* 639-641; *Biographical Cyclopedia,* 30-31.

[5] Retired from judgeship at age 70, as reported in *Sentinel,* 4 Jan. 1895.

[6] www.find-a-grave.com.

6. Robert B Peter, b. 22 Feb 1868, d. 1 Nov 1936, m. 13 Oct. 1896, Montgomery County, to Helen Olivia Lowry (b. Apr. 1871, d. 10 Sep 1917) daughter of Maj Horatio Lowry, USMC, (b. 1837, d. 1900) and Charlotte Lowry (b. 1844, d. 1901).
7. Katherine Peter, b. 9 Mar. 1871, d. 25 Dec. 1929, Annapolis, MD, m. 5 Nov. 1890, Montgomery County, to Hugh Nelson, b. 7 May 1858, d. after 1930, son of Rev. Dr. Cleland Nelson, President of St. John's College, Annapolis, and Rector of St. Anne's Parish, and his second wife, Mary Hagner Nelson.[1]
8. Arthur Peter b.16 Nov 1873, d. 24 Oct 1943, m. July 1918, to Edith Marshall of Louisville, Kentucky[2] (b. 1883, d. 19 Oct. 1964), daughter of Humphrey and Virginia Marshall, buried Oak Hill Cemetery.

DEATH: 6 August 1893. Buried (with wife) in Oak Hill Cemetery, Georgetown.

NOTES: He opposed that an oath be required before a citizen could vote. He was generally known as a champion of the poor. In addition, he was a trustee of the Rockville Academy. He lived on North Adams Street, in Rockville.[3]

JOHN FREELAND PETER (1853-1878)

Admitted to Montgomery County Bar 1874[4]

BIRTH/PARENTS: John Freeland Peter was born 15 November 1853 to George Peter (b. 28 Nov. 1829, d. 6 Aug. 1893) and Eliza Lavinia Gassaway Peter, b. 26 April 1831, d. 11 May 1909. John was the eldest son. His father and his younger brothers, Edward Compton Peter, Robert Brewer Peter and Arthur Peter, were also lawyers.

LEGAL CAREER Admitted to the Montgomery County bar in 1874.

MARRIAGE: No marriage or children.

DEATH 31 March 1878.[5] Buried at Oak Hill Cemetery, Washington, D.C.

---

[1] McIntire, *Annapolis Families,* 513.
[2] *Sentinel,* 26 July 1918.
[3] *Portrait and Biographical Record,* 639-641; *Biographical Cyclopedia,*30-31.
[4] Scharf, 668
[5] Pippenger, *Oak Hill Cemetery* .

SOMERVILLE PINKNEY (1800-1843)

Admitted To Montgomery County Bar 1837[1]

BIRTH/PARENTS: Somerville Pinkney was born 3 January 1800 in Annapolis, MD to Jonathan Pinkney (d. Dec. 1827) and Elizabeth(Munroe) Pinkney (d. Feb. 1823).[2].

LEGAL CAREER: President/Director of Annapolis & Elkridge Railroad 1837-1838[3]; a subscriber to capital stock of Annapolis & Potomac Canal[4].

MARRIAGE: 4 Dec. 1828 to Mary Franklin Deale, b. 7 Feb. 1807, d. 4 Jan. 1889.[5]

CHILDREN:[6]

1. Jonathan Edward Pinkney, b. 1830, d.-5 May 1832.
2. Elizabeth Pinkney, d. Oct. 1835, infancy.
3. Ann Franklin Pinkney, b. 14 Mar. 1833, d. 25 Apr. 1915, unmarried.
4. Mary Franklin Pinkney, b. 15 Sep. 1837, d. 26 Mar.1901.

DEATH: 21 Feb.1843.[7]

WILLIAM P. PRESTON (1811-1880)

Admitted to Montgomery County Bar 1844[8]

BIRTH/PARENTS: William P. Preston was born about 1811 in Virginia[9] His parents have not been identified.

LEGAL CAREER: "Lawyer" in Baltimore [10] Admitted to practice before the Carroll County Court 4 Sep. 1861. This listing includes attorneys regularly practicing before the Carroll County Bar, as well as "those eminent attorneys from other parts of the State, who have been specially admitted for the trial of particular causes[11]."

MARRIAGE: On 25 August 1846, to Marguerite Wickham Smith, b. abt. 1813, daughter of Andrew Smith.[12]

CHILDREN: possibly: May Wickham Preston, born abt. 1850[13]

---

[1] Scharf, 668, listed as Sommerith Pinkney.
[2] McInire, *Annapolis Families, 557.*
[3] Dixon, National Intelligencer, 12 Jun. 1837; McIntire, *Op.Cit.,* 558.
[4] Dixon, *National Intelligencer,* 12 Aug. 1836.
[5] McIntire, *Annapolis Families,* 558.
[6] McIntire, *Annapolis Families, 558.*
[7] McIntire, *Annapolis Families,* 558.
[8] Scharf, 668.
[9] 1880 Federal Census.
[10] 1860 Federal Census
[11] Scharf, Vol. 2, 819.
[12] Hollowak, *Marriages and Deaths (Baltimore) Sun. 1837-1850,* 479.
[13] 1860 Federal Census.

DEATH: 25 October 1880[1] in Baltimore.

NOTES Baltimore City directories list him as an Attorney:[2]

1845 Wm P Preston 51 Fayette St
1860 Wm P Preston 65 W Fayette
1878 Wm P Preston 173 N Calvert

ELIJAH BARRETT PRETTYMAN (1830-1907)

Clerk of Montgomery County Court 1863-1885

BIRTH/PARENTS: Elijah Barrett Prettyman was born 20 Feb. 1830 in Williamsport, PA to Rev. William Prettyman (1792-1875) and Eliza Barrett Prettyman (1792-1861).[3]

EDUCATION: Earned a BA degree at Dickinson College in 1848[4].

LEGAL CAREER: Studied law in the office of Judge Richard J. Bowie of Rockville, but never practiced law, He spent most of his career in education. In 1850 he became principal of Brookville Academy in Montgomery County, and held that position for 11 years[5]. He was elected clerk of the Montgomery County Court in 1863 and was reelected to that position several times, serving until 1885. In 1886 he was named chief clerk of the House of Delegates, and for the succeeding four years, he was deputy naval officer of the Port of Baltimore. Later he served as principal of the State Normal School of Baltimore, and then as state superintendent of public instruction[6].

MARRIAGE: On 5 June 1855, to Lydia Forrest Johnston, b. 2 Feb 1832, d. 22 Nov. 1917, daughter of Zachariah Forrest Johnston (1803-1859) and Ann M. Holland Johnston (1808-1870).

CHILDREN:

1. Charles W. Prettyman, b. 1857, d. 5 May 1921, Rockville, MD, m. Rosetta V. Bouic (1857-1945), daughter of Judge William Veirs Bouic.
2. Forrest J. Prettyman, b. 7 Apr. 1860, d. 12 Oct. 1945, m. Oct. 1888, Elizabeth Rebecca Stonestreet, (b. 5 Jun 1861, d. July 1933, in Fredericksburg, VA.) daughter of Dr. E. E. Stonestreet[7].

---

[1] Arps, *Maryland Mortalities (Baltimore) Sun*, 186.
[2] Found on *Ancestry.com.*
[3] MCHS Prettyman Family File, FGS andsketch of "Elijah Barrett Prettyman" in Steiner, *Men of Mark,* Vol. 1, 291.
[4] MCHS Prettyman Family File.
[5] Biographical sketch above, and one from the Maryland Teacher Yearbook, 1909-1910, in Prettyman Family File.
[6] MCHS Prettyman Family File.
[7] MCHS Cemetery Card File.

3. Mariam Prettyman, b. 2 Jul 1864, d. 10 Nov. 1919, m. Dec. 1884, to Albert J. Almony, b. 23 Dec. 1858 d. 15 Oct. 1939,[1] son of Jarrett Almony (d. 1861) and Mary Ann (Burke) Almony.
4. Eliza Barrett Prettyman, b. 1866, d. 1 July 1954, Rockville[2], m. Oct. 1914, to Alexander Kilgour (b. 1855, d. April 1917).[3].
5. Ann J. Prettyman, b. 1869, m. Hugh H. Magruder (d. 20 Dec. 1929, Baltimore, MD).[4]
6. Lydia F. Prettyman, b. 6 Jan. 1873, d. 23 Sep 1943.[5]

DEATH Died 9 Dec. 1907, in Rockville. Buried in Rockville Cemetery.[6]

NOTES He was a member of the Methodist Episcopal Church, the Masonic Lodge, the Maryland Historical Society, and the Maryland Academy of Sciences.

WILLIAM MONTGOMERY STEWART (1799-1872)

Admitted to the Montgomery County Bar 1830[7]

BIRTH/PARENTS: William M. Stewart was born about 1799 to William Stewart (1776-1853) and Margaret Helen Beall Stewart (1772-1847). She was the sister of Upton Beall[8] the Montgomery County Clerk.

LEGAL CAREER:. Little is known about his education or career. He appears in the court deed records as a trustee in cases involving his family, as early as 1831, and this may have been the reason for his entry into the clerks' book as an attorney.[9]

MARRIAGE: No record of marriage or children found. He appears in the D.C. censuses living with sisters in 1860 and 1870, the latter giving his occupation as "lawyer."

DEATH: 9 November 1872 in Georgetown, buried in Rock Creek Cemetery[10].

HATTERSLY WORTHINGTON TALBOTT (1842-1912)

Admitted to Montgomery County Bar 1866[1]

---

[1] MCHS Cemetery Card File, for Albert J. Almony.
[2] *Sentinel,* 8 July 1954, wife of the late Alexander Kilgour.
[3] Malloy, *Sentinel Abstracts,* 9 Oct. 1914, 13 Apr. 1917.
[4] Malloy, *Sentinel Abstracts.*
[5] MCHS Cemetery Card File, on card with parents, buried Rockville Cemetery.
[6] Bowman, *Sentinel Abstracts*, 13 Dec. 1907; MCHS Cemetery Card file.
[7] Scharf, 666.
[8] "The Brooke Beall Family and the Johns Family," manuscript by Eleanor Vaughn Cook, Montgomery County Historical Society.
[9] Montgomery County Land Records.
[10] Pippenger, *District of Columbia Interments 1855-1874,* 342.

BIRTH/PARENTS Hattersly Worthington Talbott was born 26 August 1842, in Howard County, MD to Edward Alexander (b. March 1818, d. 1 Nov.1890) and Mary Jane (Wareham) Talbott. (b, 23 Feb. 1820, d. 26 Feb.1883).[2]

EDUCATION: Howard Latin School[3],Ellicott City, Maryland, a private school kept by Reverend Cyrus Huntington, pastor of the Presbyterian Church in Ellicott City. Attended St. John's College in Annapolis, from 1859 until May 1861, when war disrupted the school.[4] Taught school in 1861 while reading law with William H. G. Dorsey, James M. Jackson of West Virginia and George W. Sands of Howard County, Maryland.

LEGAL CAREER: Moved to Montgomery County and admitted to the Bar in 1866. Mayor of Rockville three terms (i.e. 6 years); Delegate to Democratic National Convention in 1884; Elected on Democratic ticket as Presidential Elector for the 6th Congressional District in 1888[5] Chairman of the State Central Committee from 1894 to 1896; Maryland State Senator from 1894 to 1896.

MARRIAGE: On 10 February 1874, in Hagerstown, MD, Laura Williams Holland, (1844-1925) daughter of Zachariah (1806-1867) and Laura (Williams) Holland (1814-1861)[6] Her maternal grandfather was Gen. Otho Holland Williams (1776-1852).

CHILDREN[7]

1. Otho Holland Williams Talbott, b. 12 April 1875, d. 10 April 1931, m. 15 Jun 1904, at Christ Episcopal Church, Rockville,[8] Katherine M. Choate, (b. 28 Sep 1871, d. 6 Mar. 1950).[9] Chief Deputy in Office of Clerk of Circuit Court of Montgomery County in 1927.
2. Hattersley Worthington Talbott, Jr., b. 23 Sep 1876, d. 23 July 1937[10]. Residing in New Orleans in 1927, he returned to Montgomery County before 1931.

DEATH He died on 1 May1912, of heart failure. He is buried in Rockville Cemetery.[11]

---

[1] Scharf, 668.
[2] Shirk, *Descendants of Richard and Elizabeth (Ewen) Talbott,* 168.
[3] Scharf, p. 719.
[4] *Portrait & Biographical, 719-720; also Shirk.*
[5] *Ibid.*
[6] Shirk, *286*
[7] Shirk, 286.
[8] Malloy, *Sentinel,* 769 (17 Jun 1904 & 17 Apr 1931).
[9] MCHS Cemetery File cards.
[10] MCHS Cemetery File Cards.
[11] Christ Episcopal Church Records, Church file, MCHS and *Sentinel,* May 3, 1912.

NOTES: Law practice partner with Joseph H. Bradley and then Charles W. Prettyman. Member of the Board of Trustees of the Rockville Academy from 1881; served as President of Academy. Secretary/Treasurer 1879-1880 and 1882 of the Mutual Building Association of Montgomery County, MD. Vestryman of Christ Episcopal Church, Rockville, Maryland; Vice President of Montgomery County National Bank; Director of B&O Railroad 1886-1890; Mason. Lived at 100 Forest Avenue, Rockville, MD. Member of The Society of the War of 1812.

WILLIAM THOMPSON (1812-1872)

Admitted to Montgomery County Bar 1832[1]

BIRTH/PARENTS: William H. Thompson was born 14 Feb. 1812 to Richard Thompson (b. 1788, d. after 1860) and Rebecca (Peddicord) Thompson (b. 1790, d. bef 1860).

LEGAL CAREER: In August of 1832 he had an office in Rockville adjoining the Maryland Free Press. He served as Sheriff of Montgomery County in 1849, and as Chief Judge of the Orphans Court from 1863 to 1872 at the time of his death; during that time the Books of the Orphans Court were labeled WTofR.

MARRIAGE: Chloe Ellen Pope (1817-1911[2]) daughter of Nathaniel and Sarah (St.Clair) Pope.

CHILDREN No children.

DEATH 23 Jan. 1872[3], buried in Goshen Cemetery, Laytonsville, MD.

ROBERT G. THRIFT (1836 -1877)

Admitted to Montgomery County Bar 1864[4]

BIRTH/PARENTS: Robert G. Thrift was born abt.1836 to James M. Thrift (abt 1795-1845) and Charity Ducket Boyd Thrift (1796-1868). His mother had married first Horace D. Waters (1787-1823), and on the 1850 census she and 14 year old Robert Thrift were living with Horace Waters[5] (1823-1903), her son by her first marriage.

EDUCATION: Attended the University of Virginia Law School.[6] On the 1860 census for Washington, D.C., he was listed as a lawyer, age 23, living with his brother in law, also an attorney, Edward Swan, who had married Marie L. Thrift[7], his older sister.

---

[1] Scharf, 667.

[2] Tombstone in Goshen Methodist Church Cemetery. *Sentinel,* 7 July 1911. "died Thurs. last week at the home of her niece, Mrs. William Magruder, near Laytonsville.

[3] *Sentinel,* 26 Jan. 1872.

[4] Scharf, 668.

[5] Hurley, *1850 Census Montgomery County,* 71.

[6] Ancestry.com: U. S. School Catalogs : 1765-1935 : accessed 5 Mar. 2014.

[7] Ancestry.com, 1860 Federal Population Census, Washington, D.C., accessed 30 July 2016; Manuel, *Montgomery County Marriage Licenses,* Edward Swan to Maria Louisa Thrift, 12 Nov. 1844.

MARRIAGE: No record of marriage or of children.

DEATH: 17 Jun 1877 in Washington, D.C. He was a member of the Rockville and D.C. Bars. He was buried in Germantown, Montgomery County, Maryland[1].

NOTES: According to Equity Records (STS-2, Folio 514) dated March 1849, at the time of his death James Thrift owned 235 acres of *Aix La Chappell*[2]. In the 1850 Federal Census cited above, Robert G. Thrift is listed at age 14 with $1,000 real estate value and attending school. During the Civil War, Robert registered for the draft in Maryland's 4th District. He is listed as a lawyer, single, and born in Maryland.[3]

JOHN S. TYSON (1797-1864)

Admitted to Montgomery County Bar 1839[4]

BIRTH/PARENTS John Shoemaker Tyson was born 7 Nov. 1797 to Jesse Tyson and Margaret (Hopkins) Tyson of Baltimore, MD.[5]

EDUCATION: He was educated at West Town College, near West Chester, PA, an institution of the Society of Friends. After graduating he studied law and practiced principally in the Court of Claims in Baltimore, where he became a judge.[6]

LEGAL CAREER: In 1825 he was elected to the Maryland House of Delegates, where he distinguished himself by a speech on the "Jew Bill," in which he advocated abolition of the restriction upon the class of people who were then not allowed to vote or hold office.[7]

MARRIAGE 1 December 1829, to Rachel P. Snowden, b. in 1809, d. 2 May 1889, daughter of John and Rachel (Hopkins) Snowden of Birmingham, near Laurel, MD.[8]

CHILDREN[9]

1. Cornelia Tyson,b.1836.
2. John Snowden Tyson, b. 1837, d. 26July 1890, m. Mary Roberts, daughter of Levi F. Roberts. He was a civil engineer and studied law in the office of his father. He was admitted to the Howard County Bar in 189, and elected as a Delegate from Howard County to the Maryland Legislature in 1864.
3. Anna Maria Tyson,b.1838.
4. Ida Tyson, b. 1845.

---

[1] *Sentinel*, 22 Jun 1877

[2] MCHS, Swan/Swann Family File.

[3] Ancestry.com: Civil War Draft Registration Records, 1863-1865 : accessed 5 Mar. 2014.

[4] Scharf, 667.

[5] Cook, *Montpelier & the Snowden Family,* 167-168.

[6] Cook, *op.cit., 167-168.*

[7] Cook, *op.cit., 167-168.*

[8] Cook, *op.cit., 167-168.*

[9] Cook, *op.cit., 167-168.* Powell, *1850 Census Anne Arundel Co., Howard District, p. 263*

DEATH: 3 October 1864 in Ellicott City, MD. He is buried at Birmingham family cemetery.

LYCURGUS C. (L.C.)VALDENAR (1822-1864)

Admitted to the Montgomery County Bar 1846[1]

BIRTH/PARENTS Lycurgus C. Valdenar was born abt. 1822 to Francis Valdenar (b. 1797-1883) and Elizabeth Culver Valdenar (1793-1876). His sister, Mary Virginia Valdenar, b.17 Oct. 1824, was married to Josiah Harding (1817-1894).

LEGAL CAREER . He first appears as a witness to the will of Margaret Valdenar in 1841, Probably his grandmother, and then to Michael Lyddane's will in 1842. He was admitted to the bar in 1846.

MARRIAGE No record found of marriage or chidren.

DEATH: 3 January 1864 in Cincinnati, Ohio, of Ashland Co., Kentucky, "in his 42nd year" formerly of Montgomery County, MD.[2]

NOTES: He was not located on the 1850 or 1860 census.

JOHN WESLEY VEITCH (1833-1892)

Admitted to Montgomery County Bar by 1866[3]

BIRTH/PARENTS: John Wesley Veitch was born 9 January 1833[4] near Bladensburg, Prince George's County,[5] to John Veitch (b. 1785[6], d. bef. 1862) and Caroline Morsell Veitch (b. 1796, d. 24 April 1862[7]).

LEGAL CAREER: In 1860 he became a member of the Prince George's County Bar;[8] By 1866 he was practicing law in Montgomery County and by 1868 in Frederick County[9].

---

[1] Scharf, 668, "L.C. Valdeman".
[2] Dixon, *National Intelligencer,* 26 Jan. 1864.
[3] Pugh's notes, found in Advertisements for legal services in the *Sentinel, 5 Jan. 1866.*
[4] www.findagrave.com: Col. John Wesley Veitch.
[5].Baltz, *Prince George's County, Marriages and Deaths*, 561.
[6] Wilcox, ed., *1850 Census of Prince George's County:* 5,6.
[7] Baltz, *Prince George's County, Marriages and Deaths,* 561 in her 66th year.
[8] Van Horn, *Out of the Past,* 352.
[9] Advertisements in the *Sentinel*, 5 Jan. 1866 & 4 Sep. 1868, from Pugh's notes.

In 1870, elected to and served in the Maryland House of Delegates. He was in Montgomery County at least until September 1873[1], when he moved to Garrett County, where he became State's Attorney in 1876.

MARRIAGE: On 8 May 1865[2] to Annie Eliza Howard, b. abt. 1842, d. 5 Mar 1916, Rives Station, Prince George's County[3]., daughter of Edward Howard, (b. 20 May 1798, d. 15 Feb. 1877)[4] and Annie Eliza Buckey Howard (b. 1808, d. 1882[5]) of Frederick County[6].

CHILDREN

1. Percy H. Veitch, 1870-1952.
2. Margaret Lyle Veitch, (b. 1876) m. in 1898, George H. Palmer (1870-1918)

DEATH: 11 October 1892, Garrett County, Maryland of paralysis[7].

NOTES He was a trustee of the Palmos Council of the American Legion of Honor in Garrett County, where he had been admitted to the bar in 1873[8].

JOHN T. VINSON (1825-1903)

Admitted to Montgomery County Bar 1846[9]

BIRTH/PARENTS: John T. Vinson was born 6 January 1825 in Poolesville, MD to Colonel Thomas Fogg Warham Vinson (1785-1843[10]) and Polly (Hickman) Vinson[11] b. 3 Mar. 1788, d. 16 Nov. 1875, Baltimore, MD.[12]

EDUCATION: Rockville Academy. Studied law with Honorable Richard Johns Bowie.[13]

LEGAL CAREER: Admitted to Bar 1846. While still young he accepted an appointment as Clerk in Treasury Department in Washington, D.C., and, after several promotions became the Auditor for the District of Columbia. In 1882 he received the Republican nomination for Associate Judge of the 6th Judicial Circuit[14], for a 15 year term, and he

---

[1] Baltz, *Prince George's County, Marriages and Deaths*, 561.
[2] www.ancestry.com (accessed 25 June 2014).
[3] *The News* (Frederick, MD) 7 Mar.1916.
[4] Holdcraft, 605, Mt.Olivet Cemetery, Frederick.
[5] Holdcraft, 605, age 74 at death.
[6] Williams & McKinsey, *History of Frederick County,* 1563.
[7] *Sentinel,* 14 Oct. 1892.
[8] Scharf, 1524, 1540, 1542,
[9] Scharf, 668.
[10] MCHS Cemetey Card File, Thomas F. W. Vinson, buried Sept. 1943, age 58, Rockville Baptist Church Cemetery.
[11] *Sentinel*, 13 February1903, copy of obituary in MCHS Family File.
[12] Removed from Rockville Cemetery 29 Dec. 1888 and reinteered in Oak Hill Cemetery. Her dates from MCHS family file.
[13] *Sentinel,* 13 February 1903, copy of obituary in MCHS Family File.
[14] Bowman, *Sentinel,* 13 Oct. 1882.

served until his mandatory retirement at seventy years of age in 1895[1] An act failed in the legislature to allow him to continue to serve out 15 years.[2]

MARRIAGE: On 15 August 1861 to Frances Rachel Prout (1834-1888) daughter of William Prout, of Washington, D.C.

CHILDREN:[3]

1. Thomas Vinson (1862-1924), never married.
2. Julia Prout Vinson, b. 4 Apr. 1864, d. 25 Jun. 1950,[4] m. 11 Nov. 1901, George Minor Anderson, b. Oct. 1857, d. 7 Aug. 1927. He was also an attorney in Rockville.
3. Mary Gordon Vinson, b. 10 Sep. 1867, d. 20 Jul. 1947, m. on 27 Jun. 1888, Edward C. Peter, b. 18 Jun. 1862, d. 22 Aug. 1923. He was another attorney.
4. Nanny Stoddard Vinson, b. 1868, d. 18 Feb.1960, unmarried[5].
5. Forresta Vinson, (1870-1871), died of measles.
6. Robert William Vinson, twin, b. 1872, d. 16 Jan.1958, never married.[6]
7. Richard Bowie Vinson, twin, (1872-1905), never married.

DEATH: On 7 February 1903. Buried at Oak Hill Cemetery, Georgetown, D.C.[7]

NOTES: Founder of Montgomery County National Bank and Director; Trustee of Rockville Academy; Vestryman of Christ Episcopal Church. Elected to Town Council of Rockville in 1898[8]; served until 1902.

RUDOLPH WATKINS (1844-1909)

Admitted to Montgomery County Bar 1875[9]

BIRTH/PARENTS: Rudolph Watkins was born about 1844 in Georgetown, Washington, D.C.[10] to George S. (1815-1890) and Caroline Henry Ashton (1814-1851) Watkins.

LEGAL CAREER: Register of Wills in 1891.[11]

MARRIAGE: 21 January 1868[1] to Mary Catherine Hunter, b. ca. 1844, d. 25 January 1933,[2] daughter of Thomas (1812-1857) and Susana Key (Scott) (1818-aft. 1905) Hunter.

---

[1] *Sentinel,* 13 February 1903, copy of obituary in MCHS Family File.

[2] Bowman, *Sentinel,* 6 April 1894 & 11 Jan. 1895.

[3] Pippinger, *Oakhill Cemetery,* dates for most of the children are from memorials in the family plot.

[4] MCHS Family File : Anderson Family compiled by Eleanor Cook.

[5] "Death of 'Miss Nannie' Ends Rockville Era," *Sentinel,* 18 Feb. 1960, clipping in MCHS Vinson Family File., confirms that her three brothers who reached adulthood, had never married..

[6] Copy of obituary in Family File, "Robert W. Vinson, 86, Rockville Druggist, Dies," from the Evening Star, 17 Jan. 1958.

[7] *Pippenger, Oak Hill Cemetery,* Vol 1, 237.

[8] Bowman, *Sentinel,* 6 May 1898.

[9] Bowman, *Sentinel,* March 26, 1875.

[10] 1860 Census, Washington, D.C. living in household of G. S. Watkins; parents names form Ancestry Family Tree.

[11] Bowman, *Sentinel,* May 29, 1891.

CHILDREN[3]

1. George Simpson Watkins, b. 23 Oct. 1868, d. 21 April 1888. Buried in St. Mary's Old Catholic Cemetery, Rockville.
2. Susanna Ashton Hunter , b. 27 March 1870, m. Nov. 11, 1902 to J. Richard Durrett.[4] Living in Denver, Colorado in 1909 and 1933.
3. Mary Julia Watkins, b. 31 March 1872, m. J. Frederick Chatard of New York, on 1 Jun 1898 by Father Kenner at Tarrytown.[5] In 1909 & 1933, living in Los Angeles, California.
4. Rudolph Lewis Watkins Jr., b. 6 Mar 1874, d. 8 Nov. 1893 of typhoid. Buried in St. Mary's Catholic Old Cemetery, Rockville.
5. Maria L. A. Watkins, b. 27 Dec 1875, married November 1902 to James Herbert Wilson.[6] Lived in Bethesda, MD and Washington, D.C. in 1933.
6. Ramsey Watkins, b. ca. 1878. Living in North Dakota from at least 1909 through 1933.
7. Joseph Watkins, b. 15 Jun 1879.
8. Louis Watkins, b. 7 Sep 1880, d. 24 Feb 1886 of brain fever.
9. Thomas Hunter Watkins, b. 15 May 1882, m. 1 March 1905 to Mary E. Lelly of Valentine, Nebraska, where they went to live. In 1933, he was living in New York City.
10. Ogden Blackson Watkins, b. 24 Oct 1884, d. March 1892 of measles. Buried in St. Mary's Catholic Old Cemetery.

DEATH: 8 Nov. 1909 in Washington, D.C. at St. Margaret's Hospital[7]

NOTES: In 1883, he opened store in Derwood, and was appointed first postmaster.[8] He was a Democrat, member of Democratic State Central Committee.[9] His farm on present day Route 355, near Derwood, was put up for sale in 1896.[10]

RICHARD MORTIMER WILLIAMS (1841-1882)

Admitted to Montgomery County Bar 1868[11]

---

[1] St. Mary's Catholic Church Rockville, MCHS Church records file.
[2] *Sentinel, Nov. 12, 1909,* in her 89th year, Mollie, b. in Baltimore.
[3] Hurley, *Watkins Family book 4,* p. 172-174.
[4] Bowman, *Sentinel, November 21, 1902.*
[5] Malloy, *Sentinel Abstracts,* p. 74.
[6] Bowman, *Sentnnel,* November 14, 1902.
[7] *Sentinel,* 12 Nov 1909. Notice.
[8] Bowman, *Sentinnel, March 9, 1883 & April 1883.*
[9] Bowman, op.cit., Oct. 5, 1888
[10] Bowman, *op.cit.,* 1896.
[11] Scharf, 668.

BIRTH/PARENTS: Richard Mortimer Williams was born 13 March 1841 in Poolesville, to Richard Walter Williams (b. 2 Oct. 1814, d. 31 Jan. 1890) and his first wife Charlotte Caroline (Larned) Williams (b. 8 July 1815, d. 14 Feb. 1844).[1]

EDUCATION: He studied at St. James College (sic) [St. John's?] and read law under Judge Richard Johns Bowie.[2]

LEGAL CAREER: Admitted to the Montgomery County Bar in 1868 as R. M. Williams. He formed a law partnership with Judge Bowie.

MARRIAGE: On 15 Nov. 1864, to Rose Anderson (b. 13 July 1841, d. 2 Jan. 1910), daughter of Dr. John Wallace (b. abt 1808, d. 8 Jul 1867) and Myra (Magruder) Anderson (b. abt 1813, d. 5 Apr 1872) of Rockville, MD. See sketch of her brother, James Wallace Anderson.

CHILDREN:

1. Jane Elizabeth Beall Williams, b. 19 Jan. 1867, d. 2 Nov. 1920, in Seattle, WA, m. 19 July 1893, to Henry Lincoln Reynolds., They lived In Seattle, where he was a patent attorney.
2. Hugh Blair Williams, b. 12 Dec. 1868, d. 21 July 1869.
3. Rose Florence Williams, b. 10 Feb. 1871, d. 2 May 1916, unmarried.
4. Richard Maurice Williams, b. 22 Sep. 1872, d. 13 Dec. 1944, in Minneapolis, MN, m. 27 Feb. 1897, to Llewlyn ("Louella") Nixon. He was a merchant for many years in Philip, SD.
5. Walter Anderson Williams, b. 19 Jan. 1874, d. 26 Feb. 1947, m. 30 June 1909, to Emma Barry Abert, daughter of Charles and Martha Wilson (Stonestreet) Abert. He was employed by the D.C. Government and lived in Rockville, MD.

DEATH: 16 June 1882, in Baltimore, MD. He had been attacked and robbed outside his home six months earlier and left paralyzed and speechless. He was first buried in Monocacy Cemetery, Beallsville[3] but later was moved to Rockville Cemetery in a lot with his wife, Hugh Blair and Rose Florence Williams.[4]

NOTES: He lived in Rockville at the corner of West Montgomery (Commerce Street) and Williams Street, #222 W. Montgomery Ave.[5] He was Commissioner of Rockville in 1867 and 1868.

---

[1]The Williams Family, typescript by Ann Perry Williams, p. 27-29.
[2] Obituary, *Sentinel*, 23 June 1882.
[3] Frain, *Monocacy Cemetery,* 54.
[4] Cemetery Card File, MCHS Library.
[5] MD Hist Trust Site Inventory Form.

FLAVEL SCOTT WOOTTON (1828-1853)

Admitted to Montgomery County Bar 1850[1]

BIRTH/PARENTS: Flavel Scott Wootton was born 30 Oct. 1828 to Dr. John B. Wootton (1782-1840) and Elizabeth Lynn Magruder Wootton (d. 1861) who were married on 17 Jun 1806[2].

EDUCATION : 1850 Federal Census of Montgomery County, MD lists Flavel as "student" and 20 years of age[3]

MARRIAGE No record of marriage or children.

DEATH On 27th March 1853, died in an accident on the B&O Railroad above Cumberland, in his 23rd year, formerly of Rockville, but then listed of Mt. Pleasant, Henry County, Iowa.[4]

NOTES His brother, Lewis Beall Wootton, was also a lawyer.-+

HENRY EDGAR WOOTTON (1837-1894)

Admitted to Montgomery County Bar 1865[5]

BIRTH/PARENTS: Henry Edgar Wootton was born 13 Oct. 1837 at Nottingham, Prince George's County, to Turner Wootton, M.D. (1797-1855) and Olivia Caroline (Hopewell) Wootton (b. 6 Feb. 1807, d. 17 Jul.-1894).[6]

EDUCATION: Georgetown University (1855) and Yale Law School.[7]

LEGAL CAREER: He practiced in Ellicott City, Howard County, MD and was Maryland State's Attorney after the Civil War.[8]

MARRIAGE: 13 Oct. 1868[9] to Ada O'Donnell of Baltimore.

CHILDREN : No children.

DEATH: 20 April 1894 at his residence in Ellicott City, age 57 years, buried at St. John's Cemetery of Howard County (MD).[10]

---

1 Scharf, 668.
2 Hurley, *Montgomery County Families:* v.2, 246 247, 250.
3 Hurley, 1850 Federal Census, Montgomery County. 143.
4 Jacobs, *Genealogical Abstracts from some 19th Century Newspapers,* 43. Reference to the *Daily National Intelligencer,* 4 April 1853.
5 Scharf, 668.
6 Hurley, *Montgomery County Families, v. 2,* 251-252 and MCHS Cemetery Card Index.
7 Hurley, *Op.cit.,* 252.
8 *Sentinel,* 20 April 1894.
9 O'Neill, *Obituaries and Marriages in The [Baltimore] Sun : 1866-1870, v.2,* 532.
10 *Sentinel,* 20 April 1894.

NOTES: He enlisted on 3 June 1864 as a private in the 10th Virginia Cavalry, CSA and then reportedly served in Co. A, First Maryland Cavalry.[1]

LEWIS BEALL WOOTTON (1815-1839)

Admitted to Montgomery County Bar 1837[2]

BIRTH/PARENTS: Lewis Beall Wootton was born 24 Dec.1815 to Dr. John B. Wootton (1782-1840) and Elizabeth Lynn (Magruder) Wootton (d. 1861) who were married on 17 Jun 1806.[3]

EDUCATION: Attended Union College, Schenectady, New York (a junior in 1834).[4]

MARRIAGE: No record of marriage or children.

DEATH: c. 1839[5]

BRICE THOMAS BEALE WORTHINGTON (1820-1856)

Admitted to Montgomery County Bar 1847[6]
Admitted to Prince George's County Bar 1842[7]

BIRTH/PARENTS: Brice Thomas Beall Worthington was born 2 April 1820 to Dr. Beale Magruder Worthington b. abt 1783 of Anne Arundel County, and his wife Elizabeth Ricketts Worthington of Montgomery County. They were married in 1811.[8]

LEGAL CAREER: Presented by Thomas S. Alexander for admission to Prince George's Bar during the April 1842 term. Served as Mayor of Annapolis from 1851-52.[9]

MARRIAGE: By license dated 28 November 1848 to Margaret Ellen Sellman (b. 1829, d. 2 Dec.-1863) daughter of Richard Sellman (b. 18 July 1799, d. 12 Feb. 1861) and Eleanor (Watkins) Sellman. (b. 10 Sept 1805, d. 1 Sept. 1863).[10]

---

1 Hurley, *Op.cit.,* 253.
2 Scharf, 668
3 Hurley, *Montgomery County Families,* Vol. 2, 246-252 "Wootton Family"
4 www.Ancestry.com: Digitized content license: *Catalogue of the Officers and Students in Union College, 1833-34* (Worcester, MA, American Antiquarian Society).
5 Hurley, *op.cit.* Appears to come from unsourced materials in Wootton Family File, MCHS.
6 Scharf, p 668
7 Van Horn, *Out of the Past*, 322
8 www.ancestry.com, Sons of the American Revolution Membership Applications, 1889-1970 for Brice Thomas Beale Worthington, accessed 28 Jan 2015.
9 http://msa.maryland.gov/megafile/msa/speccol/sc3500/sc3520/013800/013859/html/13859bio.htm accessed 28 Jan 2015
10 Sellman, *John Sellman of Maryland* ..., 68-9; Marlborough Towne Chapter, NSDAR, comp., *Tombstone Inscriptions of Southern Anne Arundel County,* Baltimore: Gateway Press, 1971, 32;

CHILDREN[1]

1. Richard Sellman Worthington, b. 23 Nov. 1849, d. 15 Mar. 1904, Washington, D.C., m. 20 June 1889, in Rockville, Frances Nicholas Nelson, b. 27 Aug. 1855, d. 22 Feb. 1934, Pottsville, PA.[2]
2. Rosa Worthington (b. 1851, bp. 6 July 1851.)
3. Brice Thomas Beale Worthington, Jr., b. 11 Nov. 1851, d. 3 Nov. 1930, m. 9 Dec. 1844, in Davidsonville, Ellen H. Sellman, b. Apr. 1847, d. 19 Dec. 1929.
4. Eleanor Worthington, (b. 1853, bp. 30 Aug. 1853.)

DEATH Died 29 Nov. 1856. Buried 2 Dec. 1863, in St. Anne's Cemetery, Annapolis, MD.[3]

PERRY WORTHINGTON (1811-1836)

Admitted to Montgomery County Bar 1834[4]

BIRTH/PARENTS: Perry Worthington was born 26 Feb 1811 in Montgomery County,[5] to William Worthington (1760-1837) and his 2nd wife Ruth (Perry) Worthington (1765-1827)[6].

EDUCATION: In William Worthington's will, dated 1831, Perry is listed as his son and described as "a minor preparing to study Law." A codicil in February 1837 noted that Perry was deceased. The will was probated later that year[7]. It is possible that he went to Allegany County to read law with his uncle[8], Roger Perry (1767-1835), well established as a lawyer in Cumberland from 1805. (See this volume: Roger Perry.)

LEGAL CAREER: In 1835 he was appointed to the correspondence committee at a meeting at the Court House in Cumberland, Maryland. The meeting was called to hasten the completion of the C & O Canal by Chief Justice John Buchanan and Judges Abraham Shriver and Thomas Buchanan.[9] There is a listing in the Allegany County Bar for a P. Worthington, which is undated.[10]

MARRIAGE: Unmarried

DEATH: His untimely death was noted in the *Port Gibson (MS) Correspondent* and the *Daily National Intelligencer.*

---

[1] msa.maryland.gov/megafile, op.cit., accessed 28 Jan 2015

[2] McIntire, *Annapolis Families*, 783.

[3] McIntire, *Annapolis Families,* 783; Gurney, *Cemetery Inscriptions, Anne Arundel* V.I, 166.

[4] Scharf, 668.

[5] Prince George's Parish Records; however, tombstone says age 22 when he dies in 1836 (1814).

[6] MCHS Family File : Worthington.

[7] Malloy et.al., *Abstracts of Wills, 1826-1876,* 179. Will of William Worthington, Montgomery County, Maryland : Liber V, folio 183, 12 Sep 1831, probate 12 Dec 1837.

[8] Hurley, *Our Maryland Heritage: Book 10: Perry Families,*, 1998, 20.

[9] Dixon, *National Intelligencer 1834-1835,* 213.

[10] Scharf, 1353.

"At Port Gibson, Miss. on the 25th December, Perry Worthington, Esq. of Montgomery County, Maryland, in the 22nd year of his age, after an illness of ten days. Mr. W. was a member of the Bar, and a young gentleman of high character and amiable manners. He had just settled in Port Gibson, with the view of practicing his profession, and was esteemed and respected highly by those with whom he formed an acquaintance."[1]

Inscribed on his headstone "This monument erected by his brother Thomas Worthington Esq. of Rockwell, MD."[2]

JOHN EDWIN YOUNG (1833-1861)

Admitted to The Montgomery County Bar 1855[3]

BIRTH/PARENTS: John E. Young was born 10 Feb. 1833 to John B. Young (b. abt 1805) and Eliza (Aldridge) Young (b. abt 1806).[4] They were married in Loudoun County, 20 March 1832.[5]. His mother, Eliza Young was living in his household in 1860.[6]

EDUCATION: Probably Rockville Academy. See note below.

MARRIAGE Mary E. Dyson (b. 5 May 1833, d. 2 Jun 1860), daughter of Dr. Bennett Dyson of Hilltop Township, Charles County, MD.[7]

CHILDREN :

1. Edwin Bennett Young, b. ca. 1858[8]
2. Sara Elizabeth Young, (15 Apr. 1860-15 Apr 1862)

DEATH 17 Sep.1861, buried at Union Cemetery, Leesburg, VA

NOTES In the 1850 Federal Census for Montgomery County, John E. Young and Aldridge Young are recorded as students born in Virginia residing with Oliver W. Treadwell. In the *Montgomery County Sentinel* there was a notice dated 23 July 1858 that Rockville Academy announced the resignation of Principal O. W. Treadwell . Assuming that Aldridge is John E. Young's younger brother and that Mr. Treadwell was their teacher it is possible that the Young brothers did attend Rockville Academy. John E. Young, in his

---

[1] claibornecountyms.org/1800news.html, *Daily National Intelligencer* Washington, D. C. Jan. 25, 1837; accessed 23 Oct 2013.

[2] www.Findagrave.net accessed 23 Oct 2013. There is no record of Thomas Worthington being admitted to the bar, he appears as a farmer, on the census records.

[3] Scharf,668.

[4] Duncan, *Loudon County, Virginia: Will Book Abstracts,* 189 will of John Edwin Young names his mother Eliza Young and her husband, John B. Young..

[5] Wertz, *Marriages of Loudoun County,* 173.

[6] Duncan, *1860-Loudoun County Census Index,* 258. J. Edwin Young was listed as an attorney at law. Eliza Young, 54, b. MD livened in same household. Also Edwin B., age 2, Mary E., 27, and Sarah E. 2 months.

[7] Frain, *Union Cemetery, Leesburg, VA, Plats A&B, 1784-1995,* 21.

[8] Duncan, *op.cit., Loudoun County Census Index.*

Will bequeathed to his son Edwin Bennett Young his law library. In the 1900 Federal Census, Aldridge Young is recorded in Baltimore, MD residing with his nephew, Edwin G. Young (b. 1858).[1]

[1] U.S. Federal Census, 1900: Baltimore County, MD

BENCH AND BAR OF MONTGOMERY COUNTY

PART III: 1875-1900 FORMATION OF BAR ASSOCIATION

MONTGOMERY COUNTY LAWYERS

Primarily those who were admitted to the bar before the formation of the Montgomery County Bar Association in 1894 are included in this section. Many were still active into the mid 19th century, in family law firms. You will see many family ties among the attorneys and the other professions of medicine and ministry. Often a teaching career was combined with study in a law office, leading to the practice of law.

Scharf's list of lawyers only goes to 1880, but from Sentinel notices and other sources a few others dates of bar admission have been identified.

Most of the attorneys in this section, were educated at colleges in Law, and practiced in the profession either as lawyers, judges, or legislators. They were among the founders and first signers of the Bar Association constitution for the county. Many were involved in the development of Montgomery County through politics and through real estate.

The Montgomery County Bar Association lists the following men as their founders: George M. Anderson, Thomas Anderson, William Veirs Bouic Jr. (profiled in previous section) Thomas Dawson, James B. Henderson, Frank Higgins, Alexander Kilgour, Philip D. Laird, Edward C. and Robert B. Peter, Charles W. Prettyman, Samuel Riggs of R., H. Maurice Talbott were all briefly profiled in the Montgomery County Bar Association's own history.[1]

---

[1] Bar Association of Montgomery County, Centennial Pictorial 100 Years of Legal Tradition, 1894-1994.

FRANK ALMONEY (1854-1926)

ADMITTED TO MONTGOMERY COUNTY BAR 1876[1]

BIRTH/PARENTS Franklin Almony was born in November 1854 to Jarrett (1816-1861)[2] and Mary Ann (Burke) Almoney (1822-1884)[3] proprietors of the Montgomery House Hotel in Rockville by 1860[4] where they had moved around 1852. His parents were married and living in Carroll County, Maryland in 1840, where they continued to reside in 1850.[5]

EDUCATION He graduated from Rockville Academy in 1872[6]

LEGAL CAREER He was admitted to the Montgomery County Bar in 1876[7]

MARRIAGE Unmarried[8]

DEATH He died 25 May 1926 at the Chestnut Lodge Sanatorium where he had been a patient for several months. He was associated with *The Advocate* for 44 years with his brother Albert J. Almoney.[9] He is buried in Rockville Cemetery.[10]

GEORGE MINOR ANDERSON (1856-1927)

Admitted to Montgomery County Bar in 1892

BIRTH/PARENTS: George Minor Anderson was born in 9 April 1856[11] on a farm in Montgomery County, Md. to Col. James Wallace Anderson and Mary Minor Anderson, who were married 18 May 1830. His father's sketch is in previous section.

EDUCATION: He was educated at the Rockville Academy and St. Johns College in Annapolis, MD. He was admitted to the U. S. Military Academy at West Point in September, 1878 but resigned in December 1880. He was elected county surveyor in 1888 but gave up surveying while in Mississippi because he became seriously ill with malaria. He took up the study of law at the National Law School in Washington.

LEGAL CAREER: In 1892 he was elected to the Maryland House of Delegate and served one term. He practiced law for a time in Rockville and later took a position as an attorney

---

1 Scharf, 668
2 Malloy, *Sentinel,* 4, 13 Dec. 1861. Stated he was Rockville resident for 9 years.
3 *Washington Post,* 3 July 1884
4 Hurley, *1860 Census*, 158-9.
5 Ancestry.com, 1840 & 1850 Census.
6 *Sentinel,* 5 July 1872
7 *Sentinel,* 11 April 1876
8 *Sentinel*, 28 May 1926, claimed he was a native of Baltimore.
9 *The Daily News* (Frederick MD) 25 May 1926
10 MCHS Cemetery File : Almoney, Frank
11 He was baptized 8 Sep 1865, and confirmed 18 April 1886 in Christ Episcopal Chuch Rockville, which provides an earlier date of birth (April 1856) than that recorded on his tombstone of October 1857. See Church record file, cemetery record file and Anderson family file at MCHS.

with the Department of Justice. Around 1913, he became an auditor with the Court of Claims and remained in this position until his death in 1927.[1]

MARRIAGE: On 11 November 1901 to Julia Prout8 Vinson (b. 4 April 1864, d. 2 June 1950),[2] daughter of Judge John Thomas Vinson 1. (1825-1903) and Frances Rachel Prout (1834-1888).

CHILDREN:

1. Thomas Minor Anderson b. 28 Oct. 1902; d. 3 Jan. 1981, m. 1927, Berthy Girola, (b. 25 Aug. 1901[3], d. 13 Nov. 1980)[4] daughter of M.Natalie Girola of Neuchatel, Switzerland. Thomas Minor Anderson followed in his ancestor's footsteps and also became an attorney after attending Rockville Academy, St. Alban's School and University of Virginia Law School.[5] He served as a Circuit Court Judge, later a Juvenile Court Judge, and Judge of the Special Appeals Court.

DEATH George Minor Anderson died 7 August 1927, at the age of 70 at his home. He is buried at Rockville Cemetery.

THOMAS ANDERSON (1835-1900)

Admitted to Montgomery County Bar 1855
President of the County Bar Association

BIRTH/PARENTS: Thomas Anderson was born 19 Sept., 1835 to Col. James Wallace Anderson and Mary Minor Anderson, who were married 18 May 1830. His brother is subject of the above sketch.

EDUCATION: Attended Rockville Academy and studied law with his father and John Brewer.

LEGAL CAREER: He was a prominent lawyer in Rockville from 1855 to 1900, during which time he participated in many of the important cases in the county. He was a partner of William Viers Bouic, Sr. in the firm of Bouic and Anderson until 1867, when Bouic was elected to the bench. In 1870 he entered partnership with Bouic's son, William V. Bouic, Jr., which continued until Anderson's death.[6]

---

[1] MCHS Family File : Anderson Family,1.4.1.8 "Biography of George M. Anderson" prepared by George M. Anderson, S. J.
[2] MCHS Family File : Anderson Family compiled by Eleanor Cook.
[3] MCHS Family File, Anderson George Minor folder.
[4] Death notice in MCHS Biography file cards.
[5] MCHS Biography File : Thomas Minor Anderson : Montgomery County Sentinel 8 Jan. 1981.
[6] *Sentinel Abstracts, 26 Jan. 1900*

MARRIAGE :

1. 11 Feb 1873,[1] Martha Wootton (b. 15 Apr. 1833, d. 4 Jan. 1882)[2], daughter of Dr. Turner Wootton and Olivia C. Wootton; She was the sister of Dr. Edward Wootton.
2. 18 April 1887, Ella Darne, (b. 19 Mar. 1850, d.10 May 1914)[3] daughter of the late Capt. Alexander H. C. Darne,[4] (1819-1907) and Mary Gassaway Darne (1824-1859) and "niece of Sen. George Peter."[5]

CHILDREN: Both marriages were childless.

DEATH: 19 Jan. 1900, at his residence in Rockville. Buried in Rockville Cemetery[6].

NOTES He was interested in the history of Montgomery County, and a historical sketch he delivered at the 1876 centennial celebration in Rockville is widely quoted. He was president of the county bar association and the Rockville Cemetery Association.[7]

WILLIAM WALLACE ANDERSON (1851-1922)

Admitted to The Montgomery County Bar 1881[8]

BIRTH/PARENTS: William Wallace Anderson was born 13 Nov. 1851 in Rockville, MD to Dr. John Wallace Anderson (b. abt 1808, d. 8 July 1867) and Mira Magruder Anderson (b. abt 1815, d. 5 Apr. 1872)[9].

LEGAL CAREER: Shortly after admission to bar he moved to Washington, D.C., then to Kentucky, where he was in 1885, when he received an appointment from the President to be the agent for the Indians of the Crow, Creek and Lower Brule Agency in Dakota[10]. He later returned to D.C., where he lived and practiced law, while spending time on a ranch in South Dakota.

MARRIAGE: On 15 Dec. 1881, in Washington, D.C to Martha Bradley, (b. 12 Dec. 1851, d. 1 Aug. 1923) daughter of Henry Bradley (b. 1808, d.1 Dec. 1876) and Mary (Prout) Bradley (b. 1811, d. bef. 1876).[11]

---

[1] Malloy, *Sentinel Abstracts,* 8

[2] MCHS Cemetery card file, Rockville Cemetery..

[3] MCHS Cemetery card file, Rockville Cemetery.

[4] *Seninel Abstracts,* 15 May 1914.

[5] Malloy, *Sentinel Abstracts,* 8, 22 April 1887.

[6] MCHS Cemetery card file.

[7] *Sentinel Abstracts,* 26 Jan. 1900.

[8] Scharf, 668.

[9] MCHS Anderson Family File; approx.. birthdates from census records; obit. For Mira Anderson in *Sentinel.* She died testate in Montgomery County.

[10] Proquest Historical Newspapers, *The Washington Post,* 4 Dec. 1885.

[11] MCHS Cemetery card file and Anderson family file.

CHILDREN:

1. Mary B. Anderson, b. 9 Oct. 1882, d. 14 Apr. 1964, only child living with parents from 1900 through 1920 censuses in Washington, D.C

DEATH: He died 17 Oct. 1922. Buried in Rockville Cemetery[1].

NOTES: His brother James W. Anderson and his father were also attorneys. In December 1912 he was a speaker at the Rockville Womens Club meeting, on "The Government and the Indians."[2]

RICHARD ROBINSON BEALL (1859-1903)

Admitted to the Montgomery County Bar 1880[3]

BIRTH/PARENTS: Richard Robinson Beall was born 31 Mar 1859 to Thomas John Beall, b. 27 Jul 1831, d. 9 Feb. 1897, and Catherine Goldsborough Owen Beall, b. 17 Aug. 1837, d. 11 Mar. 1910[4]. They lived on Locust Hill, inherited from Washington Winder Owen, Esq.[5]

LEGAL CAREER:. On the 1880 census, he was living with his father in Montgomery County, and listed his occupation as Attorney at Law. On the 1900 census, he was living in Washington, D.C., with his wife and daughter, and his occupation was listed as lawyer.

MARRIAGE: 6 Aug. 1891, by license in Washington, D.C., to Mary Ellen (Nellie). Middleton[6] (b. 12 Nov 1862, d. 13 Mar 1914)[7] daughter of Rueben Middleton (b. 27 Jan 1814, d. 24 Apr 1876)[8] and Mary Ellen Hyatt Middleton (abt 1825-1865).

CHILDREN:

1. Dorothy Middleton Beall, b. 26 Mar 1892, d. 02 Apr 1971, m. 15 Aug. 1914, James Harrison LeFeaver of New York. Had issue.[9]

---

[1] MCHS Cemetery card file, for William W. Anderson; his wife and daughter are listed with him.

[2] Proquest Historical Newspapers, *The Washington Post,* 29 Dec. 1912.

[3] Scharf, 668

[4] Newspaper death notice clippings in Beall Family file, in Alexander Beall file for Thomas J. and Catherine G. Beall.

[5] Farquhar, *Historic Montgomery County, Maryland,* 207-208,

[6] Pippenger, *District of Columbia Marriage Records Index,1885-1892,* 25.

[7] MCHS Alexander Beall Family File includes newspaper death notices and family information. Her marriage announcement stated she was a daughter of the late Col. Richard Middleton, but no record for him has been found. She is living with Ruben Middleton, in her married sister's family (Catherine Hyatt Middleton & Lemuel Clark), on the 1870 census in Prince George's County from research on Ancestry.com. After her father's death, by 1880, she was living with her Hyatt grandparents. In the marriage announcement she was listed as the niece of the presiding minister, Rev. J. A. Regester, of St. John's, Georgetown, who married her mother's half sister, Harriett (Hattie) Hyatt.

[8] Prince George's County Marriage and Census Records, Prince George's County deeds on line at mdlandrec.net , and newspaper abstracts by Balch. Date of death in *Gasch's Funderal Home Records*, published by PG County.

[9] MCHS Alexander Beall Family File.

DEATH 21 April 1903, Washington, D.C.[1]

GEORGE BIBB BROWN (1869-1959)

Admitted to Montgomery County Bar 1893

BIRTH/PARENTS: George Bibb Brown was born 16 November 1869 in Montgomery County, Maryland, to Thomas J. and Caroline M. (Bibb) Brown. He was baptized George Minos Bibb Brown at St. Mary's Catholic Church, Rockville, MD.[2] Thomas J. and Caroline M. (Bibb) Brown planned to establish a residential community on their property in 1895 called Brown's Station on the Metropolitan Branch of the B & O Railroad.[3]

EDUCATION: Gonzaga High School, Washington, DC National University, Washington, DC in 1893 and Georgetown University Law School, Washington, DC .[4]

LEGAL CAREER: Admitted to the Montgomery County Bar on 6 Jun 1893[5]; an original signer of the Montgomery County Bar Association Constitution in 1895.[6] In 1900 the census listed him as an Attorney at law, ten years later, in 1910 he was listed as street car conductor. According to a granddaughter, Lucy Banting, "after a controversial case in which he represented a black family, they took away his license to practice law."[7]

MARRIAGE: On 18 Nov. 1893, at St. John's Church, Forest Glen, MD, Lucinda B. Anderson "of Wheaton" (b. 25 Jun. 1869, d. 11 Feb. 1912), daughter of Charles H. Anderson (b. 1825, d. 25 Jan. 1895)[8] and Lavinia Brown Anderson (b. 24 Oct. 1828, d. bef 1870). Marriage record noted dispensation of impediment, in that they were first cousins.[9]

CHILDREN:

1. George Minos Brown, b. Feb. 1897, d. after 1959, m. 28 April 1926, in Alexandria, VA., Marie L. Jett[10]. Filed for divorce in 1932.[11]
2. Henry Ashton Brown, b. 1902, d. 9 Jul 1929 (buried St. John's Cemetery)[12] Unmarried.

DEATH: 26 May 1959 at the home of a granddaughter at 2753 Woodley Place, Washington, DC. He is buried at St. Rose of Lima Cemetery, Cloppers, MD.

---

[1] Death notice clipping in MCHS Alexander Beall Family File.

[2] MCHS Church Card file.

[3] *Gaithersburg, The Heart of Montgomery County*, 21.

[4] *Sentinel, June 1893,* and MCHS Biography File, Brown, George Bibb, obituary from *Washington Star,* 26 May 1959.

[5] *Sentinel,* June 1893.

[6] Thompson, *Western Gateway, 98.*

[7] Cook, "The Anderson-Brown Family of Montgomery County, Maryland," 33.

[8] *Sentinel,* 25 Jan 1895.

[9] MCHS Church Records file, marriage of George Bibb Brown. Also Hurley, 1860, 1870, 1880 census records Charles H. Anderson and family.

[10] Sentinel, 7 May 1926.

[11] *Sentinel,* 3 Feb 1932.

[12] *Sentinel,* 12 Jul 1929.

NOTES: Owned a 170 acre farm near Gaithersburg, MD; he and his father won numerous awards at the Montgomery County Agricultural Fair for their horses. George Minos Bibb Brown lived during his later years in Silver Spring, MD where he was a member of the Holy Name Society of St. Michael's Church. He had been an invalid since an automobile accident in 1956.[1]

JAMES F. BYRNE (1858-1923)

Admitted to Montgomery County Bar 1885[2]

BIRTH/PARENTS: James Franklin Byrne was born 19 August 1858 to George F. Byrne and Mary E. McMarkham Byrne, in Martinsburg, Jefferson County, (West) Virginia. Mary McMarkham was George Byrne's second wife; they married in 1855. She died 8 Mar. 1859.[3]

MARRIAGE: Married on 23 Nov. 1892[4] to Sarah Elizabeth Jones (b. 19 Jul 1868, d. 15 Jun 1960), daughter of Leonidas and Elizabeth Isabella (King) Jones.[5] .

CHILDREN:

1. Helen Gertrude Jones, b. 20 Sep 1893, d. 7 Aug 1945, m. 27 Mar. 1915 to James William Stuart Moler.

DEATH: 23 April 1923 at Washington, D. C.[6]

NOTES: He was appointed a school teacher in Montgomery County in 1880[7], at the time of his marriage in 1892, he was the principal of the public school at Poolesville. According to entries in the Sentinel from 1887 through 1902 he attended various Teacher's Associations meetings and literary societies meetings. Both James and his father were teachers in Montgomery County. James was nominated for Justice of the Peace in 1902 and 1904[8].

WASHINGTON CATLETT (1852-1934)

Admitted to Montgomery County Bar 1877[9]

BIRTH/PARENTS: Washington Catlett was born 9 Oct. 1852 in Port Royal, VA, to George Washington Catlett (b. 1825, d. 28 May 1895, buried St. Peter's Church, Port Royal, VA) and Elizabeth Fitzhugh Catlett (b. 1825).

---

[1] MCHS Biography File, newspaper obituary.
[2] *Sentinel,* 20 Nov. 1855.
[3] MCHS Family File : Byrne : Family Bible records.
[4] *Sentinel,* 2 Dec. 1892.
[5] Hurley, *Our Maryland Heritage : King Families.*
[6] MCHS Cemetery File: Byrne, James F.
[7] *Sentinel,* 3 Sep. 1880.
[8] *Sentinel,* 21 Feb 1902, 26 Feb 1904.
[9] Scharf, 668.

LEGAL CAREER:. He passed the "necessary examination and has been admitted to the Bar of this County."[1]However, there is no evidence that he pursued a legal career, as later censuses in North Carolina showed he returned to teaching[2]. He was the Principal of the Rockville Academy at the graduation date of June 20, 1876.[3]

MARRIAGE: On 23 Dec. 1879, in New Hanover, N.C., Margaret Dudley McIlhenny[4] (b. 1 Jan. 1860, d. 8 Nov. 1930, Wilmington, NC) daughter of Thomas Cowen McIlhenny (b. 1 Jun. 1825, d. 17 Apr. 1900) and Margaret Dudley McIlhenny (b. 10 Nov. 1828, d. 21 Mar. 1881) – all buried in Oakdale Cemetery, New Hanover, N.C.[5]

CHILDREN:

1. Margaret (Patsy) J. Catlett, b. 5 Oct. 1880, d. 2 Sep. 1967, m. 3 Oct. 1906, Clarence L. Rowe.
2. George Fitzhugh Catlett, b. 21 Sep. 1883, d. 22 Mar. 1982.
3. Sarah Cowen Catlett, b. July 1886, d. 19 Jan. 1962, m. Paul Langley Cantwell.
4. Susan Catlett, b. abt 1890, no other information.

DEATH 29 August 1934, Wilmington, New Hanover, NC[6].

WARREN RAGAN CHOATE (1865-1924)

Admitted to Montgomery County Bar 1890

BIRTH/PARENTS: Warren Ragan Choate was born in Washington, D.C. on 20 Sep 1865 to Warren Choate (Jun 1842[7]-9Mar 1924[8]) and Katherine M. Ragan (1842- 24 Nov. 1924). The family moved to Rockville in 1890.[9]

EDUCATION: He attended public and private schools of Washington and took law courses at the National University and Columbia University.[10]

LEGAL CAREER: He practiced law in Washington from 1889 to 1898. He then entered the Treasury Department as a law clerk. He was appointed chief clerk to the Bureau of Corporations, Department of Commerce and Labor in March 1903.

---

[1] Bowman, *Sentinel,* 15 June 1877, p.31.
[2] www.ancestry.com, On the 1880 census he was listed in Wilmington, Hanover County, N.C., occupation teacher, as he was in 1900.
[3] Bowman, *Sentinel,* 7 July 1876, p. 12.
[4] www.ancestry.com, NC Marriage Records.
[5] Find-A-Grave.com - cemetery records.
[6] www.ancestry.com, NC Death Records
[7] U. S. Federal Census : 1900
[8] Sentinel, 14 Mar.1924
[9] Thompson, *Western Gateway*, 97.
[10] Sentinel, 18 Jan. 1924

MARRIAGE: He was married to Alice B. Fleming of Hamilton, Ohio,[1] at the Foundry M.E. Church in Washington on 4 Nov 1904.[2] She died on 23 Sep 1927 near San Francisco, CA. She is buried in Rockville Cemetery.[3]

CHILDREN : No children mentioned in any sources. No children documented on 1910 or 1920 Federal Census.

DEATH: Warren R. Choate died in Washington, D.C. at his apartment in the Albermarle on 17th and T Streets, NW, on 13 Jan 1924. He is buried at Rockville Cemetery.[4]

NOTES Warren Choate, Sr. was listed as "real estate dealer" on the 1900 Federal Census for Rockville. He was on the Board of Trustees at Washington Grove as secretary and vice-president for several years.[5]

REMUS RIGGS DARBY (1847-1916)

Judge of the Orphans Court

BIRTH/PARENTS: Remus Riggs Darby was born 25 August 1847 at Comus, Montgomery County, MD to John William Darby (b. 8 Mar. 1822, d. 22 Feb. 1889) and Ellen Ruth (Edelen) Darby (b. 16 Sep 1819, d. 11 Mar. 1896).[6]

LEGAL CAREER: Served as a Judge of the Orphans Court[7]

MARRIAGE

1. 30 October 1879 to Antoinette Griffith Chiswell (b. 26 August 1858, d. 23 May 1893), daughter of George W. and Leah (Griffith) Chiswell.[8]
2. 19 November 1895 at the National Hotel, Washington, D.C. to Clara Ireland Fowler (b. 4 August 1860, d. 14 December 1938), daughter of William and Alice (Jones) Fowler.[9]

CHILDREN:
by 1st wife

1. Emily Poole Darby, b. 24 0ct. 1880, d. 7 May 1960, m. 1. David Clark.[10], 2. on 10 Dec. 1911, William Clifton Brown (b. 8 Feb. 1882, d. 17 Nov. 1939)[11].

---

[1] Ibid
[2] Paperclips, Cutler, Dona, 184.
[3] Ibid, 163
[4] *Sentinel*, 18 Jan 1924.
[5] Edwards, *Washington Grove 1873-1937*, Appendix I
[6] Frain, *Monocacy Cemetery*, 115, 116.,
[7] *Portrait and Biographical Record of the Sixth Congressional District*, .827
[8] *Sentinel,* 7 Nov. 1879, "married NettieChiswell by Rev. H E. Hatcher at the home of the bride."
[9] *Sentinel, 22* Nov. 1911
[10] MCHS Darby family file, "Descendants of George Washington Darby" by R. H. Darby.
[11] Frain, *Monocacy Cemetery, 79.*

2. George Chiswell Darby, b. 30 Aug. 1882, d. 11 July 1938, m. 16 Oct. 1917, to Georgianna Buxton, b. 28 Oct. 1884, d. 21 May 1959,[1] daughter of William L. Buxton (1863-1951) and Ella R. Hedges Buxton (1862-1945).[2]
3. John Edwin Darby, b. 17 Sep. 1884, d. 1 Aug. 1975, m. 6 Nov.1907, to Gertrude Hyatt, (b. 9 Feb.1876, d. 25 Mar.1972) Both buried in Monocacy Cemetery.[3]
4. Genevieve Darby, b. 23 Feb. 1888, d. 15 June 1970, m 4 Nov. 1908, to Charles Thomas Brosius, (b. 27 Mar. 1879, d. 19 Apr. 1938). Buried in Monocacy Cemetery.[4]
5. Ruth Ellen Darby, b. 17 Dec. 1890, d. 10 May 1897
6. Remus Riggs Darby, Jr., b. Feb. 1893, d. 12 July 1982, m. 24 Jan. 1914, in Baltimore, MD to Della Bartgis[5] , b. 18 Dec. 1892, d. 9 June 1996[6], daughter Charles Washington Bartgis (1856-1936) and Annie A. Bartgis (1860-1944)[7] of Poolesville, MD.

by 2nd wife

7. William Leroy Darby, b. 13 Sep. 1896, d. 29 Mar' 1963, m. to Laura Allnutt, (b. 26 Apr.1896, d. 28 Dec. 1989), daughter of Nathan Smith Allnutt and Myra (Compton) Allnutt[8]. Buried in Monocacy Cemetery.[9]
8. Lawrence Jones Darby, b. 22 Sep. 1898, d. 4 June 1987, m. 23 Nov. 1922, to Arlene C. Johnson., daughter of Mr. and Mrs. B. O. Johnston of Wytheville, VA.
9. Alice Rebecca Darby, b. 29 March 1900[10] d. 4 Oct. 1995, m. 26 June 1924, to William Franklin Griffith, b. 1899, d. 17 June 1978 Buried in Monocacy Cemetery.[11].

DEATH: 10 July 1916, buried in Monocacy Cemetery, Beallsville, MD

NOTES John W. Darby and R. R. Darby, were listed as Millers in Barnesville, in 1879 Directory;[12] Remus Riggs Darby was a Democrat; County Commissioner 1895-1897[13]

HENRY BRADLEY DAVIDSON (1860-1930)

Admitted to Montgomery County Bar in 1882[14]

---

[1] Holdcraft, *Names in Stone,* 300. Both buried in Mt. Olivet Cemetery in Frederick, MD.
[2] MCHS Buxton family file.
[3] Frain, *Monocacy Cemetery,* 131.
[4] Frain, *Monocacy Cemetery,* 181.
[5]*Sentinel*, 30 Jan. 1914
[6] MCHS Biography Files, obituary from *Frederick Post,* 10 June 1996.
[7] Holdcraft, *Names in Stone,* 115, parents buried in Middletown Lutheran Cemetery.
[8] Hurley, *1900 Montgomery County Census,* 335.
[9] Frain, *Monocacy Cemetery,* 156.
[10]Hurley, *The Griffith Family*,.72.
[11] Frain, *Monocacy Cemetery,* 116.
[12]Boyd, *History of Montgomery County*, 119.
[13]MacMaster, *A Grateful Rembrance,* 400.
[14] *Sentinel,* 9 June 1882.

BIRTH/PARENTS: Henry Bradley Davidson was born 30 June 1860[1] to Dr. James Henry Davidson, b. 2 Sep. 1828, d. 8 Mar. 1886 and Sarah Slater (Bradley) Davidson b. 13 Nov 1838, d. 7 July 1889.[2] [3]

MARRIAGE:

1. June 1887 in Baltimore to Nannie Cunningham[4]. b. 25 September 1862, d. 22 October 1888,[5] at her home at 3024 Q St., Washington, DC of "Typhoid fever"[6]
2. On 2 January 1890, (license in Montgomery County) to Mary Stannard Porter. b. 1 April 1862, in Indiana, PA, d. 5 Sep. 1935 in New Bedford, PA. After the death of her husband she lived with her stepdaughter Louise in Edgemore, Bethesda.[7]

CHILDREN:

by 1st wife:

1. Louise Armstrong Davidson, b. 17 May 1888 in Georgetown, Washington, DC, unmarried, d. 18 Dec. 1973. Buried in Oak Hill Cemetery. Lived in Edgemore, Bethesda, MD.

by 2nd wife:

2. Henry Bradley Davidson, Jr., b. 10 Sep. 1892, in Bethesda, m. 1. Jessica Alward (divorced), m. 2. Elizabeth Bishop Dunn of Philadelphia, and probably m. 3. Elva Statler[8]
3. Richard Porter Davidson, (Lt. Col.) b. 7 Sep. 1900 in Washington, D.C., d. 2 Nov. 1957, Cooperstown, N.Y.;[9] m. 1. 5 April 1824, in Washington, D.C. to Elizabeth Gordon Hannah, (b.1 Dec. 1901, d. 9 Apr. 1943 Fairfax County, VA, daughter of David Hannah; m. 2. in Cooperstown, NY to Mabel Elmore Rucker. Lived near Fairfax, VA; assistant to Gen. Louis B. Hershey, director of the Selective Service.

DEATH: 21 July 1930 in Atlantic City, N.J.. Buried in Oak Hill Cemetery, Georgetown, D.C.

NOTES: The Davidson family owned property in Montgomery County between Bethesda and the District Line. Henry Bradley Davidson [10] was a member of the Bethesda Presbyterian Church where he was an Elder.

---

[1] Pippenger, *Oak Hill Cemetery*, Vol. 1, 301.

[2] Pippenger, *Oak Hill Cemetery*, Vol. 2, 166.

[3] Martin, *James Davidson of the Maryland Line,* 14, she lists birthdate as August 30, 1860. Manuel, *Marriage Licenses,* Sarah S. Bradley to James H. Davidson, 11 Oct. 1859.

[4] Martin, *Op.Cit.*

[5] Pippenger, *Oak Hill Cemetery*, Vol. 2, 166.

[6] *Sentinel,* 26 October 1888

[7] Martin, *Op.Cit.*

[8] *News,* March 4, 1935.

[9] *Find-A-Grave,* via Ancestry, accessed 24 June 2016.

[10] MCHS Church Records file.

JAMES D. DAWSON (1846-1909)

Admitted to Montgomery County Bar before 1880

BIRTH/PARENTS: James D. Dawson was born 16 Feb. 1846, in Rockville, MD, to Lawrence Allnut Dawson, b. 2 Oct. 1807, d. 6 Aug 1875, and Mary Elizabeth Kiger Dawson , b. Oct. 1814, d. 31 Dec. 1877.[1]

EDUCATION: His father and a brother were also attorneys.

LEGAL CAREER:. He was a member of the Rockville Bar, listed as a lawyer in 1880 on the census.[2] He was a clerk of the court in 1885, and appointed a States Attorney in 1887[3]. He moved to Seattle in the fall of 1889.

MARRIAGE: 21 Oct. 1895, to Henrietta Hoffman, b. Nov. 1847, d. 17 May 1926, of Spokane, WA.[4]

CHILDREN: One stepson, Frederick Dawson, b. March 1892, probably born Frederick Hoffman.

DEATH: 30 Jan. 1909 at the Dawson homestead in Rockville, leaving his wife, Henrietta Dawson of Spokane, WA.[5]. Buried in Rockville Cemetery.

NOTES: City Directories accessed on Ancestry, show that in 1901, James Dawson, lawyer, and Henrietta Dawson, a student at the business college, listed as boarding at same address. Unable to find further information.

THOMAS DAWSON (1857-1924)

Admitted to Montgomery County Bar before 1895

BIRTH/PARENTS: Thomas Dawson was born 6 Oct. 1857, in Rockville, MD, to Lawrence Allnut Dawson, b. 2 Oct. 1807, d. 6 Aug. 1875, and Mary Elizabeth Kiger Dawson, b. Oct. 1814, d. 31 Dec. 1877.[6]

EDUCATION: His father and a brother were also attorneys.

LEGAL CAREER:. Member of Law firm of Dawson, Dawson and Welsh[7]. He was appointed Postmaster at Rockvile under President Harrison. In 1895, he was a candidate for States Attorney, as a Republican; in 1897 served as Clerk of Court.[8]

---

[1] MCHS Dawson Family File.
[2] Hurley, *1880 census for Montgomery County, 257,* James Dawson, 34, was head of household, as the the eldest of 5 siblings, with George C., 33, Mary 29, Ann 24, and Thomas 23 years old.
[3] *Sentinel,* 25 Sep. 1885, and 26 Aug. 1887.
[4] MCHS Dawson Family File.
[5] *Sentinel,* 5 Feb. 1909; MCHS Cemetery Card File, on Lawrence Dawson family marker.
[6] Allnutt, *Genealogy Database printouts including the Upper Montgomery County MD families of Allnutt, Chiswell, Darby, Dawson, White. "Dawson Family Registry*
[7] Obituary from *Sentinel,* 3 Oct. 1924.
[8] *Portrait and Biographical Record,* 608.

MARRIAGE: On 3 Jan 1889, he married Mary Alice Peter, b. 23 Feb. 1859, d. 19 Oct. 1928, daughter of George Peter, also an attorney, b. 28 Nov 1829, d. 6 August 1893, and Eliza Lavinia Gassaway Peter, b. 26 April 1831, d. 11 May 1909.

CHILDREN

1. Lavinia Dawson, b. Feb. 1890, d. 28 Dec. 1961, married John Henderson (b. 16 Oct. 1887, d. 14 Jul . 1959).
2. Thomas L. Dawson, b. 15 Sep.1892, d. 14 Sep. 1944, married Anne Frazier Dawson (d. 13 Dec. 1980, age 80).
3. Elizabeth Dawson (1896-1979) in Cloverly, MD) married George R. Canby (1884-1970).
4. Mary Dawson, b. 24 Jul. 1898, d. 27 Jun. 1965, married Thomas Hyde, (b. 5 Nov. 1891, d. 9 Sep. 1949).

DEATH: 24 Sept. 1924, buried in Rockville Cemetery.

NOTES: Member of Masonic Lodge, King Solomon's Council Vestryman for 40 years and Registrar of Christ Episcopal Church for 27 years.[1]

JAMES ALBY HENDERSON (1871-1926)

Admitted to Montgomery County Bar in 1893

BIRTH/PARENTS: James Alby Henderson, was born 7 Jun. 1871, to James Barnes Henderson (b. 23 Mar.1845, d. 27 May 1917) and Clara Smith Adamson Henderson, b. 13 July 1846, d. 8 Dec. 1926.

EDUCATION: He received his degree in law from Georgetown University Law School in June 1893[2].

LEGAL CAREER: "Attorney at law," listed as occupation on 1900 census.[3]

MARRIAGE: On 3 Feb. 1915, Washington, D.C., to Mabel Anderson Spencer, (b. Dec. 1895, still living in 1940 in Washington, D.C.) daughter of Thomas H. Spencer (b. 10 Apr. 1867, d. 5 May 1913) and Cora Caroline Couch Spencer (b. 15 Nov. 1863, d. 4 Aug. 1937, buried High Point, N.C.).

---

[1] Obituary from *Sentinel,* 3 Oct. 1924.
[2] Bowman, *Sentinel,* 2 June 1893.
[3] Hurley, *1900 Census Montgomery County,* 234.

CHILDREN:

1. Helen Neel Henderson[1], b. Nov. 1919[2], d. Oct. 1973[3], lived in Washington, D.C.

DEATH: 2 Nov. 1926, listed in father's cemetery plot, Rockville Cemetery[4].

NOTES: His father, James Barnes Henderson was also an attorney.

FRANK HIGGINS (1861-1922)

Admitted to Montgomery County Bar about 1891

BIRTH/PARENTS: Frank Higgins was born 22 May 1861 in Rockville, MD, to John Hamilton Higgins and Sophia Dorothy "Dora" Barnard Higgins[5].

EDUCATION: Graduated from the National Law School and admitted to the bar in 1891.[6]

LEGAL CAREER: Listed as "Attorney at Law" on 1900 census. Offices across from the Court House. Ran unsuccessfully for Attorney General on the Prohibition ticket in 1891.[7]

MARRIAGE: 21 October 1885 to Roberta Baker (b. 6 July 1862, d. 5 Nov. 1936), daughter of Reuben Baker of Georgetown.[8]

CHILDREN:[9]

1. Roberta Philippa Higgins, b. 26 Sept. 1886, d. 6 Dec. 1958, unmarried. Buried in Rockville Cemetery.
2. Laura Mildred Higgins, b. 16 March 1889, d. 9 Nov. 1964, m. 26 Jan. 1912 in Wilmington, DE to Valentine Wilson, son of C. A. Wilson of Washington, D.C. Lived in Rockville; buried in Rockville Cemetery.
3. Frank Hamilton Higgins,, b. 3 July 1890, d. 26 May 1957, m. 10 May 1920 in Chambersburg, PA, to Mary Cecil Garrett of Rockville (b. 26 Apr 1898, d. 20 Nov. 1969). Both buried in Forest Oak Cemetery, Gaithersburg.
4. Margaret Tayloe Higgins, b. 17 April 1894, d. Aug. 1964, m. 15 March 1924 to Thomas Ray Cockman. Lived in Colorado.

---

[1] Malloy, *Sentinel,* 19 Nov. 1926.

[2] www.ancestry.com, 1920 Federal Census, Washington, D.C., enumerated 10 Jan. 1920, Helen N. Henderson was listed as one month old. She was living in household of her Spencer grandparents, along with her parents. In 1930 Federal Census, her mother was head of household, and Caroline Spencer, her grandmother, and an uncle also were in the home.

[3] www.ancestry.com, SSDI. Unable to find obituary or other verifying information.

[4] Malloy, *Sentinel,* 5 Nov. 1926; MCHS Cemetery Card File.

[5] Hurley, *Higgins Families,* 11.

[6] Bowman, *Sentinel,* 5 June 1891.

[7] *Sentinel,* July 24, 1936.

[8] Hurley, *Higgins Families, 11.*

[9] Hurley, *Higgins Families, 11* and MCHS Family File and Cemetery Card Index.

5. Cornelia Cecilia Bevans Higgins, b. 26 March 1898, d. 30 May 1898. Buried in Rockville Cemetery. Twin.
6. Lawrence Augustus Higgins, b. 26 March 1898, d. 5 Oct 1966, unmarried. Buried in Rockville Cemetery. Twin.

DEATH 25 September 1922. Buried in Rockville Cemetery[1].

NOTES Active in the Prohibition Party and attended various Party Conventions. Trustee of the public schools of the 4th District. Belonged to the Montgomery County Anti-Saloon League. Belonged to the Rockville Christian Church. In 1889, ran for the County Surveyor on the Prohibition Party ticket and was a member of the party's executive committee.[2]

WILLARD HINKLEY (1862-1891)

Admitted to Montgomery County Bar 1890

BIRTH/PARENTS: Willard Hinkley was born about 1861 to George Hinkley, b. 30 Dec 1826, d. 4 Mar 1866[3] and Eltinge Mary (Lodor) Hinkley, b. abt. 1833, d. 4 Oct. 1921.[4]

LEGAL CAREER: Admitted to the Montgomery County Bar in March 1890.[5] Shortly after being admitted to the bar he moved to Spokane Falls, Washington to practice law.[6] Soon thereafter he returned to Gaithersburg, probably because of illness.

MARRIAGE: Unmarried.

DEATH He died in Alexandria, Virginia 1 Feb. 1891.[7]

NOTES In 1888 he was given a teaching position at Bailey's School.[8]

HOBART HUTTON (1848-1896)

Admitted to Montgomery County Bar in 1880

BIRTH/PARENTS Hobart Hutton was born on 16 April 1848 in Montgomery County to. Rev. Orlando Hutton (1815-1891) and Sidney Claire Buchanan Hutton (1816-1904).[9] Rev. Orlando Hutton was an Episcopal minister who came to Montgomery County in 1844, and

---

[1] MCHS Cemetery Card Index.
[2] *Sentinel*, 16 August 1889.
[3] Cemetery Card Index, MCHS, buried St. John's Olney, born in Baltimore. Bowman, *Sentinel, 3-9-1866, "a teacher in the public schools"*
[4] Sentinel Abstracts.
[5] Sentinel, 1890 Mar 28
[6] Sentinel, 1890 July 18
[7] Sentinel, 1891 Feb 6
[8] Sentinel, 1888 Jun 22
[9] Hutton, (typescript), MCHS Library, 16.

was a long time minister at St. John's Episcopal Church, Olney. He also taught at the Brookeville Academy.[1]

EDUCATION Probably at Brookeville Academy; attended Hobart College.[2]

LEGAL CAREER: Admitted to the Bar of Montgomery Co. in 1880.

MARRIAGE By license dated 7 Feb. 1877, in Washington, D.C.[3] to Mary Lyons Stone of Washington, D.C.[4] (d. Aug. 1900) daughter of William J. Stone and Mary Frances Stone.[5]

CHILDREN:[6]

1. William Stone Hutton (1877-1908) m. Mary Sandys Lynch (1879-1965) of Petersburg, Va. Attended Virginia Military Academy. Went to CA.
2. Hobert Buchanan Hutton (d. 20 April 1881 "aged 6 months.")[7]

DEATH 1 Nov. 1896. Buried in "Mt. Calvary," Roxbury Mills, Howard Co.[8],

NOTES Farmed his father's property. Taught at the Maryland Agricultural College (now University of Maryland). Settled on property 'Clearfield' near Norbeck where he farmed and practiced law until his death.[9]

CHARLES M. JONES 1873-1957

Attorney at Law[10]

BIRTH/PARENTS: Charles Mace Jones was born 3 May 1873 in Cecil County, MD, to Charles Benedict Jones (1842-1901) and his first wife, Emma Jones, who were married before 1870 in Cecil County, (b. ca. 1838, d. bet 1875-1880. Charles B. Jones married 2. Lavinia Lyddane, in 1883 in Montgomery County (b. 2 July 1854, d. 9 Aug. 1948)[11]. On the 1900 Census, Charles B. Jones was postmaster in Rockville.

---

[1] MCHS Hutton Family File.
[2] Hutton, (typescript), MCHS Library, op.cit., 16.
[3] Provine, *D.C. Marriage Records 1870-1877*,
[4] Hutton, (typescript), MCHS Library, op.cit., 16.
[5] "Mary Lyons Hutton, widow of Hobert Hutton died Tues. last at the home of her mother in Washington." (Sentinel, Aug. 17, 1900).
Hutton, (typescript), MCHS Library, op.cit., 16.
[7] *Howard County Maryland Records, Vol. II*, 34.
[8] "a member of the Rockville Bar died Sunday last at his home 'Clearfield' near Norbeck in his 49th year. Buried at Mt. Calvary*, Howard Co." (Sentinel, Nov. 6, 1896) *Mt. Calvary was a mission his father started; probably his parents are buried there, also *Howard County Maryland Records, Vol. II*, 34
[9] Hutton, (typescript), MCHS Library, op.cit., 16.
[10] Occupation on 1900 census.
[11] MCHS Cemetery Card File.

LEGAL CAREER: Sept. 1893 he was a charter member of the Rockville Branch of the Washington National Building and Loan Association[1]. In 1896, he was appointed a Justice of the Peace for Montgomery County by the Governor.[2]

MARRIAGE/CHILDREN: No record of marriage or children has been found. His death notice in the Washington Post/Times Herald listed his brother Edmund L. Jones of Washington. D.C. and his sisters: Mrs. Charles A. (Harriett Jones) Beard, Sr. of Rockville, and Mrs. Herbert (Marie Jones) Diamond of Gaithersburg.

DEATH: Charles M. Jones died 23 Nov. 1957 and is buried in Rockville Cemetery. He had lived at 401 W. Montgomery Ave., where his mother had resided for 59 years at the time of her death in 1948

ALEXANDER KILGOUR, JR. (1855-1917)

Admitted to Montgomery County Bar In 1882[3]

BIRTH/PARENTS: Alexander Kilgour was born about 1855 in Rockville to Alexander (1799-1867) and Margaret Ann (Stribling) Kilgour (1815-1903). His father was also a lawyer.

EDUCATION: He read law with his brother-in-law, Judge A. W. Chilton, of Alexandria, VA.[4]

LEGAL CAREER: He began his practice of law in Rockville in 1882. He was appointed States Attorney for Montgomery County in 1895. He was a member of the Supreme Court of D.C. He was a Democrat.[5]

MARRIAGE: At the age of 59, on 3 October 1914, in Rockville, he married Eliza Barrett Prettyman (1866-1954). She was 48 years old, the daughter of Elijah Barrett Prettyman, (1830-1907) Clerk of the Court of Montgomery County and Lydia Forrest Johnston Prettyman. (1832-1917).[6]

CHILDREN: No children.

DEATH: He died suddenly on 11 April 1917, in the court room in Rockville. He had just finished addressing the jury in a case in which he was counsel. He is buried in Rockville Cemetery.[7]

NOTES: He was an Episcopalian, and a member of the Elks, Great Falls Lodge #89.

---

[1] Bowman, *Montgomery County Sentinel,* 29 Sept 1893.

[2] Bowman, *Montgomery County Sentinel,* 21 Feb 1896.

[3] *Sentinel,* June 8, 1917 in Kilgour Family File, MCHS, "Report of Committee of the Rockville Bar, on the Death of the late Alexander Kilgour."

[4] *Portrait and Biographical Encyclopedia of the Sixth Congressional District,* 758-759 &775.

[5]*Sentinel,* June 8, 1917, *Op.Cit.*

[6] Prettyman Family File, MCHS.

[7] *Sentinel,* April 13, 1917; MCHS Cemetery card file.

WILLIAM KILGOUR (1834-1907)

Admitted to Montgomery County Bar in 1885

BIRTH/PARENTS: William Kilgour was born 24 July 1834 to Alexander Kilgour (b. abt. 1799, d. 1 Sep. 1867[1]) and Margaret Ann Stribling Kilgour, (b. 1815 Frederick County, VA; d. 6 May 1903, Rockville, MD[2]). His father and brother were also lawyers.

EDUCATION: St. John's College, Annapolis, Class of 1855.[3] Read law with Judge Pearre in Cumberland, MD.

LEGAL CAREER: In 1856, he was elected to Maryland Legislature as a Democrat. Later, appointed Assistant States Attorney, and served as clerk and attorney for the Allegancy County Board of County Commissioners. In 1862- he was elected secretary of Maryland Senate. From 1862 to 1869, practiced law in Washington, D.C., and in Alexandria, VA with his brother-in-law, Judge Chilton. In 1872 – elected Commonwealth Attorney for Alexandria City and County. He returned to Rockville in 1878, and in 1890 was elected to Legislature from Montgomery County[4]. Served four years in U.S. Internal Revenue Service under President Cleveland.

MARRIAGE: On October 17, 1858, in Rockville he was married to Rose Ellen Queen, ,b. ca. 1834, buried 12 Sept. 1886, age 52,[5] in St. Mary's old Catholic Church Cemetery. She was the adopted daughter and niece of Henry Harding of Rockville, and daughter of Charles J. and Maria Queen.

CHILDREN

1. Ann Stribling Kilgour, (1859-1877).
2. Mary Carter Kilgour (b. 1863, d. 29 Jul 1930, age 66 years, buried St. Mary's Old Cemetery, Rockville)[6] unmarried.

DEATH 14 July 1907, buried in Harding Lot at St. Mary's Old Cemetery[7].

---

1 MCHS Cemetery Card file index.

2 Church Records File, MCHS Records of Christ Episcopal Church, age given as 86 years.

3 *Portrait and Biographical Encyclopedia,* 758-759.

4 *Portrait and Biographical Encylcopedia,* 758-759.

5 MCHS St. Mary's Old cemetery, unmarked grave, burial from church records.

6 MCHS Cemetery Card file, unmarked grave from church records.

7 MCHS Cemetery Card file.

PHILIP DANDRIDGE LAIRD (1846-1920)

Admitted to Montgomery County Bar about 1880

BIRTH/PARENTS: Philip Dandridge Laird was born 15 Nov. 1846 in Cambridge, Maryland[1] to William Winder Laird (1808-1848) and Williamina Elizabeth Cadwalader (Goldsborough) Laird (1813-1865).[2]

LEGAL CAREER: According to a 1914 *Sentinel* article, he was admitted to the [Dorchester County, MD] bar in 1867 and "practiced law in his native town" until he moved to Montgomery County in 1880 "where he built up a reputation as an able lawyer." He was a founder of the Montgomery County Bar Association in 1894 and signer of the organization's constitution in 1895.[3] A birthday notice for his widow, noted that he was a one-time State Senator[4].

MARRIAGE: On 2 Dec. 1885 to Ella Gaither Magruder (b. 16 Feb. 1857, d. 2 Dec 1941), daughter of William Bowie Magruder (b. 1 Nov. 1802, d. 21 Jan. 1873) and Elizabeth Worthington (Gaither) Magruder (b. 14 Dec. 1825, d. 18 Oct. 1886).[5]

CHILDREN: Ella G. Laird, b. 18 Nov. 1886, d. 3 Dec. 1886, age 15 days old.[6]

DEATH{ 27 Apr 1920 in Rockville. He is buried in Rockville Cemetery with his wife and child.[7]

NOTES: He appears in the 1880 federal census residing with his brother, Rev. William H. Laird, rector of St. Bartholomew's Episcopal Church, Laytonsville, MD.[8] He was a member of the Maryland House of Delegates from Montgomery County, 1886-1892; organized a militia company in Rockville in 1881;[9] Vestryman of Christ Episcopal Church;[10] one of the founders of the Farmer's Banking & Trust Co. in Rockville, elected secretary in 1900 and President, 1907-1910;[11] appointed Land Commissioner by the Governor in 1896;[12] elected president of the Democratic Reform Club and was a member of the "anti-machine" element of the Democratic Party in 1891.[13]

---

[1] *Sentinel,* 3 Jul 1914.
[2] Marshall, *Tombstone Records of Dorchester County,* 113.
[3] Thompson, *Western Gateway,* 98.
[4] *Sentinel,* 16 Feb. 1939, celebrated her 82nd birthday.
[5] *Sentinel,* 4 Dec. 1885.
[6] MCHS Cemetery Card File: Laird, Philip Dandridge.
[7] MCHS Cemetery Card File.
[8] Hurley, *1880 Population Census of Montgomery County,* 568
[9] *Sentinel,* 8 Dec. 1881.
[10] MCHS Church Files, Laird, Philip Dandridge.
[11] Thompson, *Western Gateway,* 53.
[12] *Sentinel,* 21 Feb 1889.
[13] Heibert and MacMaster, *Grateful Remembrance,* 405.:

GEORGE HOLT LAMAR (1867-1945)

Admitted to Montgomery County Bar 1890

BIRTH/PARENTS: George Holt Lamar was born 20 July 1867 in Auburn, AL to Dr. William Harmong Lamar (b. 13 July 1827, d. Nov. 1907, Jasper, AL[1]) and Ann Maria (Glenn) Lamar[2]

EDUCATION: Alabama Polytechnic Institute, June 1887; Georgetown University Law School, LLB in 1889; LLM in 1890.[3]

LEGAL CAREER: Admitted to the Bar in 1890; began practice in May 1891 with his brother William H. Lamar; practiced law in Maryland and Washington, D.C.; admitted to the bar of the Supreme Court in 1896.[4]

MARRIAGE 18 Apr 1894 at the Rockville Methodist Church, to Edith May Stonestreet (b. 1872, d. 4 Feb.-1945), daughter of Dr. Edward Elisha Stonestreet (1830-1903) and Martha Rebecca Barry Stonestreet .[5]

CHILDREN:

1. Rebecca Barry Lamar, b. 1896, d. 1980[6]; m. 20 Jun 1923 to Rev. Nolan B. Harmon, Jr.[7]
2. Edith Glen Lamar, b. 1900, d. 19 Aug. 1979; m. 24 Mar. 1932, 2nd wife to Richard Lawrence Waters (b. 12 Mar. 1893, d. 13 April 1961, Carson City, NV).[8] [9]
3. Lucille Allen Lamar, b.1903; m. 9 Oct. 1924 to Homer Stafford Bryant.
4. Edward Stonestreet Lamar, b.1905, d. 16 Aug. 1979, m. Mary Elizabeth Wood.[10]
5. Anita Lamar, b. 1909, d. 1998[11]; m. November 1937 in East Orange, NJ, to Charles F. Schley.[12]
6. George Holt Lamar, Jr., b. 1914.[13] living in Dundalk, MD in 1979.

DEATH: 10 Jun 1945. He and his wife are buried in Rockville Cemetery.[14]

---

1 *Sentinel,* 22 Nov. 1907.
2 Sketch appears in *Tercentenary History of Maryland,* Vol. IV, 783-786.
3 *Tercentenary History,* 784.
4 *Tercentenary History,* 784.
5 *Sentinel,* 20 Apr. 1894 and Hickey, *Send for the Doctor,* 90-93.
6 www.FindAGrave.com : Nolan B. Harmon : accessed 4 April 2014
7 *Sentinel,* 22 Jun. 1923
8 Hurley, *Waters Families,* 190.
9 *Sentinel,* 24 Mar. 1932
10 Obituary clipping from *Washington Post,* 19 Aug. 1979, MCHS Biography files.
11 www.Ancestry.com : Social Security Index : Anita Schley
12 *Frederick Post,* Nov. 1937 and *Sentinel,* 25 Nov. 1937. "married last Saturday."
13 www.Ancestry.com : 1930 Federal Census : Maryland : Montgomery County : Rockville, accessed 4 Apr 2014
14 MCHS Cemetery File : Lamar, George Holt

NOTES: He was president of the Montgomery County School Board, 1906-1912, member of the Legal Advisory Board for Montgomery County during World War I; active in enacting prohibition legislation; served as CEO of the Alpha Tau Omega Fraternity.[1]

WILLIAM HARMONG LAMAR (1859-1928)

Admitted to Montgomery County Bar 1885

BIRTH/PARENTS: William Harmong Lamar was born 11 December 1859 in Auburn, AL, to Dr. William Harmong Lamar (b. 13 July 1827, d. Nov. 1907, Jasper, AL[2]) and Ann Maria (Glenn) Lamar.[3]

EDUCATION: Alabama Polytechnic Institute, 1881; Georgetown University Law School, LLB in 1884; LLM in 1885.[4]

LEGAL CAREER: Admitted to the Rockville and Washington Bars soon after earning his law degree; began practice in May 1891 with his brother George Holt Lamar; practiced law in Maryland and Washington, D.C.; a member of the Maryland legislature in 1894; Assistant Attorney for the Department of Justice, 1906-1913; Assistant Attorney-General and Solicitor of the Post Office Department, 1913-.1921.[5]

MARRIAGE: On 21 June 1887 in Macon, Georgia, to Virginia Longstreet Lamar (b. 1865, d. 12 Dec. 1911), daughter of Supreme Court Justice Lucius. Q. C. Lamar and Viriginia Lafayette Longstreet Lamar.[6] She was a second cousin of his father[7].

CHILDREN[8]

1. Virginia Longstreet Lamar, b. 1889, m. Robert C. Matthews. Living in Knoxville, TN in 1928[9].
2. Augusta Glenn Lamar, b. 1891, m. 8 Nov. 1912, Frederick N. Henderson (b. 1870, d. April 1918, Camp Oglethorpe, Georgia), buried Rockville Cemetery, son of Judge James B. and Clara Hendersonof Rockville. She m.2., before 1928. Robert Lytle of College Park, MD.[10]
3. Lucius Q. C. Lamar, (1892-1954), m. August 1916, in Bel Air, MD., Priscilla Dawson Gibbons, daughter of Mr. and Mrs. William H. Gibbons of Baltimore, MD[11].
4. William Harmong Lamar, III, b. 21 Mar. 1897, Rockville, MD, d. 24 May 1970, Rockport, MA. Buried Baltimore, MD.

DEATH He died 10 Feb. 1928. He is buried in Arlington National Cemetery along with his wife.[1]

---

[1] Thompson, *Western Gatewa,y* 98.
[2] *Sentinel,* 22 Nov. 1907.
[3] *Tercentenary History of Maryland,* V. II, *152.*
[4] *Tercentenary History of Maryland,* V. II, 152.
[5] *Tercentenary History of Maryland,* V. II, 153-156.
[6] *Sentinel,* 15 Dec. 1911. Obituary notice for Virginia Longstreet Lamar.
[7] *Tercentenary History of Maryland,* V. II, *158.*
[8] http://trees.ancestry.com/tree/13440215/person/-68926454 accessed 21 May 2014. *Tercentenary History of Maryland,* 158 names his two sons and two daughters without dates.
[9] *Sentinel,* obituary of William Harmong Lamar, Feb. 17, 1928.
[10] *Sentinel,* obituary of William HArmong Lamar, Feb. 17, 1928.
[11] *Sentinel,* 11 Aug. 1916.

NOTES He was a member of the Greeley Relief Expedition in 1883; elected to Maryland Legislature in 1894; served during the Spanish-American War in 1898; and, was a member of the general telegraph and telephone administration board during the period of government control, 1918-1919.[2]

FRANCIS PRESTON BLAIR LEE (1857-1944)
AKA "BLAIR LEE"

Admitted to Montgomery County Bar in 1883[3]

BIRTH/PARENTS: Francis Preston Blair Lee was born on 9 August 1857 in Silver Spring, MD[4] to Rear Admiral Samuel Phillips Lee (b.1812) of Virginia and Elizabeth Blair Lee (b. 1819, d. 1906) of Kentucky [5] She was the daughter of Francis Preston Blair,and Eliza Violet Gist[6]; and sister of Montgomery Blair, President Lincoln's Postmaster General, and Francis Preston Blair, Jr., U.S. Senator.

EDUCATION: He was educated at Emerson Institute and graduated from Princeton College in 1880, followed by two years at the Columbia Law School in Washington. He was admitted to the Bar at Rockville, Md and Washington, D.C. in 1883.

LEGAL CAREER: He opened his law office in Washington. In 1896 he received his nomination for the Sixth Congressional District as a Democrat. He served in the U.S. Senate from 1914-1917. He ran unsuccessfully for Governor.

MARRIAGE: In October 1891 he was married to Miss Annie Clymer Brooke, (1870-1903) daughter of Edward Brooke and Annie Clymer Brooke of Birdsborough, Berks County, PA. She died December 24, 1903 in Birdsboro, after an illness of several years.[7]

CHILDREN :

1. Edward Brooke Lee, b. 23 Oct. 1892, d. 21 Sep. 1984,[8] m. Elizabeth Wilson, had issue: Francis Preston Blair Lee, Edward B. Lee, Jr. and Elizabeth Lee who married David Scull.[9]
2. Phillip Blair Lee, b. 27 Dec. 1895, Washington, D.C., d. Sep. 1983 in Philadelphia; m. abt 1926 to Elizabeth Wayne Lee. Had issue.[10]
3. Arthur Fitzgerald Lee, b. 1900, d. 1905.[11]

---

[1] www.FindAGrave : Lamar, William H. accessed 21 May 2014.
[2] *Tercentenary History of Maryland*, V. II, 152, 155
[3] Portrait and Biographical Record, p. 781, sketch of Blair Lee
[4] Portrait and Biographical Record, p. 781, sketch of Blair Lee
[5] "Elizabeth Blair Lee, of Famous Family, dead" *Washington Post,* Sep. 14, 1906, Proquest Historical Newspapers.
[6] Smith, *Francis Preston Blair,*7-9.
[7] "Death of Mrs. Blair Lee," *Washington Post,* Dec. 25, 1903, Proquest Historical Newspapers.
[8] *Find-A-Grave.com.,* accessed 27 May 2016.
[9] Farquhar, *Old Homes,* 283, sketch of Silver Spring and Blair and Lee families.
[10] *Ancestry.com,* WWI Draft registration, Social Security Death Index, 1930 & 1940 Federal Census records, living on W. Allen St. in Philadelphia, occupation was Banker.
[11] *Find-A-Grave.com.,* accessed 27 May 2016

DEATH 25 Dec. 1944 at Norwood, Sandy Spring, MD. Services from Grace Episcopal Church. Buried in Rock Creek Cemetery, Washington, D.C.[1]

STEPHEN MELTIAS LYDDANE (1817-1889)

Judge of the Orphans Court 1887

BIRTH/PARENTS: Stephen M. Lyddane was born 10 Feb. 1817 to James Lyddane (d. 1843[2]) and Ann Adams Lyddane. (1780-aft. 1850)[3]

LEGAL CAREER: 1840-1847 Justice of the Peace; 1848 County Commissioner for three terms; again in 1869 elected County Commissioner for 6 years; 1887 Judge of Orphan's Court; Democratic Party, Catholic[4]

MARRIAGE: 8 Aug. 1848, to Sarah Hilton (Braddock) Smith, b. 12 Jan 1827, d. 29 Jan 1911; Sarah Braddock had first married 8 May 1845, in Montgomery County, to Charles Smith (b. 1817, d. 13 Aug. 1845)[5]. She was the daughter of William Braddock (b. 23 Aug. 1789, d. 11 Sep. 1830) and Elizabeth Hilton Braddock (b. 13 Oct. 1795, d. 29 May 1878).[6]

CHILDREN:

1. Gertrude Lyddane, b. 7 Sep 1850, d. 16 Jul.-1930, m. William Dorsey, b. 26 Jan 1848, d. 25 Mar. 1920.[7]
2. Elizabeth Lyddane, b. 19 June 1852, d. 26 June 1853.
3. Grace Lyddane, b. 11 Mar. 1854, d. 23 Jan. 1930, m. 30 Oct 1876[8], Charles H. Quigley, b. 23 Sep 1851, d. 3 Mar. 1919. On Stephen Lyddane monument.
4. Nicholas Lyddane, b. April 1855, d. Sept. 1855.[9]
5. Anna (Nannie) Lyddane, b. 23 Aug. 1856, d. 12 Nov. 1888, m. Oct 1886, in Baltimore, MD, David H. Warfield, who m. 2. 25 Nov. 1892, Kate R. Fields.[10]
6. Joseph Lyddane, b. 16 Mar. 1858, d. 29 Jun 1858.[11]
7. Bessie Lyddane, b. 18 Jul 1863, d. 23 Oct. 1931, buried in Rockville Cemetery[12]

---

[1] "Funeral Today for Blair Lee, Former Senator" *Washington Post,* Dec. 28, 1944, Proquest Historical Newspapers.

[2] Malloy et.al., *Montgomery County Wills,* probated 4 Jul 1843.

[3] Hurley, 1850 Montgomery County Census, age 70, living with son Thomas Lyddane.

[4] Portrait and Biographical, 1898, Pg. 571

[5] Malloy, Montgomery County Marriages, 34, 200; MCHS Cemetery Card file, buried in the Baptist Church Cemetery, transferred to Rockville Cemetery. MCHS Church Card file, notes William Braddock paid for 2 Smith graves in the Baptist Cemetery..

[6] MCHS Braddock Family File, papers on family of William Braddock from Gharlotte R. Gregory, Sep. 1989.

[7] MCHS Cemetery Card File, Stephen Lyddane monument in Rockville Cemetery.

[8] Malloy, *Sentinel Abstracts,* 305; license dated 26 Oct. 1876.

[9] MCHS Braddock Family File.

[10] Malloy, *Sentinel Abstracts,* 381.

[11] MCHS Braddock Family File.

[12] Montgomery County Historical Society Family File, Lyddane

DEATH: 2 Sept 1889; buried Rockville Cemetery[1].

ARTHUR PETER (1873-1943)

Admitted to the Montgomery County Bar about 1894

BIRTH/PARENTS: Arthur Peter was born 16 November 1873 in Rockville, Maryland, the youngest son of George Peter (b. 28 Nov. 1829, d. 6 Aug. 1893) and Eliza Lavinia Gassaway Peter, , b. 26 April 1831, d. 11 May 1909. His father and his older brothers, John Freeland Peter, Edward Compton Peter, and Robert Brewer Peter, were also lawyers.

EDUCATION: Rittenhouse Academy of Washington and Rockville Academy [2]. Studied law with his father and Judge James Henderson. Graduated from the National Univversity of Washington, D.C., as First in Class in 1894.[3]

LEGAL CAREER Part of Peter family of lawyers, his law office was in the Washington Loan and Trust Building, of which company he was Chairman of the Board of Directors at his death. He had worked in the Office of Arthur A. Birney, U.S. attorney for D.C., and a partnership with Hon. J. J. Hemphill, M.C., on several important trials.

MARRIAGE 2 July 1918 to Edith Marshall a daughter of Humphrey Marshall of Louisville, Kentucky.[4] She was born 29 Jan. 1885, died 19 Oct. 1964.

CHILDREN:

1. Humphrey Marshall Peter, b. 29 March 1919, twin, d. 1 Nov. 1959.
2. Arthur Peter, Jr., b. 29 March 1919, d. 30 Sept. 1992.

DEATH 24 October 1943.[5] Buried at Oak Hill Cemetery, Washington, D.C.

EDWARD C. PETER (1862-1923)

Admitted to Montgomery County Bar 1883

BIRTH/PARENTS Edward Compston Peter was born 18 June 1862 to George Peter (b. 28 Nov. 1829, d. 6 Aug. 1893) and Eliza Lavinia Gassaway Peter, b. 26 April 1831, d. 11 May 1909. He was also an attorney, and his sketch is in the earlier section.

EDUCATION: Rockville Academy. Studied law under his father George Peter and his law partner, James B Henderson.

LEGAL CAREER: Beginning in 1887, he served two 4-year terms as States Attorney. Originally a Democrat, Edward and his brother Arthur switched parties and joined the

---

[1] Malloy, *Sentinel Abstracts, 233;* MCHS Cemetery card file.
[2] *The Washington Post,* Oct. 25, 1943, ProQuest Historical Newspapers, "Arthur Peter, DC Banker is Dead at 69"
[3] *Sentinel,* June 15, 1894.
[4] *Sentinel,* July 26, 1918
[5] Pippenger, *Oak Hill Cemetery*

anti-machine forces. In 1889 he gained the upper hand in the machine from father George Peter. In 1895, he signed the constitution of the Montgomery County Bar Association. In 1896, he became a Partner with {James] Alby Henderson. In 1900, the Peter brothers allied with Democrat Blair Lee. They were powerful in Montgomery County politics. In 1900, he became 1st Vice President of the Farmers Banking and Trust Co. From 1910 until his death in 1923, he served as an Associate Judge of Circuit Court. Upon Judge Edward Peter's death, his brother Robert B. Peter (a founder of the Bar Assn.) succeeded him as judge.

MARRIAGE On 27 June 1888, to Mary Gordon Vinson, b. 10 Sep 1867, d. 20 July 1947, daughter of Judge John Thomas Vinson (b. 6 Jan. 1825,[1] d. 7 Feb. 1903) and Fannie Rachel Prout Vinson (b. 1837, d. 27 Dec. 1888) both buried at Oak Hill Cemetery.[2]

CHILDREN:

1. Frances Vinson Peter, b. 29 Apr. 1889, d. 29 Jan. 1974, m. Albert Manoury Bouic, b. 20 Aug. 1882, d. 1 May 1969, son of William Veirs Bouic, b. 20 Jul 1846, Rockville, Md., d. 12 Oct.1906, Rockville, Md., and Alice A. Almoney Bouic b. 26 Dec. 1845, d. 22 Aug. 1922. [3]
2. George Lane Peter, b. 9 Oct. 1894, d. 13 Jan. 1954, m. 1 Aug. 1936, Blanche Fulks (b. 26 Aug. 1903, d. 16 May 1991) daughter of Oscar Fernando Fulks (1876-1952) and Edith Maud Watkins Fulks (1883-1951)[4].
3. John Vinson Peter, b. 14 Mar. 1898, d. 30 Mar.1963, m. 10 Jun. 1924, to Gertrude Veirs[5] (b. 18 Nov. 1899, d. 27 Jan. 1988) daughter of. Charles Veirs (b. 25 Feb. 1859, d. 13 Dec. 1935) and Rose Lyddane Veirs (b. 25 June 1859, d. 3 Feb 1963).[6]
4. Edward Peter, b. 23 Dec. 1904, d. 1 Apr. 1953, m. 1. in Sep. 1927, Anita Phillips Smith.[7], (b. 22 Apr 1905, Philippine Islands, where her father was stationed; d. 2 Jan. 1992, Miami, FL) daughter of Gilbert Coles Smith (b. 1870, d. 1921, buried Arlington National Cemetery) and Anita Veronica Phillips Smith[8] (b. 1882, d. 1958). Marriage ended in divorce. Married 2. Esther James, b. abt 1905, d. 27 Feb. 1963, buried in Rockville Cemetery with Edward Peter.[9]

DEATH 22 August 1923, buried in Rockville Cemetery.

NOTES From his obituary: Evidently Edward had been in poor health, but on this day he seemed better and attended the Rockville Fair and visited with friends during

---

[1] Retired from judgeship at age 70, as reported in *Sentinel,* 4 Jan. 1895.
[2] www.find-a-grave.com.
[3] MCHS Cemetery Files, card of William Veirs Bouic, Jr. Family plot at Rockville Cemetery.
[4] *History of Gaithersburg*, Fulks family.
[5] *Sentinel,* 13 Jun 1924.
[6] MCHS Cemetery Records, both buried in Rockville Cemetery.
[7] *Sentinel,*23 Sep. 1927.
[8] MCHS Peter Family File.
[9] MCHS Cemetery Card File.

day. In the evening he walked downtown with his wife and dropped dead in Vinson's Drug Store. At the Fair, the next day, there was a moment of silence for Judge Peter[1].

ROBERT BREWER PETER (1868-1936)

Admitted to Montgomery County Bar 1893

BIRTH/PARENTS: Robert Brewer Peter was born 22 February 1868 in Rockville, MD to George Peter (b. 28 Nov. 1829, d. 6 Aug. 1893) and Eliza Lavinia Gassaway Peter, b. 26 April 1831, d. 11 May 1909.

EDUCATION: Rockville Academy and Hampton Sidney College. Taught several years in Indian schools in South Dakota. Studied law at National University of Washington DC, graduated in 1893 (second in his class)[2].

LEGAL CAREER After returning from South Dakota, he was appointed Deputy Clerk of Circuit Court while studying law. He later served as a Montgomery County Circuit Court Judge[3].

MARRIAGE On 13 Oct. 1896, in Montgomery County, to Helen Olivia Lowry, (b. Apr. 1871, d. 10 Sep. 1917), daughter of Maj. Horatio Lowry, USMC, (b. 1837, d. 1900) and Charlotte Lowry (b. 1844, d. 1901).

CHILDREN

1. Robert Peter, Jr., b. 1898, d. 5 June 1951[4], buried Rockville Cemetery, m. in 1931, Mary Fackler Tyler (b. 1904, d. 9 Jun. 1996)[5] daughter of the Rev. Frank Ames Tyler (b. 1875, d. 21 Aug. 1953) and Margaret Linthicum Tyler. (d. 19 March 1951).

DEATH 1 November 1936 of a heart attack. Buried in Rockville Cemetery

CHARLES WESLEY PRETTYMAN (1857-1921)

Admitted to Montgomery County Bar, c1881

BIRTH/PARENTS: Charles W. Prettyman was born 1 April 1857 in Brookville, MD[6] to Elijah Barrett Prettyman (b. 20 Feb 1830, d. 9 Dec 1907) and Lydia Forrest Prettyman, (b. 2 Feb. 1832, d. 22 Nov. 1917). His father was also an attorney, see earlier section.

EDUCATION: Randolph-Macon College, Ashland, Virginia and the Law School, University of Maryland, 1879, (ranked 4th out of 33)[1]

---

[1] *Sentinel,* 22 August 1923.

[2] *Portrait and Biographical Record*, 641.

[3] *Portrait and Biographical Record,* 641; obituary published in *Sentinel,* 5 Nov.1936.

[4] MCHS Biography Files, obituary published April 1951, he was an attorney, and former former Democratic State's Attorney and State Senator from Montgomery County.

[5] MCHS Biography files, obituary published in Gazette, 28 June 1996.

[6] Centennial Pictorial, 100 Years of Legal Tradition, 1894-1994., p. 19. Findagrave.com

LEGAL CAREER: Associated with law practice of W. H. Talbott in Rockville [2] Owned his own law practice in Rockville[3] One of founding members of the Montgomery County Bar Association; President, 1910-1924[4] Ran as a candidate for State's Attorney, in 1887[5]

MARRIAGE: By license dated 7 Dec. 1881[6] to Rosetta (Rosa) Vauclin Bouic (24 Feb 1857-29 Mar 1945), daughter of Judge W. V. Bouic, b. 12 May 1816, d. 4 May 1896, (see entry)[7] and Mary Ann Matilda Veirs Bouic, b. 2 June 1821, d. 1 Oct 1888.

CHILDREN[8]

1. William Forrest Prettyman (b. 5 July 1883, d. 12 Oct 1972) buried Rockville Cemetery; m. 23 July 1914, Bella K. Bond., (b. July 1857, d. Feb. 1920)[9]. He was also an Attorney, and served as President of Montgomery Co Bar Association in 1927.
2. Charles Aubrey Prettyman (1886-1890) buried in Rockville Cemetery.

DEATH: 5 May 1921 Rockville, Maryland. Buried Rockville Cemetery[10]

SAMUEL RIGGS (1869-1943)

Admitted to Montgomery County Bar 1892

BIRTH/PARENTS: Samuel Riggs[11] was born 15 August 1869 near Laytonsville, MD, to Reuben Riggs (b. 29 Nov. 1839, d. 1 Aug.1910) and Martha Hughs (Canby) Riggs (b. 26 Nov.1841, d. 6 June 1897)[12].

LEGAL CAREER: In law practice with George Minor Anderson from 1892-1898. in Rockville[13] in1893 he was appointed Attorney for the County Commission.[14] In 1895, he ran unsuccessfully for County Commissioner.[15] He was a charter member of the new Bar Association of Montgomery County.[16]

---

1 Sentinel, 7 Nov 1957 (MCHS, Prettyman Family file) and Sentinel, 6 June 1879, p. 3
2 Centennial Pictorial, p. 19.
3 Federal Census, 1910 and 1920.
4 Centennial Pictorial, pp. 21, 23
5 Sentinel, 10 June 1887, p. 3
6 Marriage Licenses, Montgomery County, 1798-1898 p. 256.
7 Findagrave.com
8 MCHS Cemetery Files
9 Hurley, *Montgomery County 1900 Census;* Malloy et.al., *Sentinel Abstracts,* 13 Feb. 1920.
10 MCHS Cemetery Files; findagrave.com
11 Styled "Samuel Riggs of R," i.e. "of Reuben," his father. Also known as "Captain"
12 Riggs, *Riggs Family,* 273, 280, 281; MCHS library cemetery card file.
13 Thompson, *Western Gateway,* 96
14 *Sentinel,* 24 Nov. 1893.
15 *Sentinel,* 19 July 1895.
16 *Sentinel,* 14 Aug. 1896.

MARRIAGE: 4 October 1897 in Media, PA, to Ida Frances Lowry (1866-1942), daughter of Maj. Horatio Barnard. Lowry, USMC, (1837-1901) and his wife, Charlotte Huntingdon Young Lowry (1842-1900). .[1] Her parents are buried in Rockville Cemetery.[2]

CHILDREN:

1. Samuel Brownell Riggs, b. 18 Nov. 1898, d. 23 Jul. 1937, m. Ernestine Pessou of New Orleans, LA. After his death, she moved to Evanston, Illinois[3].
2. Reuben Riggs, b. 12 Jul. 1902, d. 7 Mar. 1980, m. 1. 25 Sept. 1926, Claudia Gartrell (b. 1906, d. 16 Mar. 1976[4]) daughter of Charles and Virginia (Groomes) Gartrell, they were divorced. She m. 2. James Wilson. Reuben m. 2. Mabel Elizabeth Linthicum, (b. 1914, d. 16 Mar. 1955[5]); m. 3. Margaret Teller, (b. 1909, d. 30 Jan. 1996) widow of Capt. Steadman Teller[6].
3. Barnard Lowry Riggs, b. 11 Jun. 1910, d. 26 May 1961[7], m. 8 Feb. 1933, Ruth Dronenburg (b. 18 Sep 1911, d. 14 Aug. 2001)[8], daughter of Clifton Dronenburg (b. 26 Jul 1879, d. 18 Jan. 1943) and Katherine E. (Ricketts) Dronenburg (b. 27 Nov. 1890, d. 3 Jan. 1982)[9] of Clarksburg, MD[10].

DEATH: 19 Dec. 1943 at his home in Rockville. Buried in Rockville Cemetery.

NOTES: Served in Spanish American War with rank of captain. Later served in Philippine Islands, where he was breveted for gallantry in action and received the Silver Star medal. His later volunteer work included trustee of the School Board and a volunteer with the Rockville Fire Company. He was also a founding board member of the Sandy Spring Bank. Elected County Commissioner for Montgomery County in 1917. Later employed by the DC Water Department, from which he retired about 15 years before his death.

HENRY MAURICE TALBOTT (1851-1934)

Admitted to Montgomery County Bar by 1882[11]

BIRTH/PARENTS: Henry Maurice Talbott was born 22 January 1851 in Shepherdstown, West Virginia. He was baptized at St. Peter's Episcopal Church, Poolesville, Maryland on

[1] Riggs, *Riggs Family, 280-281;* Malloy, *Sentinel,* 21 Oct.1898.
[2] MCHS Cemetery Card index, card for Lowry, H. B. (Maj.) USMC. Includes wife and children.
[3] Riggs, *Riggs Family,* 291.
[4] Gartrell, *The Gartrells {1540-2000],* 264.
[5] MCHS Biography File, newspaper obituary on card of Reuben Riggs.
[6] MCHS Biography File, newspaper obituary on card of Reuben Riggs.
[7] MCHS Cemetery Card File. Buried Rockville Cemetery.
[8] find-a-grave.com. Accessed 12 Jan. 2017.
[9] MCHS Cemetery Card, buried Clarksburg Methodist Church.
[10] *Sentinel,* 23 Feb. 1933.
[11] Thompson, *Western Gateway*, 97.

8 Sep. 1851.[1] His parents were Benson Talbott (b. 24 Jan 1821, d. 30 Dec. 1902) and Maria (Hyde) Talbott[2] (b. 11 Jul 1828, d. 15 Jun 1903).

EDUCATION: Columbian University of Washington, D. C., class of 1872.[3]

LEGAL CAREER: He had a general practice in Rockville, MD; pled cases before Supreme Courts of Maryland and Washington, D.C., and in 1886 he formed the law partnership of Talbott and Talbott with his brother, William Hyde Talbott.[4]

MARRIAGE On 4 Jan. 1875 at Dunbarton M.E. Church, Georgetown to Cora E. Wilson,[5] (b. 20 Nov. 1852, d. 2 Nov. 1900), buried in Rockville Cemetery.[6]

CHILDREN[7]

1. Estelle Hyde Talbott b. 4 Apr 1876, d. 6 Jun 1904, m. in Nov. 1898, to Benjamin Canby Riggs[8] (b. 3 Aug 1871, d. 26 Dec. 1906).
2. Thomas Maurice Talbott, b. 14 Nov. 1878, d. 22 Jan. 1952, m. Sep. 1904, at Ascension Church, Gaithersburg, Katherine Munro (1881-1970), daughter of Mr. and Mrs. David Munro of Gaithersburg[9].
3. Helen Wilson Talbott, b. 16 Aug. 1883, d. 30 Sep. 1957, m. F. Bernard Welsh (b. 23 Oct. 1880, d. 27 Jun 1954). Both buried in Rockville Cemetery.
4. Evelyn Wailes Talbott, b. 1885, d. 19 Nov. 1953, m. 1. 16 Jan. 1904, in Baltimore, Hugh Craig Glascott (divorced c. 1907-1908)[10] m. 2. Feb. 1913, in Washington, John Darby Bowman[11] (b. 30 Nov 1880, d. 28 May 1954), both buried in Monocacy Cemetery.

DEATH: Henry Maurice Talbott died 3 Nov. 1934, buried in Rockville Cemetery.[12]

---

[1] MCHS Church Records : Talbott, Henry Maurice.
[2] *Portrait and Biographical*, 649-650.
[3] *Portrait and Biographical,* 649-650.
[4] Thompson, *Western Gateway*, 97.
[5] Malloy, *Sentinel,* 355, 15 Jan. 1875.
[6] MCHS Cemetery Files, Talbott, Henry Maurice card.
[7] MCHS Talbott Family File, and Cemetery Card files.
[8] Malloy, *Sentinel Abstracts,* 318 (11 Nov. 1898)
[9] Malloy, *Sentinel Abstracts,*769. (23 Sep. 1904).
[10] Malloy, *Sentinel, 317.* (29 Jan. 1904, 17 May 1907, 13 Nov. 1908).
[11] Malloy, *Sentinel,* 84 (21 Feb. 1913).
[12] *Sentinel,* 8 Nov. 1934

WILLIAM HYDE TALBOTT (1861-1941)

Admitted to Montgomery County Bar c. 1886

BIRTH/PARENTS William Hyde Talbott was born 5 July 1861, near Poolesville, MD, to Benson Talbott (b. 24 Jan 1821, d. 30 Dec. 1902) and Maria (Hyde) Talbott (b. 11 Jul 1828, d. 15 Jun 1903).[1]

EDUCATION: Public schools and Columbian College, Washington, D.C. He then followed the grain commission business in Georgetown for three years before he returned to Rockville and read law under his brother, Henry Maurice Talbott.[2]

LEGAL CAREER In 1886, he joined his brother, Henry Maurice Talbott, in the law firm of Talbott and Talbott; practiced law in Hagerstown, 1887-1891; ("Wm. Talbott, formerly of the Rockville Bar, has been admitted to practice in Hagerstown"[3]) and then returned to the law firm of Talbott and Talbott, which dissolved in 1923. He signed the Montgomery County Bar Association constitution in 1895. He gave his attention primarily to real estate matters.[4]

MARRIAGE: On 2 Sep 1885, in Poolesville, to Bertha Hall[5] (b. 30 Sep. 1864, d. 17 Oct. 1937)[6]

CHILDREN

1. Sadie Marie Talbott (1887-1968)[7] m. May 1921, at home of bride's parents, by Rev. Richard S. Owens, Walter G. Ellison of Waynesboro, Virginia.[8]
2. William Randolph Talbott (1888-1953) m. July 1918, in Rockville Presbyterian Church, Laura Magruder Higgins (1888-1985), daughter of Mr. and Mrs. John J. Higgins of Rockville.[9]

DEATH On 5 Feb. 1941; buried at Rockville Cemetery.

MILTON GEORGE URNER (1839-1926)

Representative 6th Congressional District

---

[1] *Portrait and Biographical*, 649-650; they are buried in Rockville Cemetery, MCHS Cemetery Card file.

[2] *Portrait and Biographical*, 649-650.

[3] *Sentinel*, 24 Feb. 1888.

[4] *Portrait and Biographical*, 649-650 and Thompson, *Western Gateway* 97.

[5] *Malloy, Sentinel Abstracts,* 355. (4 Sep 1885).

[6] MCHS Cemetery File, Talbott, William Hyde card.

[7] www.findagrave.com.

[8] Malloy, *Sentinel Abstracts,* 264. (20 May 1921).

[9] Malloy, *Sentinel Abstracts,* 769. (5 Jul 1918).

BIRTH/PARENTS Milton George Urner was born 29 July 1839 to Samuel Urner (b. 25 Dec.1797, Chester Co., Pa.; d. August 1872, Frederick County, MD) and his second wife, Susanna (Norris) Urner (b. 30 Oct. 1802, d. March 1853, daughter of Amos Norris). His first wife was Elizabeth Snader (b. 23 Jan. 1800, d. 8 Oct 1828).[1]

EDUCATION: Dickinson Seminary, Williamsport, PA, and, later Freeland Seminary in Montgomery County, PA. 1856-1857. He began the study of law in the office of the Hon. Grayson Eichelberger in Frederick City.[2]

LEGAL CAREER: Admitted to Frederick Co. Bar in October 1863. In politics he was an active supporter of the Republican Party. In 1871 he was elected State's Attorney for Frederick County. In 1878 he was elected to the House of Representatives from the 6th Congressional District of Maryland, his opponents being George Peter, Democrat and Horace Resley, Greenbacker.

MARRIAGE: 10 January 1866 to Laura A. Hammond (b. 31 May 1845, d. 31 July 1923) daughter of Dr. Richard T. Hammond (b. 14 Mar. 1815, d. 3 Feb. 1896), and Mary Agnes Cramer Hammond,(b. 21 July 1823, d. 18 May 1894)[3], of Woodsboro, Frederick County. They were the parents of ten children, six were living and named at the time of the sketch in Williams' History; three others identified from tombstone records.

CHILDREN

1. Walter Grayson Urner, b. 26 Oct. 1867, d. 14 July 1930, of Washington, D.C.
2. Hammond Urner, b. 4 Dec. 1868, d. 27 Sep 1942,[4] m. 3 May 1893 to Mary L. Floyd of South Carolina. He was a prominent Frederick Attorney, who became Chief Judge of the 5th Judicial Circuit and Associate Judge of the Court of Appeals of Maryland.
3. Samuel Percy Urner b. 15 Nov. 1869, d. 17 Nov. 1869.
4. Milton G. Urner, Jr., b. 18 Dec. 1871, d. 25 Nov. 1936, also a member of the law firm of Urner and Urner.
5. Laura Eugenia Urner (1873-1952) who married William E. Gaver, M.D., of Mount Airy, MD.
6. Richard Summerfield Urner, b. 10 Oct. 1875, d. 16 Jan. 1876.
7. Mary Susannah Urner, b. 13 Dec. 1880, d. 5 July 1881.
8. Jonas Paul Urner, b. ca. 1884, a civil engineer who moved to the Argentine Republic.
9. Helen Agnes Urner, b. ca. 1887, who remained unmarried.

DEATH 9 Feb. 1926, buried in Mt. Olivet Cemetery, Frederick, MD.

---

[1] Williams, *History of Frederick County,* Vol. II, p. 990-992.

[2] *Ibid.*

[3] Holdcraft, *Names in Stone,* 518.

[4] Holdcraft, *Names in Stone,* 1168.

JAMES P. B. VEIRS (1866-1956)

Law School Graduate in 1894

BIRTH/PARENTS: James P. B. Veirs was born about 1866 to William Augustus Veirs (b. 1828, d. 6 Jan. 1892)[1] and Rebecca Thomas Biays Veirs (1833-1918) daughter of Philip Grable Biays and Jane C. T. Magruder Biays.

EDUCATION: Graduated in 1894 from the National University Law School in Washington, DC. [2]

LEGAL CAREER: No record of an actual law practice, used education in pursuit of public affairs.

MARRIAGE: Jan. 1924 to Louise Fechtig, divorced Dec. 1927[3]. No record of children.

DEATH: 7 March 1956. Buried in Rockville Union Cemetery.[4]

NOTES: In 1895, he ran on the Primary Ticket for House of Delegates, as a Democrat. He was one of the organizers of the Rockville Fire Department and a member of Rockville Athletic Club[5]. He was active in civic affairs and, at the time of his death, it was noted that he was a staunch Republican and one of Rockville's oldest and wealthiest residents, with an estate of $1,724,000. His family settled in Rockville in early 1800s, and owned Veirs Mill. In 1934 he joined the Independent Democrats to form the Fusion Party, which took over from the Democrats in 1936. His immediate survivors were his nephews, Stephen C. Cromwell and Julian M. Whiting, sons of his sisters Jane B. Bradley and Kate Whiting.[6]

BOWIE FRANKLIN WATERS (1870-1949)

Admitted to Montgomery County Bar 1893[7]

BIRTH/PARENTS: Bowie Franklin Waters was born in January 1870 in Germantown, MD, to Horace Waters (b. 25 May 1823, d. 17Nov 1903)[8] and Mary Jane Priscilla Etchison Waters (2nd wife) who were married on 24 Oct 1866. She is also known as Mary Poultney Jones Etchison (b. 1839, d. 3 Apr 1924).[9]

EDUCATION Graduated from Rockville Academy and earned his law degree from Georgetown University, June 1893, when he was also admitted to the Montgomery County Bar.[10]

---

[1] Bowman, *Sentinel,* 8 Jan. 1892.
[2] Bowman Sentinel Abstracts Jan 1, 1893-Dec. 31, 1896
[3] Sentinel Gen. Abstr. 1900-1934 Vol II
[4] MCHS Veirs Family File, obituary.
[5] Bowman, *Sentinel,*. Jan 1, 1893-Dec. 31, 1896
[6] MCHS Vertical files, copy of obituary from the *Washington Star* in 1956.
[7] *Sentinel,* 9 Jun. 1893.
[8] MCHS Cemetery Files : Waters, Horace.
[9] Hurley, *Waters Family,* 178-179.
[10] *Sentinel,* 2 & 9 Jun. 1893.

LEGAL CAREER: Attorney for the Board of County Commissioners; two terms as States's Attorney; member of the Maryland and Montgomery County Bar Association.[1]

MARRIAGE: On 26 Dec. 1907 to Laura Gassaway[2] (b. abt 1881, d. 21 Apr. 1972), daughter of William Augustus Gassaway (b. 11 Sep 1837, d. 3 Oct. 1909) and Mary Elizabeth (Farrow) Gassaway (b. 7 Mar. 1843, d. 31 Aug. 1905)[3].

CHILDREN:

1. Bowie Jennings Waters, b. 14 Sep 1908, d. 13 Dec 1963,[4] m. 12 Oct. 1933, Hilda Rebecca Scarff, b. abt. 1912, daughter of P. B. Scarff of Frederick.[5]
2. John Horace Waters, b. 5 Jun 1918, d. 7 Apr 1980, m. 24 Aug. 1943, Dorothy Rogers, b. 28 Oct. 1920,[6] daughter of Mr.and Mrs. R. M. Rogers.[7]

DEATH In October 1949, buried at Neelsville Presbyterian Cemetery, Germantown, MD.[8]

NOTES: He was an agent for United States Fidelity and Guaranty Co. of Baltimore, Director and Vice President of the Germantown Bank, and a Mason.[9]

RICHARD WHITE (1856-1927)

Admitted to The Montgomery County Bar 1880[10]

BIRTH/PARENTS: Richard White was born 5 Sept 1856 in Poolesville, Montgomery County to Thomas Henry White, b. 20 Sep 1831, d. 19 Jan. 1930, and Mary Ellen Gott White, b. 14 Oct. 1834, d. 26 May 1890.[11]

EDUCATION: He went to the University of Virginia for a summer course of law lectures in 1878.[12] He read law with George Peter in Rockville, and had received an A.M. degree from St. John's College in Annapolis[13].

LEGAL CAREER:. He is listed twice on the 1880 census – once in the town of Rockville, where he appears to be boarding with a Caroline Price, listed as a lawyer, and living next

---

[1] *Sentinel*, 28 Oct. 1893.
[2] *Sentinel,* 20 Dec. 1907.
[3] Frain, *Monocacy Cemetery,* 46.
[4] Frain, *Monocacy Cemetery,* 46.
[5] Hurley, *Waters Family,* 183.
[6] Hurley, *Waters Family, 183.*
[7] *Sentinel,* 2 Sep. 1943.
[8] MCHS Cemetery File, Waters, Bowie Franklin.
[9] *Sentinel,* 28 Oct 1949.
[10] Scharf, 668.
[11] Huley, *White Families,*34-35.
[12] Bowman, *Sentinel,* 5 July 1878.
[13] Biographies in *History of Butte County, California,* by George C. Mansfield, 675-6, and in 1913 Edition of *Who's Who on the Pacific Coast,* cited in write up on his *Find-A-Grave.*

door to the family of John W. Warner, a lawyer born in Virginia.[1] He is also listed in his parents' home. Interestingly in both places, there are school teachers also in the residence. He may be the Richard White who was appointed one of the school commissioners for the county in January 1880[2]. In spring of 1881 he left Poolesville for California, where he proposed to practice law.[3] In Butte County he held several offices with the Board of Education, and with the Court System, ending his career there as a Judge.

MARRIAGE: 30 Dec 1891, Butte County, California, to Florence Earll, b. 5 Sep 1865, Austin, NV, d. 7 Aug. 1944, Butte Co., CA, daughter of William Earll (1832-1905) and Nancy Strickland Earll (1833-1925).

CHILDREN:

1. Margery White, b. 26 Sep 1892, d. 12 Sep 1984, m. to Lt. Stephen Carson Whipple (1889-1958).
2. Nancy Ellen White, b. 1901.

DEATH 10 April 1927, Chico, Butte County, California.[4]

GLENN HOWARD WORTHINGTON (1858-1934)

Admitted to Frederick County Bar 1888
Chief Judge 6th Judicial Circuit[5]

BIRTH/PARENTS: Glenn Howard Worthington was born 22 April 1858[6] in the Urbana District of Frederick County to John T. Worthington (b. 31 Mar. 1826, d. 28 Mar. 1908) and Mary R. (Simmons) Worthington (b. 16 May 1832, d. 5 June 1902).[7]

EDUCATION: Public schools of Frederick County, Frederick City College, read law at the University of Maryland School of Law and graduated in May 1887.[8]

LEGAL CAREER: Admitted to Frederick Bar, January 4, 1888; Maryland Bar, April 19, 1895[9]; named State's Attorney in 1899; appointed a Judge of the Sixth Judicial Circuit, which is composed of Montgomery and Frederick Counties, on 6 Nov. 1907 by Gov. Warfield.[10]

---

[1] Hurley, 1880 Census, p. 209, 260. Hurley read his occupation at his father's home as laborer, but viewing the original on ancestry it actually says "lawyer."
[2] Bowman, *Sentinel,* 2 Jan. 1880.
[3] Bowman, *Sentinel,* 13 May 1881.
[4] *Find-A-Grave.com,* accessed 22 Oct. 2016.
[5] Williams, T.J.C., *History of Frederick County,* 728.
[6] *Zion Episcopal Church, Urbana, MD,* transcript by Dr. B.F. McPherson, from the Frederick County Public Library Maryland Room Collection, 9.
[7] Williams, T.J.C.,*History of Frederick County*, 728-9; Holdcraft, *Names in Stone,* 1264.
[8] Williams, T.J.C., *History of Frederick County*, 728-9.
[9] http://msa.maryland.gov/megafile/msa/speccol accessed 21 Jan 2015
[10] Bowman, *Sentinel, 1905-1908,* 134.

MARRIAGE 30 April 1890 to Julia Alvey (b, 18 Dec. 1867, d. 30 July 1951), daughter of Hon. Richard H. Alvey and Julia Hays Alvey, of Hagerstown, Maryland[1].

CHILDREN[2]:

1. Ruth Worthington, 1891-1968, m. Robert Henderson Pfeil.
2. Richard Alvey Worthington,1891-1895.
3. Glen Bayard Worthington b. 24 Apr. 1892, d. 7 Feb. 1896, buried Mt. Olivet Cemetery.[3]
4. Julian Alvey Worthington, b. 4 Oct. 1893, d. 12 Jul. 1894, buried Mt. Olivet Cemetery.[4]
5. Richard Alvey Worthington, b. Dec. 1895, m. 1928, Elizabeth Ruth Smith.
6. Julia Worthington, b. Oct. 1897, m. 1920, Lorenzo W. Martin.
7. Margaret Worthington b. 1898, d. 26 May 1899.
8. Dorothy Worthington, 1901-1986, m. Paul de Hoff Reed.
9. John Clarke Worthington, b. 26 Aug. 1904, d. 30 July 1985, m. Nina Elizabeth Brown, b. 17 Jan. 1906, d. 26 April 1978, daughter of Edward Brown and Elizabeth Hall Brown.

DEATH: 7 Aug. 1934 at City Hospital after a 4 week illness;[5] buried in Mt. Olivet Cemetery, Frederick, Maryland.

NOTES: Taught school before attending law school and continued in the field while earning his degree, appointed School Examiner for Frederick County in 1888. He resigned the post in 1891 to pursue a legal profession. He was an active member of the Democratic party, served on the State Board of Education, and belonged to several fraternal organizations. He was a member of the Protestant Episcopal Church.[6]

---

[1] Long & Eader, *Engelbrecht MarriageLedger,* 140; Williams, T.J.C., *History of Frederick County,* 728.

[2]Some details from family trees on *Ancestry.com.*

[3] Holdcraft, *Names in Stone,* 1264.

[4] Holdcraft, *Names in Stone,* 1264.

[5] *Washington Post,* 9 Aug 1934.

[6] Williams, *History of Frederick County, 728-9.*

BIBLIOGRAPHY:

MCHS REFERENCES

The Montgomery County Historical Society (MCHS) recently identifying itself as "Montgomery History" has several special collections that were used extensively in researching this volume. Among these are:

MCHS Cemetery Card File – which contains the readings of most of the small cemeteries in the county, as well as Rockville Cemetery, done by volunteers in the 1970s and 1980s for the Genealogy Club of MCHS. Updates have come from church records, and some cemetery records as well as library volunteers

MCHS Church Card File – contains an index to church records of marriages, births, and membership from various church record manuscripts.

MCHS Family files. There are over 1000 files containing various manuscripts and research notes of Montgomery County families.

Sentinel Abstracts: MCHS has a collection of the Montgomery County Sentinel Newspaper from 1855 through 1969, which were microfilmed several years ago. There are several abstracts of them, so references to the Sentinel, may be to the Abstracts by Bowman from 1855 through 19xx) or by Malloy et. al., 1855 through 1935, (see below) or to clippings in the family files, and/or bibliography files, or from a card index covering 1935 to 1945. MCHS also has an Access Database index to marriage and death notices from the Sentinel, 1945 through 1969.

BOOKS/MANUSCRIPTS

_____*The Biographical Cyclopedia of Representative Men of Maryland and District of Columbia*, Baltimore, National Biographical Publishing Co., 1879.

_____*Biographical Directory of the American Congress, 1774-1961; the Continental Congress Septmeber 5, 1774 to October 21, 1788 and The Congress of the United States, from the first to the eighty-sixth Congress, March 4, 1789, to January 3, 1961, Inclusive,* Washington, D.C., Government Printing Office, 1961. [BDAC]

_____*Carroll County Cemeteries: Volume One: Southeast* through *Volume Seven: Northwest.* Westminster, MD: Carroll County Genealogical Society, 1989 to 2004.

_____*Dictionary of American Biography,* Vol. I, Abbe to Brazer, ed. By Allen Johnson; Vol. II, Brearly to Cushing, Vol. III, Cushman to Fraser, Vol. IV. Fraimces to Hibbard, ed. Allen Johnson and Dumas Malone; Vol. V, Hibben to Larken, Vol. VI, Larned to Millington, Vol. VII. Mills to Platner, Vol. VIII, Platt to Steward, Vol. IX, Sewell to Trowbridge, Vol. X, Troye to Zunser, ed. By Dumas Malone; and Vol. XI Supplements One (ed. By Harris E. Stark, 1944) and Two (ed. By Robert Livingston Schuyler & Edward T. James, 1958). Originally published as 20 volumes with 2 later supplements, New York, Charles Scribner's Sons, 1930-1936. Reprint ca. 1964.

_____*Gaithersburg: The Heart of Montgomery County*. Gaithersburg, MD: The City of Gaithersburg, 1978

_____*Heads of Families at the First Census of the United States, taken in the year 1790, Maryland.* Baltimore: Southern Book Co., 1952.

_____*Howard County Maryland Records, Volume II: More Cemeteries*, Columbia, MD: Howard County Genealogical Society, 1981.

_____*Portrait and Biographical Record of the Sixth Congressional District, Maryland, Containing Portraits and Biographies of many well known Citizens of the past and present, together with portraits and biographies of all the Presidents of the United States*. New York: Chapman Publishing Co., 1898.

_____*Prince George' s County, Maryland, Indexes of Church Registers, 1686-1885, Protestant Episcopal Church, Vol. I: King George's Parish, Queen Anne's Parish; Vol. II St. Paul's Parish, Prince George's Parish,* Riversdale, MD: Prince George's County Historical Society, 1979.

_____ *St. John's College Alumni Register, 1793-1967.* Annapolis, MD: St. John's College, 1968.

_____*Tercentenary History of Maryland,* (illustrated). *Volume II Biographical.* Chicago & Baltimore: S. J. Clarke Publishing Co., 1925; *Volume IV, Embodying Biographical Records of Colonists, Pioneers, Judges, Governors, Military Officers, Etc.,* compiled principally by Henry Fletcher Powell. Chicago & Baltimore: S. J. Clarke Publishing Co., 1925.

Andersen, Patricia, *Montgomery County Land Record Miscellany Libers A-E, Selected Abstracts, 1777-1794; F, F-7 and G Abstracts, 1795-1797,* Lewes, DE, Colonial Roots, 2010.

Andersen, Patricia, *Montgomery County Maryland, Land Record Abstracts 1797-1803, from Libers H, I/J, and K, Millsboro,* DE, Colonial Roots, 2014.

Arps, Walter E., Jr., *Heirs & Orphans: Anne Arundel County, Md., Distributions, 1788-1838,* Silver Spring, MD: Family Line Publications, 1985

Arps, Walter E., Jr., *Maryland Mortalities 1876-1915, from the (Baltimore) Sun Almanac,* Westminster, MD: Willow Bend Books, 1999.

Aud, Kathleen L. & Susan E., *Our Ancestors*, the authors, 1972.

Bailey, Chris H., compiler, *The Stulls of "Millsborough": A Genealogical History of John Stull, "the Miller," Pioneer of Western Maryland, Volume I, Descendants of Col. John Stull of Hagerstown, Mary Stull Greathouse and Margaret Stull White*, Author, 2000.

Baldwin, Jane Cotton. *Maryland Calendar of Wills.* Vol. 1-8. Baltimore, MD: Kohn & Pollock, 1904-1928. Series continued, Vol. 9-16 Westminster, MD: Family Line Publications, 1991-1995.

Baltz, Shirley V. and George E., compilers, *Prince George's County Maryland, Marriages and Deaths in Nineteenth Century Newspapers,* 2 volumes, Bowie, MD: Heritage Books, 1995.

Baltz, Shirley Vlasik and Catherine Marwin Mayhew. *A Chronicle of BelAir, "Part Two: The Descendants of Samuel and Ann Tasker Ogle."* Author, 1984.

Barnes, Robert, comp. *Marriages and Deaths from Baltimore Newspapers, 1796-1816.* Baltimore, MD: Genealogical Publishing Co., 1978.

Barnes, Robert, comp. *Marriages and Deaths from the Maryland Gazette, 1727-1839.* Baltimore, MD: Genealogical Publishing Co., 1973

Bishop, Charles Lawrence, *Frederick's Other City, Mount Olivet Cemetery*, Frederick, MD: Mount Olivet Cemetery Committee of the 150th Anniversary, 2002.

Bogart, Bryan Wilhelmus. *A History of the National Capital: from its Foundation through the Period of the Adoption of the Organic Act.* New York: Macmillan, 1914-1916.

Bowie, Effie Gwynn. *Across the years in Prince George's County, A Genealogical and Biographical History of Some Prince George's County, Maryland and Allied Families.* 1947. Reprint. Baltimore: Genealogical Publishing Co., 1975.

Bowie, Walter Worthington : *The Bowies and Their Kindred.* 1899. Reprint. Cottonport, LA: Polyanthos, Inc., 1971.
Bowman, John D., *Guide to Selections from the Montgomery County Sentinel, Maryland, January 1, 1856 – December 31, 1875,* Westminster, Md: Heritage Books, 2005.
Bowman, John D., *Guide to Selections from the Montgomery County Sentinel, Maryland, January 1, 1876 – December 31, 1881,* Westminster, Md: Heritage Books, 2005.
Bowman, John D., *Guide to Selections from the Montgomery County Sentinel, Maryland, January 1, 1882 – December 31, 1887,* Westminster, Md: Heritage Books, 2005.
Bowman, John D., *Guide to Selections from the Montgomery County Sentinel, Maryland, January 1, 1888 – December 31, 1892,* Westminster, Md: Heritage Books, 2006.
Bowman, John D., *Guide to Selections from the Montgomery County Sentinel, Maryland, January 1, 1893 – December 31, 1896,* Westminster, Md: Heritage Books, 2007.
Bowman, John D., *Guide to Selections from the Montgomery County Sentinel, Maryland, January 1, 1897 – December 31, 1901,* Westminster, Md: Heritage Books, 2007.
Bowman, John D., *Guide to Selections from the Montgomery County Sentinel, Maryland, January 1, 1902 – December 31, 1904,* Westminster, Md: Heritage Books, 2008.
Bowman, John D., *Guide to Selections from the Montgomery County Sentinel, Maryland, January 1, 1905 – December 31, 1908,* Westminster, Md., Heritage Books, 2009.
Bowman, John D., *Guide to Selections from the Montgomery County Sentinel, Maryland, January 1, 1909 – December 27, 1912,* Westminster, Md., Heritage Books, 2010.
Bowman, John D., *Guide to Selections from the Montgomery County Sentinel, Maryland, January 1, 1913 – December 31, 1916,* Westminster, Md., Heritage Books, 2011.
Brown, Helen E., comp. *Index to the Register of Prince George's Episcopal Parish, Prince George's and Montgomery Counties, 1711-1845.* Genealogical Records Chairman, Maryland State Society, Daughters of the American Revolution, 1961.
Brashear, Charles and Shirley Brasher McCoy, *A Brashear(s) Family, History, Vol. 1, The First 200 Years of Brasear(s) in America.* San Diego, CA and Smithfield, N.C.: Authors, 1998.
Brumbaugh, Gaius Marcus, *Maryland Records: Colonial, Revolutionary, County and Church from Original Sources,* 2 Vols. Baltimore: Genealogical Publishing Co., Inc., 1985 reprint. Originally published in 1915.
Callcott, Margaret Law, editor, *Mistress of Riversdale, the Plantation Letters of Rosalie Stier Calvert, 1795-1821,* Baltimore, Md., Johns Hopkins Press, 1991.
Carothers, Bettie Stirling, compiler. *1776 Census of Maryland.* Westminster, MD: Family Line Publications, 1992.
Clark, Eugene and Edythe. *The Spirit of Captain John.* New York: Carton Press, Inc., 1970.
Coldham, Peter Wilson. *Settlers of Maryland, 1751-1765.* Baltimore: Genealogical Publishing Co., 1996.
Cook, Eleanor Mildred Vaughn, *The Anderson-Brown Family of Montgomery County, Maryland,* manuscript book, 128 pp + Appendix containing genealogy, and index.
Cook, William G., compiler, and Mrs. Carol-Jean Webster, editor, *Montpelier & the Snowden Family,* Author, 1976.
Darby, Rodney H. *All About Darbys,* Rockville, MD: Author, 1999.
Delaplaine, Edward S. *The Life of Thomas Johnson: Member of the Continental Congress, First Governor of the State of Maryland, and Associate Justice of the United States Supreme Court,* New York: Frederick H. Hitchcock, the Grafton Press, 1927.

Dixon, Joan M., *National Intelligencer Newspaper Abstracts, 1800-1805*, Westminster, MD: Heritage Books, 1996.

Dixon, Joan M., *National Intelligencer Newspaper Abstracts, 1806-1810*, Westminster, MD: Heritage Books, 1996.

Dixon, Joan M., *National Intelligencer Newspaper Abstracts, 1811-1813*, Westminster, MD: Heritage Books, 1997.

Dixon, Joan M., *National Intelligencer Newspaper Abstracts, 1814-1817*, Westminster, MD: Heritage Books, 1997.

Dixon, Joan M., *National Intellig.encer Newspaper Abstracts, 1818-1820*, Westminster, MD: Heritage Books, 1998.

Dixon, Joan M., *National Intelligencer Newspaper Abstracts, 1821-1823*, Westminster, MD: Heritage Books, 1998.

Dixon, Joan M., *National Intelligencer Newspaper Abstracts, 1824-1826*, Westminster, MD: Heritage Books, 1999.

Dixon, Joan M., *National Intelligencer Newspaper Abstracts, 1827-1829*, Westminster, MD: Heritage Books, 1999.

Dixon, Joan M., *National Intelligencer Newspaper Abstracts, 1830-1831*, Westminster, MD: Heritage Books, 1999.

Dixon, Joan M., *National Intelligencer Newspaper Abstracts, 1832-1833*, Westminster, MD: Heritage Books, 2000.

Dixon, Joan M., *National Intelligencer Newspaper Abstracts, 1834-1835*, Westminster, MD: Heritage Books, 2000.

Dixon, Joan M., *National Intelligencer Newspaper Abstracts, 1836-1837*, Westminster, MD: Heritage Books, 2001.

Dixon, Joan M., *National Intelligencer Newspaper Abstracts, 1838-1839*, Westminster, MD: Heritage Books, 2002

Dixon, Joan M., *National Intelligencer Newspaper Abstracts, 1840*, Westminster, MD: Heritage Books, 2003.

Dixon, Joan M., *National Intelligencer Newspaper Abstracts, 1841*, Westminster, MD: Heritage Books, 2003.

Dixon, Joan M., *National Intelligencer Newspaper Abstracts, 1842*, Westminster, MD: Heritage Books, 2004.

Dixon, Joan M., *National Intelligencer Newspaper Abstracts, 1843*, Westminster, MD: Heritage Books, 2006.

Dixon, Joan M., *National Intelligencer Newspaper Abstracts, 1844*, Westminster, MD: Heritage Books, 2005.

Dixon, Joan M., *National Intelligencer Newspaper Abstracts, 1845*, Westminster, MD: Heritage Books, 2006.

Dixon, Joan M., *National Intelligencer Newspaper Abstracts, 1846*, Westminster, MD: Heritage Books, 2006.

Dixon, Joan M., *National Intelligencer Newspaper Abstracts, 1847*, Westminster, MD: Heritage Books, 2007.

Dixon, Joan M., *National Intelligencer Newspaper Abstracts, 1848*, Westminster, MD: Heritage Books, 2007.

Dixon, Joan M., *National Intelligencer Newspaper Abstracts, 1849*, Westminster, MD: Heritage Books, 2007.

Dixon, Joan M., *National Intelligencer Newspaper Abstracts, 1850*, Westminster, MD: Heritage Books, 2007.

Dixon, Joan M., *National Intelligencer Newspaper Abstracts, 1851*, Westminster, MD: Heritage Books, 2008.

Dixon, Joan M., *National Intelligencer Newspaper Abstracts, 1852*, Westminster, MD: Heritage Books, 2008.

Dixon, Joan M., *National Intelligencer Newspaper Abstracts, 1853*, Westminster, MD: Heritage Books, 2008.

Dixon, Joan M., *National Intelligencer Newspaper Abstracts, 1854*, Westminster, MD: Heritage Books, 2008.

Dixon, Joan M., *National Intelligencer Newspaper Abstracts, 1855*, Westminster, MD: Heritage Books, 2008.

Dixon, Joan M., *National Intelligencer Newspaper Abstracts, 1856*, Westminster, MD: Heritage Books, 2008.

Dixon, Joan M., *National Intelligencer Newspaper Abstracts, 1858*, Westminster, MD: Heritage Books, 2008.

Dixon, Joan M., *National Intelligencer Newspaper Abstracts, 1859*, Westminster, MD: Heritage Books, 2009.

Dixon, Joan M., *National Intelligencer Newspaper Abstracts, 1860*, Westminster, MD: Heritage Books, 2009.

Dixon, Joan M., *National Intelligencer Newspaper Abstracts, 1867*, Westminster, MD: Heritage Books, 2009.

Dixon, Joan M., *National Intelligencer Newspaper Abstracts, 1868*, Westminster, MD: Heritage Books, 2009.

Dixon, Joan M., *National Intelligencer Newspaper Abstracts, Jan. 1, 1869-Jan. 8, 1870*, Westminster, MD: Heritage Books, 2009.

Dixon, Joan M., *National Intelligencer Newspaper Abstracts, Special Edition: The Civil War Years, July 1, 1863-December 31, 1865,* 2 volumes. Westminster, MD Heritage Books, 2001

Doliante, Sharon J. *Maryland and Virginia Colonials; Genealogies of Some Colonial Families.* Baltimore: Genealogical Publishing Co., 1991.

Donnelly, Sister Mary Louise, *Maryland Elder Family and Kin, William Elder, 1707-1775, Emmitsburg, Md. Pioneer,* Burke, VA, author, 1975.

Duncan, Patricia B., *1860 Loudon County, Virginia Federal Population Census Index*, Westminster, MD: Willow Bend Books, 2002.

Duncan, Patricia B., *Loudon County, Virginia Will Books Abstracts : Books 2A-3C.* Westminster, MD: Willow Bend Books, 2001.

Eader, Edith Olivia & Trudie Davos-Long. *The Jacob Engelbrecht Death Ledger of Frederick County, Maryland, 1820-1890.* Monrovia, MD: Paw Prints, Inc., 1995.

Eckert, Grace Dunlop. *A Portrait of Old Georgetown.* Richmond, VA: The Dietz Press Inc., 1951.

Edwards, Philip K, *Washington Grove: 1873-1937: a history of the Washington Grove Camp Meeting Association*, Washington Grove: author, 1988.

England, C. Walter, comp., *John England and His Descendants,* Manuscript Typescript, author, 1975.

Farquhar, Roger Brooke, *Historic Montgomery County, Maryland, Old Homes and History,* Silver Spring, MD: Author, 1952.

Fogle, Patricia A. *Frederick County, Maryland: Church and Cemetery Records, Vol. 4.* Westminster, MD: Willow Bend Books, 2000

Frain, Elizabeth R. *Loudoun County, Virginia Death Register, 1853-1896.* Westminster, MD: Willow Bend Books, 1998.

Frain, Elizabeth R., *Monocacy Cemetery, Beallsville, Montgomery County, Maryland,* Lovettsville, VA, Willow Bend Books, 1997.

Frain, Elizabeth R., *Union Cemetery, Leesburg, Loudoun County, Virginia, Plats A&B, 1784-1995,* Lovettsville, VA, Willow Bend Books, 1995.

Gartrell, William J., *The Gartrells [1540 to 2000],* 2 vols., Frederick, MD, author, 2000.

Griffith, R. R. *Genealogy of the Griffith Family: the Descendants of William and Sarah Maccubbin Griffith.* Baltimore: Press of William K. Boyle & Son, 1892.

Gurney, John Thomas, ed., *Cemetery Inscriptions of Anne Arundel County, Maryland,* 2 volumes. Chelsea, MI, Bookcrafters, Inc., 1982, copyright by Anne Arundel Genealogical Society.

Helfenstein, Ernest, *History of All Saints Parish, Frederick County, Maryland, Second Ed., Rev. & expanded by Jean Davis, Carroll H. Hendickson, Jr., Arthur Potts, C. Lynn Price,* Frederick, MD., All Saints' Church, 1991.

Heterick, Elizabeth B. *Five Families "Beall" of Maryland: Their Intermarriages and descendants as traced: "Colonel Ninian Beall: Immigrant into Maryland."* self-published, n.d.

Hickey, Clarence R., *Send for the Doctor, the Life and Times of Dr. Edward E. Stonestreet, 19th Century Physician & Civil War Surgeon, Montgomery County, Maryland,* Rockville, MD: Montgomery County Historical Society, 2009.

Hiebert, Ray Eldon and Richard K. MacMaster. *A Grateful Remembrance the Story of Montgomery County, Maryland.* Rockville, MD: Montgomery County Government & Montgomery County Historical Society, 1976.

Hienton, Louise Joyner. *Prince George's Heritage Sidelights on the Early History of Prince George's County, Maryland from 1696 to 1800.* Baltimore, MD: author, 1972.

Holdcraft, Jacob Mehrling, *Names in Stone: 75,000 Cemetery Inscriptions From Frederick County, Maryland*, 2 vol. Ann Arbor, MI: author, 1972.

Hollowak, Thomas E., *Index to Marriages and Deaths in the (Baltimore) Sun. 1837-1850,* Baltimore, Genealogical Publishing Co., 1978.

Hurley, William N., Jr. *1850 Census, Montgomery County Maryland.* Bowie, MD: Heritage Books, 1998.

Hurley, William N., Jr. *Montgomery County, Maryland, 1860 Census.* Bowie, MD: Heritage Books, 1998.

Hurley, William N., Jr. *Montgomery County Maryland, 1870 Census.* Bowie, MD: Heritage Books, 1999.

Hurley, William N., Jr. *1880 Population Census of Montgomery County Maryland.* Bowie, MD: Heritage Books, 1999.

Hurley, William N., Jr. *1900 Population Census of Montgomery County Maryland.* Bowie, MD: Heritage Books, 2000.

Hurley, William N., Jr., *Maddox: A Southern Maryland Family*, Bowie, Md., Heritage Books, 1994.

Hurley, William N., Jr., *Montgomery County Families: A Collection of Genealogies of Early Families of Montgomery County, Maryland,* 2 volumes, Bowie, MD, Heritage Books, 2004.

Hurley, William N., Jr. *Our Maryland Heritage, The Davis Families of Montgomery County Maryland, Book Twenty-Two.* Bowie, MD: Heritage Books, 2001.

Hurley, William N., Jr. *Our Maryland Heritage, The Griffith Families of Maryland, Book Thirty-Three.* Westminster, MD: Family Line Publications, 2002.

Hurley, William N., Jr. *Our Maryland Heritage, The Harding Families of Montgomery County Maryland, Book Thirty-Nine.* Bowie, MD: Heritage Books, 2002.

Hurley, William N, Jr., *Our Maryland Heritage: The King Families, Book Five,* Bowie, MD:, Heritage Books, Inc., 1997.

Hurley, William N, Jr., *Our Maryland Heritage: Book 10: Perry Families,* Bowie, MD: Heritage Books, 1998.

Hurley, William N, Jr., *Our Maryland Heritage: The Waters Families of Maryland, Book Thirty-Two,* Bowie, MD: Heritage Books, Inc., 2002.

Hurley, William N, Jr., *Our Maryland Heritage: The White Families Book Sixteen,* Bowie, MD: Heritage Books, Inc., 1999.

Hutton, S. Janney, *"Records of the Direct Family of Ulric Hutton (1855-1929) AND Mary Brooke (Janney) Hutton (1864-1947) to December 31, 1969,* (typescript) MCHS Library, n.d., n.p..

Jacobs, Marion and Charles. *Confederate Soldiers & Allies with Montgomery County Connections, An Alphabetical Listing of Biographical Data.* Typescript. Rockville, MD: MCHS, 2009.

Jacobs, Marian Waters, compiler, *Genealogical Abstracts from some 19th Century Montgomery County, Maryland, Frederick County, Maryland and Washington, D.C. Newspapers,* manuscript at MCHS, n.d., n.p.

Jacobs, Marian Waters and Mary Gordon Malloy, compilers, *People, Places, and Potpourri,* Rockville, MD: manuscript at MCHS, 1988

Jenkins, Edward Felix, compiler. *Thomas Jenkins of Maryland 1670, His Descendants and Allied Families.* Baltimore: Gateway Press, Inc., 1985 for Maryland Historical Society.

Jewell, Aurelia M., compiler. *Loudoun County, Virginia Marriage Records to 1881.* Berryville, VA: Virginia Book Company, 1975.

Kanely, Edna Agatha, *Directory of Ministers and the Maryland Churches They Served, 1634-1990*; 2 Vol. Westminster, MD: Family Line Publications, 1991.

Keddie, Leslie & Neil, *Prince George's County, Maryland Wills, Liber T No #1, 1778-1783,* np, The Family Tree Bookshop (Waldo (Woof!) Books), 200?.

Keddie, Leslie & Neil. *Prince George's County Maryland Wills, Liber TT, 1818-1822.* np, The Family Tree Bookshop (Waldo (Woof!) Books), 2005.

Kelleher, Polly P., John L. Funk, Robert C. Young and James W. Witt. *John Pigman and His Descendants.* Columbia, MO: Pigman Publishing Co., 1991.

Long, Trudie Davis & Edith Olivia Eader. *The Jacob Englebrecht Marriage Ledger of Frederick County, Maryland, 1820 – 1890.* Monrovia, MD: Paw Prints, Inc., 1994.

Mackenzie, George Norbury, LL.B., editor with Nelson Osgood Rhodes, on Volume 7. *Colonial Families of the United States in which is Given the History, Genealogy and Armorial Bearings of Colonial Families who Settled in the American Colonies from te Time of the Settlement of Jamestown, 11th May 1607 to the Battle of Lexington, 19th April 1975.* Orig. pub. 1912. Reprint. Baltimore: Genealogical Publishing Co.,1966.

Mallick, Sallie A. & F. Edward Wright. *Frederick County Militia in the War of 1812.* Westminster, MD: Family Line Publications, 1992.

Malloy, Mary Gordon, Jane C. Sween and Janet D. Manual. *Abstracts of Wills, Montgomery County, Maryland, 1776-1825.* Washington, D.C., Gray Printing Co. by authors, 1977.

Malloy, Mary Gordon, Jane C. Sween and Janet D. Manual. *Abstracts of Wills, Montgomery County, Maryland, 1826-1875.* Silver Spring, MD: Family Line Publications: 1987.

Mann-Kenny, Louise. *Rosedale, the Eighteenth Century Country Estate of General Uriah Forrest, Cleveland Park, Washington, D.C.* Washington, D.C.: author, 1989.

Manuel, Janet Thompson. *Marriage Licenses Montgomery County Maryland, 1798-1898.* Silver Spring, Md., Family Line Publications, 1987.

Marine, William M. *The British Invasion of Maryland, 1812-1815.* Baltimore: Genealogical Publishing Co., 1977.

Marlborough Towne Chapter, NSDAR, comp., *Tombstone Inscriptions of Southern Anne Arundel County*, Baltimore: Gateway Press, 1971.

Marshall, Nellie M., comp., *Tombstone Records of Dorchester County, Maryland : 1678-1964,* Dorchester County(MD) Historical Society, 1965.

Martin, Margaret Wilmot, *James Davidson of the Maryland Line and some of his descendants,* 38 pages with index; author, 1966. With supplement, 1970. MCHS Library.

McGuckian, Eileen S. *Rockville: Portrait of a City.* Franklin, TN: Hillsboro Press, 2001.

McIntire, Robert Harry. *Annapolis Maryland Families.* Baltimore, MD: Gateway Press, 1980.

Morrow, Dale Walton and Deborah Sue Jensen. *Wills of Washington County, Maryland, an Index: 1776-1890.* Authors, 1977.

Morrow, Dale W. editor, *Washington County Maryland Cemetery Records*, Vol. VI, recorded by Samuel Webster Piper, Westminster, MD: Family Line Publications, 1994.

Morrow, Dale W. editor, *Washington County Maryland Cemetery Records*, Vol. VII, recorded by Samuel Webster Piper, Westminster, MD: Family Line Publications, 1994.

Myers, Margaret E., *Marriage Licenses of Frederick County, 1778-1810,* 2nd. Ed., Westminster, MD, Family Line Publications, 1994.

Newman, Harry Wright. *Anne Arundel Gentry: A Genealogical History of some early families of Anne Arundel County, Maryland.* Revised and Augmented. Vol. 1, Annapolis, author, 1970; Vol. II, author, 1971; Volume Three, author, 1979.

Newman, Harry Wright. *The Maryland Dents.* Richmond, Va.: Dietz Press, Inc., 1963

O'Neill, Francis P., *Index of Obituaries and Marriages in The [Baltimore] Sun : 1866-1870,* 2 volumes, Westminster, Md., Family Line Publications, 1996.

Palmer, Lewis, compiler, *Descendants of John and Mary Palmer*, Chester, PA: 1910. Copy at MCHS Library.

Papenfuse, Edward C., Alan F. Day, David W. Jordan, and Gregory A. Stiverson. *A Biographical Dictionary of the Maryland Legislature, 1635-1789,* Vol. 1: A-H, Baltimore, MD: The Johns Hopkins University Press, 1979; Vol. 2: I-Z, Baltimore, MD: The Johns Hopkins University Press, 1985.

Peden, Henry C., Jr. *Revolutionary Patriots of Charles County, Maryland, 1776-1783.* Westminster, MD: Family Line Publications, 1997.

Peden, Henry C., Jr. *Revolutionary Patriots of Montgomery County, Maryland, 1776-1783.* Westminster, MD: Family Line Publications, 1996.

Peden, Henry C., Jr. *Revolutionary Patriots of Washington County, Maryland, 1776-1783.* Westminster, MD: Family Line Publications, 1998.

Pippenger, Wesley E. *District of Columbia: Guardianship Index: 1802-1928.* Westminster, MD: Willow Bend Books, 1998.

Pippenger, Wesley E. *District of Columbia: Interments (Index to Deaths): January 1, 1855 to July 31, 1874.* Westminster, MD: Willow Bend Books, 1999.

Pippenger, Wesley E., compiler. *District of Columbia Marriage Licenses, Register 1, 1811-1858*. Westminster, MD: Family Line Publications, 1994.

Pippenger, Wesley E., compiler. *District of Columbia Marriage Licenses, Register 2, 1858-1870*. Westminster, MD: Family Line Publications, 1996

Pippenger, Wesley E., compiler. *District of Columbia Marriage Records Index, October 20, 1885 to January 20, 1892 (Marriage Record Books 21 to 30)*. Westminster, MD, Willow Bend Books, 2003.

Pippenger, Wesley E. *Georgetown, District of Columbia: Marriage and Death Notices, 1801-1838,* Bowie, MD: Heritage Books, Inc, 2004

Pippenger, Wesley E. *District of Columbia: Probate Records, Wll Books 1 Through 6, 1801-1852 and Estate Files, 1801-1852*, Westminster, MD: Family Line Publications, 1996.

Pippenger, Wesley E., compiler. *Oak Hill Cemetery, Georgetown, D.C., Monument Inscriptions and Burial Data*, 2 volumes. Privately published for the Oak Hill Cemetery Preservation Foundation, 2006.

Powell, Henry Fletcher, compiler, see *Tercentenary History of Maryland, Vol. IV*, above.

Powell, John W., compiler, *1850 Census Anne Arundel Co., MD including Howard District,* Pasadena, MD, Anne Arundel Genealogical Society, 1991.

Prall, Richard Dwight. *The Crabb Family,* 2 Vol. Albuquerque, NM: New York Book Binders, 1997.

Proctor, John Clagett, editor in chief, *Washington Past and Present,*4 volumes. New York: Lewis Historical Publishing Co., 1930.

Provine, Dorothy, Compensated Emancipation in the District of Columbia, Petitions under the Act of April 16, 1862, Westminster, MD., Heritage Books, 2008.

Provine, Dorothy, *District of Columbia Marriage Records 1870-1877,* Willow Bend Books, Lovettsville, Va., 1997.

Quynn, William R., ed., *The Diary of Jacob Engelbrecht,* Frederick, MD: Historical Society of Frederick County, Inc., 2001.

Rice, Millard Milburn. *New Facts and Old Families, from the Records of Frederick County, Maryland*. Redwood City, CA: Monocacy Book Co., 1976.

Riggs, John Beverly, *The Riggs Family of Maryland, A Genealogical and Historical Record including a study of several families in England,* Baltimore, MD: The Lord Baltimore Press, 1939.

Riley, Elihu S. *The Ancient City: A History of Annapolis, In Maryland: 1649-1887.* Annapolis, MD: author, 1887.

Sargent, Jean A., editor, *Stones and Bones, Cemetery Records of Prince George's County Maryland*. Bowie, MD: Prince George's County Genealogical Society,1984 with inserted Addenda and Errata, 1988 and Addendum, 2000.

Scharf, Col. J. Thomas. *The Chronicles of Baltimore, being a complete history of "Baltimore Town" and Baltimore City from the Earliest Period to the Present Time*. Baltimore: Turnbull Brothers, 1874.

Scharf, J. Thomas. *History of Maryland, From the Earliest Period to the Present Day,* 3 Vol. 1879, Facsimile reprint. Hatboro, Pennsylvania: Tradition Press, 1967.

Scharf, John Thomas, *The History of Baltimore City and County*. Philadelphia, PA: Louis H. Everts, 1881

Scharf, J. Thomas. *History of Western Maryland, Being a History of Frederick, Montgomery, Carroll, Washington, Allegany and Garrett Counties from the earliest period to the present day including biographical sketches of their representative men,* 2 Vol. 1882. Reprint. Baltimore: Regional Publishing Co., 1968.

Sellman, W. Marshall, *John Sellman of Maryland and Descendants,* Cincinnati, Ohio, author, 1975.

Shirk, Ida Morrison (Murphy), comp. *Descendants of Richard and Elizabeth (Ewen) Talbott.* Baltimore, MD, Genealogical Publishing Co. Inc., 1995.

Smith, Elbert B., *Francis Preston Blair,* New York: The Free Press, 1980.

Steiner, Bernard C., Ph.D., *Men of Mark in Maryland, V. I,* Washington, DC: Johnson-Wynne Co., 1907

Sween, Jane C., *All You Want to Know About the Magruders and a Little Bit More,* unpublished manuscript, 1986. Montgomery County Historical Society Library. (MCHS).

Thompson, Noma. *Western Gateway to the National Capital: Rockville, Maryland,* Washington, D.C., Stewart Printing Co., 1949.

Toomey, Daniel Carroll, *The Maryland Line Confederate Soldiers' Home and Confederate Veterans' Organizations in Maryland,* Baltimore, MD, Toomey Press, 2001.

Tyler, Samuel. *Memoir of Roger Brooke Taney, LL.D.* Baltimore: John Murphy & Co., 1872.

USDAR, Marlborough Towne Chapter. *Tombstone Inscriptions of Southern Anne Arundel County.* Baltimore, MD: Gateway Press, 1971.

Van Horn, R. Lee. *Out of the Past: Prince Georgeans and Their Land.* Riverdale, MD: Prince George's Genealogical Society, 1976.

Vogt, John & T. William Kethley, Jr., compilers, *Loudoun County Marriages, 1760-1850,* revised edition with index, Athens Georgia: Iberian Publishing Co., 1985.

Warfield, J. D., *The founders of Anne Arundel and Howard Counties, Maryland. A genealogical and biographical review from wills, deeds and church records.* 1905. Reprint. Westminster, MD: Heritage Books, 2008.

Wearmouth, Roberta J., *Abstracts from the Port Tobacco Times and Charles County Advertiser, Vol. two: 1855-1869.* Bowie, Md., Heritage Books, 1991

Wertz, Mary Alice, compiler, *Marriages of Loudoun County Virginia 1757-1853,* Baltimore, MD: Genealogical Publishing Co., Inc., 1985.

White, Frank F., Jr., *The Governors of Maryland, 1777-1970,* Annapolis, Md., Hall of Records Commission, Publication No. 15, 1970.

Wilcox, Shirley Langdon, ed., *1850 Census of Prince George's County,* Bowie, MD: Prince George's County Genealogical Society, 1978.

Williams, Thomas J. C. *History of Washington County, Maryland: from the earliest settlements to the present time.* 2 Vols. 1906. Reprint. Baltimore, MD: Genealogical Publishing Co., Inc., 1968, 1992

Wright, F. Edward, *Maryland Militia War of 1812, Vol. 1, Eastern Shore.* Silver Spring, MD: Family Line Publications, 1979. *Vol. 2, Baltimore.* Silver Spring, MD, Family Line Publications, 1979. *Vol. 3 Cecil & Harford Counties.* Silver Spring, MD: Family Line Publications, 1980. *Vol. 4, Anne Arundel & Calvert.* Silver Spring, MD: Family Line Publications, 1981. *Vol. 6, Prince George's County.* Silver Spring, MD: Family Line Publications, 1985. *Vol. 7, Montgomery County.* Silver Spring, MD: Family Line Publications, 1986.

Wright, F. Edward. *Newspaper Abstracts of Frederick County,1811-1815,* Silver Spring, MD: Family Line Publications, 1987.

Wright, F. Edward. *Western Maryland Newspaper Abstracts,1806-1810,* Volume 3. Westminster, MD: Family Line Publications, 1992.

PERIODICALS

Maryland Historical Magazine,
Vol. 84, No. 3, Fall 1989, Sam Meyer, "Religion, Patriotism, and Poetry in the life of Francis Scott, Key," 267-274.

Montgomery County Story,
Dryden, Steve "Keeping Up with the Joneses" Vol. 49, no 2, May 2006.
Fitzsimons, Mrs. Neal (Mavis) "The Audubon Naturalist Society and its home, Woodend," Vol. 17, No. 3, August 1974
Sween, Jane C., "Maryland and Montgomery County in the Evolution of the United States Constitution," Vol. 30, no. 2

Records of the Columbia Historical Society:
Clark, Allen C., "Rev. Stephen Bloomer Balch, A Pioneer Preacher of Georgetown, Vol. 15, 1912, p. 73-95.

INDEX

Abert
Allen McLane, 68
Charles, 67, 142
Charles, Jr., 67
Constantia, 68
Ellen, 67
Ellen Matlack, 67
Emma Barry, 142
John James, 67
Maria Bache, 67
Martha Wilson (Stonestreet), 142
Mary Warner, 67
Robert Walker, 67
Sophia Bache, 67
Adams
Ann, 170
Adamson
Clara Smith, 106, 160
Jane Smith, 54
John Jr., 38
Lloyd, 54
Margaret Ann Alby, 106
Walter Hilleary, 106
Alby
Margaret Ann, 106
Aldridge
Eliza, 146
Alexander
Amelia, 83
Allen
Alethea Van Horne, 59
Robert, 59
Allen
Thomas G, 38
Allison
Maria Key Taney, 57
Richard T., 57
Allnutt
Ann, 95
Myra (Compton), 157
Nathan Smith, 157
Almoney
Albert J., 149
Alice A., 75, 172
Jarret, 75, 77, 149
Mary Ann (Burke), 75, 77, 149
Almony
Albert J., 134
Alice, 76
Franklin (Frank), 149
Jarrett, 134
Mariam Prettyman, 134
Alvey
Julia, 182
Richard H, 182
Alward
Jessica, 97, 158
Anderson
Alice, 69
Alice M. Lawn, 69
Berthy Girola, 150
Charles, 101
Charles H., 153
Edward, 69
Eleanor, 120
Elizabeth Wallace, 68
Ella Darne, 69, 151
Frances Virginia, 69
George, 69
George Minor, 69, 140, 149, 150, 174
James, 8
James B., 152
James W., 120
James Wallace, 68, 70, 142, 149, 150
James, Dr., 68
John Wallace, 70, 142, 151
Josephine L., 101
Julia Prout Vinson, 69, 140
Lavinia Brown, 153
Lillie Minor, 69
Lucinda B., 153
Martha Bradley, 151
Martha C. (Love), 101
Martha Wootton, 69, 151
Mary Bowie Sprigg, 70
Mary E., 69
Mary Minor, 69, 120, 149, 150
Meliora Ogle, 8
Mira Magruder, 70, 151
Myra (Magruder), 142
Osborn Sprigg, 70
Rebecca Maria Harriett, 8
Richard, 69
Richard S., 101
Rose, 142
Samuel Sprigg, 70
Sarah (Sallie) Thrift, 69

Thomas, 69, 75, 150
Thomas Minor, 150
William Bowie, 70
William Wallace, 151
Anderson
James Jr., 38
Andre
John, Major, 47
Annan
James R., 44
Priscilla J. Perry, 44
Ashton, 3
Anna Sophia, 4
Caroline Henry, 4, 140
Cecilia, 4
Eleanor Hawkins, 3
Henry, 4, 65
Jane C., 4
Mary, 4
Mary Dent, 3
Rebecca Latham, 3
Sarah B., 4
Awl
Aimee Rebecca Motter, 122
Francis Asbury, 122
Bache
Henrietta Constantia, 67
Richard, 67
Sophia Burrell, 67
Bacon
Ann, 117
Baer
Elizabeth Shellman, 50
George, 127
Henry, 50
Matilda Chase Ridgely, 50
Michael Shellman, 50
Bailey
Mary Catherine, 91
Baker
Josephine, 96
Roberta, 161
Rueben, 161
Balch
Adam Weber, 5
Aletha Matilda Boteler, 6
Alexandrine Macomb, 6
Anna Beall, 5
Anna Jay, 5
Catherine Elizabeth Spencer, 5
Elizabeth Beall, 5
Emily Swift, 5
Frances Carter, 6
Harriet Cornelia, 5
John Wilson, 6
Lewis P. W., 6
Stephen Bloomer, 5
Stephen Fitzhugh, 6
Sylvester Whitefield, 6
Thomas, 5
Virginia Melancthon, 5
Balch.
Lewis P. W., 5
Baldwin
Maria Bache Abert, 67
William D., 67
Barnard
Sophia Dorothy "Dora", 161
Barnes
Mary King, 41
Samuel, 44
Barrett
Eliza, 133
Barry
Martha Rebecca, 167
Bartgis
Annie A., 157
Charles, 157
Della, 157
Batcheller
Harriet Carolina, 85
Battee
Richard Harwood, 49
Sophia Ridgely, 49
Beach
Annie Lee, 71
Charles W., 70
Edwin, 71
Emma Virginia, 71
Fannie, 71
Frances Coleman Woodbridge, 70
John Newton, 71
Sylvester, 71
Beale
George William, 77
Mary Anna Bouic, 77
Beall
Alethea Elizabeth, 59
Amelia (Beall), 59
Amelia Beall Van Horne, 59
Ann Trueman Greenfield, 59
Bessie, 72
Brooke, 63
Catherine Goldsborough Owen, 152
Dorothy Middleton, 152
Eleanor, 12
Eleanor Brooke, 13
Elizabeth, 5
Elizabeth Fenimore Cooper, 72
Elizabeth Wootton, 63, 72
Ellen, 72
Emma Cooper, 72
Fanny, 72
George, 59
Jane Robb, 105
John, 64, 72
Lewis, 63, 72
Lucy, 38
Luella Ophelia (Doty), 72
Margaret, 96
Margaret Helen, 134
Margaret Johns, 44, 63
Mary, 72
Mary Ellen (Nellie). Middleton, 152
Priscilla Beall, 95
Rezin, 59
Richard Robinson, 152
Roger, 72
Samuel, 13
Samuel Wootton, 72
Sarah, 64
Singleton Wooten, 72
Thomas John, 152
Upton, 44, 63, 72, 105, 134
Walter Truman Greenleaf, 59
Bean
Prudence, 126
Beanes
William, 33
Beard
Charles A., 164
Harriett Jones, 164
Beardsley
Andromeda Smith, 55
Governor, 55
Beckenbaugh
George, 116
Isabella C., 116
Martha (Vanes), 116
Belt
Addison, 126
Elizabeth Ann, 11
Elizabeth Ann (Carrington), 126
Julia, 126
Martha Anna Carrington, 122
Beltzhoover
Elizabeth, 41
Benton
Thomas Hart, 73
Berry
Jeremiah, 124
Ruth (Gassaway), 124
Biays
Jane C. T. Magruder, 179
Philip Grable, 179
Rebecca Thomas, 179
Bibb, 4
Caroline M., 153
George R., 4

Mary Rebecca Latham Ashton, 4
Binney
Horace, 94
Birney
Arthur A., 171
Biscoe
Elizabeth, 87
Blair
Betty, 74
Caroline Rebecca Buckner, 74
Eliza Violet Gist, 73, 169
Elizabeth, 169
Ellen Abert, 67
Francis Preston, 73, 169
Gist, 74
John S., 67
Maria, 74
Mary Elizabeth Woodbury, 74
Minna, 74
Montgomery, 73, 169
Montgomery, Jr., 74
Woodbury, 74
Blunt
Ellen Lloyd Key, 35
Simon Fraser, 35
Bohrer
Benjamin, 22
Maria Forrest, 22
Bomford
Elizabeth (or Louisa), 115
Booth
Elizabeth, 65
Bordley
Henrietta Marie, 50
John Beale, 50
Margaret (Chew), 50
Boteler
Aletha Matilda, 6
Eliza, 116
Bouic
Albert Manoury, 76, 172
Alice A. Almoney, 75, 172
Alice Almony, 76
Charles Norman, 75
Dorcas Veirs Fletchall, 76
Ella Clark, 77
Eulalie Louise, 77
Frances Peter, 76, 172
Henry Vauclin, 75
Isabel, 75
Louis Aubrey, 75
Margaret Wilbourne, 75
Mary A. Rosetta, 76
Mary Ann Matilda (Veirs), 75
Mary Ann Matilda Veirs, 174
Mary Anna, 77
Peter Amiable Tranquille, 76
Rosetta (Rosa) Vauclin, 174
Rosetta V., 133
Rosetta Vauclin, 77
W. V., 174
William Garner, 75
William Veirs, 76, 133, 172
William Veirs, Jr., 75
William Veirs, Sr., 75, 76
Bourne
Sarah, 49
Bowie
Allen, 17
Carolina Lansdale, 70
Catharine L. Williams, 78
Catherine, 21
Catherine Worthington (Davis), 17
Elizabeth, 17
Kitty Beanes Duckett, 21
Margaret, 92, 93
Margaret Crabb Johns, 77
Mary A., 92
Mary Crabb Johns, 17
Priscilla Fraser, 20
Richard J, 133
Richard J., 80
Richard Johns, 77, 93, 139, 142
Ruth Cramphin, 17
Thomas Johns, 17
Washington, 54, 77, 92
Washington, Col., 17
William, 21
Bowman
Evelyn Wailes Talbott, 176
John Darby, 176
Boyd
Charity Ducket, 136
Boyle
Edwin, 7
Ellen Slemaker, 7
James, 6
John Henry, 7
Llewellyn, 7
Mary (Brewer, 6
Mary Ann, 7
Susan Maccubbin, 7
Violetta, 7
Braddock
Charles, 79
Elizabeth Hilton, 170
John, 78, 79
John, Jr., 80
Joseph, 78, 79, 80
Laura Locke, 78
Mary, 78
Mary Hilton, 78, 79
Sarah Ann Locke, 80
Sarah Hilton, 170
William, 170
William Locke, 79
William Perry, 79
Bradford
Gov., 127
James Morgan, 82
Sophia Elizabeth, 82
Bradley
Abraham, 80
Abraham Thomas, 80
Alice, 81
Eliza M. Thomas, 81
Hannah (Smith), 80
Hannah T., 80
Henry, 151
Jane B., 179
Joseh H.,Jr., 81
Joseph H., 136
Joseph Habersham, 80
Lucy Sherman Tuttle, 80
Martha, 151
Mary, 80
Mary (Prout), 151
Mary Duncan, 81
Mary Harriss, 80
Sarah D., 80
Sarah Slater, 158
Brashears
AnnCook, 13
Anne, 13
Belt, 13
Elizabeth C., 63
Brent
Dorothy Leigh, 7
Harriet Cottringer, 81
Joseph Lancaster, 8
Maria Fenwick, 8
Robert, 7, 81
Robert Young, 81
William Cottringer, 81
William L., 7, 8
Brewer
Amelia Alexander, 83
Bessie Stonestreet Greene, 83
Catharine Musser Medairy, 84
Catharine Susanna, 85
Catherine, 84
Charles, 85
Eleanor, 84
Elizabeth Morris, 85
Elizabeth Sophia, 82
Elizabeth Stewart, 83

Elizabeth Stewart (Buchanan), 82, 109
Elizabeth Stewart Buchanan, 84, 85
Ellen, 109
Ellen Russell, 83
George, 83
Harriet Carolina Batcheller, 84
Hattie Batcheller, 85
James, 82
James Chiswell, 81, 83
John, 83, 86, 130
John Buchanan, 82, 84
John Chiswell, 82, 83, 84, 85, 109
Joseph, 82
Lloyd Archibald, 83
Lucy Briscoe, 83
Mary, 84
Mary McPherson, 83
Mary Octavia, 82
Mary Robertson Chiswell, 81, 84
Matilda Provost Russell, 86
Maude Stalnaker, 83
Nicholas, 82, 83, 84
Nicholas IV, 85
Rosalind Caldwell, 83
Sarah Caroline, 85
Sophia Bradford, 82
Thomas Leverett, 85
Virginia Fletcher, 83
Virginia Fletcher Russell, 83
William, 81, 83, 84, 85
William P., 82
William Russell, 83

Brice
Ariana Frisby, 50
John, 50
Sarah (Frisby), 50

Bridges
James Taliafero, 106
Sarah Isabel Henderson, 106

Briscoe
R. S., 38

Brooke
Anne, 19
Annie Clymer, 169
Deborah Snowden, 38
Edward, 169
James, 38
Jane Lynn, 19
Monica, 56, 57
Richard, 19, 38

Brosius
Charles Thomas, 157
Genevieve Darby, 157

Brown
Alice, 65
Amos, 93
Caroline M. (Bibb), 153
Edward, 182
Elizabeth Hall, 182
Emily Poole Darby, 156
Frances Thompson, 65
Frank, 105
George Bibb, 153
George Minos, 153
George Minos Bibb, 154
Henry, 65
Henry Ashton, 153
Lavinia, 153
Lucinda B. Anderson, 153
Lydia, 93
Marie L. Jett, 153
Nina Elizabeth, 182
Ridgely, 93
Sarah Ridgely (Griffith), 93
Thomas J, 153
William Clifton, 156

Bruce
Ariana, 33
Elizabeth, 33
Henrietta Jones, 33
Jane, 32, **33**

Bryant
Homer Stafford, 167
Lucille Allen Lamar, 167

Buchanan
Anne Maria Cooke, 8
Anne Ogle, 9
Elizabeth Stewart, 82, 84, 85, 109
Harriett Rebecca, 9
James Anderson, 9
John, 9, 145
Meliora Ogle, 9
Sidney Claire, 162
Thomas, 8, 145
Thomas Cribb, 9

Buck
Harry H., 75
Isabel Bouic, 75

Buckey
Annie Eliza, 139
Catherine, 97

Buckner
Caroline Rebecca, 74

Buhrman
Ann, 121

Burbage
Fanny Ann, 45

Burgess
Ann, *10*
Dennis, 89
Edward, 9, 10
Eleanor Griffith, 26
Elizabeth, *10*
Elizabeth Magruder, 10
Ephraim, *10*
Helen Maccubbin, 10
Jane, *10*
Jane (McElfresh), 9
John, *9*, *10*, 26
Margaret, 10
Mary, 10
Sally/Sarah, 10
Sarah Worthington Dorsey, 26
Thomas, *10*

Burke
Mary Ann, 134

Burr
Aaron, 40, 41

Burroughs
Elizabeth Smith Locke, 79

Butler
Ann, 26

Butt
Richard, 38

Buxton
Ella R. Hedges, 157
George Chiswell Darby, 157
Georgie, 157
William L., 157

Byrne
family, 58
George F., 154
James Franklin, 154
Mary E. McMarkham, 154
Sarah Elizabeth Jones, 154

Cadwallader
Anna Maria, 48

Cahill
Joseph Aloysius, 86
Philip J, 86
Sophia Ann Cecilia (Elder), 86

Caldwell
Mr., 80
Rosalind, 83

Calmes
George, 44
Lucy, 44
Mary (Price), 44

Calvert
Edward Henry, 87
Elizabeth (Biscoe), 87
Rosalie Stier, 87
Washington Custis, 87

Campbell
Aeneas, 11, 12
Alvin Cook, 14
Ann, *12*
Ann Arnold Taney, 56
Elizabeth Sowers, 14

Hester, 12
Iver, 14
James, 11, 12
James Mason, 56
John, 14
Kitty White, *12*
L, 12
Lydia, *12*
Lydia Cartwright, 12
Mary M., 14
Canby
Elizabeth Dawson, 160
George R., 160
Martha Hughs, 174
Cantwell
Paul Langley, 155
Sarah Cowen Catlett, 155
Caperton
Eliza Jane Mosher, 88
Hugh, 88
Hugh Elmwood, 88
Imogene, 88
James Mosher, 88
Jane, 88
Mary Jane Erskine, 88
Caranahan
Dr., 77
Carpenter
Hugh, 88
Carr
Clarissa Van Horne, 59
Rev., 59
Carrington
Elizabeth Ann, 126
Carroll
Charles, 104
Mary Clare, 104
Carter
Catharine, 90
Charles Adam, 90
Elizabeth Ann Harding, 90
Eva (Russell), 75
Harry Lee, 75
Henry Harding, 90
James Caldwell, 90
John, 88, 89
John A., 89
John Alexander, 88, 90
Mary Ann Harding, 90
Mary Anna Harding, 27
Mary Catherine Holmes Magruder, 89
Mary M. Gunton, 90
Rebecca J., 89
Robert W., 27, 89
Robert W., Jr., 90
William, 90
William John, 90
Cartwright
Lydia, 11
Cashell
Amanda E., 91
Catherine Groomes, 91
Edgar Hill, 92
Elizabeth B. Edmonston, 91
Elizabeth Emily Groomes, 92
Elizabeth Henrietta, 92
Ella Virginia Ferry, 92
Ellen Rebecca Groomes, 92
Francis Hazel, 92
George, 91
Harriet A. Jones, 91
Hazel Butt, 91
James Groomes, 91
Marie Catherine Weller, 92
Mary Ellen Hodges, 91
Thomas Franklin, 92
William Lycurgus, 92
Catlett
Elizabeth Fitzhugh, 154
George Fitzhugh, 155
George Washington, 154
Margaret Dudley McIlhenny, 155
Margaret J., 155
Sarah Cowen, 155
Susan, 155
Washington, 154
Chaney
Henrietta, *11*
Charlton
Ann Phoebe, 33
Chase
Catherine, 15
Jeremiah Townley, 56
Samuel, 40, 47
Chatard
J.Frederick, 141
Mary Julia, 141
Chesley
Jane G., 121
William Fitzhugh, 121
Chichester
Eliza Miller Hallowell, 93
George Mason, 92
Harriet Ridgely, 93
Lydia Brown, 93
Lydia W., 93
Margaret Bowie, 93
Mary A. Bowie, 92
Mary Richard, 93
Nathan, 92
Washington Bowie, 92, 93
Washington Bowie, Jr., 93
Chilton
A. W., 164
Alexandria, 112
Martha Matilda Kilgour, 112
Mr., 37
Chiswell
Antoinette Griffith, 156
George W., 156
Leah (Griffith), 156
Mary Robertson, 81, 84
Choate
Alice B. Fleming, 156
Katherine M., 135
Katherine M. Ragan, 155
Warren, 155
Warren Ragan, 155
Clagett
Alexander, 12
Ara Rebecca, 128
Eleanor Beall, 12
Elizabeth, 84, 109
Elizabeth Ann, 124
Elizabeth Perry, 12
James H., 128
Margaret Ann (Wilcoxin), 124
Margaret Burgess, 10
Mary Thrift, 128
Nathaniel, 124
NinianMagruder, 10
William, 12, 13
Clark
Catherine Hyatt Middleton, 152
Charles, 42
David, 156
Emily Poole Darby, 156
Lemuel, 152
Martha (Crawford), 42
Thomas, 42
Clarke
Catherine Bowie, 21
Daniel, 21
Jane, 126
Margaret Howard, 21
Matthew St. Clair, 126
Clarkson
Catherine Elizabeth Spencer, 5
Freeman, 5
Clay
Henry, 3
Clymer
Annie, 169
Cockman
Margaret Taylor Higgins, 161
Thomas Ray, 161
Coleman
Frances, 71
Collins
Elizabeth, 115

Collinson
Sarah, 103
Combs
H. Wheeler, 128
Comer
George C., 96
Mary (Mollie) Dawson, 96
Compton
Myra, 157
Cone
Elijah, 72
Emma Agnes (Beall), 72
Contee
Charity Henley, 32
John, 32
Cook
Ann, 13
Elizabeth (Johnson), 13
George, 13
James, 13
John, 13, 14
John, 38
Mary M., 14
Thomas, 13
Cook
Thomas, 13
Cook
John, 13
Cook
George, 13
Cooke
Anne Maria, 8
Nathan, 39
Rachel, 39
Rachel Magruder, 39
Cooper
Bernard John, 116
Elizabeth Fenimore, 72
Isaac, 72
James Fenimore, 72
Mary (Morris), 72
Mary Elizabeth Lee, 116
Cottringer
Garrett, 81
Harriet, 81
Couch
Cora Caroline, 106, 160
Courts
Charity Henley, 32
Elizabeth, 32
John, 32
Cox
Clement, 77
Richard S., 80
Coxe
Daniel, 94
Mary Griffith, 94
Rachel Smith, 94
Richard D., 94
Richard Smith, 94
Susan Boudinot Griffith, 94
Susan Bradley, 94
Susan Warren Wheeler, 94
William, 94
William Griffith, 95
Crabb
Ann (Snowden), 15
Catherine Chase, 15
Charles Henry, 15
Elizabeth Ridgely, 15, 100
Elizabeth Ridgely Griffith, 15
Emeline, 15
Henry Wright, 15
Jeremiah, 15
Lydia Ridgely, 15
Mary L. Summers, 15
Matilda, 15
Nancy (Anne) Snowden, 15
Richard J., 15
Sarah Griffith, 15
Cramer
Mary Agnes, 178
Cramphin
Mary Jackson, 16
Ruth, 17
Thomas, 16, 17
Thomas Jr., 16
Crapster
William T., 128
Crawford
David, 42
John, 128
Martha, 42
Rebecca, 128
Cresap
Mary, 40
Mary Whitehead, 40
Michael, 40
Cromwell
Stephen C., 179
Culver
Elizabeth, 138
Cummins
Alexandrine Macomb Balch, 6
George David, 6
Cunningham
Nannie, 96, 158
Cuyler
Agnes, 104
Emily Potter, 104
Dall
Meliora Buchanan, 9
Robert, 9
Darby
Alice Rebecca, 157
Antoinette Griffith Chiswell, 156
Arlene C. Johnson, 157
Della Bartgis, 157
Ellen Ruth (Edelen), 156
Emily Poole, 156
Genevieve, 157
George Chiswell, 157
Gertrude Hyatt, 157
John Edwin, 157
John William, 156
Juliana, 117
Laura Allnutt, 157
Lawrence Jones, 157
Remus Riggs, 156
Remus Riggs, Jr., 157
Ruth Ellen, 157
William Leroy, 157
Dare
Elizabeth Ridgely, 49
Nathaniel C., 49
Darne
Alexander H. C., 69, 151
Ella, 69, 151
Mary A. Gassaway, 69
Mary Gassaway, 151
Dashiell
Alfred Henry, 49
Ann Ridgely, 49
Davidson
Elizabeth Bishop Dunn, 97, 158
Elizabeth Gordon Hannah, 97, 158
Elva Statler, 97, 158
Henry Bradley, 96, 158
Henry Bradley, Jr., 97, 158
James Henry, 96, 158
Jessica Alward, 97, 158
Louise Armstrong, 96, 158
Mabel Elmore Rucker, 97, 158
Mary Stannard Porter, 96, 158
Nannie Cunningham, 96, 158
Richard Porter, 97, 158
Sarah (Slater), 96
Sarah Slater (Bradley), 158
Davis, 9
Allen Bowie, 17
Anne Wilkins, 17
Catherine Worthington, 17
Charles, 55
Dolly Madison Smith, 55
Elizabeth (Howard), 17
Ephraim, 17
Ignatius, 63
Jefferson, 18, 98, 99

Margaret Wootton, 63
Rebecca Comfort (Dorsey), 17
Sarah, 25
Thomas, 17
Thomas John, 17
Varina, 99
Varina Banks Howell, 98
Dawes
Annie E., 117
Isaac, 117
Juliana Darby, 117
Dawson
Amelia Hollyday Somerville, 95
Ann, 159
Ann Allnutt, 95
Anne E., 96
Anne Frazier, 160
Elizabeth, 160
Fannie Knight, 96
Frederick, 159
George C., 95
George C.,, 159
Henrietta Hoffman, 95, 159
Henry A., 96
James D., 95, 159
James Mackall, 95
John Lawrence, 95
Josephine Baker, 96
Lavinia, 160
Lawrence Allnut, 159
Lawrence Allnutt, 95
Louise Weaver, 95
Mary, 159, 160
Mary (Mollie), 96
Mary A. Peter, 130, 160
Mary Elizabeth Kiger, 95, 159
Rose Newell Williams, 96
Thomas, 96, 130, 159
Thomas L., 160
Day
Charles A.H., 98
Enoch G., 97
John E., 98
Julia Ann (England), 97
Mary C., 98
Thomas, 97
William H., 98
Deale
Mary Franklin, 132
Dent
Anna Sophia, 4
George, 4
Mary, 3
Diamond
Herbert, 164
Marie Jones, 164
Diffendorfer
Juliana, 76
Dixon
James, 44
Donaldson
George M., 123
Sarah Turpin Ould, 123
Dorsey
Ann, 20, 25
Anna Maria, 30
Anne Brooke, 19
Charles Ridgely, 19
Charles S. W., 18
Charles S.W., 98
Charles Samuel Worthington, 99
Charles Worthington, 99
Clement, 20
Comfort, 99
Comfort W., 99
Comfort Worthington, 18, 98, 99
Deborah (Dorsey), 49
Edward, 25
Eleanor Harrison, 19
Eliza, 130
Elizabeth, 25, 49
Elizabeth Worthington, 99
Ely, 49
Gertrude Lyddane, 170
Gustavus Warfield, 124
Hopewell Hebb, 30
James M., 20
John, 19
John TW, 100
John Worthington, 18, 19
Madge, 123
Margaret Owen, 124
Maria Ann, 20
Mary, 99
Mary Hammond, 19
Mary Pue Ridgely, 99
Mary Pue Ridgley, 18
Mary Ridgley, 99
Mary Riggs Griffith, 124
Mary Tolly Worthington, 99
Milcah (Goodwin), 17
Milcah Goodwin, 98, 99
Priscilla, 18
Priscilla Hebb, 20
Priscilla Ridgley, 18
Rachel, 25
Rebecca Comfort, 17
Rebecca Hanson, 19
Richard Brooke, 20
Robert E., 20
Rosetta Lynn, 20
Samuel Owings, 124
Samuel W., 18
Samuel Worthington, 19, 98
Sarah, 99
Sarah (Todd), 25
Sarah Anne Ellis, 98
Sarah Duvall, 20
Sarah Worthington, 26
Susan Robertson, 20
Thomas, 98
Thomas B., 18, 99
Thomas Beale, 17, 18, 98, 99
W. H. Goodwin, 18
Walter, 30
William, 170
William H. G., 98
William H.G., 135
William Hammond, 19
William Hammond, Jr., 20
William Henry Goodwin, 99
Doty
Luella Ophelia, 72
Dove
Elizabeth Ann Harding Carter, 90
John Maury, 90
Mrs., 90
Drake
Louisa Hannah, 43
Driscoll
Mary, 120
Dronenburg
Clifton, 175
Katherine E. (Ricketts), 175
Ruth, 175
Duckett
Allen Bowie, 20, 24
Catherine Bowie, 21
Catherine Goldsborough, 24
Elizabeth Worthington Goldsborough, 21
Kitty Beanes, 21
Marcella Elizabeth, 21
Margaret Howard, 21
Richard, 24
Richard Jacob, 21
Thomas, 20, 21, 24
Dudley
Margaret, 155
Duncan
Mary, 81
Sarah, 24
Dunlop
Sarah N. Peter, 130
William, 130
Dunn
Elizabeth Bishop, 97, 158
Dupont
Francis G, 93
DuPont
Alexis Felix, 93

Mary Richards Chichester, 93
Durrett
Richard, 141
Susanna Ashton Hunter, 141
Duvall
Elizabeth Whitaker Hawkins, 20
Grafton, 20
Sarah, 20
Dyer
Alexander, 4
Rebecca Latham, 3
Dyson
Bennett, 146
Mary E., 146
Earll
Florence, 181
Nancy Strickland, 181
William, 181
Eccleston
Archbishop, 115
Edelen
Ellen Ruth, 156
Edelin
Christopher, 39
Eleanor, 39
Rebecca Johnson, 39
Edgerton
Sarah, 110
Edmonston
Elizabeth B., 91
Margery, 38
Eichelberger
Grayson, 178
Elder
Sophia Ann Cecilia, 86
Ellis
Sarah Anne, 98
Ellison
Sadie Marie Talbott, 177
Walter G., 177
Elmendorf
Mary, *11*
Emack
John D., 59
Mary Ann Van Horne, 59
England
Amos, 100
Andrew, 97
Annie L. Griffith, 101
Catherine (Buckey), 97
Emily Howard, 100
Harriet V., 100
Henry Clay, 100
John Glisan, 100
John Glisan, Jr, 101
Julia Ann, 97
Mary Ridgely, 101
Susan R., 100
Thomas H., 100
English
David, 56
Erskine
Mary Jane, 88
Etchison
Mary Jane Priscilla, 179
Mary Poultney Etchison, 179
Evans
Josephine L. Anderson, 101
Madge, 101
Susan, 101
William Tecumseh, 101
Ewen
Edward, 124
Falvey
Elizabeth Jones, 110
Thomas R., 110
Farrow
Mary Elizabeth, 180
Fay
H. A., Capt., 105
Fechtig
Louise, 179
Fenwick
Henrietta Lancaster, 8
James, 8
John L., 8
Maria, 8
Ferry
Ella Virginia, 92
Fields
Kate R., 170
Fish
Eleanor, 91
Fitzhugh
Elizabeth, 154
Fleming
Alice B., 156
Fletchall
Dorcas Veirs, 76
John, 76
Fletcher
Virginia, 83, 86
Floyd
Mary L., 178
Forrest
Ann, 22
Ann Maria Summers, 22
Anna Maria Summers, 102
Benjamin, 95
Benjamin S., 38
Benjamin Stoddert, 22, 102
Charles Wayman, 103
Elizabeth, 22
George Plater Plate, 22
Henrietta Raley, 21
Henry, 102, 103
Jane [Love], 102
Maria, 22
Rebecca Plater, 102
Samuel, 33
Thomas, 21
Uriah, 21, 102
Fowler
Alice (Jones), 156
Clara Ireland, 156
William, 156
Franklin
Benjamin, 67
Sarah, 67
Freeland
Sarah Norfleet, 130
Fulks
Blanche, 172
Edith Maud Watkins, 172
Oscar Fernando, 172
Gaither, 9
Elizabeth (Howard), 17
Elizabeth Worthington, 166
George Riggs, 19
Pauline, 123
Rebecca Hanson Dorsey, 19
William, 17
Galloway
Joseph, 39
Mary, 39, 52
Gantt
Benjamin Edward, 23
Edwin Thomas, 23
John Mackall, 22
Lucy Sprigg, 23
Susannah Mackall, 22
Thomas, 22
William Turner, 23
Gantt
Thomas, 62
Garrett
Mary Cecil, 161
Gartrell
Charles, 175
Claudia, 175
Virginia (Groomes), 175
Gassaway
Eliza Dorsey, 130
Eliza Lavinia, 130, 131, 160, 171, 173
John, 130
Laura, 180
Mary, 151
Mary A., 69
Mary Elizabeth, 180
Ruth, 124
William Augustus, 180
Gaver

Laura Eugenia Urner, 178
William E., 178
Gear
Carrie, 125
Carter, 125
Rebecca, 125
George Dent, 4
Gibbons
Priscilla Dawson, 168
William H., 168
Girola
Bertha, 150
Natalie, 150
Gist
Eliza Violet, 73, 169
Glascott
Evelyn Wailes Talbott, 176
Hugh Craig, 176
Glenn
Ann Maria, 167, 168
John, 98
Mary, 116
Glisan
Rebecca, 100
Goldsborough, 166
Amelia Poe, 24
Catharine, 21
Catherine, 24
Charles Henry, 24
Edward Yerbury, 24
Leander W, 24
Nicholas Worthington, 24
Robert, 23
Sarah Duncan, 24
Sarah Worthington, 24
Sarah Yerbury, 23
William, 23, 24
Williamina Elizabeth Cadwalader, 166
Goodwin
Milcah, 17, 98, 99
Gordon
Anne E., 46
Gott
Lydia Nichols, 103
Mary Ellen, 180
Richard, 103
Sarah Collinson, 103
William Collinson, 103
Gould
Ashley Molgram, 85
Elizabeth, 115
Elizabeth Morris Brewer, 85
Grady
Wm, 126
Grahame
10. Caroline Worthington Goldsborough Johnson, 30
Thomas J., 30
Gray
Barney, 33
Martha, 125
Green
John, 22
Greene
Bessie Stonestreet, 83
Greenfield
Ann Trueman, 59
Griffith
Alice Rebecca Darby, 157
Ann, 25
Annie L., 101
Catherine, 24, 29
Charles, 25
Charles Greenberry, 15
Eleanor, 26
Eleanor Jacob, 25
Elizabeth, 26
Elizabeth Ridgely, 15, 25, 26
Henrietta Elizabeth Wilcoxin, 101
Henry, 25
John Hammond, 25
Joshua, 26
Katherine Howard, 25
Leah, 156
Lyde, 26
Lydia Ridgely Crabb, 15
Mary Riggs, 124
Michael Berry, 15
Orlando, 25
Philemon, 15, 25
Rachel, 25
Rachel Warfield, 25
Ruth, 25, 26
Samuel, 25
Sarah, 25
Sarah (Ridgely), 15
Sarah Davis, 25
Sarah Griffith Crabb, 15
Sarah Ridgely, 93
Sarah Warfield, 25
Susan Boudinot, 94
Uriah, 101
William, 94
William Franklin, 157
Grimes
Greer Brown, 55
Sophia Smith, 55
Groomes
Catherine, 91
Eleanor (Fish), 91
Elizabeth Emily, 92
Elizabeth Henrietta (Cashell), 92
Ellen Rebecca, 92
Hanson, 92
James, 91
Gruber
Jacob, Rev., 45
Gunton
Mary M., 90
Hagner
Mary, 131
Hall
Ann Buchanan Pottenger, 52
Ann Griffith, 25
Barbara, 52
Bertha, 177
Elisha, 27
Elizabeth, 182
Elizabeth Bowie, 78
Jacob, 27
Letitia, 52
Mary, 52
Nicholas, 25
Ruth, 27
Thomas B., 52
Hallowell
Eliza Mille, 93
Hamilton
Lucy Briscoe Brewer, 83
Martha Crawford, 42
Murray, 83
Wilhelmina, 42
William, 42
Hammond
Agnes Cuyler, 104
Alice, 104
Ann (Dorsey), 25
Ariana, 118
Edward, 103, 104
Elizabeth Meriweather, 103
Elizabeth Merriweather, 104
Emily Potter Cuyler, 104
Frank Lloyd, 104
George Maccubbin, 104
John, 25
L. T., Dr., 118
Lloyd Thomas, 103
Lola Augusta, 104
Mary, 19, 49
Mary Agnes Cramer, 178
Richard Creagh, 104
Richard T., 178
Ruth, 25
William Allen, 104
Hannah
David, 97, 158
Elizabeth Gordon, 97, 158
Hanson
Alexander C., 31
John, 47
Hanson
Alexander Contee, 113
Harding
Ann Butler, 26

Catharine Jane, 27
Catherine Ann (Robb), 105
Catherine Ann Robb, 26, 90
Charles Adam, 27
Edward, 26
Elizabeth Ann, 26
Henry, 26, 90, 105, 165
Josiah, 138
Mary Ann, 90
Mary Anna, 27
Mary Virginia Valdenar, 138
Violetta E. Lee, 27
W.R., 105
William R., 27, 105
Harmon
Nolan B., 167
Rebecca Barry Lamar, 167
Harris
Rebecca, 62
Harrison
Charles, 19
Dorothy Hanson, 32
Eleanor, 19
Mary, 19
Robert Hanson, 32
Harriss
Mary, 80
Harwood
Elizabeth Lloyd, 34
Richard, 62
Hawkins
Elizabeth Whitaker, 20
Haxall
Alice Brown, 65
William Henry, 65
Heaton
Cecelia, 112
James Decatur, 112
Margaret McIlhany, 112
Hebb
Hopewell, 30
Priscilla, 20
Hedges
Ella R., 157
Henderson
Augusta Glenn Lamar, 168
Clara, 168
Clara Smith Adamson, 105, 160
Frederick N., 168
Frederick Neel, 106
George Peter, 106
Gussie Glenn Lamar, 106
Helen Neel, 161
James, 171
James Alby, 106, 160, 172
James B., 130, 168, 171
James Barnes, 105, 160, 161
James S. H., 105
John, 160
Lavinia Dawson, 160
Mabel Anderson Spencer, 106, 160
Margaret Adamson, 106
Mary M. Welsh, 106
Richard, 51
Rosanna Neel, 105
Rose Mary, 106
Sarah Isabel, 106
Vernon Lee, 106
Walter H., 106
Henley
Charity, 32
Hepburn
Samuel, 89
Hermance
John, 23
Mary Sprigg, 23
Hershey
Louis B., 97, 158
Hickman
Joshua, *11*
Margaret, *11*
Polly, 139
Sarah, 11
Solomon, 11
Higgins
Cornelia Cecilia Bevans Higgins, 162
Frank, 161
Frank Hamilton, 161
John Hamilton, 161
John J., Mr. and Mrs., 177
Laura Magruder, 177
Laura Mildred, 161
Lawrence Augustus, 162
Margaret Tayloe, 161
Mary Cecil Garrett, 161
Roberta Baker, 161
Roberta Philippa, 161
Sophia Dorothy "Dora" Barnard, 161
Hilleary
Susan Smith, 55
Walter Henry, 55
Hilton
Elizabeth, 170
Hinkley
Eltinge Mary (Lodor), 162
George, 162
Willard, 162
Hodges
Henry, 91
Mary Catherine (Bailey), 91
Mary Ellen, 91
Hoffman
Emily Louisa Key, 36
Frederick, 159
Henrietta, 95, 159
Philip Rogers, Dr., 36
Hoge
Moses, 28
Holland
Ann M., 133
Capel, 57
Laura Williams, 135
William, 57
Zachariah, 135
Holmes
Ann, 89
Hook
Daniel, 10
Sarah Burgess, 10
Hopewell
Olivia Caroline, 143
Hopkins
Rachel, 137
Howard
Annie Eliza, 139
Annie Eliza Buckey, 139
Charles, 34
Edward, 139
Elizabeth, 17
Elizabeth Phoebe Key, 34
Elizabeth Ridgely (Crabb), 100
Elizabeth Ridgely Crabb, 15
Emily, 100
John Eager, Gen., 34
Joseph, 21
Margaret, 21
Martha, 21
Rebecca Ann Key, 36
Thomas Worthington, 15, 100
William, Dr., 36
Hubbell
Levi N., 72
Mary Morris (Beall), 72
Hughes
Barnabas, 47
Elizabeth, 47
Elizabeth Waters, 47
James, 47
Hunt
Ann Meade, 28
James, 27
James Watkins, 28
Ruth Hall, 27, 28
Thomas Poage, 28
William, 28
William P., 28
William Pitt, 27
Hunter
Mary Catherine, 140
Huntington
Cyrus, Rev., 135

Hurley
Catherine (Kitty), 58
Thomas, 58
Hutton
Hobart, 162
Hobert Buchanan, 163
Mary Lyons Stone, 162
Mary Sandys Lynch, 163
Orlando, 162
Sidney Claire Buchanan, 162
William Stone, 163
Hyatt
Gertrude, 157
Harriett (Hattie), 152
Mary Ellen, 152
Hyde
Maria, 176, 177
Mary Dawson, 160
Thomas, 160
Isaac
Jemima, 25
Jackson, 10
Andrew, 34
Andrew, President, 56
James M., 135
Mary, 16
Jacob
Eleanor, 25
Jemima Isaac, 25
John Jeremiah, 40
Mordecai, 25
James
Esther, 172
Jay
Anna, 5
Jefferson
[President], 40
Thomas, 7, 19, 21
Jenkins
Elizabeth (Gould), 115
Martha Ann deValcourt, 115
Thomas Courtney, 115
Jett
Marie L., 153
Johns
Elizabeth, 15
John, 30
Juliana Johnson, 30
Margaret, 44, 63
Margaret Johns, 77
Mary Crabb, 17
Priscilla, 44
Johnson
10. Caroline Worthington Goldsborough, 30
Ann Washington, 39
Anna Maria Dorsey, 30
Arlene C., 157
Baker, 29
Catherine W., 29
Dorcas Sedgwick, 13, 29, 31
Elizabeth, 13
Elizabeth Rousby Key, 36
Henry, 36
J., 13
James, 31
James Thomas, 31
Juliana, 30
Margaret Ann, 39
Margaret L. Skinner, 31
Maria Ann Dorsey, 20
Mary Jane Fitzhugh Potts, 48
Mary Jane Potts, 30
Matilda, 30
Nancy M. Richards, 31
Nicholas, 29
Nicholas Worthington, 29
Rebecca, 31, 39
Rebecca (Johnson), 31
Reverdy, 104
Thomas, 13, 29, 30, 31, 49
William, 20, 30, 39
Worthington, 30, 48
Johnston
Ann M. Holland, 133
B.O., 157
Lydia Forrest, 133
Lydia Forrest, 164
Zachariah Forrest, 133
Jones
Ariana, 32
Cecelia Kilgour, 112
Charles, 32
Charles Benedict, 163
Charles Courts, 33
Charles Mace, 163
Dorothy Hanson Harrison, 32
Eleanor Brewer, 84
Eleanor Courts (Nelly), 33
Elizabeth, 110
Elizabeth (Clagett), 109
Elizabeth Clagett, 84
Elizabeth Isabella (King), 154
Ellen Brewer, 109
Emma ( ), 163
Harriet, 164
Harriet Amelia, 91
Helen Gertrude, 154
Henrietta, 33
Henry, 32
Hill, 91
Jane (Yates) Tyler, 32
John Courts, 32
Joseph H (Rev.), 109
Joseph Hawkins, 84
Lavinia Lyddane, 163
Leonidas, 154
Louisa, 32
Marie, 164
Mary Ann, 32
Mary Courtney, 91
Samuel, 112
Sarah, 33
Sarah Elizabeth, 154
Spencer Cone, 84, 109
Susanna (Sucky) Courts, 33
Jordan
Margaret, 37
Keene
Eleanora (Ellen) Martin, 41
Lawrence, 41
Maria Martin, 41
Richard Raynal, 41
Kemp
Henry, 14
Kenner
Father, 141
Key
Alice, 35
Ann Arnold Ross, 35
Ann Phoebe Charlton, 33
Ann Plater, 36
Anna Arnold, 34
Anne Arnold, 36
Anne Phoebe Charlton, 56
Cecelia Brown, 3
Charles Henry, 35
Daniel Murray, 34
Edmund, 89
Edward, 34
Elizabeth, 34
Elizabeth Lloyd Harwood, 34
Elizabeth Phoebe, 34
Elizabeth Rousby, 36
Ellen Lloyd, 35
Emily Louisa, 36
Frances Rebecca, 60
Frances Scott, 61
Francis, 3, 35
Francis Scott, 33, 36, 56
Francis Scott, Jr., 34
George Barton, 36
John Ross, 33, 34, 56
Louise Emily, 36
Margaret Johns, 89
Maria Lloyd, 34
Maria Louisa Sewell, 36
Mary Brent Sewell, 36
Mary Lloyd, 36
Mary Tayloe Lloyd, 34
Philip, 3

Philip Barton, 33, 34, 35, 36, 61
Rebecca Ann, 36
Rebecca Jowles Sothoron, 3
Richard Ward, 60
Virginia Ringold, 34
Kiger
George W, 95
Mary Elizabeth, 95, 159
Rebecca (Rice), 95
Kilgore
James, 37
Margaret (Jordan), 37
Sarah (Edgerton), 110
William, 110
Kilgour
2. Elizabeth Cornelia Wootton, 114
Alexander, 113, 134, 164
Alexander, Jr., 112
Alexandria, 110, 165
Ann E, 113
Ann Elliza Shelme, 112
Ann Stribling, 165
Cecelia, 112
Charles, 113
Charles I., 38
Charles J., 112, 113
Charles Jordan, 37, 113, 114
Charlotte, 114
Eliza Barrett Prettyman, 134
Elizabeth Barrett Prettyman, 112
Fannie Claiborne Beaufort, 114
Francis Stribling, 112
Isabella, 114
James, 113
James McIlhaney, 114
James McIlheny, 37
John A. T, 113
John A. T., 112
John Allen Thomas, Jr., 113
John Mortimer, 37, 113
Judge, 14
Louisa McIlhany, 113
Louisa McIlheny, 37
Louisa T. McIlhany, 37
Margaret Ann (Stribling), 164
Margaret Ann Stribling, 111, 165
Margaret McIlhany Heaton, 112
Martha Matilda, 112
Martha Wilson Wootton, 37, 114
Mary Adelaide Wootton, 114
Mary Carter, 165
Rose Ellen Queen, 112, 165
Sarah Edgerton, 112
Virginia, 112
William, 112, 165
King
Elizabeth, 128
Kunkel
Anna Mary McElfresh, 118
Jacob M., 118
Lackland
James, 38
James Cooper, 15
John, 38
Margery Edmonston, 38
Matilda (Crabb), 15
Laird
Ella Gaither Magruder, 166
Philip Dandridge, 166
William Winder, 166
Williamina Elizabeth Cadwalader (Goldsborough), 166
Lamar
Anita, 167
Ann Maria (Glenn), 167, 168
Augusta Glenn, 168
Edith Glen, 167
Edith May Stonestreet, 167
Edward Stonestreet, 167
Elizabeth, 20, 38
George Holt Jr., 167
Gussie Glenn, 106
John, 38
Lucille Allen, 167
Lucius Q. C., 168
Mary Elizabeth Wood, 167
Priscilla Dawson Gibbons, 168
Rebecca Barry, 167
Susanna Tyler, 38
Virginia Longstreet, 106, 168
Virginia Longstreet Lamar, 168
William Harmong, 106, 167, 168
William Harmong, III, 168
Lancaster
Henrietta, 8
Lanham
Edward, 54
Elizabeth, 54
Susannah (Page), 54
Lansdale
Elizabeth Ann, 26
Violetta, 70
Larned
Charlotte Caroline, 142
Laura Lock, 80
Lawn
Alice M., 69
Lear
Benjamin Lincoln, 114
Elizabeth (or Louisa) Bomford, 115
Frances (Bassett) Washington, 114
Frances Dandridge Henley, 114
Maria Morris, 115
Mary Long, 114
Tobias, 114
Lee
Annie Clymer Brooke, 169
Arthur Fitzgerald, 169
Benjamin, 27
Blair, 172
Edward Brooke, 169
Eleanor Lansdale Belt, 27
Elizabeth Blair, 169
Elizabeth Collins, 115
Elizabeth Wayne, 169
Elizabeth Wilson, 169
Francis Preston Blair, 169
Henry "Light Horse Harry", 115
Mary Elizabeth, 116
Mary Ida, 116
Phillip, 47
Phillip Blair, 169
Richard Bland, 115
Richard Henry, 116
Robert E., 115
Samuel Phillips, 169
Sarah, 47
Violetta, 27
Zaccheus Collins, 115
LeFeaver
Dorothy Middleton Beall, 152
James Harrison, 152
LeFevre
Emma Cooper (Beall), 72
George, 72
Leigh
Dorothy, 7
Lelly
Mary E., 141
Letton
Anna Maria, 102
Lewis
Elizabeth, 64
Mary Edward, 129
Lincoln
President, 57, 74
Lindley
Elizabeth King, 128

John Clark, 128
Linstead
Anna Maria Letton, 102
Thomas, 102
Linthicum
Mabel Elizabeth, 175
Margaret, 173
Lloyd
Edward, 34
Mary Tayloe, 34
Lock
Laura, 80
Locke
Laura, 78
Sarah Ann Locke, 80
Sarah Mary Smith, 78, 79
William Bruce, 78, 79
Lodor
Eltinge Mary, 162
Long
Mary, 114
Longstreet
Virginia, 106
Love
Jane, 102
Jean, 32
Martha C., 101
Lowry
Charlotte, 131, 173
Charlotte Huntingdon Young, 175
Helen Olivia, 131, 173
Horatio Barnard, 175
Horatio, Maj. USMC, 131, 173
Ida Frances, 175
Luckett
Montjoy B., 116
Lyddane
Ann Adams, 170
Anna (Nannie), 170
Bessie, 170
Gertrude, 170
Grace, 170
James, 170
Lavinia, 163
Michael, 138
Rose, 172
Stephen M., 170
Thomas, 170
Lynch
Eliza Boteler, 116
Isabella C. Beckenbaugh, 116
John Alexander, 116
Mary Sandys, 163
Lynn
Ann Woodson (Nancy) Venables, 39
Catherine, 38
Caty, 39
David, 20, 38, 39, 52
David, Jr., 39
Eleanor Edelin, 39
Elizabeth, 38
Elizabeth Lamar, 20
Francina Cheston, 52
George, 39
Jane, 19, 38
John, 39
Mary Galloway, 39, 52
Rosalie, 38
Rosetta, 20
Sarah, 38, 39
Lytle
Augusta Glenn Lamar, 106, 168
Robert, 106, 168
Maccubbin
Helen, 10
Mary Ann Rawlings, 7
Nicholas, 104
Samuel, 7
Susan, 7
Mackall
Benjamin, 89
Susannah, 22
Mackubin
Eleanor Carroll Maccubbin, 104
George, 104
Mary Catherine, 104
Maddox
Catharine Jane Harding, 27
Charles J., 27
Martha Harris, 27
William Theobold, 27
Madison
James, 7, 55
Magruder
Agdin (Ogden), 89
Alexander, 39
Ann H., 89
Ann Holmes, 89
Ann J. Prettyman, 134
Elizabeth, 10, 88
Elizabeth Lynn, 37, 38, 63, 143, 144
Elizabeth Worthington (Gaither), 166
Ella Gaither, 166
Harriet Elizabeth, 39
Hugh H., 134
Jane C. T., 179
Joseph, *10*
Julian, 39
Levin, 38
Lloyd, 89
Lucy B., 89
Lucy Beall, 38
Margaret Ann Johnson, 39
Martha Wilson, 39
Mary Catherine Holmes, 89
Mary Jackson, *10*
Mira, 70, 151
Myra, 142
Rachel, 39
Samuel Wade, 38
William Bowie, 166
Zadok, 39, 40
Mahan
Alexander, 94
Mary Griffith Coxe, 94
Mallory
James, 67
Johnson Baltzer, 98
Mary C. Day, 98
Sophia Bache Abert, 67
Mallory and Watts, 62
Mantz
Anna Mary Burkhardt, 118
Francis, 118
Theresa, 118
Marken
Ann Buhrman, 121
Effie Buhrman, 121
Josiah Recher, 121
Marshall
Edith, 131, 171
Humphrey, 131, 171
Virginia, 131
Martin
Benjamin, 40
Eleanora (Ellen), 41
Elizabeth Sophia, 41
Hannah, 40
Julia Worthington, 182
Juliet, 40
Lorenzo W., 182
Luther, 40, 47
Maria, 41
Mary, 117
Mary Cresap, 40
Mason
Abram Barnes, 41
Elizabeth Ann Armistead, 41
Elizabeth Beltzhoover, 41
George, 41
John, 3
John Thomson, 41
John Thomson, Jr, 41
Mary Barnes, 41
Mary King Barnes, 41
Mary Thrift, 69
Melchoir Beltzhoover, 41
Thomson, 41

Virginia Wallace, 41
Matthews
Robert C., 168
Virginia Longstreet Lamar, 168
Maynard
Samuel, 7
McCannon
Eliza Asbury, 52
James, 52
McCormick
Alexander, 59
Eliza Van Horne, 59
McCutchen
Ann Bacon, 117
Annie E. Dawes, 117
John, 117
John H. G., 117
Julia, 117
Mary Martin, 117
McElfresh
Anna Mary, 118
Ariana, 118
Ariana Hammond, 118
Casper Mantz, 118
Francis, 118
Henry, 118
Jane, *9*
John Hammond, 118
Theresa Mantz, 118
McIlhaney
Cecelia, 111
Elizbeth Johnson, 37
James, 37
Margaret Tribbey, 37
McIlhany
Louisa T., 37
McIlhenny
Margaret Dudley, 155
Thomas Cowen, 155
McIlheny
Louisa, 37
McMarkham
Mary E., 154
McPherson
Alexander, 30
Matilda Johnson, 30
Meade
Ann, 28
Medairy
Catharine Musser, 84
Meriweather
Elizabeth, 103
Merrick
Catherine Boarman Thomas, 119
Mary B. Wickliffe, 119
Richard T., 129
Wiliam Matthew, 119
William D., 129
William Duhurst, 119
William Matthew, 119
Metzger
Amanda E. Cashell, 91
William, 91
Middleton
Catherine Hyatt, 152
Mary Ellen (Nellie)., 152
Mary Ellen (Nellie). Middleton, 152
Mary Ellen Hyatt, 152
Rueben, 152
Miles
Eleanor Hawkins, 3
James, 3
Miller
Ellenora Elder, 9
Mines
Elizabeth Wootton, 63
Elizabeth Wootton Beall, 72
John, 63, 72
John Lewis Beall, 73
Mary, 73
Minor
Eleanor Anderson, 120
Franklin, 120
George, 69, 120
Mary, 69, 120
Mary Driscoll, 120
Mary Thift, 120
Mary Virginia, 120
Robert, 120
Moler
Helen Gertrude Jones, 154
James William Stuart, 154
Morris
Margaret Cecelia, 46
Maria, 115
Mary, 72
Robert, 81
Morse
Martha Crawford, 43
Nathan, 43
Morsell
Caroline, 138
James S., 120
Joshua, 120
William F. C., 121
Morton
Judith, 39
Mosher
Eliza Jane, 88
Elizabeth Magruder, 88
James, 88
Motter
Aimee Rebecca, 122
Alan, 122
Bessie Estella, 122
Effie Buhrman Marken, 121
Emily, 122
George, 122
Helen, 122
Jacob, 121
Jemima (Troxell), 121
Jessie, 122
John Columbus, 121
Lola, 122
Roger, 122
William, 127
Muir
Lydia W. Chichester, 93
William Sawtell, 93
Mulliken
Margaret, 17
Mullikin
Sophia Oden, 87
Muncaster
Harriet Elizabeth Magruder, 39
Otho Z., 39
Munro
David, Mr. and Mrs., 176
Katherine, 176
Munroe
Elizabeth, 132
Murdoch
Ann Letitia, 48
Eleanor, 47
Eleanor Charlton, 47, 48
George, 47, 48
Murray
James, 47
Neel
Joseph, 105
Rosanna, 105
Negro
James, 61
Kitty Ann, 61
Mariah, 61
Mary, 61
William, 61
Neilson
Deborah Ridgely, 49
Robert, 49
Nelson
Anna Maria, 9
Carrington Scott, 122
Cleland, 131
Emeline (Crabb), 15
Frances Nicholas, 145
Hugh, 131
John, 118
John Scott, 122
Katherine Peter, 131
Martha Anna Carrington Belt, 122
Mary Hagner, 131

Nathan, 15
Roger, 8
Nevins
Mary Lloyd Key, 36
William, 36
Nicholls
Edward, 42, 43
Francis Redding Tillou, 42
Louisa Hannah Drake, 43
Martha Crawford, 43
Mary, 43
Robert Hamilton, 43
Thomas C., 42
Thomas Clark, 43
Wilhelmina Hamilton, 42
Nichols
Lydia, 103
Nixon
Llewlyn ("Louella"), 142
Noland
Catheine, *12*
Thomas, *12*
Norris
Amos, 178
Susanna, 178
O'Donnell
Ada, 143
Offutt
Hannah, 64
James, 64
Mary, 64
Rachel, 64
Rebecca, 64
Sarah Beall, 64
Ogle
Meliora, 8
Samuel, 8
Ord
James, 38
Orme
Archibald, 15
Elizabeth (Johns)., 15
Richard Johns, 15
Ould
Jessie Bright, 123
Kate, 123
Madge, 123
Madge Dorsey, 123
Martha Gwynn, 123
Robert, 123
Robert C., 123
Samuel Riggs Gaither Ould, 123
Sarah Turpin, 123
Sarah Turpin Ould, 123
Owen
Catherine Goldsborough, 152
Edward W., 124
Elizabeth Ann Clagett, 124
Margaret, 124
Ruth (Gassaway), 124
Thos, 126
Washington, 124
Washington Winder, 152
Owens
Richard S., 177
Owings
John H., 128
Packer
Mary, 61
Page
Susannah, 54
Palmer
Carrie Gear, 125
George H., 139
Henrietta M. (Reed), 125
Jessie, 125
Margaret Lyle Veitch, 139
Martha Gray, 125
Moses Gray, 125
Walter Gray, 125
William P., 125
Patterson
George C., 126
Henry, 126
Jane Clarke, 126
Julia Belt, 126
Prudence Bean, 126
Thomas, 126
Virginia, 126
Peach
Richard, 87
Pearre
Catherine Marian (Springer), 127
Elizabeth G. Shoup, 127
Elizabeth Smith, 127
Florence Worthington, 127
George A., Jr., 127
George Alexander, 127
Georgia, 127
James Graham, 128
Mary, 127
Mary Worthington, 127
William, 127
Peddicord
Ara Rebecca Clagett, 128
Ella May, 129
Harriet (Lindley) Whipps, 128
James Clagett, 129
MaggieWashington, 129
Mary Edward Lewis, 129
Mary Rebecca, 129
Rebecca, 136
Rebecca Crawford, 128
Thomas John, 128
Washington Asbury, 128
Pendleton
Alice Key, 35
George, 35
Perine
David Maulden, 116
Mary (Glenn), 116
Mary Elizabeth Lee, 116
William Buchanan, 116
Perry
Augustus Emory, 129
Benjamin, 12
Charles, 44
Edith, 129
Elizabeth Magruder, 12
Estelle Frances Tayloe, 44
George C., 44
James Wilson, 62
Magruder, 45
Marcus, 45
Martha, 62
Mary Callie Thaw, 129
Mary Jane Ross, 129
Mary Louisa Van Lear, 44
Mary M., 45
Priscilla J., 44
Priscilla Johns, 44
Rebecca Harris, 62
Richard Ross, 129
Roger, 44, 145
Ruth, 127, 145
Thomas Johns, 44
William, 45
Pessou
Ernestine, 175
Peter
Anita Phillips Smith, 172
Arthur, 131, 171
Arthur, Jr., 171
Blanche Fulks, 172
Edith Marshall, 131, 171
Edward, 76, 172
Edward C., 140
Edward Compston, 130, 171
Edward Compton, 131, 171
Eliza Lavinia Gassaway, 130, 131, 160, 171, 173
Esther James, 172
Frances, 76
George, 69, 84, 105, 130, 131, 160, 171, 172, 173, 178, 180
George Gibson, 130
Gertrude Veirs, 172
Helen Olivia Lowry, 131, 173
Humphrey Marshall, 171
John Freeland, 130, 131, 171
John Vinson, 172

Katherine, 131
Mary A., 130, 160
Mary Fackler Tyler, 173
Mary Gordon Vinson, 130, 140, 172
Mary V., 76
Robert B., 131, 172
Robert Brewer, 131, 171, 173
Robert Jr., 173
Sarah N., 130
Sarah Norfleet Freeland, 130
Pfeil
Robert Henderson, 182
Ruth Worthington, 182
Phillips
Anita Veronica, 172
Eunice, 113
Pigman
Anna (Waters), 45
Anne E. Gordon, 46
Bene Smallwood, 45, 46
Charles Henry Jordan, 46
Fanny Ann Burbage, 45
Hanson Briscoe, 46
Harriet Ann, 46
Margaret Cecelia Morris, 46
Mary Elizabeth Shriver, 46
Nathaniel, 45, 46
Philip Augustus Smallwood, 45
Summerfield, 46
William Pinkney, 45
Pinkney
Ann Franklin, 132
Elizabeth, 132
Elizabeth(Munroe), 132
Jonathan, 132
Jonathan Edward, 132
Mary Franklin, 132
Mary Franklin Deale, 132
Somerville, 132
Plater
Ann, 36
Elizabeth Rousby, 22, 36
George, 22
George, Governor, 36
Rebecca, 22, 102
Platt
W. H., 105
Poe
Amelia, 24
Edgar Allen, 115
Pope
Chloe Ellen, 136
Nathaniel, 136
Sarah (St.Clair), 136
Porter
Mary Stannard, 96, 158
Pottenger
Ann Buchanan, 52
Potts
Ann Letitia Murdoch, 48
Arthur, 47, 48
Cornelia Ringgold, 48
Eleanor Murdoch, 47, 48
Elizabeth, 48
Elizabeth Hughes, 47
George Murdoch, 48
Harriet Murdoch, 48
John Lee, 48
Mary Jane, 30
Mary Jane Fitzhugh, 48
Philip Thomas, 48
Rebecca, 48
Richard, 47, 48
Samuel H., 48
Sarah Ann, 48
Sarah Lee, 47
William, 47, 48
Powers
Madge Ould, 123
William Francis, 123
Prettyman
Ann J., 134
Charles W., 133, 136
Charles Wesley, 77, 173
E. B., 126
Elijah Barrett, 77, 133, 164, 173
Eliza Barrett, 133, 134, 164
Elizabeth Barrett, 112
Elizabeth Rebecca Stonestreet, 133
Forrest J., 133
Lydia Forrest Johnston, 133
Lydia F, 134
Lydia Forrest, 173
Lydia Forrest Johnston, 77, 164
Mariam, 134
Rosetta (Rosa) Vauclin Bouic, 173
Rosetta Vauclin Bouic, 77
William, 133
Price
Caroline, 180
Jane, 49
John Lewis, 49
Mary, 44
Sarah Bourne, 49
Prout
Fannie Rachel, 130, 172
Frances Rachel, 69, 140, 150
Mary, 151
William, 140
Queen
Charles J, 165
Maria, 165
Rose Ellen, 112, 165
Quigley
Charles H., 170
Grace Lyddane, 170
Ragan
Katherine M., 155
Ramsey
Caroline Henry, 4
Caroline Henry Ashton, 4
Charles, 4
Randolph
Elizabeth G., 87
John, 40
Rawlings
Mary Ann, 7
Ray
Alfred, Jr., 91
Mary Ellen Hodges, 91
Reed
Dorothy Worthington, 182
Eleanor, 125
Elijah, 125
Elizabeth Forrest, 22
Henrietta M., 125
Paul de Hoff, 182
Upton, 22
Regester
Harriett (Hattie) Hyatt., 152
Rev. J. A,, 152
Resley
Horace, 178
Reynolds
Henry Lincoln, 142
Jane Elizabeth Beall Williams, 142
Rice
Rebecca, 95
Richards
Nancy M., 31
Richardson
Henrietta M. (Reed), 125
Ricketts
Elizabeth, 144
Katherine E., 175
Ridgely
Ann, 49
Daniel B., 49
Deborah, 49
Edward Dorsey, 50
Elizabeth, 25, 26, 49, 60
Elizabeth Dorsey, 49
Greenbury, 49
Jane Price, 49
Lucy Stringer, 49
Mary Hammond, 49
Mary Pue, 99
Matilda Chasw, 50

Richard, 49
Sarah, 15
Sophia, 49
Ridgley
Charles Carnan, 18
Mary Pue, 18
Priscilla Dorsey, 18
Riggs
Amon Edward, 25
Barnard Lowry, 175
Benjamin Canby, 176
Claudia Gartrell, 175
Ernestine Pessou, 175
Estelle Hyde Talbott, 176
Mabel Elizabeth Linthicum, 175
Margaret Teller, 175
Martha Hughs (Canby), 174
Reuben, 174, 175
Ruth Dronenburg, 175
Ruth Griffith, 25
Samuel, 174
Samuel Brownell, 175
Ringgold
Anna Maria Cadwallader, 48
Cornelia, 48
Samuel, 48
Ringold
Virginia, 34
Ritchie
Stephen Olin, 74
Robb
Adam, 26
Catherine Ann, 26, 90, 105
Elizabeth Ann Lansdale, 26
Jane, 105
Roberts
Levi F., 137
Mary, 137
Robertson
Susan, 20
Rogers
Dorothy, 180
R.M., 180
Rose
Helen, 61
John, 61
Rose
John, 61
Ross
Ann Arnold, 35
Ariana Frisby Brice, 50
Catherine W. Johnson, 29
Charles Bordley, 50
David, 50, 51
Edmond, 50
Elizabeth Bordley, 51
Henrietta Marie Bordley, 50
J. W., 109
James Brice, 50
John Bordley, 50
Margaret Ariana, 50
Mary Jane, 129
Sarah Corbett, 50
Thomas Bordley, 51
William, 29, 84
William Stuart, 51
Rousby
Elizabeth, 22, 36
Rowe
Clarence L., 155
Margaret Catlett, 155
Rozer
Charles B., 69
Frances Virginia Anderson, 69
Francis Whetenhall, 69
Mary E. Anderson, 69
Rucker
Mabel Elmore, 97, 158
Russell
Catherine, 75
Eva, 75
Matilda Provost, 86
Virginia (Fletcher), 86
Virginia Fletcher, 83
William W., 83, 86
Sams
Isaac, 98
Sands
George W., 135
Saunders
Hannah T. Bradley, 80
William H., 80
Scarff
Hilda Rebecca, 180
P.B., 180
Schley
Anita Lamar, 167
Anna Maria (Shelman), 51
Buchanan, 53
Charles F., 167
Eliza Ashbuy McCannon, 52
Ellen N. Stull, 52
Frederick Augustus, 51
Frederick Augustus, Jr., 52
George, 52
James McCannon, 52
John Jacob, 51
Mary Buchanan, 53
Mary Hall, 52
Roger Brooke Taney, 53
Sarah Rebecca Roman, 53
Thomas Hall, 53
William, 127
William Henry, 52
Schoolcraft
Martha Gwynn Ould, 123
Oliver J., 123
Scott
Dred, 56
Scull
David, 169
Elizabeth Lee, 169
Sedgwick
Dorcas, 13, 29, 31
Sellman
Eleanor (Watkins), 144
Ellen H., 145
Margaret Ellen, 144
Richard, 144
Sewell
Maria Louisa, 36
Mary Brent, 36
Robert, 36
Sheckles
John, 10
Mary Burgess, 10
Shellman
Elizabeth, 50
Shelman
Anna Maria, 51
Shelmerdine
Ann Elliza, 113
Eunice Phillips, 113
Stephen, 113
Sheridine
Upton, 31
Sherman
Charles A., 80
Sarah D. Bradley, 80
Shoup
Elizabeth G., 127
Shriver
Abraham, 145
Edwin Thomas, 46
Harriet Ann Pigman, 46
Mary Elizabeth, 46
Sickles
Daniel E., General, 34
Simmons
Mary R., 181
Skinner
Margaret L., 31
Slater
Sarah, 96
Slemaker
Ellen, 7
Smith
Andromeda, 55
Anita Phillips, 172
Anita Veronica Phillips, 172
Anna Jane Clagett, 106
Charles, 170
Dolly Madison, 55
Elizabeth Lanham, 54
Elizabeth Ruth, 182

Gilbert Coles, 172
James, 127
James Madison, 55
Jane, 54
John, 53, 55
Margaret Bowie Chichester, 93
Robert, 53, 54, 55
Samuel, 55
Sarah Elizabeth, 55
Sarah Hilton, 170
Sophia, 55
Susan, 55
Warrington Gillet, 93
Snader
Elizabeth, 178
Snowden
Ann, 15
Deborah, 38
John, 137
Rachel (Hopkins), 137
Rachel P., 137
Somerville
Amelia Hollyday, 95
James, 95
Priscilla Beall, 95
Sothoron
Rebecca Jowles, 3
Sowers
Elizabeth, 14
Spencer
Cora Caroline Couch, 106, 160
Mabel Anderson, 106, 160
Thomas H., 106, 160
Sprecher
Annie Lee Beach, 71
Daniel Boteler, 71
Sprigg
Carolina Lansdale Bowie, 70
Elizabeth, 62, 63
Mary Bowie, 70
Osborn, 70
Osburn, 43
Samuel, 70
Violetta Lansdale, 70
Springer
Catherine Marian, 127
St.Clair
Sarah, 136
Stalnaker
Maude, 83
Statler
Elva, 97, 158
Steele
Anne Buchanan, 9
Henry, 34
Maria Lloyd Key, 34
Nevett, 9
Stephen
Charles H., 5
Virginia Melancthon Balch, 5
Stevenson
Elizabeth Maynadier Taney, 57
William, 57
Stewart
Margaret Helen Beall, 134
William, 134
William M., 134
Stone
Mary Frances, 163
Mary Lyons, 163
William J., 163
Stonestreet
Dr. E. E., 67, 133
Edith May, 167
Edward Elisha, 167
Elizabeth Rebecca, 133
Martha, 67
Martha Rebecca Barry, 167
Martha Wilson, 142
Storke
Johannis Greenfield Dent, 4
Mary Ashton, 4
Stribling
Cecelia (McIlhaney), 111
Francis, 111
Margaret Ann, 111, 164, 165
Strickland
Nancy, 181
Stringer
Lucy, 49
Stuart
Jeb, 78
JEB, 95
Joseph Noble, 4
Mary Ashton, 4
Stull
Ellen N., 52
Letitia Hall, 52
Otho H. W., 8
Otho Holland Williams, 52
Summers
Ann Maria, 22
Anna Maria, 102
Anna Maria Letton, 102
John Letton, 102
Mary L., 15
Rueben, 102
Zadock, 15
Surratt
John H., 80
Swan
Edward, 136
Marie L. Thrift, 136
Swift
Emily, 5
Talbott
Benson, 176, 177
Bertha Hall, 177
Cora E. Wilson, 176
Edward Alexander, 135
Estelle Hyde, 176
Evelyn Wailes, 176
Hattersley Worthington, Jr., 135
Hattersly Worthington, 135
Helen Wilson, 176
Henry Maurice, 175, 177
Katherine M. Choate, 135
Katherine Munro, 176
Laura Magruder Higgins, 177
Laura Williams Holland, 135
Maria Hyde, 176, 177
Mary Jane (Wareham), 135
Otho Holland Williams, 135
Sadie Marie, 177
Thomas Maurice, 176
W. H., 174
William Hyde, 177
William Randolph, 177
Taney
Alice Carroll, 57
Ann Arnold, 56
Anne Louisa White, 58
Anne Phoebe Charlton Key, 56
Augustus, 57, 68
Augustus Brooke, 57
Catherine (Kitty) Hurley, 58
Elizabeth Maynadier, 57
Ellen Mary, 57
Joseph Augustus, 58
Maria Key, 57
Mary Henley, 58
Mary Young, 58
Michael, 57
Michael, V., 56
Monica (Brooke), 56, 57
Roger B., 51
Roger Brooke, 5, 45, 56, 57, 58
Sophia Brooke, 57
Thomas Augustine, 57
Tayloe
Anne, 38
Estelle Frances, 44
John, 22
John, 38
Tayloe
John, 38
Taylor
Francis, 57

Sophia Brooke Taney, 57
Teller
Margaret, 175
Steadman, 175
Thaw
Jean Hood, 129
John, 129
Mary Callie, 129
Thomas
Catherine Boarman, 119
Elizabeth Merriweather Hammond, 104
George, 104
Thompson
Anne Arnold Key, 36
Chloe Ellen Pope, 136
Frances, 65
Rebecca Peddicord, 136
Richard, 136
William E., 36
William H., 136
Thrift
Charity Ducket Boyd, 136
James M., 136
Maria L., 136
Mary, 69, 128
Robert G., 136
Sarah M. (Sallie R.M.), 69
Todd
John Moore, 4
Rezin, 25
Sarah, 25
Sarah B.. *See*
Sarah Griffith, 25
Torrey
Catharine Susanna Brewer, 85
Morris Whitmore, 85
Trail
Ariana McElfresh, 118
Charles Edward, 118
Trapnell
J., 121
Treadwell
Oliver W., 146
Tribbey
Margaret, 37
Troxell
Jemima, 121
Turner
Anna Arnold Key, 34
Daniel, 34
Turpin
Sarah, 123
Thomas J., 123
Tuttle
Asahel, 80
Lucy Sherman, 80
Tyler
Frank Ames, 173
Jane, 32
Margaret Linthicum, 173
Mary Fackler, 173
Susanna, 38
Trueman, 89
Tyson
Alexander H., 36
Anna Maria, 137
Cornelia, 137
Ida, 137
Jesse, 137
John Shoemaker, 137
John Snowden, 137
Margaret (Hopkins), 137
Mary Roberts, 137
Rachel P. Snowden, 137
Rebecca Ann Key, 36
Urner
Elizabeth Snader, 178
Hammond, 178
Helen Agnes, 178
Jonas Paul, 178
Laura Eugenia, 178
Mary L. Floyd, 178
Mary Susannah, 178
Milton G., 130
Milton George, 178
Richard Summerfield, 178
Samuel, 178
Samuel Percy, 178
Susanna (Norris), 178
Susanna Norris, 178
Walter Grayson, 178
Valdenar
Elizabeth Culver, 138
Francis, 138
Lycurgus C., 138
Margaret, 138
Mary Virginia, 138
Van Horne
Alethea, 59
Alethea Elizabeth Beall, 59
Amelia Beall, 59
Archibald, 59
Clarissa, 59
Eliza, 59
Gabriel Peterson, 59
Mary (Van Sant), 59
Mary Ann, 59
Rezin, 59
William, 59
Van Lear
Mary Louise, 44
Van Sant
Mary, 59
Vandervender
Charles, 112
Virginia Kilgour, 112
Vanes
Martha, 116
Veirs
Charles, 172
Dorcas, 76
Gertrude, 172
James P. B., 179
Juliana (Diffendorfer), 76
Louise Fechtig, 179
Mary Ann Matilda, 75, 76
Rebecca Thomas Biays, 179
Rose Lyddane, 172
Samuel C., 62, 76
William Augustus, 179
Veitch
Annie Eliza Howard, 138
Caroline Morsell., 138
John, 138
John Wesley, 138
Margaret Lyle, 139
Percy H., 139
Venable
Ann Woodson (Nancy), 39
James, 39
Judith Morton, 39
Vinson
Fannie Rachel Prout, 130, 172
Forresta, 140
Frances Rachel Prout, 69, 140, 150
John T., 139
John Thomas, 69, 130, 150, 172
Julia Prout, 69, 140, 150
Mary Gordon, 130, 140, 172
Nanny Stoddard, 140
Polly (Hickman), 139
Richard Bowie, 140
Thomas, 140
Thomas Fogg Warham, 139
Wailes
Evalina, 77
Walker
Dudley, 4
Hannah, 54
Jane C. Ashton, 4
Wallace
Mary Key Watts, 61
Robert, 61
Wareham
Mary Jane, 135
Warfield
Anna (Nannie) Lyddane, 170
Charles Alexander, 60
David H., 170
Elizabeth Ridgely, 60
Gov., 181
Henry Ridgely, 60

John, 25
Kate R. Fields, 170
Rachel, 25
Rachel Dorsey, 25
Sarah, 25
Warner
John W., 67, 181
Mary, 67
Warren
John, 94
Susan, 94
Washington
Ann, 39
Frances (Bassett), 114
George, 22, 114
George C., 38
Martha, 114
Waters
Bowie Franklin, 179
Bowie Jennings, 180
Charity Ducket Boyd, 136
Dorothy Rogers, 180
Edith Glen Lamar, 167
Elizabeth, 47
Ellen Russell Brewer, 83
Hilda Rebecca Scarff, 180
Horace, 136, 179
Horace D., 136
Joel, 26
John Horace, 180
Laura Gassaway, 179
Mary Jane Priscilla Etchison, 179
Richard Lawrence, 167
Ruth Griffith, 26
William Brewer, 83
Watkins
Agnes (Morton), 28
Caroline Henry Ashton, 4, 140
Edith Maud, 172
Eleanor, 144
George S., 4, 140
George Simpson, 141
Joel Joseph, 28
Joseph, 141
Louis, 141
Maria L.A., 141
Mary Catherine Hunter, 140
Mary E. Lelly, 141
Mary Julia, 141
Ogden Blackson, 141
Ramsey, 141
Rudolph, 140
Rudolph Lewis, Jr., 141
Susanna, 28
Susanna Ashton, 141
Thomas Hunter, 141
Watts
Elizabeth Ann Key, 61
Frances, 60
Frances Rebecca Key, 60
George, 60
Helen Rose, 61
Mary, 62
Mary Key, 61
Mary Packer, 61
Philip Hamond, 61
Phillip, 60
Richard Key, 60
Richard Key, 62
Richard Key, Jr, 61
Watts
Richard Key Jr., 61
Watts
Elizabeth Ann Key, 61
Watts
Richard, 61
Weaver
Louise, 95
Weems
Ann Maria, 27
Arabella, 27
Catharine Ann, 27
Charles Adam, 27
John Lewis, 27
Joseph, 27
Sylvester, 27
Thomas Richard, 27
William Augustus, 27
Weightman
Richard Hanson, 94
Susan Bradley Coxe, 94
Weller
Marie Catherine, 92
Welsh
Anna Jane Clagett Smith, 106
F. Bernard, 176
Helen Wilson Talbott, 176
Mary M., 106
Rachel Griffith, 25
Samuel, 25
Warner W., 106
Wever
Adam, 5
Elizabeth Willis, 5
Whelan
Lola Augusta Hammond, 104
Whie
Florence Earll, 181
Whipple
Margery White, 181
Stephen Carson, 181
Whipps
Harriet (Lindley), 128
Henry, 128
White
Ambrose A., 58
Anne Louisa, 58
Ella Clark Bouic, 77
Evelina Wailes, 77
Margery, 181
Mary, 58
Mary Ellen Gott, 180
Nancy Ellen, 181
Nathan Smith, 77
Richard, 180
Thomas Henry, 180
Whitehead
Mary, 40
Whiting
Julian M., 179
Kate, 179
Wickliffe
Mary B., 119
Wilbourne
Margaret, 75
Wilcoxin
Henrietta Elizabeth, 101
Wilkins
Anne, 17
William, 17
Williams
Alice Bradley, 81
Catherine L., 78
Charlotte Caroline (Larned), 142
Elizabeth Bowie Hall, 78
Emma Barry Abert, 142
Fannie Knight, 96
Hugh Blair, 142
Jane Elizabeth Beall, 142
Laura, 135
Llewlyn ("Louella") Nixon, 142
Otho Holland, 78, 135
Richard Maurice, 142
Richard Mortimer, 70, 142
Richard Walter, 142
Rose (Anderson), 70
Rose Anderson, 142
Rose Florence, 142
Rose Newell, 96
Walter Anderson, 142
Walter W., 81
Willson
Anna Maria Letton, 102
Anne E. Dawson, 96
Martha Wootton, 63
William, 102
William M., 96
William Murdock Beall, 63
Wilson
C. A., 161
Claudia Gartrell, 175

Cora E., 176
Elizabeth, 169
Elizabeth (Sprigg), 62
Elizabeth Sprigg, 63
Isabella George, 116
James, 175
James Herbert, 141
Josiah, 62, 63
Laura Mildred Higgins, 161
Maria L.A. Watkins, 141
Martha, 39
Valentine, 161
Winsor
Arnold T, 38
Wirt
William, 28, 68
Wood
Mary Elizabeth, 167
Woodbury
Levi, 74
Mary Elizabeth, 74
Wooten
Ann, 23
Mary Sprigg, 23
William Turner, 23
Wootton
Ada O'Donnell, 143
Edward, 151
Elizabeth, 63, 72
Elizabeth (Sprigg) Wilson, 62
Elizabeth C. Brashears, 63
Elizabeth Lynn (Magruder), 37, 114
Elizabeth Lynn Magruder, 63, 143, 144
Elizabeth Sprigg, 63
Flavel Scott, 143
Henry Edgar, 143
John, 114
John B., 63, 143, 144
John, Dr., 37
Lewis Beall, 143, 144
Margaret, 63
Martha, 63, 69, 151
Martha Perry, 62
Martha Wilson, 37, 114
Mary, 63
Olivia C., 69, 151
Olivia Caroline (Hopewell), 143
Richard, 62, 63
Singleton, 63
Thomas Sprigg, 63
Turner, 62, 63, 64, 69, 151
Turner, M.D., 143
Worthington
Alice Brown, 65
Beale Magruder, 144
Brice Thomas Beale, Jr., 145
Brice Thomas Beall, 144
Catherine, 17, 29
Catherine Griffith, 24, 29
Charles Hathaway, 65
Comfort, 18
Dorothy, 182
Eleanor, 145
Elizabeth (Booth), 65
Elizabeth Ricketts, 144
Elizabeth Ruth Smith, 182
Ellen H. Sellman, 145
Frances Nicholas Nelson, 145
Glen Bayard, 182
Glen Howard, 181
John Clarke, 182
John T., 181
Julia, 182
Julia Alvey, 181
Julian Alvey, 182
Margaret, 182
Margaret Ellen Sellman, 144
Margaret Mulliken, 17
Mary, 127
Mary R. (Simmons), 181
Mary Tolly, 99
Nicholas, 24, 29
Nina Elizabeth, 182
Perry, 145, 146
Reuben, 127
Richard Alvey, 182
Richard Sellman, 145
Rosa, 145
Ruth, 182
Ruth (Perry), 145
Ruth Perry, 127
Sarah, 24
Thomas, 17
William, 145
William M., 65
William Nicholas, 65
Yates
Jane, 32
Young
Aldridge, 146
Charlotte Huntingdon, 175
Edwin Bennett, 146
Eliza (Aldridge), 146
John B., 146
John E., 146
Mary, 58
Mary E. Dyson, 146
Nicholas, 58
Sara Elizabeth, 146

Made in the USA
Monee, IL
13 September 2026

62975270R10125